STROLLING IN THE RUINS

STROLLING IN THE RUINS

The Caribbean's Non-sovereign Modern in the Early Twentieth Century

Faith Smith

DUKE UNIVERSITY PRESS
Durham and London
2023

Project Editor: Erin Davis
Designed by A. Mattson Gallagher
Typeset in Adobe Text Pro by Westchester Publishing Services
Printed and bound by CPI Group (UK) Ltd, Croydon, CR0 4YY
Library of Congress Cataloging-in-Publication Data
Names: Smith, Faith, [date] author.
Title: Strolling in the ruins : the Caribbean's non-sovereign modern
in the early twentieth century / Faith Smith.
Description: Durham : Duke University Press, 2023. | Includes
bibliographical references and index.
Identifiers: LCCN 2022041263 (print)
LCCN 2022041264 (ebook)
ISBN 9781478019688 (paperback)
ISBN 9781478017042 (hardcover)
ISBN 9781478024316 (ebook)
Subjects: LCSH: Black people—Caribbean, English-speaking—
History. | Black nationalism—Caribbean, English-speaking. |
Nationalism in literature. | Caribbean, English-speaking—History—
20th century. | Caribbean, English-speaking—Politics and
government—20th century. | Great Britain—Colonies—America. |
BISAC: SOCIAL SCIENCE / Ethnic Studies / Caribbean & Latin
American Studies | SOCIAL SCIENCE / Black Studies (Global)
Classification: LCC F2131 .S66 2023 (print) | LCC F2131 (ebook) |
DDC 972.9/04—dc23/eng/20221122
LC record available at https://lccn.loc.gov/2022041263
LC ebook record available at https://lccn.loc.gov/2022041264

Cover art: *Alchemy of the Soul, Elixir for the Spirits*, 2015. Video
still from a five-channel video installation produced by the
Peabody Essex Museum with María Magdalena Campos-Pons
and Neil Leonard for the exhibition *Alchemy of the Soul: María
Magdalena Campos-Pons* (January 9, 2016–April 3, 2016).
Image courtesy of Chip Van Dyke. Copyright courtesy of the
Peabody Essex Museum.

To Miss Bidda and her generations

Contents

Acknowledgments   *ix*

Introduction
Introducing a Quiet Period
        1

1   Cuba, South Africa, and the Anglophone
    Caribbean's New Imperial Century
        33

2   Ruination's Intimate Architecture
        68

3   Photography's "Typical Negro"
        118

4   Plotting Inheritance
        144

Coda
    186

        Notes   *191*
        Bibliography   *229*
        Index   *257*

Acknowledgments

Many aspects of the production of this book, as well as my travels to the archives, to conferences, and to literary and art festivals, were funded by Brandeis's Theodore and Jane Norman Fund and other travel awards from the Dean's office; the Center for German and European Studies; and the generosity of the Rothenberg family, which funds Jane's Awards to faculty in the Latin American, Caribbean and Latinx Studies Program. Many thanks to Magdalena Campos-Pons, Simon Tatum, and Studio Campos-Pons for the wonder of this book cover; and to the generosity of ChaeRan Freeze and Brandeis's Department of Women's, Gender, and Sexuality Studies for related resources. I thank Ryan Kendall and many others who produced this book, and Liz Smith, Erin Davis, and Mary Horan for the meticulous attention that they brought to the copyediting process. During my year at the National Humanities Center in Durham, the staff and the fellows, including Paula Sanders and Kathryn Burns, were extremely generous to me. There, and at the National Endowment for the Humanities seminar "Visions of Freedom for the Americas: Eugenio María de Hostos and José Martí in Nineteenth-Century New York" (when I thought I was writing about Martí and Firmin), colleagues were very supportive. I thank Evelyn Higginbotham, Vera Ingrid Grant, Donald Yacovone, Raquel Deborah Kennon, and everyone who was so kind to me during my year at Harvard's Hutchins Center for African and African American Research. When my body turned on me the first time, lovely Paul Kaplan kept his overcoat on, in an office that shared a thermometer with my office.

I thank scholars of the nineteenth and early twentieth centuries, many of whom have been personally kind to me, and whose scholarship, including new editions, has made that period so vivid: Veronica Gregg, Michelle A. Johnson, Brian L. Moore, Patrick Bryan, Erna Brodber, Lara Putnam, Diana Paton, Matthew Smith, Bridget Brereton, David Scott, Lise Winer, Harvey Neptune, Michelle Stephens, Teju Niranjana, Maureen Warner-Lewis, Rupert Lewis, Evelyn O'Callaghan, Stephen Steumple, Yarimar Bonilla, Belinda Edmondson, Hazel Carby, Vincent Brown, Saidiya Hartman, Gordon Rohlehr, Rhoda Reddock, Marika Sherwood, Pat Mohammad, Wayne Modest, David Trotman, Catherine Hall, Krista Thompson, Joy Lumsden, Tim Barringer, Nicole Aljoe, Elizabeth Dillon, Susan Gillman, Peter Hulme, Rhonda Cobham-Sander, Donette Francis, and Leah Rosenberg, among many others.

Thanks to the librarians at the National Library of Jamaica, and the Special Collections and ISER Library, University of the West Indies, Mona; the Government Archives of Trinidad and Tobago and Special Collections, UWI, St. Augustine; the newspaper section of the British Library, and the National Archives, UK; and over many, many years, the Interlibrary Loan and Document Scan divisions of Brandeis's Goldfarb Library. My Brandeis colleagues in African and African American Studies, the English Department, Latin American, Caribbean and Latinx Studies, Women's, Gender and Sexuality Studies, Creativity, the Arts and Social Transformation, the African Diaspora Cluster Writing Workshop, and the Mandel Center for the Humanities, provided generative space to air my work. I thank the Tufts University graduate students in Christina Sharpe's class, and again in Sonia Hofkosh and Modhumita Roy's class. I appreciate the generous support of graduate students and faculty at Florida Atlantic University during the semester that I taught there. I had many supportive listeners at meetings of the Caribbean Studies Association, Association of Caribbean Historians, Modern Language Association, Society for Caribbean Studies, Dark Room Collective, and Black Portraiture—and at talks organized by William Ghosh for the Oxford University Caribbean Studies Network; Ben Aslinger and Tzarina Prater in Bentley University's Department of English and Media Studies; and Sruti Bala at the University of Amsterdam. Conferences organized by Northwestern University's Comparative Literature Department, Honor Ford-Smith and Anthony Bogues, Deborah Thomas and John Jackson, and by Pat Noxolo, Rivke Jaffe, and Lucy Evans in Toronto, Philadelphia, Amsterdam, and Leicester were extremely generative, as were many *Small Axe* seminars organized by David Scott, Kelly Baker Joseph, Alex Gill, Kaiama Glover, Patricia Saunders, Deborah Thomas, and Donette Francis. Kimberly Juanita Brown and the Dark Room Collective, Jennifer Stern, and Robin

Lydenberg thought that I could say something meaningful about visuality and made sure that I had the resources to do so.

Over many years and courses, I have learned to think about many of the texts I discuss here with my students at Brandeis: thank you for your intellectual generosity. As a student myself at the University of the West Indies, Mona, I encountered many of the themes explored here in the classrooms of Caribbeanists who introduced me to canonical texts in Modernist, African American, African, and Victorian literary traditions; it was in Mervyn Morris's West Indian Literature class that I first heard Claude McKay's spoken voice.

I remain deeply grateful for the lifesaving support of Karen Wood, Claire Cronin, and Abram Recht.

Ken Wissoker's support for this project has been unflagging, and touching. Thanks to the anonymous reviewers who understood where I was going and helped me to get there.

To those who read or listened to versions of these chapters with such insight and grace, thank you: Sue Houchins, Thandeka, Bernadette Brooten, Sue Lanser, and Florence Ladd; Caren Irr and David Sherman; Aliyyah Abdur-Rahman and Ulka Anjaria; Brian Horton, V Varun Chaudhury, Brandon Callender, and Ulka Anjaria (again!); Sue Lanser (again!). Michelle Stephens and Yolanda Martinez San-Miguel read an early prospectus generously and supportively. At a critical point, Dean Susan Birren saw that I was drowning, and helped me, and that led me to the supportive community of Enid J. Schatz, Laveria Hutchison, Susan Callaway, and Yang Hu. Mary Campbell asked about royalty, Wangui Muigai asked about newspaper advertisements; John Plotz asked about the Rockefellers; Kanika Batra and I confided with each other about Claude McKay as if he is an uncle who haunts our dreams; Rachel Goffe asked about women traveling to the city to sell provisions; Tom King asked about the pinch of time; Carina Ray talked to me about Casely Hayford; Olive Senior said, "Look for the smallest possible detail on which to hang your story"; and Jasmine Johnson, Shoniqua Roach, and Sika Dagbovie-Mullins pressed me in different ways about Black women's ruination and pleasure. In the Phillips Reading Room, Jeanne Penvenne offered moral support. Thanks to Peter Desmond for many leads. Donette Francis, Mari Negron, and Elora Chowdhury continue to show me that the writing process can be joyfully supportive. In Port of Spain, walking back and forth between the Government Archives on St. Vincent Street and the Bocas Literary Festival must have fed my ideas about space and imagination; many thanks to so many lovely hosts and interlocutors over many years, including

Martha and Jamal Thomas, Charles and Denise Pennycooke, Marjorie Thorpe, and Nicholas Laughlin. Kevin Adonis Browne reminded me to think about Belmont's proximity to the Savannah. The directors of the "Yard Campus," marvelous Sunity Maharaj and Rawle Gibbons, showered me with love, showed me where C. L. R.'s aunts lived, and continue to remind me that I should make the work I do publicly accessible. In Jamaica, Mervyn and Helen Morris, Winifred Mullings, Patrick Robinson, and Val Carnegie talked to me about Westmoreland.

Whether known or unknown to me personally, these losses remain shocking to me: Barbara Stewart, Robert McKinley, Sean Morgan, Huntley Watson, Hope Smith, Katrina Scott-George, Christopher Edmondson, Garth Trotz, Hilton Rowley, Fernando Coronil, Jacqueline Barker, Sarita Bhalotra, Charles Mills, Steven Gregory, Sandra Bland, Donna McFarlane, Steve Adler-Golden, Christina Yuna Lee, Garfield Ellis, Karl Nyangoni, Victor Chang, Shirley Smith, Peggy Aljoe, Teresita Martínez-Vergne, Margaret Vendryes, Tejumola Olaniyan, Colin Robinson, Leslie Brown, José Muñoz, Sara Danius, and Greg Hampton. Laura Cade Brown.

Many friends fed me, kept my spirits up, took turns taking me to my radiation appointments, and taught me that you can be deeply theoretically engaged with global and local abjection while you are laughing. Gilberto Rosa-Duran, who came into Boston to sit and work with me in the public library, Kareem Khubchandani, Stacey Lantz, Jacqui Alexander, Lisa Pannella, Megan Finch, Diana Filar, Christina Sharpe, Dionne Brand, Patty Moonsammy, Alissa Trotz, Ifeona Fulani, Carroll Smith-Rosenberg, Alvia Golden, Andil Gosine, Jennifer Morgan, Herman Bennett, Rhonda Frederick, Derron Wallace, M. Jacqui Alexander, Lyndon Kamal Gill, the Pedder family, Rivke Jaffe, Wayne Modest, Supriya Nair, Chad Williams, Madeleine Lopez, Darrell Moore, Frederick Harris; Patricia Powell, Helen Klonaris, Kim Robinson, Patrick Sylvain, Sigrun Svarsdottir, and Erin Kelly; Sean McGuffy, Rosie Gordon-Wallace, Vanessa Pérez-Rosario, Kezia Page, Michael Bucknor, Suze Prudent, Gina Pugliese.

Leah Rosenberg, Njelle Hamilton, Angela Pérez Mejía, the Jackson-Thomases of Broad Street many times over, Roxanne, Ron, Brandon and Danielle Chambers, Ethan Geringer-Sameth, Barbara Lewis; Marc and Dora Older, Betsy Plumb, Mark Schafer, Patrick Grant, Gayle Grant, Gaurav Desai, Supriya Nair, Val and Barbara Carnegie, Chinyere Brown, Lynette Joseph-Brown, Jeannine Verrett-Hempstead, Jehanne-Marie Gavarini, Ronald Cummings, Avinash Singh, Dawn Skorczewski, Lewis Kirshner, Holly Fritz,

Dave Sherman, Charlotte Daniels, Teju Niranjana, Sandra Pouchet Paquet, Basil Paquet, Régine Jean-Charles, Joel Dawson, Alok Kapoor, Régine Jean-Charles, Matthew Chin, Chris Cozier, Irenée Shaw, Greg Childs, Patricia Saunders, Shalini Puri, Robin Feuer Miller, Carolyn Allen, Harleen Singh, Lynell Thomas, Jyoti Puri, Gillian Brown-Isabelle, Annie Paul, Michelle Rowley, Tracy Robinson, Belinda Edmondson, Marisol Negron, Elora Chowdhury, Donette Francis, Philippa Lawrence, Janet Lawrence, Marjorie Salvodon. My extended family of Smiths, Crooks, Browns, Simmonds, Hessons, Neils, Haughtons, and Hamiltons.

To say that Grace, Bertrand, Sharon, Hannah, and Johnathon Smith have cloaked me with unconditional love is to understate their unflagging love and care. It has taken me years to figure out how closely I have been circling my parents' birthplaces with this project: Blauwearie, in the parish of Westmoreland, Jamaica (1929) and Ciego de Ávila in Camagüey Province, Cuba (1931). Bless you both.

INTRODUCTION

Introducing a Quiet Period

In the last week of February 1900, revelers in Trinidad's capital, Port of Spain, embodied the postures of General Piet Cronjé and his Boer troops surrendering to British forces in southern Africa's Orange Free State, for that season's Carnival masquerade. Standing in formation on the Savannah on Pretoria Day later that year, Trinidadians in Port of Spain joined others in the colony and across the globe in saluting British victories in southern Africa. "In the reign of Victoria / We marched on Pretoria." This *we* in the Trinidadian calypsonian Duke of Marlborough's tribute to the victory is the sort of anglophile sentiment that might explain why this era of anglophone Caribbean history sounds disconcerting to later generations, or at any rate uncomplicated in its imperial loyalty. The cultural production of this pre-1930s period earns the ignominy of retrospective dismissal when later writers claim that they are the first to be other than embarrassingly mimetic.[1] In this sense turn-of-the-century anglophone Caribbean time seems nondescript, out of joint. It is *too late*, after insurgent acts making slavery unsustainable led to the 1833 Emancipation Act, and after postabolition *hataclaps* such as the state's murder of hundreds of protesters in Morant Bay, St. Thomas, Jamaica in late 1865, and of religious celebrants near San Fernando, Trinidad in late 1884.[2] *Too soon*, before discourses that tend to be claimed for early nationalism such as Trinidad's Beacon period of the 1920s and 1930s, and the labor strikes and demonstrations that swept through the region in the late 1930s. And generally too proud of its imperial identity to be included in lineages of resistance or of the nation-to-come. But what if we do not think of this period of anglophone Caribbean life in terms of mimicry or belatedness, of anticipating or refusing nationalism or a nation (a future that we know is down the road), but instead as sizing up alliances at a moment when every Caribbean territory, whether sovereign such as Haiti, or part of the Spanish, French, British, Dutch, or Danish empires, is keenly aware of being wedged between some European imperial project and increasingly also US imperial inclinations? Genealogies of the anglophone Caribbean should attend to this era's own sense of its ability to frame its past and its future and listen keenly to its "distinctive debate about modernity."[3]

Strolling in the Ruins focuses on two British Caribbean territories in the last years of the nineteenth century and the beginning of the twentieth: a "quiet period" that "remains understudied" in the British Caribbean.[4] If *quiet* runs against the grain of resistance and other concepts that we have come to value, what happens when we cannot prove resistance without a doubt; when resistance seems less interesting as a goal or disposition than other aspects of a spectacular event; or when, without other kinds of legibility, all we have is quiet?[5] In this "quiet period," what might the obscure or nondescript give us? Quiet is also violent routinization, as in the "intensity" of "many, many small cases" through which "the weight of the law is most intensely felt," when police and magistrates wield the power that most working-class people experience from the judicial system.[6] This is an intensity that suggests the *hum* of law and a building up (by wearing down) of the capacity to endure its violence; a *humdrum* that is repetitive, unrelenting, probably unremarked. Hum is also a "modality of quiet," an "undervalued lower range of quotidian audibility" that enlists us to attend to its very banality.[7]

Most of this book's *action*, such as it is, occurs on the cusp of events that could be said to mark time more productively, including a period identified with a "global imaginary of Caribbean intellectuals in the US," the beginning of the first World War in 1914, and Haiti's occupation by US Marines in 1915.[8] For Caribbean subjects in Trinidad and Jamaica confronting and shaping their discursive milieux at the convergence of multiple temporalities and geographies, what do sovereignty and freedom mean at this particular nodal point of empire? European interests across the Caribbean concede and contest US supremacy while continuing a pivot to Africa, Asia, and the Pacific intensified from the mid-nineteenth century. The United States stabilizes its interests in the region in the wake of the Spanish American War, which allows it to open the new century with considerable political, military, and economic power in Cuba, Puerto Rico, Guam, the Philippines, and Hawai'i. For the United

States, this growth follows decades of internal colonization of First Nation and Mexican communities and land, the codification of citizenship as coterminous with whiteness, an exponential increase of public lynchings, and legal enactments of exclusion and segregation including *Plessy v. Ferguson* (1896). At this time, the United States looks ahead to the military occupation of Haiti and the Dominican Republic and the purchase of the Danish Virgin Islands in the next decade.

As I track these imperial maneuvers in the context of the massive and consequential movement of Caribbean people to the Panama Canal zone, Costa Rica, the United States, and other locations, I pay even more attention to what it means to move back and forth, and often on foot, between two colonies' rural environs and their respective capitals, Port of Spain and Kingston. In these cities "peopled mainly by single women," streets, markets, and botanical gardens are charged sites of encounters between jamettes, queens, nightwomen, and new women, and the men who are so unnerved by them that their texts are a powerful expression of the energies and anxieties of this historical moment.[9] As nonwhite and nonelite people attempt to take advantage of new opportunities for accumulation and mobility in this moment, or at least try to secure relief from oppressive regimes of labor and surveillance, and as white, near-white, and nonwhite élites strive to retain moral and economic dominance, in part by mocking others as social upstarts, someone must bear the brunt of this mockery or learn to deflect it onto others. These are processes of destabilization and reinvention that mark a particular *conjuncture*: "a period during which the different social, political, economic, and ideological contradictions that are at work in society come together to give it a specific and distinctive shape"; "the set of material conditions within which one is compelled to think and to act."[10]

Migration is the great feature of anglophone Caribbean life in the later nineteenth and early twentieth centuries, as travelers from these territories and from Haiti, the francophone Caribbean, the Indian subcontinent, China, and West Africa, entering or leaving the Caribbean, fan out across the region as well as Central, South, and North America to work—sometimes also attempting to return, with supplemented families and capital, to the territories they left. Centering British Caribbean people and their journeys in this period, Lara Putnam refers to "all the lands that migrants . . . made part of the British Caribbean world," syntactically attributing a transformative cartographic and agential power to travelers who, compelled to leave hard times in one territory, often find themselves fueling antiforeigner nationalism in the territories that they helped to make prosperous.[11] Noting an almost exact temporal overlap of two patterns of migration in particular—1838–1917 for Asian indentured labor into the Caribbean, and the 1850s to 1920s for Caribbean migrants to Panama—the collaborators of the digital humanities project "Panama Silver, Asian Gold: Migration, Money, and the Birth of Modern Caribbean Literature" point out that it was the accumulation of these two groups of laborers that helped to fund the education and the social mobility of the intellectuals identified with the nationalist struggles and cultural production of the 1940s and 1950s, including the Windrush generation of writers, even as the mobility and accumulation of these laborers would be repudiated as crass.[12]

Before the phalanx of social scientists and reformers peering into barracks and tenement yards and bedrooms in order to speak with authority about the intimacies of working-class Afro- and Indo-Caribbean people, a period that we associate with the 1920s–50s, Kodak-wielding tourists emboldened by US triumph in the Spanish American war, or religious leaders and newspaper editors debating the effects of unmarried parenthood train their eyes on people who are returning from cutting cane and chopping lumber and building canals and fighting others' wars elsewhere, and also on people who have not left the region at all. *Strolling in the Ruins* is as interested in discerning their response to being the object of this surveillance, as it is in their own participation in the consumption of racist media coverage of, say, events in southern Africa in 1900.

If the Caribbean offers a unique vantage point from which to reconsider itineraries that have tended to define and overshadow the early twentieth century, including modernist ones that consign the region to an aesthetic periphery, or nationalist ones which privilege particular events or dispositions, then seeing "the anglophone Caribbean [as] . . . a shadowy presence and bridge between the British metropolis and the US global superpower," presses us to reimagine both this historical moment and our relationship to it.[13] A bridge affords a vantage point from which to consider the adjacency of two imperial powers, while a "shadowy presence" suggests the immaterial, the inconsequential, or the ghostly. Neither roiled by political clamor for change like its hispanophone and Haitian neighbors, nor apparently desirous of being so, the anglophone Caribbean can barely be discerned in relation to its noisy neighbors nor in relation to its own noisier pasts and futures. So-called riotous events in Montego Bay, Jamaica in April 1902, and the March 23, 1903 Water Riot in Port of Spain are significant, but they feel relatively minor compared to political upheaval elsewhere, an impression intensified by the trek of political exiles from the nineteenth century and continuing into the new century, from Venezuela to Trinidad, and from Cuba and Haiti to Jamaica.[14] Depending on the commentator, this means that the British Caribbean is stable and level headed, or that it is stifled: *Strolling in the Ruins* asks what is breathing quietly, or seething, beneath nonrevolutionary "stability" and "order."

Caribbean people avidly watch the flexing of British imperial muscles at this turn-of-the-century moment. On the African continent alone they are following news about southern Africa, as we have seen, as well as the Gold Coast, where British forces contend with French and German troops for gold, cocoa, and rubber, under the rubric of bringing stability to the region and ending slave trading and human sacrifice; and news about the Ovonramwen, the Oba of Benin, forced to cede his sovereign power to the British during the so-called Punitive Expedition in 1897, as bronzes from his royal court are carted off to a future in European and North American museums. Some Caribbean people also cheer on family members and neighbors—those West Indian soldiers who, serving in the West India Regiment as part of the British army, help quell the *insurgency* of what is reported in the papers as Ashanti or Anglo-Ashanti *expeditions* and establish a British protectorate. Watching one Ashanti sovereign after another exiled to the Seychelles for objecting to the levying of tributes or to the attempt by British military figures to sit on the Golden Stool, the royal throne of the Ashanti, Caribbean people sometimes have firsthand knowledge of the fate of sovereign powers who challenged European claims to their land and commodities. King Ja Ja of the West African state of Opobo was punished for trading in palm oil on his own terms with exile to St. Vincent in the 1880s; and the French military authorities exiled King Béhanzin of Dahomey to Fort de France, Martinique, in 1894.

His title starkly setting out the available alternatives for the British Caribbean, Louis Meikle, a Jamaican-born and US-trained doctor living in Trinidad, published *Confederation of the British West Indies Versus Annexation to the United States of America: A Political Discourse on the West Indies* in 1912. Meikle directed his attention to the racial consequences of US annexation for people who were not, as he put it, "White! White!! White!!!"[15] As the United States inherits military, economic, and political dominance from Spain and other empires, in the Caribbean and elsewhere, and in the latest phase of its own long-standing relationship to the Caribbean, we are interested in how this involvement can be made legible when, unlike its own internal continental expansion, or unlike Europe, the United States eschews formal settlement. Performing nonmonarchical imperial governance, its directives not necessarily made by *Congress* or *the president* or *the republic*, US power asserts itself in the wake of older orders of conquest and enslavement, including on its own soil. This is demonstrated when US magnate Andrew Carnegie suggests that the United States ought to exchange the recently acquired Philippines for the British Caribbean and Bermuda.[16] It is evident in the social power of estate managers, hotels, railway stations, and ships connected to the United Fruit Company in towns with banana cultivation across Central America and the Caribbean, as well as in offshore naval squadrons performing friendly maneuvers.[17] Moreover, European imperial assertions have to be understood as shifting in reaction to the more insistent presence of the United States. How does power issuing from a monarchy measure up against power without this? We are tracking, then, "how sovereignty *feels*" in this era: how do Caribbean people and territories incite or inspire, as well as manage and endure this multifaceted imperial posturing?[18]

The Vocabulary of Sovereignty

One way of making sense of the Duke of Marlborough's *we* ("In the reign of Victoria / We marched on Pretoria") is that imperial power provides the vocabulary through which people in the region imagine power or freedom. To choose the moniker "Duke," as George Jamesie Adilla does, is to identify his public persona as a calypsonian with a meaningful sign of imperial power. When I hear "Lord Kitchener" today I do not think of the British military figure, Horace Herbert Kitchener, who assumed command of the British forces in southern Africa in late 1900, after leading Egyptian and British forces in the defeat of the Khalifa and the Mahdist state encompassing Khartoum-Sudan. I think of the beloved calypsonian Aldwyn Roberts who used that sobriquet, and who dominated the Trinidad Carnival scene from the 1950s: surely a sign of nationalist or postcolonial triumph (the "right" Kitchener gained posterity in the end), but the very choice of the name attests to its considerable symbolic power. Though Horace Kitchener was identified with terrible human devastation in both military campaigns—thousands of Sudanese died, including civilians, and the treatment of Boer prisoners both in the British concentration camps and on the battlefield earned him negative press (press which did not bemoan the nonwhite constituencies whose lives and land were being upended)—this devastation did not, for many around the world, diminish the idea of British imperial power as essentially moral.

In this period of major regal transfers in the British context (Queen Victoria's reign of sixty-four years ended with her death in 1901, and when her successor and eldest son, Edward VII, died on the throne in 1910, he was succeeded by his son George V), we will have many occasions to see how fictional characters and their creators take the power of their status as British colonial subjects as a given. The interest in royalty who are other than European or white (interest that I read as parallel or entangled, rather than necessarily oppositional or contradictory) also suggests how the *office*, the position of authority and its attendant power, fascinates. "There is no black princess in Trinidad," a newspaper in that colony declared in 1909, disputing information published in a Barbadian paper: "To say the least it is vulgar to have a horde of the great unwashed running behind her carriage shouting 'de princess' as she drives about, or to have them actually peering at her, at very close quarters, when she pays a visit. . . . She is an Algerian lady of color who carries no title whatsoever."[19] What appealed to this Trinidadian crowd about this visitor, why did the newspaper's tone appear to be one of irritation or even outrage (rather than neutrality), and was the term "black princess" the newspaper's, in the process of negating this fact, or the crowd's?

To their consternation, eighteenth- and nineteenth-century Caribbean slaveholders and colonial authorities had found themselves contending with strong notions of African sovereignty expressed in terms of royalty. In spiritual traditions such as *Kumina*, ritual specialists and queens presided over *nation* business, crossing various phases, and dimensions of the human and spirit world.[20] In Cuban *cabildos* and Trinidad *convois*, organizations of enslaved people and free people of color appointed kings and queens surreptitiously or in plain sight.[21] In Antigua in 1736, preparations by the Leeward Islands élite for an annual ball to commemorate King George II's 1727 coronation were interrupted by the uncovering of a plot by enslaved people to kill all the whites, and "they intirely to possess the island."[22] One of the leaders of the thwarted plot, Court-Tackey, had been "crowned King of the Coromantees" about two weeks earlier, with two thousand enslaved people in attendance, in an elaborate Akan ceremony understood to be a sovereign's declaration of imminent military exercises and a call to prepare for war. We could say that even as they attached different readings of the past and future to their present moment, the timing of their plan to coincide with the celebration of the anniversary of a British sovereign's coronation meant that they also acknowledged and exploited the importance of the way that the colonial state marked time. Gendering the assignment of regal titles in the planning of insurgencies such as the Ladder Conspiracy in 1840s Cuba, Aisha Finch notes that whether women were themselves organizers or facilitated access to strategic points of entry because of their proximity to the domestic quarters of slaveholding families, it was their perceived ties to male organizers that appeared to shape the granting of the designation "queen" or "second queen," however extensive or limited their involvement.[23]

One inspiring and troubling assertion of sovereignty was the transformation of Haitian president Henri Christophe into King Henri I, and of Haiti into a kingdom, with days of festivities to mark the June 1811 coronation of King Henri and Queen Marie-Louise. A few months later when, in Cuba, the artisan and military veteran José Antonio Aponte was tried as the leader of a conspiracy to overthrow the government and slavery in that Spanish colony, his familiarity with King Henri Christophe's coronation and with Haiti's willingness to assist its enslaved territorial neighbors; his artistic renderings of the Vatican with black priests and cardinals, and of the fifteenth-century king and kingdom of Ethiopia enjoying diplomatic popularity in Rome and throughout Europe all proved incriminating.[24] Haiti's sovereign maneuvers terrified its neighbors in the region and around the world, and attempts to rehearse the republic's emancipatory gestures on plantations across the region inspired harsh retaliation, as well as scorn for King Christophe and his court.[25]

In the early twentieth century, at least two territories offered immediate examples of formidable non-European sovereign power, when Emporer Menelik II of Ethiopia/Abyssinia led his troops in the routing of Italian forces in the Battle of Adwa in 1896, and when Japan defeated Russia in the Russo-Japanese War of 1904–5. Newspaper accounts of negotiations with Emperor Menelik as the British pursued military strategies in Khartoum and Egypt, or about the fêting of Prince Fushimi in the US White House and at the St. Louis World's Fair in Missouri, may have conveyed a sense of non-Western imperial power that the US and European powers either respected or had no choice but to engage.[26] Such reports may have expanded an idea of imperial power as more than the white-dominant civilizational cast that was often its presumed register (though it will be clear that this book never concedes a displacement of British imperial power but rather tries to understand how Caribbean people contended complexly with its material and symbolic weight). Certainly Abyssinia's victory had powerful reverberations for global Black diasporic visions of freedom, and it fulfilled a biblical prophecy that Ethiopia would "soon stretch out her hands unto God."[27]

While an "Algerian lady" found herself designated "black princess" by a Trinidad crowd, Prince Ludwig Menelik presented himself to the Berlin public as the nephew of Abyssinia's Emperor Menelik in 1907, three years after appearing throughout Jamaica and in Bristol, England as Royal Prince Thomas Mackarooroo, "second heir to the throne of Ceylon."[28] A member of what Robert Hill has designated *Aethiopis vagantes*, "a group of wandering "'Ethiopians,' consisting largely of West Indians, who, along with a smattering of African Americans and continental Africans, traversed the Atlantic world promoting their special 'Ethiopian' lineage and pedigree," he was the kind of figure about whom Marcus Garvey cautioned his followers decades later: "Keep a close eye on African princes, African chiefs, princesses and all such fake personalities."[29] Prince Ludwig likely undermined both the dignity of the Abyssinian royal court and global Black discourses of uplift and respectability, and we could think of "Mackarooroo" as a caricature, its strung-together syllables an indication of the ease with which the demand for *Anywhere, Africa-or-Asia* could be satisfied by African-descended people in the Americas—what Simon Gikandi has discussed in terms of a perverse preference for a familiar primitivism.[30] Claiming kinship with Ceylon as well as Abyssinia is a nod to some specific contemporaneous inspiration that I have so far failed to notice, or perhaps to the popularity of *The Cingalee or Sunny Ceylon*, a play performed on London, Broadway, and Kingston stages throughout 1904, its all-white cast of characters of Cingalese belles and nobility, and European administrators and governesses, possibly giving Prince Ludwig resources for performances of parallel sovereignty, even as the play normalized the violence of British management of tea plantations and the annexation of the Kandy.[31]

At the same time Prince Ludwig also demonstrated that the Abyssinian king was as susceptible to imposture as any other royalty; that there were multiple and complex ways to pay tribute to the power of the Abyssinian throne at a moment when the African continent was being thoroughly reimagined on Europe's terms; that Abyssinian royalty was a powerful counterweight to, even if not necessarily always a repudiation of, European imperial power; and that Abyssinian sovereign power elicited global desires for kinship whether, as here, with a claim to be a nephew, or, within a few decades, as beloved and long-anticipated Messiah. Steeped as we are in discourses of Rastafari that have challenged the political and theological underpinnings of British colonial rule from at least the 1940s to the present, the incident reminds us that diasporic inclinations are sometimes refracted through empire, or at any rate under its auspices—that the diasporic and the imperial, far from being mutually exclusive spheres, are better understood relationally, as not only thwarting and displacing but also shaping or enlivening each other.

Whether disrespectful returnee, unrepentant hustler, or visionary seeking to show that unfairly taxed colonial subjects in the Caribbean were Emperor Menelik's rightful heirs, Prince Ludwig was cast as *bogus* and *fake*, and we could interpret this at least partly to a tradition of ridiculing and sometimes punishing transatlantic Black speech and attire as excessive, since the prevailing vocabulary (not to mention violent military and legal force) of imperial power being worked out globally by European states and the United States could not be other than inappropriate when utilized by those perceived as innately subordinate. In this decade before the House of Saxe-Coburg and Gotha became the House of Windsor, assumptions of authority, wealth, and access that were not embodied in and endorsed by white personhood and institutions reeked especially of impostorship. Minstrel shows performed on stages across the Caribbean and North America, and caricatures and anecdotes published in leading periodicals and broadsides all circulated and codified particular readings of the nonwhite body. *Strolling in the Ruins* looks closely at the authorities' often punitive exercise of surveillance of those presumed to be exceeding their allotted social roles, but also pays particular attention to the bystanders (offenders-in-waiting, in the logic of the state) of the same class as the presumed impostor. Whether neighbors, police informants, or oglers in court, we want to presume their ability to discern multiple levels of signification in these figures transformed by arrest or salacious newspaper reports into spectacular performers, even as they understand that the spectacle being made out of their peers is meant to elicit their own submissiveness. We want to attend to the capacity of performer and bystander to turn such occasions into "intellectual sites of inquiry," to see each performance as both test and warning.[32] We are on the lookout for performers who, whether quietly, or in the expansive gestures and itineraries of Carnival revelers or *Aethiopis vagantes*, rehearse loyalty to all kinds of sovereigns, and to their own sense of personal sovereignty, employing their bodies (or being read by others) as "canvasses of dissent" or as acquiescent.[33]

Postcards from the Present

I have come to the anglophone Caribbean's "quiet" early twentieth century with inclinations located at the intersection of Caribbean, feminist, Black diasporic, and postcolonial studies; and steeped in the nationalist agendas and timelines that have designated the cultural production of figures based in the Caribbean, Europe, North America, Asia, and Africa from the 1950s through the end of the twentieth century as the ideal expression of freedom struggles, civil rights projects, and independence movements. From our contemporary moment marked by exhaustion and cynicism regarding questions of power and sovereignty, but also by buoyancy and resilience in popular, quotidian, and activist arenas, it is tempting to think that there are lineages of struggle and terror, as well as postures of endurance, that might show how people have always lived with apparent setbacks. When has this happened before, and what can we learn from it? This is what the early twentieth century stands to teach us.

Yarimar Bonilla has proposed that Caribbean people share "non-sovereign" status with one another, whether their individual territories have remained colonies, sponsored successful revolutions, experienced flag independence, or they are departments and commonwealths.[34] If this has always been true, and if this book probes one moment's clear-sightedness about and negotiation of this realization, then I take from Bonilla's need to state it, an uneven sense across the region of the long-standing truth of this condition. No doubt I am prepared to hear Bonilla's insights because of my own post-post-independence disillusionment in the anglophone Caribbean context, though this does not of course mean that everyone registers our present this way. Disillusionment implies an expectation that things would have gone another way, and it also offers a chance to understand the past differently, or to reimagine the future. Centering Caribbean women and girls, and queer Asian migrants, respectively, Donette Francis and David Eng problematize the kind of narration of emancipation, independence, and liberalism that excludes those who "had already experienced the failure of colonial and independent nation-states to deliver happy endings" or who "remain subjects in waiting."[35]

The last few years have brought constant reminders of both the region's complex non-sovereign contexts and the suturing and severing of pasts to and from the ongoing present. When the Jamaican armed forces cracked down brutally on a western Kingston community for its support of Christopher

Dudus Coke in 2010—support expressed in divine and regal terms—they were punishing but also making more visible a figure whose business interests and patronage equaled and even transcended that of the government and the state. Extending across the United States as well as deep inside the city's neighborhoods, Coke's influence represented a parallel sovereignty, even as his extradition to the United States and subsequent incarceration rehearsed Caribbean sovereignty's limits.[36]

Reports about the treatment of Windrush-era migrants to the United Kingdom ("freely landed" travelers who became presumptive British citizens) were striking to me in the context of the continuing revelations of historians who are "following the money," as they trace the court claims of British citizens who sought part of the twenty million pounds in compensation granted to slaveholders for the loss of their human property when slavery was abolished in the British Caribbean in 1833.[37] In the 2020 summer of corporate apologies for antiblackness, the compound interest and other instruments of accumulation that continue to activate the wealth from enslavement and the postemancipation period were missing from the calculated phrasing ("the indefensible wrongdoing that occurred during this period," "it is inexcusable that one of our founders profited from slavery") that insists that the past came to an end in the past.[38] Catherine Hall, Nicholas Draper, and Keith McClelland remind us of the "invisibility" of slave-ownership in British history: "It has been elided by strategies of euphemism and evasion originally adopted by the slave-owners themselves and subsequently introduced widely in British culture."[39] In the turn-of-the-century period covered by this book, Britons (in sleights of hand that we will note for other constituencies as well), who "never shall be slaves," owned and managed slaves, magnanimously "emancipated" them, and continued to profit from the legacies of enslavement.

The right to claim a range of sexual and gender identities in the region, sometimes terrifying and heartening on the same day in its consequences, is often met with popularly endorsed appeals to colonial law to enforce heterosexuality and gender conformity. The so-called cross-dressing law, Section 153 (1) (xlvii) of the Summary Jurisdiction (Offences) Act of 1893, deeming it illegal for anyone "being a man, in any public way or public place, for any improper purpose, [to] appear in female attire; or being a woman, in any public way or public place, for any improper purpose, [to] appear in male attire," and which allowed Guyanese authorities to charge a group of gender-nonconforming persons with being wrongly attired in female clothing in 2009, was struck down on November 13, 2018.[40] Appeals to colonial law in postcolonial time, enforced by the keen, quotidian scrutiny of armed forces who suss out purported mannish women and effeminate men, came to seem eerily familiar to me as I watched Caribbean people in early twentieth-century newspapers, novels, and poetry whose sartorial choices, movements, and congress with intimate partners of another race, or with night-time visitors in their bedrooms on their employers' property, rendered them out of place and subject to both the weight of the law, enforced by police, and the disapproving scrutiny of their neighbors. Thus the nonheterosexual and gender-nonconforming expressions that are currently the default assumption of what constitutes sexual transgressions, and that incur ongoing and violent scrutiny by the state and its citizens, are continuous and entangled with the violations that were assumed to deserve such scrutiny in the past.[41]

My twenty-first-century present is also marked by cynicism and despair about two 1960s projects charged (perhaps burdened) with expectations of political and social freedom: the political independence of some anglophone Caribbean territories in the wake of decolonization across Africa and Asia, on the one hand, and the US Civil Rights Act of 1964, on the other; but also the radical projects (including Black Power movements in the Caribbean and the United States, and the Cuban and Grenadian revolutions) that promised to counter the liberal constraints of those formal, legislated agendas. This disillusionment has been analyzed in the contexts of interrogating Caribbean governments' ramped-up scrutiny and punishment of citizens' sexual behavior to compensate for their economic and political paralysis, and reassessing who had been included in promises of freedom at the time of anglophone Caribbean independence;[42] and in reconsidering the assumption that African American leaders' involvement in the highest echelons of the wielding of US state violence by the early twenty-first century was a good and inevitable outcome of the civil rights movement.[43] Two commentators reflect on our present in terms of outlasting ruination: of "living *on* in the wake of past political time, amid the ruins, specifically, of postsocialist and postcolonial futures past," in the case of the Caribbean; and as a time, in the US context, that is "simultaneously postfree and not yet free," requiring a modality that "eschews the heroism of black pasts and the promise of liberated black futures in order to register and revere rapturous joy in the broken-down present."[44] What does this sense of having outlived the future allow us to see more clearly about the past, or about what we have taken for granted regarding its proper narration?

Whose Modern?

Focused on forms of self-fashioning that allow Caribbean subjects at the turn of the twentieth century to feel that they can live to see another day, we have to keep in mind how our sense of time in the contemporary moment frames what sounds aesthetically or ideologically feasible in these historical texts. These texts are bound to disappoint, though hopefully productively.[45] The stilted prose, forged letters, and misrecognized kin of some of the novels examined here feel melodramatic for an era that has come to be defined in terms of the emergence of modernist agnosticism and ironic detachment. The setting for some of the texts is the country estate that is the near-rural second home of cocoa planters, or that is the actual site of working sugar mills and cattle pens—striking, on the cusp of an era in which novelists join anthropologists and social workers in scrutinizing the intimate lives of young single women moving from a rural landscape to the yard/*yaad* of the city. It is also striking from a future in which the politically transformative act is to burn down the estate's great house or otherwise harm its owner or occupants, or at least to stroll through the ruins contemplating its demise.[46]

Drawing on Sylvia Wynter's foundational opposition between *plot* (as land and as literary form) and market-driven *plantation*, Curdella Forbes points out that undermining those who own and monitor land has now come to define a Caribbean ethos of what she calls "sly disobedience."[47] Squatting on Crown lands becomes part of an enduring struggle (between the perceived heirs of plantation owners, and others who either own much smaller units of land or who do not own land at all) over the public right to share space "at the nexus between Backra's plantation and family land, praedial larceny and reclamation, enemy territory to be 'captured' and territory that is mine—in other words, between Backra's plantation and plot-as-family-land/community-space."[48] This plantation-plot confrontation, at least in its *narration*, posits the great house–residing owners as aligned with local and external capitalist interests, as probably but not necessarily white and near-white, and as hostile to the interests of an Afro- and Indo-descended class identified with rural and urban nonelites. But what happens when nonwhite people lay claim to *plantation* instead of *plot* in this dyad? Perhaps it is only a coincidence that estate ownership is solidly white in Jamaican novels discussed here, and by contrast eastern Caribbean protagonists (who want to take their place in the great house as owners, and as part of the trajectory of proving their moral right to befriend, share power with, and inherit—or recover—the wealth of local and visiting white élites, and to do so utilizing the vindicating discourses of a global African-descended Talented Tenth) affirm their African descent no matter how physically white-appearing they may be.[49] Somehow the allure of the plantation-as-pastoral (bucolic, restorative, ameliorating) appears to transcend legacies of violence, and in such narratives we must attend to how strategies of "euphemism and evasion" noted by Hall, Draper, and McClellan are utilized not only in British "national" life, but on behalf of a range of social subjects within the Caribbean as well.

As batons are passed from one imperial robber baron to the other across the globe, we are mapping the narrative contortions of plotting African-descended owners who inherit patriarchal authority successfully from white Caribbean estate owners, and we are keeping an eye on the fictional characters whose aspirations fail to garner them a share in this reimagining. This is partly a question of the right to own land, or at least to tread freely on it, in this moment of massive uprooting and displacement and newly levied "poll" and "hut" taxes across the African continent, when US African Americans are violently dangled above the earth to reinforce their dispossession, and when visiting whites assured of a Caribbean that is populated by safely subordinated nonwhites and free of yellow fever, stroll around the region *armed* with cameras.[50]

Both the right to claim and share space and the right to suture the present to particular pasts and futures are shaped by long-standing perceptions of the Caribbean's inauspicious relationship to time and modernity, and by Caribbean peoples' recalibration of such perceptions. Whether "alternative," "divergent," or a "time-lag" according to some theorizations of modernities experienced simultaneously and differently, the Caribbean has long been positioned as not-quite-modern even as the region enabled the capital accumulation that was key to the "West's" modernity.[51] The same history of enslavement casts Caribbean people and their geographical location as eternally abject, never properly modern, even when (or perhaps *because*), as in the case of Haiti, this history includes the radical overthrow of both slavery and colonial rule. British Caribbean people struggle to reconcile multiple temporalities while recognizing that the history of being enslaved, as well as of having had slaves, taints the region in a way that it never seems to taint the British *at home*. Casting this period as an *interregnum* in an *English* context, a sort of undistinguished Edwardian pause before the explosion of the First World War, understates the momentous imperial accumulation so critical for familial and national inheritance.[52] How is Englishness, but also imperial power more generally, able to narrate itself as merely or even primarily "national," in this moment of tremendous, violent, and enriching involvement across the globe, and when and how do Caribbean and other imperial subjects make note of this?

Attending to the entanglement of affiliations, newly emergent and long-standing, in this moment, we see Caribbean people observing (but also *embodying*, as in the Carnival lyrics and postures to celebrate developments in Pretoria) European imperial powers' consolidation of the turn to direct rule in Africa and Asia over the course of the nineteenth century, as if moving on to greener pastures, while the United States moves in to the Caribbean to consolidate economic interests. Keeping British "strategies of euphemism and evasion" in mind we want to pay attention to the capacity of old money to narrate itself as ruined, as finished, or to claim wonderment when transported to new arenas of exploitation. Part of this historical period's experience of modernity is the discernment of plantation slavery and other older orders of exploitation (even if cast as belated) in the jingoism of the present of a new century: connecting estate time, for example, to the imperial war-front in southern Africa because British accumulation there is continuous with centuries of accumulation in the Americas. "Remembering the wrong things at a wrong moment" is Lisa Yoneyama's prescription for a productive "unsettling" and "unlearning," in her discussion of the "cold war ruins" of power in Asia and the Pacific—a mid-twentieth-century context for the United States' inheritance of power from Europe.[53] We want to see how the perception of an imperial turning away from or toward the Caribbean leaves unresolved questions—about estate accumulation, for example—in its wake.

How are Africa, the United States, and the Caribbean newly configured in relation to each other, in relation to these imperial arrangements? Placing contemporaneous novels from different global spaces in dialogue with each other, as in chapter 4, illustrates how fictional characters in the Caribbean, West Africa, and North America conceptualize time in relation to questions of inheritance, "traditions," and empire, but also suggests what can be made explicit and what is left unsaid.[54] The US-based novel, explicit in its critique of slavery's entanglement with imperialism, represents continental Africans as biding time for a US-based messiah. The West African novel discusses polygamy (a taboo subject for the US and Caribbean novels) as a viable cultural institution that is comparable rather than inferior to European contexts of intimacy and kinship, bearing out Rhonda Cobham-Sander's characterization of a "face-off" between two entities (Africa and Europe) with "established institutions through which to articulate the significance of commonly held beliefs and widely dispersed practices."[55] Somewhat similarly to the use of West African polygamy to assess and critique European morality, late nineteenth-century Indian nationalists conceded Europe's superiority in technological, scientific, and economic realms, seeking to transform "traditional culture" where applicable, but reserving *ghar*, an inner realm that was inaccessible and spiritually superior to the worldly, European-dominated domain of *b̄ahir*: a way to make peace with the colonizing power while preserving an untouchable, inner sanctum, even as it idealized a sphere of confining protection for élite women.[56] That is to say, middle-class Indian intellectuals, as with their West African counterparts, experience European colonialism, in its direct official and settler dimensions, as relatively recent, with a "traditional-modern" axis, however "invented," grounded in a mutual understanding of lifeworlds that precede the colonizing power. Their debates with colonial officials about marriage and other issues entail at least a rhetorical acknowledgment of multiple customary systems, whether or not these are honored in practice. But this is not the case for the Caribbean, subject to direct colonial settlement, anchored in racial enslavement and then indentureship from the late fifteenth century.

"Our uprootedness is the original model of the total twentieth century disruption of man," notes Sylvia Wynter in 1968 about the Caribbean. "[Ours was] the first labor force that emergent capitalism had totally at its disposal.... We anticipated, by centuries, that exile, which in our century is now common to all."[57] But this displacement is recognizable as modern only when (non-Caribbean) others experience it later in time, or when these others are socially legible *as modern* when they experience it. Indispensable to metropolitan prosperity at the cost of its own underdevelopment ("Not an inch of this world devoid of my fingerprints . . . and my filth in the glitter of gems"), the region's perceived lack of modernity has sometimes been deliberately highlighted in order to attract tourists imagined as modern. And researchers searching for pristine, premodern cultures have also been disappointed when the Caribbean seemed insufficiently noncoeval.[58]

Invoking a time before European conquest (in the course of asserting that the colonized were not just passive victims, for example) can be interpreted as denying the reality of "a single, shared world, a world brought into being by European conquest," and the extent to which "colonial power transformed the ground on which accommodation or resistance was possible in the first place."[59] I read Lisa Lowe's call for "an actively acknowledged loss within the present" not as synonymous with longing for a return to a world before conquest, but rather as an active engagement with "what could have been" that reminds us that our conceptions of freedom in the present and for the future utilize the same modes of liberal-humanist registers of affirmation and forgetting that undergirded conquest, enslavement, and indentureship.[60] Moreover, a "transformed ground" brings to mind Melanie Newton's caution that concession of the violent efficiency of the erasure of the indigenous presence in the Caribbean at the moment of conquest (Europeans' "scourging of the human landscape"—"*as if the Antilles were empty lands*") further instantiates, rather than simply describes, the absence of a retrievable past that preceded the plantation economy; a past that is thus unavailable even for ongoing and dynamic reflection.[61]

This historical period is still often referred to by the names of either of two successive British monarchs, whose lives and reigns are thus held to have the meaning that merits this comprehensive designation, or the power to conscript colonial subjects (and then all of us, in the aftermath, who use such designations) into conceding such significance, with statues and parades and Empire Days across the globe celebrating Victoria and Edward (rather than, say, Henri, Shaka, Ovonramwen, Yaa Asantewaa, Prempeh, Cixu, Puyi).[62] With fireworks and other events marking Empire Day, colonial authorities seek to impose official time and a collective memory, and this is in keeping with the celebration of British royal successions and coronations, but also with more mundane events and commemorations linked to plantation schedules, or to marital unions and the wealth passed on to the children of such unions. But other kinds of events ("outside" children, devotees' timekeeping propitiation of various *lwas*, the quiet observance of the anniversary of a successful runaway attempt, for the one committing *marronage*/escape and for those left behind) are a reminder of the "invisible rhythms and punctuations concealed beneath the surface of each visible time."[63]

No doubt, the sovereigns I have just referred to parenthetically are celebrated periodically and ritually in Trinidad, Jamaica, and elsewhere in the first decade of the twentieth century, in rituals known, unknown, forbidden, or permitted by the authorities, alongside ("beneath the surface of") other rituals observed or reluctantly conceded over time: saints days and missionary Sundays, tazia processions to the banks of a river or the sea, the colors and abstentions required by orisha and *lwa*. Standing or moving together as one, participants mark an anniversary or salute some personage, but we cannot register their exuberance, hostility, or ambivalence with certainty, any more than we can assume what memories are summoned up or what ideas are being fashioned. The notion of a community's single ritual bonding feels useful in its ability to capture a sense of sharing a deep affiliation based on religious, imperial, diasporic, or other contexts. In this way we imagine people being conscious, wherever they are in the world, of rooting for the same side, whether in Adwa in 1896, or Pretoria in 1900. This is to invoke the vivid and also heavily critiqued image of the "meanwhileness" of "imagined communities."[64] We might imagine Venezuelans exiled in Trinidad at the turn of the century—consuming the same media as others in Trinidad but *reading into* particular news items and imagining that they share coded interpretations with others across the region—as an example of beating time differently in the same space or similarly across different geographical spaces. Thinking of the way that each one of several constituencies in a single nation "*originates* its present in the past differently," offers a useful way of visualizing people who share a national or other space without sharing a sense of marking time together.[65]

Orlando Patterson's definition of "natal alienation" rests on this inability to integrate the experiences of the past *freely* with one's ongoing present and future. It is not that people do not manage to achieve this integration, but that even their success in doing so, secretly and under duress, is liable to be reprimanded harshly when discovered and is not recognized as significant or legitimate by the status quo: no *mus-and-bound-ness* compels law or custom to affirm or recognize such attempts.[66] This is why we must pay such keen attention to people being "dressed down" ("bused," "traced") rhetorically in public, in the presence of laughing bystanders. The prohibition on what can be uttered, worn, or otherwise performed becomes attached to the memories that such people feel free to pass on to their descendants. While some have the freedom to talk about an event, or to invoke a time in the past and integrate it into the ongoing present, others are enjoined to be silent.[67]

This severing of the past had been important for a sugar economy that required people with different traditions to work side by side "producing capitalism's first real commodities," under duress and "without kinfolk. That was also modernizing, because the minimal cells of tradition-perpetuation are familial," and we have already referred to this capacity. "Because the basis for operating in terms of known status categories was under constant pressure from migration and external coercion," Caribbean people became adept at "socializing without recourse to previously learned forms . . . [practicing] an acquired matter-of-factness about cultural differences in social style or manners."[68] But what have been the consequences of this adroitness in the absence of "kinfolk" and "tradition-perpetuation" for notions of *kinship itself*, when, as Hortense Spillers notes, "'kinship' loses meaning, since it can be invaded at any given and arbitrary moment by the property relations?"[69] How does this vulnerability to "invasion" shape the understanding of how one is anchored to the past, as one turns to the future? When an inherited heterogeneity signals impurity—a bastard modernity, in effect, that might very well add value to the laborer *in the zone of labor,* but that also signals the laborer's devalued social status—who is made to bear the weight of this presumed stigma?

Reproducing Bad Time

Tracking the Black woman's actual and perceived embodiment of this stigma is one of this book's preoccupations. How time in her company or kinship with her must be sloughed off in order to thrive is a phenomenon and conundrum that wends its way through the meditation on inheritance in chapter 4, and in the way that, in chapter 3, she enlivens the intellectual and sexual lives of socially mobile men, even as law and custom render her deeply entangled in their political and social downfall. These early twentieth-century scenarios have their precedent in immediate and distant pasts. Enslaved and free Black women in the United States used baptisms, legal briefs, manumission attempts, and other strategies to "shield" their children from "exposure," understanding that they could not leave to chance their children's eligibility for future freedom; and as "tithable labor" they attracted a tax that had to be paid by their owners, marital partners, or themselves, depending on their status.[70] In Trinidad "bastardy" ordinances forcing powerful men to acknowledge the paternity of single women's children (a magnanimous concession, as they saw it, that was now being turned into a legal obligation) required these mothers to prove that they were not "immoral"; and in Cuba "*sin otro apellido*" or "*sin segundo apellido*" ("without any other surname" or "without second surname") identified persons of color with a single surname, the mother's name, as socially "illegitimate."[71]

Even as the neutralizing of tradition can be freeing (or can be instrumentalized as such) some social subjects appear to render time and space especially fraught, even unbearable, and we will be interested in how, as Grace Kyung-won Hong frames it, "the inheritance of *disinheritance*," the passing on and passing down of "the status of *nothingness itself*, social death" is a characteristic and an inclination perceived to course through the body and personhood of female-identified descendants of enslaved people and those who are adjacent to them.[72] I read newspapers, novels, and other texts in part to see how "the time of inheritance" is negotiated—in the quest for a parental legacy that is socially legible and luminous, or that, since it cannot be named, is erased in the claim to have birthed oneself.[73] In the generic distribution of sympathy or time—a poem's allocation of allusions and echoes within and across its lines, syllables, and stresses, or a novel's staging of "different characters who jostle for limited space within the same fictive universe," I read male narrators and personae struggling to save face, as in chapter 4 where even the *wealthy* nonwhite female partner is unable to take the hero comfortably into a viable future, since she brings a claim to inherit on her own behalf or a threatening energy, sexuality, and intellect that has to be contained.[74]

Given Garvey's injunction to "keep a close eye on African princes, African chiefs, *princesses*" what scope do women ("real" princesses or otherwise) have to be globally or locally mobile, or to make their bodies "canvases of dissent," given the social expectations attached to particular gendered and sexed bodies? Women's bodies and clothing are key markers of "culture," or its absence, as when in the late 1880s a visitor to Trinidad had proposed that African-descended women "twist[ed] their unhappy wool into knots and ropes in the vain hope of being mistaken for the purer race" of women he identified as Indian indentured immigrants.[75] Read as attractive, demure, and exotic (at least to *visitors*), the latter's presumably "happy" hair, their saris, and their bejeweled bodies signify *Indian* authenticity, and thus a transient status in relation to the geographical and cultural space of the Caribbean. But their jewelry is more usefully read, as Joy Mahabir has pointed out, as "a way of storing wages" on their bodies, of making visible their earnings as cane cutters and other workers in the Caribbean, making plain and "unenigmatic" both the labor that earned them these wages and the labor by silversmiths in their community of smelting their wages into jewelry, but also indulging in the pleasure of adorning the body.[76] Standing side by side with other workers in the Caribbean's transnational and multiethnic plantation economy, "socializing without recourse to previously learned forms . . . [practicing] an acquired matter-of-factness about cultural differences in social style or manners," these workers defy the observation that "the African and the Asiatic will not mix."[77]

It is precisely a repeated failure to meet the expectations of onlookers—whether members of their own class, middle-class nationalist leaders (local or diasporic), or well-meaning and hostile élites—that makes women the source of anxiety. Statements such as "the African and Asiatic will not mix" are uttered as a caveat to the observation that women with "unhappy wool" desire to be "mistaken" for "purer" women of another ethnic group. *But they will not mix.* Uttered as a *description*, it is actually prescriptive—a prediction and a command. For such unauthorized identification and substitution cannot work in an economic system guaranteeing the prosperity of property holders, and for which the importation of one group of laborers in the postemancipation period in the 1830s and after, had been designed to thwart the ability of another group to offer its labor strategically in those seasons when the plantation needed it most urgently, so that higher wages could supplement sovereign attempts to make life elsewhere, away from the plantation. Read as *lazy* for not making the prosperity of sugar, cocoa (or later on banana) industries their priority, African-descended workers are compared unfavorably to imported, indentured workers whose presence keeps wages depressed, and who are thus read as hardworking, possessed of a superior ancestral civilization, and disappointingly transient in relation to the stable economic future that their industry guarantees for élites.

Both groups are read and misread *culturally* and *morally* in relation to these economic considerations. African-descended people are unmoored from an African continent presumed to generate anything but civilizational *purity*, and are read as doggedly connected to the Americas, even when (as with West African indentured laborers) they are born elsewhere. On the other hand indentured laborers from the Indian subcontinent are read as exotic and transient, even though by the early twentieth century it is possible that they are born in the Caribbean or that they have lived there for generations; their *docility* is as harshly guaranteed by surveillance and punishment as the *insubordination* of African-descended people is penalized; their patriarchal family arrangements are a rebuke to licentious homes in which (Afro-Caribbean) women appear to be head of their households, *except* when Indo-Caribbean women are violently and sometimes fatally punished by male partners for moving themselves and their portable, jeweled banks to another household; and their industry and thrift is praised in relation to the supposedly wild spending of other groups on clothing and celebration, except when it is condemned for paralyzing the economy.

Women hoping to be "mistaken for" (or drawn into closer proximity to, or desired by?) other women risk jeopardizing ethnic, religious, sexual, gendered, and other boundaries that keep different groups of laborers adjacent to but not organizing for better conditions with one another, or that justify paying higher wages to men who share their households. Desired as both "steady . . . cheap, submissive" labor and as unwaged nurturers of "men, children, the aged and the ill," working-class women are confounding for middle- and upper-class women reformers who may be spared from the vulnerability of public, manual labor, but are similarly enmeshed in nurturing roles that might reward them with symbolic honor but are no less demeaning or contradictory.[78] Even as women in the region meet or defy the expectations of visiting spectators, they are the subject of sometimes heated debate by male leaders of their ethnic communities who, like Garvey writing from Jamaica ("Our women are prostituted") or Mahatmas Gandhi writing from India ("women [who] are not necessarily wives"), use the idea of women's sexual degeneracy to argue for the compromised state of the diasporic group as a whole.[79] This is a deep disquiet about a woman's erotic and economic autonomy, and the implications of her desires, appetites, and inclinations: which male-headed household she is attached to; her maternal or nonmaternal decisions; whether she can live in a household of her own choosing and how this is linked to issues of wage parity with her male counterparts in the labor force; who exercises control about how her wages are spent; and whether she stays or returns to a place of "origin" (back to a rural location from her new home in the city, or back to another territory) or moves back and forth.[80]

A useful formulation of women's temporal relationship to modernity posits them as "inert, backward-looking and natural," as the "symbolic bearers of the nation" or some other constituency "denied any direct relation" to "agency," in contradistinction to their "forward-thrusting, potent and historic" male counterparts who bring into being registers of time and action that are discontinuous, progressive, and radicalizing.[81] This is a gendered experience of time, "progress," and attachment to a collectivity that could just as easily be uttered by at least two constituencies: by colonial and imperial authorities charging women with the responsibility of teaching children the perceived cultural origins and civilizational legacy of the group, and positing all colonial and imperial subordinates as children who require protection; and by anticolonial male nationalists, feeling feminized and infantilized by such imperial conceptions and making similar appeals to a degraded present and to promising pasts and futures, if only the women and the nonelites they understand themselves to be leading would assume their allocated positions. But far from "inert," it is precisely women's *movement*, whether from one household, workplace, merchant, or customer to another, or across geographical and other borders, that produces anxiety for onlookers, whether such onlookers are neighbors, lovers, newspaper editors, spiritual leaders, or colonial officials. Their purchasing power or their perceived yearnings shape the advertising and display of goods or stimulate the economy, even as they are viewed as provoking inappropriate desires. Though arguably all working-class people offend the status quo for some reason or another, and though condemnation for violation of gendered norms of womanhood sometimes applies to all women regardless of class and race and some men as well, it is nonwhite, working-class performances of womanhood in particular that are held to be too assertive, too public, too commercial, or otherwise unappealing as to undermine masculine authority or cast their community as insufficiently moral or modern. But they offend precisely because their modernity surpasses notions of propriety.[82]

In a 1911 poem, the female persona, a working-class Black woman, warns a Black constable whom she accuses of "palming her up" in the streets that he will feel the "pinch of time" because "you don't wait fe you glass."[83] Subjecting him to a proper "busing" in the public domain (though the Jamaican Creole *tracing* seems as apt here as the eastern Caribbean term for capturing the dramatic and public rehearsal of an opponent's genealogical history in order to shame, a strategy of self-recovery that involves the other's undoing), she dresses him down literally as she makes clear that his ill-fitting police uniform bespeaks his unsuitedness for what was generally recognized to be a socially mobile occupation for Black men. As she and her silent interlocutor know very well, the prevailing vagrancy laws render it completely legal, whatever his or her intentions may have been, for him to arrest "every common prostitute who shall be found wandering in any public place and behaving in a riotous or indecent manner, or annoying passers by soliciting them."[84] Even if what constitutes the "annoyance" is that she refuses to accept his prior "palming up," he can assault her and then lock her up for soliciting. If the poem can be read as capturing her vulnerability, it also renders *him* a victim of her verbal abuse, and as part of the social apparatus of neighbors and onlookers who conspire with the colonial authorities to thwart Black men's attempt to turn the new imperial century into new opportunities for mobility and political participation. Following Sarah Nicolazzo's lead we want to see how vagrancy laws seek to "contain socially, economically, and sexually disruptive bodies," and thus how the conjoining of sexuality and the law brings into focus a Black woman and a Black man who are both subject to vagrancy laws, but also its strolling enforcers.[85] The terrible intimacy of this moment is that on the streets, in the bedroom, everywhere, such laws, sometimes newly amended in this historical moment, circumscribe the movements and aspirations of the descendants of enslaved people as well as currently and formerly indentured people.[86] For if *she* can be arrested as a "riotous" wanderer, we will see how the men of this class are subject to arrest by other clauses of the vagrancy laws.

We also want to pay close attention to how she gets figured as an agent of the up-and-coming Black man's demise. Casting him as a victim of her sharp tongue, the poem conveys a strong sense of her rhetorical agency and autonomy, and this threatens to overshadow her vulnerability. In drawing attention to what occludes her ability to move, or to how the two of them are differently subject to the oppressive weight of the colonial machine, we want to attend to the complexity of being accused by another person of one's own social group of not waiting "fe you glass." Invoking an hourglass (and *his*, at that: *your glass*, as if there is a special time marked out for him that he has overstepped) she suggests that he has not marked time with propriety, that he is exceeding the proper, measured time for change in the social order. We are meant to hear *class* here, discernible as a sonic echo of "glass." Making her rebuke in the register of time, she can be read as supporting the status quo's efforts to stymie him. She invokes "waiting," with its genealogy of nineteenth-century colonial appeals to Queen Victoria that bypass local legislatures perceived as corrupt, and of royal responses encouraging good colonial subjects to wait patiently. Unlike the unfeeling official who can see no time for the colonial subject's relief or political participation, it is the regent and the liberal who endorse waiting, who believe in (or are prepared to go on record as having such faith in) the capacity of colonial subjects to acquire the ability to rule themselves *eventually*.[87]

There are different registers of waiting: being persuaded to be recruited for a struggle next door; figuring out how the same time is marked differently by different social actors; reading a pause as life. Waiting is a way of marking time that need not imply being subject to paternalism. To slow down is to learn to discern what is hesitant, measured, almost imperceptible, marginal, opaque—a cautionary note against our investment in transparency, and particular visions of heroism and resistance. Waiting is also the revolutionary pause, when it looks like one is waiting only because others are acting—when (as with Venezuelans waiting it out in Trinidad, or Cubans and Haitians in Jamaica) getting news, buying arms, and publishing newspapers in a *British* space is obviously an interregnum. But "you don't wait fe you glass" is also the poem's persona saying to a member of her class, if I have to wait, why shouldn't you? Why is it that the two of us must mark time differently? How will *your* not waiting—the asking price of future local leaders of their future followers—help *me*? We are trying to see how both "midnight woman" and "bobby" are thwarted by a colonial system that wants to keep most nonwhites subordinate, and to discern the specifically gendered ways in which this is worked out—for instance, how she is read as betraying Black (male) hopes and dreams as a "compromised subject," and as bestowing a "hereditary weight of betrayal."[88] Thus she is read as conservative, as waiting for class/glass and holding back the visionary who, confounding decreed boundaries of space, time, and desire, says: look, my people, a child of Mulgrave, St. Elizabeth can be a prince of Abyssinia. We want to read her as a gendered social subject who is unfairly targeted as the agent of—but who is also sometimes deeply invested in—his public shaming.

Living with Ruin

Strolling in the Ruins names both theme and disposition, as I indulge in an inclination to meander, to pursue the open-ended or provisional path, or to reconsider moments claimed as triumphant or unseemly in the later genealogies of the nation. I linger in some places but not others. I suture events together anachronistically, on the one hand; but I also hold to what may feel like a rigid temporal boundary (roughly between 1895 and 1914) on the other, because I want to slow down and spend time in a moment whose unfamiliarity promises insight. I am drawn to the narratives of strollers of this historical period, even as my use of them risks a focus on persons with more social power relative to others. Strolling has been claimed for a cultivated practice of informed and disinterested nonchalance, but leisurely strolling is a luxury in a heavily surveilled colonial state: as we will see in chapter 2, the would-be Caribbean *flâneur/flâneuse* is likely to be charged as a vagrant.

Ruins may establish that there has been some break from the past, and that something valuable should be preserved from that past, or it could be that it is the presumed break between past and present that makes the ruins significant.[89] The very designation of ruination can be linked to selective memory, retrospection, introspection, privilege, for who decides that an experience is ruinous, and how do ruins, as a consequence or remnant of disaster, conceal or idealize the regularity of some communities' experience of disaster? It is sobering to consider Michel-Rolph Trouillot's sardonic invocation back in 1990 of "quite ordinary accidents, quite ordinary tortures, quite ordinary diseases," in the wake of earthquakes in Haiti in 2010 and 2021, recent disastrous hurricanes including Ida and Maria, and volcanic eruptions in Montserrat (1995) and St. Vincent (2020–21).[90] As I have noted, it is my sense of a ruinous neoliberal present that partly drives my interest in the past I am considering here but knowing that not everyone experiences the present as ruinous in the same way, or at all, reminds me that the past is also not uniformly apprehended in this way. When a strolling poetic persona indicts Elizabethan-era, slave-trading poets for violent legacies of enslavement, the United States is absent from the accounting of that estate's ruins, save for a Faulknerian allusion to shared histories with the US South.[91] Here it is worth noting that the estate's reversion to *ruinate* (which gives this poem's persona a bitter, if complex, pleasure at this sign of the demise of imperial and colonial rule) also signals nature's reclamation of cultivated land with wild overgrowth.

As an undergraduate I strolled through a campus that was complexly palimpsestic: a ruined aqueduct identified the University of the West Indies' Mona campus as a former sugar estate; a beautiful chapel, transplanted from another estate, remains a choice location for weddings; I sat my first-year final examinations in buildings that had served as barracks for Holocaust refugees; a plaque marks the location of housing for indentured laborers from India. I do not recall feelings of consternation about daily reminders of these pasts. Visiting Havana, I have been struck by the way in which that city's iconic ruins, replete with laundry-laden clotheslines, interrogate the presumed *pastness* (of both ruins and ruin), a reading that I recognize as the tourist's capacity to idealize insecure housing.[92] At the same time, the inability or refusal to demolish and rebuild offers a register for thinking about a colonial past that is repudiated in an ongoing and dynamic way; and that in being blithely ignored (as in my campus experience) instead of mourned or otherwise carefully commemorated, is perversely claimed as at least the postcolonial right to trudge in one's own ruins.

Ruined/ruint also names the perception of a woman as fallen—sexually compromised and publicly known to be thus, and a figure who is most often filtered in what follows through the texts of a male intellectual class (of journalists, poets, novelists, policemen) who are invested in working through this perception—in order to scoff at élite investment in sentimentalizing female virtue, for instance. I am interested in commentators' use of the Black woman's ruin to gauge the moral condition of a constituency, or to insulate themselves against their own susceptibility to ruin. In such commentaries she is not always visible as ruined, as having anything of value that could be ruined, or she is considered so shameless as to exceed the capacity to perceive ruin and its consequences. But in mobilizing discourses of shame, abjection, respectability, or defiance, I am both pronouncing something ruined and making an assumption about what has been broken, in a way that affirms both her contemporaneous critics, and reformist feminist narratives in my present, and that risks leaving little room for imagining her complex analysis and negotiation of her own situation. Here I have in mind Andil Gosine's "wrecking work," where "wrecking," as an analog to "ruin," alludes both to what was destroyed in the process of enslavement, indentureship, and colonialism, and to what must be refused (what might need to be wrecked) when a vindicating respectability has meant investing in structures that prop up patriarchal and other hierarchies.[93]

In the chapters that follow, the newspapers that I have drawn from most heavily are those that have been most readily available to me, an availability that is itself made possible by the longevity and social power of particular periodicals or the institutions that publish them.[94] The leads I have pursued (or that, in being accessible to me could be said to have pursued me) have been shaped by this availability, especially with the digital access that I began to have to one of these newspapers in the last few years. In addition, while I track down a particular lead, there are many things going on in an issue, on a page, or within a column that I ignore, and that would have come to life when the paper was read (individually, or aloud to a group of listeners), pasted on walls, or used as wrapping paper.[95] Because I have my eyes trained on the prospects, in a new century, of social subjects I am identifying as descendants of slavery, in two British Caribbean colonies, people in proximity to them both come into view and risk acquiring significance only insofar as they appear to make others legible. I move between Trinidad and Jamaica as a more or less *natural* outcome of years of doing archival work on these two territories, and with the realization that there is nothing innately natural about studying them together. They are not any more similar than any other two territories would have been, and certainly not interchangeable, and those moments in which I *compare* them are few and far between, with the result that I spend far less time than perhaps I ought to have done in saying how different they are from each other. For instance, Jamaica's dance with the British imperial and colonial project has been much longer (since the seventeenth century) and with a long period of contentious assembly rule before the institution of direct, Crown colony governance in the wake of Morant Bay in 1865; whereas in Trinidad, British rule began much later (the early nineteenth century), was never other than Crown colony governance, and found itself in an Anglo-Saxon, Protestant battle with a long-entrenched and powerful bloc of hispanophone and francophone Catholic constituencies. Both territories negotiated independence from British rule in the early 1960s, but the king of England remains the head of state in Jamaica.

Adjacency is how I think about how these two colonies claim my attention, a relationship that is not about comparison, though this is not irrelevant.[96] *Adjacency* also becomes a way of thinking about how Cuban, Haitian, American, Ethiopian, Madrassee, South African, and other identities inflect Trinidadian, Jamaican, or British colonial ones. Swapping the Philippines for Bermuda and Jamaica indicates that some equivalence is being made, as when visitors or officials use the condition of indentured laborers across the world to congratulate themselves on the treatment of indentured laborers in the Caribbean.[97] While these do not feel like the same kinds of equivalences, in each case an *Asian/Pacific* example brings an operation of domination into view: "*intimacy* as spatial proximity or adjacent connection."[98] It occurs to me, completing this book, how different permutations of *Asian* adjacency have been illuminating but also sidestepped, in my pursuit of blackness. Adjacency also marks a disappearance (or transformation) into another territory's racial orders, as when Caribbean people migrate to the United States, and are therefore unmarked as *Caribbean*, and when Caribbean whiteness disappears into global whiteness.[99]

The following chapter takes shape around Cuba's Third War of Independence from Spain, 1895–98 (counting 1868–78 and 1879–80 as two earlier wars against Spanish rule), a war that was ultimately foreclosed by the US-dominated Spanish American War, 1898–1902; and the 1899–1902 conflict (between the British-dominated Cape and Natal territories, and the Afrikaaner Republics of Orange Free State and the Transvaal) that is sometimes termed the Boer War. I use these wars to signify the material and affective impact of shifts in imperial power that open the century, whether Caribbean subjects are traveling or sitting still. The bet here is that Trinidad and southern Africa, on the one hand, and Jamaica and Cuba, on the other, throw each other into unexpected relief. "Ruination's Intimate Architecture," chapter 2, uses Kingston's 1907 earthquake to track different kinds of cataclysmic shifts, and Jamaican writers' attempts to assert narrative control in the face of this. Chapter 3, "Photography's 'Typical Negro,'" analyzes the visual field that Caribbean people are navigating in this era of world's fairs and kodaking tourists.

Chapter 4, "Plotting Inheritance," analyzes selected novels' plotting of marriage and accumulation, as a political class eager to share rule figures out how professional accreditation and powerful friendships (more so than the noble moralizing of their predecessors) might be retailed into wealth and institutions that accrue value and that can be passed down. This focus on novels published in the century's first decade risks *producing* an artificial historical moment but hopefully this is offset by gaining a productive sense of fictional Caribbean aspiration to estate ownership, in the contexts of a previous generation of Caribbean writing, and of contemporary West African and African American fiction.[100] If Caribbean novelists seem averse to being explicit about the era's violence, we might read their plotlines about visiting photographers' freedom to take images of Black people standing near trees, or slanderous newspaper headlines about the romance between a Black man and a white woman, as coded allusions to contemporaneous events in the United States, and the sensational headlines about them: public lynchings and dismemberment, Black appointees to political and judicial office, and dangerous Black sexuality. Similarly, white consternation about Black characters' attendance at theatrical performances in a Caribbean novel could be read in the context of (explicitly) segregated theaters in the United States and elsewhere, blackface minstrel performances across the Caribbean and internationally, the complexly evolving repertoires of choirs performing Negro spirituals, folk songs, and European classical music throughout the Caribbean and internationally, but also the cyclical staging of Carnival, Jonkannu, and Ramleela across the Caribbean, and the complex relationships of these street-enacted performance traditions to perceived African and Asian *origins*, even as they emerged from violent plantation histories in the Caribbean. Read this way, these novelists join composers, choir directors, playwrights, and theater producers in searching for the space and form to contain (accommodate, but also tamp down) violence, endurance, and transformation, while observing élite rules of propriety.

But these allusions are not evident in these texts, and if we are looking for them, it is easy to be dismissive of these characters who recite Tennyson or who are named after characters in Jane Austen's fiction. In attending to this and in holding fast to a finite time period, I want to track something we might otherwise miss: a representation of modern social subjectivity that is not always (or is not yet?) tied to urban space, and that explicitly connects old money to the rising middle-class Black subject who is explicit about being of African descent. But perhaps I miss that these early twentieth-century writers understand that these fictions can never be more than fantasy: that the estate must yield to the urban yard as more fictionally interesting (that it is already in ruins as far as the creative classes are concerned); that in the social rather than fictional world white and functionally white estate owners in this new century continue to exert social power from a cloistered estate that is inextricably linked to white rejuvenation; and that nonwhiteness is tied to the estate through ruin (or at least nonaccumulation), including the ruin-as-picturesque that continues to ground the postcolonial leisure and tourist economy today.

Even as this book tries to keep the era's contemporaneity in view, and even as we will sometimes find that it is narrated as new and discontinuous, we will ask, which pasts come to the fore, and why? What do we keep, as we move into another phase, and how and when do we say, *that was the past*? By literalizing or idealizing aspects of the past, or by forgetting, we miss its significance for the present—how it newly configures the present and permits a new clarity and legibility. A familiar articulation cautions us to "seize hold of a memory as it flashes up at a moment of danger," lest in not recognizing that it should claim our attention in the present—that the "[image comes] to legibility at a specific time"—it "[disappears] irretrievably."[101] What if "Ceylon" and "Abyssinnia" are placeholders for an alternative that is hazy (to those who invoke it, or to me), wedged between more clearly delineated projects or eras, but also geographical spaces? When the poet Kamau Brathwaite refers to Caribbean islands as "broken fragments of the Andean chain," he is getting at this disconnectedness.[102] As with the islands off the coast of Trinidad, or the cays, knolls, and banks that connect Jamaica to the Central American isthmus, these appear shadowy only because my eyes are trained on land masses that are colonies and nations; to those traversing them frequently by boat, they are normal and distinct.

If haziness fosters an obliviousness that consecrates national boundaries, it also offers indeterminacy, a productive uncertainty about how things will turn out, in line with Lisa Lowe's conception of the past "not as fixed or settled, not as inaugurating the temporality into which our present falls, but as a configuration of multiple contingent possibilities, all present, yet none inevitable," or Raúl Coronado's invitation to be less sure about what happens at particular historical moments, in his discussion of the space that *would become* Mexico, Texas, the United States: "The future-in-past tense draws out, unfolds, and lengthens the process of 'becoming,' so that we are attuned to the various routes of 'becoming.'"[103]

One way that this historical moment is legible to me is in the image of C. L. R. James's mother reading to her young son at home in Tunapuna, Trinidad. Born in 1901, a toddler and a teenager in the years explored in this book, what did James see, looking out through the eyes of his mother, father, aunts, and other relatives, in that home of second-generation children of Barbadian immigrants?[104] Which moments in the *past* resonated for two long-lived intellectuals, alive as the new century opened, and both dying in 1911: Anténor Firmin, the Haitian social scientist and statesman so deeply committed to Caribbean regionalism, keenly following debates from the Danish colony St. Thomas, to which he had been exiled by his political opponents, and where he died at 61; and the African American poet, novelist, and activist, Frances Ellen Watkins Harper, who died in Philadelphia in her eighty-sixth year after a long career of activism against slavery and the dismantling of Reconstruction, and for women's voting rights and temperance? Which moments "flashed up" for Harper and for Firmin in the last decade of their lives? Certainly, we want to keep the *present* of the early twentieth century fully in view.[105] Yet for James and for other toddlers and tweens of the new century, which moments would "flash up in a moment of danger," as they recalled, later on in life, the events, gestures, and silences of this new century?

1

CUBA, SOUTH AFRICA, AND THE ANGLOPHONE CARIBBEAN'S NEW IMPERIAL CENTURY

See them climbing Majuba hill
See them climbing the hill to gain the victory
On Carnival day.

In the reign of Victoria
We marched on Pretoria
Our valor the world will remember
And destroyed the Boers' predomination
Now the Transvaal is ours, the population
Have raised the imperial flag of Britannia
Over South Africa.

Mboz e	The Boers, oh
Mboz mbonga Majuba	The Boers I shot at Majuba
Ta netele	I grieve
Nelezi na bodi yekiti	Wet fluid was spread
Menga ma	This blood.[1]

Just hours after his defeat at the Battle of Paardeberg in the Orange Free State of southern Africa, "General [Piet] Cronjé," head bowed and waving a white flag, surrendered in front of Trinidad revelers, in one of the bands of masqueraders crossing Port of Spain's Savannah in the Carnival celebrations in the last week of February 1900. Euphoric celebrations erupted yet again when the colony celebrated Pretoria Day in the first week of June later that year.

With the rest of the English-speaking world, Trinidad's newspaper readers, inundated with references to "*veldt*," "*laager*," "*kopje*," and other Afrikaaner words, were instructed by journalists reporting from the battlefront on the correct pronunciation of "Lord Kruger" ("g" as in "gold," not "gem") and "*Mafeking*" ("trafficking," not "safe king").[2] Almost two decades before the official consecration of Afrikaans itself as a putatively self-sufficient language rather than a racialized multi-ethnic aggregation of intimacies, histories, and tongues, such grammar lessons reminded English-speaking readers that these names and places were pivotal, tethering them to figures of regulation, comparison, and familiarity founded on earlier moments of conquest: "well known to all who have read Livingstone"; "Langalibelele," as simple as Italian; "chiefs with whom we have been at daggers drawn."[3] If British and Boer opposed each other, the banishment of King Langalibelele of the amaHlubi (in today's KwaZulu-Natal) to Robben Island a generation earlier united them in a white evisceration of Black claims to land, minerals, and sovereignty. King Langalibelele's name was made available for Creole grammar lessons in conquest, as Afrikaans shed its Creolized status on the battlefield, and "Lord Kitchener," the honorific of one of the British commanders in southern Africa, entered the Trinidadian imagination.

Within two years, Cubans celebrated the successful removal of Spain as their imperial power. Marial Iglesias Utset's discussion of their apparent affirmation of the United States gives us a clue as to how we might read the apparently euphoric Trinidadian affirmation of British supremacy suggested by calypsonian Lord Marlborough's "Now the Transvaal is ours." That is, where we might have expected resentment and humiliation when the successful defeat of Spain had to yield to US supremacy, Iglesias Utset points out that at least initially Cubans participated readily in US celebrations because they were also cheering on their emerging nation, apparently free of imperial rule:

> The receptions given a speech, spectacle, symbolic gesture, or other such event is always a dialectic, entailing creative appropriation in which the matter being treated, or material presented is transformed, reformulated, and surpassed by the person encountering it. Consequently, texts or spectacles never possess in themselves a stable, univocal meaning: rather, they are invariably "read," interpreted, in shifting, pluralistic, and contradictory ways. The transfer-of-sovereignty ceremony was intended by the US military authorities to display the force and power of the island's new masters, but this meaning was recast in different ways: in "patriotic" but

prudent and conciliatory terms in the broadside issued by the Junta Patriotica and in unrestrained nationalistic terms by the people of Havana who, despite the prohibition announced by the US authorities and the urging of "calm rejoicing," spilled into the streets to celebrate wildly, as if true independence were at hand.[4]

Certainly, Cubans—fiercely fighting to end Spanish rule for the second time in two generations and welcoming Americans and anyone else who cared to join them in this endeavor—were not synonymous with Trinidadians, who were onlookers in a southern African conflict involving their imperial power. But in the early years of the new century both Trinidadians and Cubans, keeping an eye on Spanish, US, and British forces, demonstrated that Caribbean people were always ultimately onlookers in imperial designs for domination even when (as here with the Cubans) they thought they were fighting, or had already successfully fought, to end their own.

If you lived in Trinidad or Jamaica in 1900, what did it mean to see Cuban and Boer soldiers defeating (even if occasionally) Spanish and English forces? Or to register global disapproval of European imperial power as cruel and unjust, as the world followed reports of the deliberate ruination of farmland, and the reports of starvation in the internment camps used by the British authorities in southern Africa and by "Weyler the Butcher" (the term used by US newspapers for Don Valeriano Weyler y Nicolau, the Spanish general) in Cuba to cut off Afrikaaner and Cuban guerilla forces from the communities that sustained them, depriving both fighters and civilians of food and other resources?[5] I am interested in performances elicited or refuted as these wars in Cuba and southern Africa profoundly reshape imperial alignments restricting or otherwise defining the movements, discourses, and aspirations of Caribbean people as the twentieth century begins. The very names of these conflicts—"Spanish American War" (as opposed to "Second (or Third) Cuban War of Independence"), "Second Boer War," "Anglo-Boer War," "South African War"—commemorate beleaguered or recalcitrant settler-colonists contending with predatory or virtuous outsiders for control of subject peoples who are unnamed in these designations. "Boer War" inscribes a face-off between divinely ordained Afrikaaner *trekboers* in actual or symbolic *laagers*, and encroaching Dutch and then British bids for land and mining rights, a characterization that effaces the aspirations of nonwhite groups, including Black Africans of multiple ethnicities, governance arrangements, and loyalties, and with long and deep temporal attachments to that land. For instance, not only Afrikaaners but also Black people were detained in (racially separated) concentration camps; and class and ethnic differences as well as the specific character of segregationist life would have shaped complex support for either side of this war by Black communities residing in southern African Boer- or British-ruled territories.[6]

Gestures of surrender, loyalty, dissimulation, anticipation: deciding among these or other options can imply that it is only imperial *subjects*, and not also rulers, whose postures and motives are worth considering. But if battle after battle in southern Africa revivifies Boer or British whiteness, the era's anxieties about the capacities of whiteness under pressure are also revealed: its stamina and coherence, or its enervation and lack of self-sufficiency. Imperial and colonizing powers, as well as their subjects or would-be subjects, rehearse and reconstitute themselves on shifting terrain, and we are trying to track these gestures, with particular attention to Trinidad and Jamaica, in the wake of turn-of-the-century imperial reconfigurations. The *imperfect* reproduction of the values and attributes of the powerful by those over whom they exercise this power, might very well confirm the inability of the dominated to *get it right,* but it also provokes anxieties on the part of those wielding power about approximation, utility, and originality. Encounters, through war or otherwise, transform all participants, naturalizing the nations, languages, and other entities which are held to precede the confrontation, and producing "an inbetween that transforms what it is presumed to separate and join."[7]

But how might centering the Caribbean both challenge and *sustain* racializing and imperializing maneuvers? What pasts and futures are rendered discernible or invisible when South Africa is mapped from Trinidad, or Cuba from Jamaica? Reading *Africa* from the Americas, and Cuba's revolutionary struggle from a *future* in the 1940s, this chapter explores the risk of a constantly deferred contemporaneity, as well as the promise of a temporal distance that avoids a *locking into place* when texts read outside of their proper time yield unexpected vibrations.[8] It unfolds over two sections. "Seeing Cuba from Jamaica" examines revolutionary Cuba from the point of view of a neighboring British colony contemplating its own imperial status, as well as its returning migrants from Cuba, some four decades later. "Modernism's African Itineraries" traces the gestures of constituencies in, or fighting on behalf of, southern Africans that facilitate a way to fight for rights elsewhere, or to enact performances that are simultaneously troubling and freeing. Trinidadian masqueraders and activists join a world riveted by events in southern Africa, including the sieges of Kimberley, Ladysmith, and Mafeking and the capture of Pretoria, with shifting fortunes for Boers and British in 1900, and opposition by multiple constituencies in the ensuing decade and a half to taxes, legislation, and other curtailments of Black freedom.

Seeing Cuba from Jamaica

How is Cuba visible from Jamaica, against a longer backdrop of parallel and colluding imperial interests (Cuban dogs imported to catch runaway slaves, anxiety about Cuba's slave-driven economic prosperity in the wake of Britain's abolition of slavery) but also in the present, in the shifts being registered by a tourist enjoying refreshments on the veranda of a renovated plantation? Eric Allan, a visiting New Englander (whose steamer skirts Cuba on the way to Jamaica, allowing him to identify Cuba's "most productive sugar district" from on board), separates US enterprise from the ruined properties of "sugar kings" who returned to England to enjoy the ill-gotten wealth from enslavement, and perhaps also from an earlier imperial history represented by the "cruel Spanish bayonet" of sisal plants lining the road.[9] Disentangling New England from what it shares with the Caribbean beyond foliage—"we might almost have imagined we were in some portion of the New England States, had it not been for the vine-covered crumbling walls of an old sugar mill"— he disavows Massachusetts's and Rhode Island's long-standing bankrolling of the slave trade's transatlantic shipping and of plantations in the US South and in Cuba. Sugar's ruins redound to the prosperity of the US present—"These old sugar estates are now occupied by some of the finest banana plantations on the island"—as the Boston Fruit Company (the publisher of Allan's book) is transforming the tastes of New England consumers with mangoes, pears, bananas, and coconuts, on its own estates across the Caribbean and Central America (including the plantation that Eric is touring), and as it transforms itself into the United Fruit Company, one of the most powerful institutions in the Caribbean and Central America, dominating transportation networks, tourism, and later, installing and deposing political regimes in the region.[10]

Esther Allen maps the trajectory of an estate proprietor in Matanzas, Cuba, whose great house was destroyed during the revolution in 1896, while he and his family vacationed in Puerto Rico on the way home from a trip to Europe.[11] Heading to New York instead, they stayed at a hotel for five months before visiting the rest of the United States and returning to Europe. As it became clear that history was on the rebels' side, the family mailed funds to the rebels' cause from Paris, via New York. After the great house was rebuilt in

Matanzas, they moved back to Cuba, but in a nod to US power they also used their stays in New York to petition successfully for US citizenship. Thus does capital reinvent itself in this moment of revolution and imperial transition.

To see Cuba from Jamaica is to note this British colony's substantial pro-independence Cuban presence, many Cubans having moved to Jamaica after an earlier war of independence in the 1870s. Leaders of the revolutionary movement visited the British colony: Antonio Maceo, whose family was based in Jamaica, met with Calixto García and Máximo Gómez there; José Martí visited in 1892.[12] A key site for "gun-running" and "mail delivery and collection" for the Cuban independence movement in the 1890s, on the cusp of the United States' declaration of war on Spain, Jamaica was "as close to the impending action as journalists could get." But with British patrolling of the waters in support of Spain and to thwart the export of conflict to Jamaica, "seeing Cuba in the distance" meant that Jamaica was also a site of counterrevolutionary surveillance.[13]

Not just Cubans, but other political exiles made the British colony a place to wait it out while setting things in motion elsewhere. Simón Bolívar wrote his "Carta de Jamaica" here in 1815 during a moment of reflection and recuperation, contemplating the future of New Granada, the appeal and burden of British recognition of his cause, and the need for collaboration among the territories of the Americas. In his capacity as a US commissioner for the annexation of the Dominican Republic, Frederick Douglass visited exiled Haitian president Fabre Geffrard in Kingston in 1871. Such respites and meetings made of Jamaica a mediating third space—between the territory being fought for and the capital city of an imperial power being petitioned or thwarted, say—but also shed light on the ongoing collaborative relationships within and between numerous struggles for freedom throughout the nineteenth century and now at the turn of the twentieth. But while people consult one another and wait for the next move in an interim location, they also build a life. Today Jamaicans have Spanish- and French-language names in part because of Haitian and Cuban sojourns, doubtless sometimes initially envisioned as temporary.[14] Whether revolutions succeeded or failed there were always periods of waiting that had to be endured in the meantime.

Published in 1949, *The Single Star* by W. Adolphe Roberts is striking in its engagement with late nineteenth-century revolutionary Cuba, especially when compared with another novel that also engages a moment of radical insurgency from the past and that was published in the same year, Vic Reid's *New Day*. Each Jamaican novel "sees" Cuba very differently. For Reid, identified with the intellectual generation defined by the *Empire Windrush*'s transportation of almost five hundred passengers from the British Caribbean to London the previous year (though Reid himself remained in Jamaica), the Cuban mainland is far less tangible than the cays dotting the stretch of water separating Jamaica from Cuba and providing utopic relief from characters fleeing the upheaval of Morant Bay in 1865, the present of his novel. In *The Single Star*, Cuba's vivid revolutionary spirit in the 1890s puts Jamaica's monarchical loyalties to shame. Peter Hulme contends that different geographical locations in Cuba have determined the trajectories of its exiles, so that while Havana's migrants look west to Yucatán and north to Florida, southcoast Santiago residents look to Haiti and Jamaica. Looking out from Jamaica, Roberts's western Jamaican coastline is most attuned to revolutionary Cuba, while the action of Reid's novel hovers close to eastern Jamaica and Morant Bay's Native Baptist history.[15]

Derek Walcott's play *Henri Christophe* on the Haitian Revolution also appeared in 1949, as if meditations on sovereignty and, more particularly, performances of the consequences of the radical seizure of power in nonanglophone territories were on the minds of anglophone writers at this moment.[16] At the same time, even for a period usually read as if impending decolonization were firmly on the horizon, we do not want to fall into the trap of folding in future events to a fixed idea of that moment's trajectory. Both (white Jamaican) Roberts and (Black Jamaican) Reid use white or near-white Jamaicans as their major characters at a historical moment often defined in terms of the nationalist exploration of an Afro- and Indo-Caribbean *folk* ethos. In using the 1940s to recover the late nineteenth century we risk erasing the register of retrospection. One writer sees Cuba fully and the other myopically, but the retrospective gaze of both will facilitate our examination of that moment with an eye to futures desired and foreclosed; they will allow us to practice teasing out the future conditional from the present.

Why, in this moment just after the end of the Second World War, does Cuba matter (albeit differently) to these two novelists? First, we would venture to say that for Jamaicans any portrayal of radical political or social change, particularly when accompanied by violence, could be read as an obsessive return to the moment of Morant Bay in 1865, in order to figure out and perhaps reorder its traumatic events: resistance to legal, political, and property restrictions to Black advancement; protest rooted in profound populist faith in the imperial sovereign's ability and inclination to override local administrative corruption; exaggerated fear of Black political resistance leading to brutal official retaliation; ideological repercussions in London's public life; seizing of political power from local assemblies and a return to Crown colony administration in Jamaica and elsewhere in the anglophone Caribbean. Whether Jamaicans believed, some eighty years later, that events at Morant Bay proved that political protest was worth the risk or not, or that events there proved the overreach of imperial dominance, or the danger of Black power, 1865 surely suggested the high cost of radical demands and explicit assertions of freedom.[17]

But as Walcott's play suggested, a more regional reflection (on what connected the region across differences of imperial origin, on its own *quiet* process of decolonization compared to its nonanglophone neighbors) was in play as well. The Barbadian writer George Lamming talks about the experience of going to teach English in Venezuela in the 1940s as

> a kind of blessing because it [put] me in touch with the Americas in a way that now became part of my agenda.... And it is there then that I also became aware of the political figure as monument in a people's consciousness. Because the way those Venezuelans spoke of Bolivar! I had never heard of anyone spoken of in the world of politics and struggle and war in the way they spoke of Bolivar. And if you'd make a mistake and uttered the slightest irreverence about Bolivar, you were only playing with your life. That kind of figure in the national consciousness was completely new to me.[18]

Here Venezuela is marked as the space with a genealogy of radical possibility for the anglophone south*eastern* Caribbean, much as, for Roberts at least, Cuba is for Jamaica in the northwestern Caribbean. Lamming is anything but idealistic about the material conditions of his own presence in Venezuela: the parents of his boarding school pupils want their children to master English "because of the American presence there. That language [was] going to be decisive in how they move[d] up and so on in the oil." Still, Latin America offers him "a continuity of war and fighting" that throws into sharp relief "lulls" and "imperial settlements"—the diffused moments of possibility of the anglophone region. Here "lulls" might signal impatience for a more decisive aftermath to the turbulent labor strikes in the 1930s across the British Caribbean by dockworkers and workers in sugar, oil, and other industries, that had been accompanied by demands for sweeping political reform, leading to the formation of trade unions and political parties—a turbulence vividly captured in Lamming's own future novel which would come to define the nationalist moment.[19] But we might reimagine "lulls" if we consider that this period is marked by the end of occupation, as US Marines withdraw from Haiti and the Dominican Republic in the 1930s, as well as by wartime occupation, as US Marines occupy the US base in Trinidad, and the Vichy regime takes up residence in its Caribbean colonies, at a moment when hundreds of Caribbean people served their imperial powers in wars across the globe.[20] The coronation of Emperor Haile Selassie in November 1930, and his closely watched standoff with Italy later in the decade, would prove to have profound effects on notions of sovereignty that, neither colonial nor respectably nationalist, would generate powerful alternative visions of the future.

Wartime Jamaica was marked by adult suffrage in 1944, and, in the same year, the imprisonment of journalist and future novelist Roger Mais for treason, because of his critique of Winston Churchill's reminder that the defense of British freedom was also an affirmation of imperialism. "Colonials from all parts of the British empire are fighting," Mais declared, for "the great idea of Democracy which relegates all 'niggers' of whichever race to their proper place in the scheme of political economy."[21] As those steaming toward England four years later on the *Empire Windrush* would see (or probably already suspected) the wartime labor crisis which made the metropole receptive to a massive influx of laborers from the Caribbean was by no means a straightforward affirmation of imperial fraternity. This is the age of powerful reflection on what it means to travel to the metropole but also to "return to a native land" still occupied by the imperial power.[22] In this moment of impending decolonization across the global south, Césaire would choose department status for Martinique.[23] What is newly visible about that moment when we do not assume that a particular kind of sovereignty is the endgame? What can we see when an *anglophone* territory looks across at its *hispanophone* neighbor?

In V. S. Reid's *New Day*, a small community flees Jamaica in the wake of the colonial state's violent repression of protests in Morant Bay in eastern Jamaica in 1865. When one of the leaders of the protests, Paul Bogle, pushes for secession, it is a stand against compromise with the colonial authorities that will eventually earn him execution. While the Cuban state is clearly complicit with British repression—"Governor Eyre has sent to Honduras and Cuba and America for ships and guns and sailormen enough to fight all poor people in the island"—it is land between Cuba and Jamaica that is the destination: "new land ... where what you get for your bellies shall be no' gauged by the colour o' your skin or the weight o' your pocket."[24] In these cays off the coast of Jamaica, constituting "clean water tween the Queen's land and we," different visions of freedom are negotiated among the group of sojourners. In effect, it becomes a sort of religious refuge, which at least one character finds too severe: there are no flowers, no laughter, only the Bible and *Pilgrim's Progress*; it feels like walking to Zion in a straitjacket, as she puts it. But she pays a heavy price for these divergent views of what the rest of the community has decided is a utopia; when she leaves with a ship captain, their vessel is shipwrecked off Cuba, she is raped by sailors from another vessel, and eventually dies in a Kingston brothel. This alerts us to the mapping and punishment of political dissent on the body of the woman. Cuba is part of the novel's plot in another way, when Zekiel marries a Cuban woman who eventually takes their child to live in Cuba after they split up. Eventually a grandson, Cuban-born Carlos Fernandez, goes to Jamaica to join his cousin—a lawyer who is married to a sculptor—in participating in Jamaican political life.

This last is easily read as a fictional rendering of three key figures in Jamaica's nationalist movement: Alexander Bustamante, who had lived in Cuba and Central America before returning to Jamaica to become a charismatic union leader and the leader of the Jamaica Labor Party; his cousin Norman Manley, a lawyer and the leader of the rival People's National Party; and Edna Manley, a sculptor and a prominent figure in Jamaica's nationalist arts movement. Thus does Cuba provide a way to account for Bustamante's migratory hispanophone routes and to be folded into the narrative of Jamaica's political life, as a Cuban woman, in effect, sires Cuban kin for the project of Jamaican nationalism. Finally, *New Day* shares with *The Single Star* the fact that the central figures are white or near-white figures, though Reid's novel is arguably different in that it takes seriously Black capacity and positions its protagonists in relation to a brown and Black middle class rather than, as *The Single Star* does, to a project of consolidating landed whiteness. Yet it is interesting that in *New Day* one of the characters, Ruthie, marries a British veteran of the Boer War who sends for her when he decides to put down roots in southern Africa and to "farm in the Transvaal."[25] In this novel that is often read in relation to a developing Jamaican nationalism, then, women's bodies are used to map political capital and political dissidence, kinship networks with Cuba and South Africa, and whiteness and accumulation.

If Cuba is, in *New Day*, little more than an off-stage hispanophone space from which to wait for the moment to return to the major action in the British Caribbean, in Roberts's novel Cuba is *the* critical space to imagine freedom, with important lessons for complacent Jamaicans. The deep familiarity of *The Single Star* with Cuba's landscape stems from Roberts's long-standing interest in the hispanophone and francophone region extending across the islands and to the US plantation South, and reflected in several biographies, histories, and novels that he had published by the 1940s. In 1941 he wrote *La historia de un retrato* about Martí's October 1892 visit to Jamaica. In the early 1950s he traveled across Jamaica giving lectures on Morant Bay, Bolívar, Toussaint L'Ouverture, and Martí. It is because of Roberts's efforts that there is a statue of Simón Bolívar in downtown Kingston today. Yet Roberts's long and deep regional sensibilities were further shaped by his US citizenship. He moved to the United States early in the twentieth century, living there continuously until the 1940s, and working as a journalist and publisher. Involving himself in the momentum for Jamaican self-government from New York, in the 1940s he was in the process of returning to live in Jamaica. Urging the colony's liberal and radical politicians to make a complete, republican break with the British, he was viewed with suspicion for his ideological radicalism but also for his US citizenship, which was discussed in the colony's House of Representatives.[26] It is not difficult to imagine how Roberts, whose regionalism actively affirmed francophone and hispanophone traditions, and who was not anti–United States, would be the object of suspicion in a British-oriented context, even for those sharing his anticolonial sentiments.

Roberts began writing *The Single Star* in New Orleans and moved slowly through the Cuban landscape on a trip there in 1948, with Santiago as his base. The Jamaican portion of the novel is set mainly in the town of Lucea in western Jamaica, an actual site of Cuban blockade-running in the 1890s. The novel appeared in a US edition in 1949, followed by an English edition shortly after, and by a 1956 Jamaican edition published by Pioneer, the press that Roberts managed with Una Marson. Cuba awarded him the *Orden Nacional de Mérito* in 1950 for *The Single Star*, as well as for *The Caribbean: The Story of Our Sea of Destiny*.[27] For Peter Hulme, *The Single Star* is crucial because Roberts exposes the self-interest of the United States in Cuba's revolutionary struggles (through the Jamaican sharpshooter who is the novel's protagonist and who is so trusted by Cuban revolutionary leaders that he is given critical access to both Cuban and US camps).[28] The novel depicts Cubans fighting for their own cause in battles that, in US historical accounts, tend to center the actions of US soldiers. Stephen Lloyd, the novel's protagonist, boldly tells US soldiers that as a colonial subject himself he does not want Cubans to gain their freedom from Spain, only to have to surrender it to another imperial power. On the other hand, he warns the Cubans that "occupation" is not necessarily preferable to "annexation" if the latter would continue "indefinitely." "Undoubtedly," he warns them, US soldiers "have come in the mood of colonizers."[29] Here it is possible to read Roberts using the 1890s to warn the British Caribbean in the 1940s that freedom from imperial domination meant not only severing ties with the British but being wary of the United States, which, after all, had significant military and economic interests in the Caribbean in this postwar moment.[30]

The novel has a keen sense of Jamaican and Cuban landscapes, but the waterways that connect both territories are also vividly delineated—not simply for the extent to which they can transport people to land, but because time spent on boats and ships is an opportunity to reflect on the radical possibilities of projects on both land and water. Regional ties cannot be stymied by the coast guard patrols that are all too apparent to Stephen, the Jamaican protagonist, and to Miguel and Inés, the Cuban revolutionary siblings whose family resides in exile in Jamaica, and who take Stephen with them when they both leave to rejoin the fighting in Cuba. "Retracing a romantic course," Philip reminds his new friends that indigenous people must have rowed the same course centuries earlier from the Jamaican West Coast that they now take to Cuba, that Columbus would have done so as well, after he was spurned by the governor at Santo Domingo, and that both Jamaican authorities aiding French planters during the Haitian Revolution and people fleeing Haiti had also traveled this path. If imperial patrols attempt to squelch radicalism, here characters from multiple imperial lineages in the region inspire one another to discern and build on traditions of struggle. In the spirit of theorists of ship-based radicalism and of the imaginative possibilities of tidal currents, the sea travels of the novel's revolutionaries become an important opportunity to pool information, to activate alternative histories and trajectories, and to forge regional solidarity.[31]

Cuban freedom, then, is necessarily a regional undertaking—a lesson both for the 1890s that Roberts re-creates, and for anglophone Caribbean territories strategizing decolonization in the present of the novel's publication. Here a Jamaican protagonist inspired by Cubans fighting against their imperial power maps an oceanic itinerary that precedes and challenges the imperial-colonial ties that bedevil not only their two territories, but sovereign territories like Haiti. It is hard to shake off such domination, Roberts warns, through his characters; we are always in its hold one way or another.

Cuba in the 1890s, Roberts seems to say in *The Single Star*, offers lessons for the present, and it also offers Jamaicans a rich tradition of regional histories, geographies, and radical itineraries. As with Reid's novel, Cuba also offers fictional opportunities to explore the role of the Jamaican politician Alexander

Bustamante, as if the details of Bustamante's public self-fashioning as a man with a hispanophone past had necessarily to be scrutinized and either absorbed into Jamaican lineages as in Reid's *New Day* or rejected (and Roberts makes no bones about his intense dislike of Bustamante in his autobiography). In *The Single Star* Henrietta Costello, a Jamaican governess with a murky past and a drug habit who mysteriously turns up at dinner parties, turns out to be a spy for the colonial Spanish state, and thus endangers Stephen and his Cuban comrades. On my reading, this secretive figure whose time spent in Spanish-speaking spaces is unaccounted for, and who undermines radical projects of emancipation, occupies the Bustamante slot in the novel. As a questionable figure himself in the eyes of the Jamaican state, Roberts uses his fiction to pinpoint the real alien.[32]

Though they could not be more different ideologically, Henrietta Costello and Inés are perhaps the only women in *The Single Star* who are free of futures that are tied to actual or implied sexual entanglements with men. Inés, one of the revolution's most valiant warriors, and with whom Stephen shares an intense intellectual and emotional bond, ultimately rejects his profession of love and his desire to share his life with her, when she declares that her total commitment to the revolution would not facilitate a relationship with him. Stephen is thus resigned to end his Cuban sojourn by reclaiming the family acquaintance who has long been marked out for him by his Jamaican social milieu, thus assuring him a heterosexual marital future, even if not with the guerilla soulmate of his dreams. Both women are tied to the novel's resolution; Inés because of what her rejection enables, and Henrietta Costello because the novel ends with Stephen catching sight of her in Jamaica, lining her up in his gun's sights to assassinate her, and then deciding that she is not worth the bullet. This means that a dangerous antirevolutionary is left free to roam, undermining the potentiality of future radical projects. The scene also echoes earlier moments when Stephen kills a mongoose (the savior-turned-nuisance of Jamaican landscape and agriculture), as well as a bull that threatens him and Inés's brother early in the novel. Costello is thus cast as parallel to threats to the resolution of safe futures.

These resolutions have sexual and racial implications. Inés seizes the agency to opt out of long-term heterosexual intimacy, in a novel where most other women are closely linked to intimate and familial investments: as busty barmaids, as sexual relief, as spies (though not, like Costello, for the Spanish) whose sexual congress facilitates surveillance of the enemy, or as women in ruined homesteads across the Cuban landscape who clarify what has been lost in the war. Particularly in this latter role, they are key to the novel's quiet affirmation of the racial hierarchies similarly undergirding social arrangements in reactionary Jamaica and revolutionary Cuba. That is to say, for all of its multiracial and transimperial regional solidarity, I read Roberts's *The Single Star* as affirming (whether affirming *above all*, or at least *also* affirming) the regional solidarity of white landed interests, and white women's reproductive futures are critical to this project. The fact of occasional nonwhite characters who are social equals does not dislodge this; as I've argued elsewhere, except for revolutionary leaders, the depiction of Black Cubans as indecisive and Black Jamaicans as pedantic constitutes, on my reading, a negative representation of blackness.[33]

Stephen's friendship with Inés and Miguel Carmona is rooted in an anti-imperial radicalism which I read as specifically white. Miguel invites Stephen home to meet his family, and ultimately to join him and his sister in Cuba when Stephen, brushing aside his gratitude after saving him from being attacked by the bull, notes: "In this country [Jamaica] no white person is considered a trespasser on any plantation."[34] The solidarity between Cuba and Jamaica is rooted in and maintained by a shared investment in white landownership, and presumably also the histories of labor and servitude that enable this. Here Roberts's own memories of watching the Boer War from Jamaica as a young man are illuminating: "I was a young Britisher uncritical of the eternal verities like Queen Victoria, the imperial system, and the Union Jack," until he realizes that the Boer fighters are "stockraisers and planters with a background similar to that of my own family. Fathers and sons reported together for war by taking down their rifles from the wall."[35] Rather than the enemy, therefore, he now saw Boers fighting for their "right to maintain the small Transvaal and range River republics, to be an individualistic people. . . . As for me, I had gone over to the side of the bearded farmers in their slouch hats, their bandoleers slung across plain hunters' coats, men of deadly marksmanship and hard riding." Read alongside the novel, this is a settler genealogy of nationalism for a nationalist period (the anglophone Caribbean 1940s) that we tend to read as *anti-imperial* in a different register—as the ascent to power of, certainly, a white or near-white élite, and that in its public discursive registers advocates for a better future for the brown and Black populace of which they constitute the leadership. Roberts claims the Boer War for the freedom of landed white enclaves across the region. That his earlier novels are set in Louisiana, that in *The Single Star* Stephen's father is a US-born Confederate soldier who settles in Jamaica, or that the very title of the novel gestures toward white

Texan histories of conquest, suggests a delineation of a beleaguered white plantocracy that, resenting imperial invaders, spreads its tentacles of kinship across a greater Caribbean that includes the US plantation South.

Is it the case, then, that Jamaicans and Cubans mean different things by freedom—that a writer from Jamaica's deeply hierarchical society who is preserving his fictional characters' landed interests sullies the loftier Cuban revolutionary commitment to a thoroughgoing transformation of social relations? Here discussions of the limitations of Cuban revolutionary transformation are helpful. Aline Helg's discussion of the characterization of Afro-Cubans as violent rapists, not unlike the US South after Reconstruction, and Rebecca Scott's parsing of phrasing such as "*ciudadano cubano de color*" (Cuban citizen of color) get at some of the tensions of the Cuban revolutionary project.[36] Indeed, the establishment, outlawing, and armed resistance of the Partido Independiente de Color (Independent Party of Color) that prompted a violent backlash (against the party's leadership and Afro-Cubans more generally) in 1912 demonstrated that, if blackness could not be taken for granted as an element of *cubanidad*, the specificity of a race-specific political party was read as a dangerous destabilization of *cubanidad*.[37]

From this retrospective reclamation of Cuban and Boer struggles for independence in a novel of the late 1940s, a fantastical newspaper account with implications for white futurity returns us to the early twentieth-century period. Reprinted from the *New York Evening Journal*, the 1906 story recounted the adventure-filled fortunes of a Boer prisoner of war in Bermuda, whose escape by water and land took him to Baltimore, New York City, London, and back to New York.[38] Following media reports of his fortunes, a Jamaican woman who had first glimpsed him when she attended a tennis party of British officers next door to the prison in Bermuda, attended a lecture that he gave in New York City, where he had finally landed as a journalist, and where her family now lived in Park Slope, Brooklyn after her father's engineering stint in Bermuda. What is striking is the goodwill that allows Boer misfortune to be transmuted into US prosperity, and we imagine that the couple can look forward to a nonethnic future, following Kahlil Gibran Muhammad's discussion of the racialization of citizenship in the early twentieth-century United States.[39] At the same time, perhaps the gain of unmarked whiteness in the United States comes at the expense of a loss of Jamaicanness, however this is calculated. Just as *New Day*'s near-white Jamaican femininity promises white-without-question prospects in South Africa, and a "West Indian Belle" does the same in the United States, we will see in chapter 4 how white or near-white belles are conscripted into anchoring Black and brown middle-class male futures, as fictional protagonists of this latter class (in novels written by men of this class) secure prosperous economic futures for the up-and-coming Caribbean New Negro. As heiresses of plantation lineages, white Caribbean women facilitate the ability of an upwardly mobile nonwhite class to lay claim to the inheritance of white accumulation. Thus the whiteness that stymies nonwhite aspiration in social life is transformed in fiction to whiteness that catalyzes nonwhite prosperity.

Read in relation to *New Day*'s affirmation of nonwhite prosperity, we would be tempted to read *The Single Star*'s disparaging portrayal of Black characters and Roberts's general fictional vision of a regional white paterfamilias as an assertion that it is inconceivable that a majority-Black voting citizenry could play a significant role in political life, including potential nationhood. Another way of stating this is that Roberts, the diasporic subject who imagines a complete political break from England and the Anglo-Saxon, posits (through the family of Inés and Miguel, Cuban exiles living in Jamaica, or through Stephen who would presumably have remained in Cuba if Inés had accepted his proposal) that migration and exile can be viable founding narratives for a future sovereign territory. Outsiders—the right ones, at least—rejuvenate rather than undermine the community.

Proposing that we read *The Single Star* in terms of a long 1940s, a "global anticolonial" period beginning in the mid-1930s, Susan Gillman considers *The Single Star* as part of Roberts's fictional trilogy, and in terms of his delineation of a "Mediterraneanized Caribbean."[40] Gillman reads the historical moment as a remarkable assessment of the aftermath of Reconstruction; W. E. B. Du Bois's *Reconstruction* and C. L. R. James's *Black Jacobins* are trenchant analyses that are significantly different from the narrow, parochial scope of the text that trumped them all in popularity, Margaret Mitchell's *Gone with the Wind* and its film adaptation.[41] Gillman allows us to consider this historical period as an intensive reassessment of the period of the failures of slavery's afterlives in Haiti, United States, Cuba, and Jamaica as the region's intellectuals ponder what happens when dreams of freedom are deferred.

Thus on the cusp of a renegotiation of sovereignty in Jamaica, Roberts insists that beating back imperialists is something that landed plantation owners have always done. He invites us to read his novel, but also Reid's, outside of the sole context of nationalism and the Windrush moment (as at least the latter would come to be read, retrospectively). Both novels show that social relations embedded in the plantation matrix have to be contended with in the immediate post–World War II era, and whether or not they are viewed as dying out, such relations are reworked, mourned, revivified. Roberts and Reid fictionalize armed insurgency at a historical moment of various projects of decolonization around the globe. We can read both as asking, through their respective novels: How does the earlier moment's attempt to move forward offer us something in the present? What can its achievement or failure teach us? What does our time share with theirs?

But to this *retrospective* gesture toward Cuba, we also want to see how Cuba registers in the Jamaican imagination in the present of the late 1940s, whether in the regular reports of sporting events (football and softball matches between the two territories, or the regional Central American-Caribbean athletic games in Colombia), in the report of the invitation extended to Winston Churchill to visit Jamaica during his trip to Cuba, or arguably the most pressing reason: Jamaican migrant laborers and their families in Cuba.[42] When De Lisser had compared Cuba to Jamaica in 1910 he framed the importance of both territories in terms of the "great undertaking" underway at the Panama Canal which would totally transform "the industrial and economic position of the West Indian Islands," since both islands "command" the Windward Passage which is the route to the Canal's "Atlantic side."[43] Noting that wealthy Cubans were sending their children to study in Boston and New York rather than, as previously, to Paris, he likens sailing with a group of Jamaican migrants traveling to Panama and other points in the Americas seeking gold to the Spaniards of an earlier age.

But some gold-seekers had a fraught afterlife, rejected by both sending and host territories, and in the late 1940s, this required careful attention. In 1947, for instance, it was reported that the World Federation of Trade Unions (WFTU) estimated that there were some forty thousand "West Indian workers" in Cuba, most of whom were both Jamaican and unemployed.[44] The dizzying chain of command told its own story of disavowal. Apparently promises to fulfill their requests for repatriation after the Second World War had not been honored, and the National Union of Sugar Workers of Cuba was now asking the WFTU to intervene. The WFTU had consulted the (British) Trade Union Congress (TUC) about the matter, and the latter had in turn asked the secretary of state for the colonies, who asked the National Union of Sugar Workers of Cuba for information. The secretary of state informed the TUC that the repatriation of thousands of West Indian workers in Cuba was not feasible, both because of the resulting strain on resources in an already-overpopulated British Caribbean, but also because these prospective returnees would include the *descendants* of persons who had left the English-speaking Caribbean to work in Cuba, and these descendants were *Cuban* citizens. There had been an agreement to repatriate "aged persons" and "incurables," and money had been allocated for this purpose since 1944. The secretary of state proposed that a better solution would be to get them employment in Cuba, but that the *nationalistic* policy of the Cuban government and of Cuban trade unions prevented this from happening. The article went on to note that the Cuban Sugar Workers Federation was not guilty of racial discrimination—indeed, the article pointed out, its president Jesús Hernández was a Black man— but that jobs for Cubans were their first priority. The WFTU was concluding that the British government was "passing the buck and that the proper remedy is that those workers who cannot be employed any longer in Cuba and have not become Cuban citizens" ought to be assisted by the British government in settling in British Guiana, British Honduras, Surinam, or elsewhere in Latin America.

In the context of this passing of the buck, of this denial of the very labor that had helped to sustain the Cuban sugar industry, it might be possible to read a novel about a Jamaican who goes to Cuba to assist in its war of liberation as an appeal for reciprocal solidarity. I do not claim that *The Single Star* desires to make such an appeal on behalf of Jamaican workers and their children seeking to return to Jamaica from Cuba, but rather that the novel's appearance in 1949 illuminates issues of insiders and outsiders, as well as of solidarity. Indeed, perhaps it is Reid's *New Day*, looking warily at Cuba in the distance, that better approximates Jamaica's *British* rejection of Cuban-born *returnees*, and its objection to more mouths to feed—the kind of dismissal that had sent drought-stricken and unemployed Jamaicans to seek work in Cuba generations earlier, in the first place.

Modernism's African Itineraries

Returning to Trinidad's February 1900 Carnival season: the bodily gestures of masqueraders and the names of southern African places and persons, spoken or sung, draw people intimately into the experience of war. Empire and colony provide a crucial vocabulary of affiliation in this moment. Whether supervised and scripted by colonial authorities or not, such events mobilize intense feelings across class and race, so that *loyalty* or *patriotism* are neither accurate nor irrelevant as a way of capturing such intensity. Hearing irony and dissemblance (instead of full-on loyalty) in Lord Marlborough's celebration of raising "the imperial flag of Britannia / Over South Africa" in the second song quoted at the opening of this chapter would most likely be only a function of my own postcolonial desire. At the same time, taking the song's faith in imperial power at face value opens up rather than flattens fruitful layers of meaning, including squabbles about an incremental shift from four-line calypsos sung in French Creole and in *single tone*, to English-language, double-tone, eight-line calypsos.[45] If we can see that battles in southern Africa provide the occasion for local arguments about tradition and form, and about British patriotism in a colony long dominated by francophone Catholic loyalty, then "We marched on Pretoria" begins to sound like the rehearsal of bombast in a new musical form and linguistic register, and also something that has to be insisted on, in the face of nonanglophile dissension within Trinidad.

Lord Inventor's entry for that year's calypso contest, also cited in the epigraph, invokes Majuba Hill. "Remember Majuba" was a rallying cry to spur on the British troops in memory of a huge British loss to the Boers in the 1880s. A reference to the routing of the British in the Battle of Majuba Mountain was thus a reminder that the *Boers* had triumphed in that earlier battle. Therefore, who were you rooting for when you were "climbing Majuba Hill" in February 1900? Summoning up 1880s-era British ignominy and Boer triumph, allusions to Majuba Hill also (and perhaps *primarily*) had resonances that were specific to Port of Spain's geographies of class and race. When the *Port of Spain Gazette* noted that the "Laventille Boers" remained ensconced in their encampment, a "miniature Majuba Hill, completely fortified with shot and shell, scientifically provided with entrenchments," the newspaper named a masquerade band affiliated with a working-class neighborhood in Trinidad's capital city that took pride in its defiance of the colony's police force.[46] Here working-class Afro-Trinidadian subjects identified at least nominally with a white settler power that challenged British assertion of its dominance over nonwhite subjects.

As Boers at Majuba Hill, Port of Spain, the Laventille Boers enacted an anti-British performance in a British colony, in this year of imperial jubilation. By July, Victoria Lazaro (the "Queen of the Brigade Band") and sixteen others were charged with "riotous behavior" on Pretoria Day in early June; "armed with sticks and in fighting attitude," they had caused businesses to be closed. All had their cases dismissed but three, including Lazaro, who appears to have been too fully and deeply implicated, and who was, in any case, the ringleader, as the "Queen."[47] Perhaps this *jamette*'s raced and gendered body made her band's activities all the more transgressive. Such protests, read as rebellious and attracting the violent weight of the law, remind us of the real social costs of dissident activity, even taking into account the much-vaunted sanctioned dissidence that is often identified with Carnival as an institution.[48] Though Carnival was, in Trinidad, an annual scene of working-class clashes with the law, we could surmise that enthusiastic expressions of patriotism in this year of an imperial war (fireworks, parades, knitting socks, and collecting money to send to the warfront) must have been a particular inspiration for performances of dissent. Encamped "Boers" and stick-fighting *jamettes* challenged the colonial state's curtailment of space and cramping of working-class life.

With "*Mboz mbonga Majuba*" ("The Boers I shot at Majuba") in the third extract of the epigraph, Central Africans who later migrated to Trinidad may well have been singing about their service in the Boer conflicts of the 1880s on behalf of the British, in Congolese lyrics recalled by their children and grandchildren in interviews with Maureen Warner Lewis in the 1960s. Here we are reminded of other performances and affiliations when, fighting as British subjects, cadres of soldiers from across the imperial world had been pressed into service in multiple campaigns for generations, or had expressed their disappointment or anger when the authorities' determination that they were unsuited to serve was received as a racial slight. Lyrics about bloodshed insisted that the injuries and fatalities rendered winners and losers equally vulnerable. Thus grief takes its place alongside jubilation as responses to either British or Boer victories.

With the Boer War the imperial center solicited loyalty from its Caribbean subjects, while exhibiting a convenient amnesia about older modalities of power: descendants of the mighty eastern dispersal from St. Domingue in the late eighteenth and early nineteenth centuries fleeing the Haitian Revolution and buttressing Trinidad's strong francophone cultural presence; indentured laborers to Trinidad in the later nineteenth century from across the Caribbean, China, the Indian subcontinent, and west and southern Africa. As the new century opened, Trinidadians born into enslavement, indentureship, or plantation-ownership, or their children and grandchildren, offered interesting parallels to the ongoing "conflict for control over African land and labor" in southern Africa, where British disinterest after annexing territory from the Dutch in the 1790s was transformed into centralized control to pursue the cheap labor needed for mineral extraction—a renewed interest which rattled Boer farmers' dominion over both Cape-residing enslaved labor originating from Malaya, Madagascar, and Indonesia, and a range of ethnic African constituencies.[49] Shift around the players in this narrative of southern Africa, and the Cape was not unlike Trinidad: imperial cycles of indifference and interest in a southeastern Caribbean colony with initial European conquest (replete with three fabled ships), ruled by a barely interested Spain and dominated culturally by an increasingly significant French and francophone white élite when it was annexed by the British in the early nineteenth century. In two colonies at the beginning and close of the nineteenth century, landed whites cast themselves as beleaguered in the face of white British imperial interests challenging their dominance over an array of nonwhite constituencies.

Southern Africa and the Boer War offer perspectives that risk being overlooked because of more well-rehearsed *West* African affiliations to the Caribbean shaped by enslavement and diaspora. Figure 1.1 is a photograph of one of the sites of European imperial power along the West African coast (a fort that was by turns Portuguese, Swedish, Danish, Dutch, and English, its dungeons accommodating enslaved captives for the Atlantic trade from at least the early nineteenth century). It is visually familiar today as an obvious reference to the Atlantic slave trade. But here its 1900 context potentially intervenes in and disrupts that singular reference; the fort's courtyard shows the preparation for an imminent military campaign in July 1900 and is thus a reminder of European states' accelerated gouging of the African continent at the turn of the century.

In this regard, the Boer War has the capacity to remind us that the Atlantic slave trade and its ongoing reverberations constitute a connection between the African continent and the Caribbean that is being rejuvenated by the predations of imperial conquest in this new century. Jemima Pierre has cautioned about the "isolated treatment of the transatlantic slave trade and hemispheric colonialism and slavery, on the one hand, and European colonialism of the African continent, on the other. This is a move that not only links issues of race primarily to the experience of enslavement in the New World, but also gives the New World ownership of that history while it simultaneously excludes it from postcolonial Africa."[50]

African-born indentured laborers living in the Caribbean, such as Maureen Warner-Lewis's interlocutors (or their parents), and Caribbean people in early twentieth-century South Africa remind us of other contexts besides enslavement (even as the context of enslavement is not displaced), and this keeps in view ongoing and multiple temporalities, affinities, and contexts of labor. This reminds us to seek out *imperial* and not just diasporic resonances of Caribbean invocations of West Africa (or to see how these are entangled);

FIGURE 1.1. "The Courtyard of Cape Castle, Gold Coast." From *Black and White* magazine, July 14, 1900, 45.

while in southern Africa we must keep in view histories of Afrikaaner enslavement, as well as earlier British banking and mining interests, when it suits neither British nor Boer sides to invoke them in 1900. Southern Africa helps us to see Trinidad when, as Victoria Collis-Buthelezi puts it, that region is inserted "into anglophone Caribbean early twentieth-century mappings of the Caribbean that do not emanate from a 'roots' discourse but push at the limits of the region's cartography."[51] For instance, we can contextualize Trinidadian Henry Sylvester Williams's advocacy on behalf of "Malays, West Indians, coloureds and Indians," and Indian Mohandas K. Gandhi's advocacy for indentured immigrants, in terms of two Natal-based legal activists whose political capacity *at home* in their respective British colonies was limited, if not nonexistent.[52] We could understand their advocacy as both the identification of an alternative space in which to resist imperial power (as each finds himself in South Africa in the context of being curtailed in fighting for rights in his respective British colony), but also as speaking on behalf of a diasporic other located in southern Africa—a *speaking for* that, in compensating for each activist's particular anxieties or limitations, mobilizes particular notions of tradition, modernity, and diaspora.

In the early twentieth century, southern Africa was the catalyst for all kinds of projects, performances, and anxieties. The first treasurer of what became Henry Sylvester Williams's Pan-African Association was Mrs. A. V. Kinloch, a South African on the lecture circuit in London, speaking about conditions for Black people in southern Africa, who had inspired Williams; and Marcus Garvey would later name as his inspiration for the organization that would become the Universal Negro Improvement Association (UNIA), a conversation on board ship about conditions in Basutoland with a couple who had lived there: his "heart bled" from hearing about conditions there.[53] When the Pan-African Conference was convened in London, on July 23–25, 1900, an event which drew attendees from around the world, and which is often eclipsed by the Pan-African Congresses that began meeting in 1919, events in southern Africa were central to its agenda.[54] The conference sent a letter to Queen Victoria about conditions in South Africa, and the queen sent a letter in response, assuring them that British policy would not "overlook the interests of the native people." Mr. Christian of Dominica criticized the relentless drive for profits in the quest for minerals in southern Africa, warning that the British could hardly claim moral superiority over its Boer opponents, while R. E. Phipps of Trinidad complained to the gathering that the worst civil service positions in the colonies were set aside for "the colored people."[55] I juxtapose the concerns of Christian and Phipps to underline the extent to which two British Caribbean conference participants expressed keen interest in southern Africa as well as in social and political problems in Caribbean territories. This is to underscore my point that advocacy for southern Africa was in part a way of addressing concerns about colonial conditions elsewhere.

Sylvester Williams traveled through the Caribbean drumming up support for the Pan-African Association and for South Africa in the wake of the London conference.[56] When he visited Jamaica in 1901, he learned in no uncertain terms that talking about the African continent exceeded the purview of Black spokespersons and was better left to white colonial administrators. Sylvester Williams and his organization clearly enjoyed popularity in the colony. Addressing the Kingston chapter of the Pan-African Association, one of multiple Jamaican branches of the association, he "spoke at length of the injustice and barbarity with which the natives in South Africa are frequently treated . . . and the degrading limitations placed upon the freedom of men of color in some of the towns of South Africa."[57] Perhaps predictably, most of the newspaper's multicolumn focus was devoted to the chair of the proceedings, Sydney Olivier, the English colonial official who would become governor of Jamaica a few years later. Enfolding Williams symbolically into a sort of pass system in which he had earned official recognition, Olivier declared that he found Henry Sylvester Williams "worthy of consideration" after the latter brought him letters of introduction from two friends of his in England, Mr. Harold Cox, secretary of the Cobden Club and Mr. Keir Hardie, MP. Thus he found no hesitation in chairing the meeting, though he could not see why Mr. Williams found it necessary to visit the West Indies. "Any racial association, whether calling itself Pan-African or Semitic or Keltic," he regarded "with some distrust." In Africa, Olivier pointed out, "there existed a very clear division of races. . . . But most of 'our own' black and colored people derived their origin from West African tribes very different from the Bantus," so it was "far-fetched to form an association on the basis of African birth and descent."

With "our own" signaling *our Negroes on this side of the Atlantic*, Olivier asserted white colonial knowledge about the African continent as well the proper parameters of its relationship to West Indians of African descent, chiding Williams (a Trinidad-born British colonial subject) for exceeding these parameters. Southern Africa was an erroneous point of interest for West Indians if one understood questions of history, culture, and origin, Olivier seemed to say, but he was also signaling that current economic and political arrangements in southern Africa were off-limits to Black interlopers. Here Olivier asserted authority in the context of a familiarity that was constantly invoked by administrators and missionaries as they shuttled between postings in the Caribbean and Africa or Asia, invoking the specificity of ethnic and linguistic *types*.

Olivier used humor to undermine the validity of the Pan-African Association; eliciting laughter from his audience, he noted that although Anglo-Saxons were also doing hard and menial work all over the world, under the direction of Scots, Jews, and Germans, and for the profit of these employers, they did not think it necessary to form an association; Anglo-Saxons "held their own without it." He declared that it was undesirable "to form a racial organization in opposition to other races, and to claim for any one race that it was the crown or flower of humanity." Thus Sylvester Williams (and by implication his cosmopolitan global attendees who had made southern Africa central to the London conference's focus) had no authority to speak about Africa or on behalf of Africans, but they were also being told that any organization based on racial affiliation was inappropriate. Shortly afterward readers learned that the Pan-African Association had been dissolved, but that members of the chapters in Jamaica had met to keep it going in that colony.[58]

Five years later, a Jamaican editorial amplified Olivier's insistence that "racial organization" was both evident across the globe, and unacceptable in the wake of a popular resistance movement to the imposition of an additional colonial tax in Natal led by Bambatha kaMancinza, and that resulted in the execution or flogging by British authorities of thousands of Zulu clanspeople and the exile of chieftains to St. Helena. "The Cry of Race" expressed alarm about the "detrimental influence" that events in Natal could have on "other aboriginal races in Africa."[59] "Some striking manifestations of racial self-consciousness all over the world" were notable, including the Slavs in Russia and the Balkans trying to be "one of the important races of the world." The Asian continent was of great interest as well: "Japan has given the signal, and now we hear the cry of 'China for the Chinese'" while India was expected to "claim absolute freedom" and then "make good that claim." All Asia "will decree that that vast continent shall be for Asiatics alone"—and so we are watching "'the awakening of the East.'"

But "no one has ever expected that Africa might follow on the same lines." Recent events in Natal were a warning that this was the first sign of a general movement. The obvious culprit was the "American coloured people," who were spreading their "race-antagonism" to the African continent. In the United States "the descendants of Africa are admittedly badly treated," but they erred, "under the influence of a civilization alien to them but which forces into premature growth the qualities of aggressiveness and self-assertion," their dangerous discontent, which leaders such as Booker T. Washington understood, had to be channeled into "industrial pursuits." Continental Africans used to conduct their quarrels in specific ethnic contexts, but now their American "tutors" were teaching them that "the European is the common enemy."

Using a phrase that would become identified with Marcus Garvey, the editorial pointed out that "Africa for the Africans" would become a dangerous battle cry if these tendencies were left unchecked, warning that there was a race feeling, a "racial self-consciousness" that was alarming, and that was being led by misguided ringleaders from across the Atlantic. Erasing the agency of thousands who had organized and participated in the uprising in Natal (as well as those whom we must also assume were punished even if they did not participate), the editorial separated out diasporic instigators from hypnotized continental followers, inferring without specifying ethnic categories that, when left intact, they were free of animosity toward "the European." As we saw, Olivier had invoked white ethnicities to undermine Black claims for "racial association," and this editorial invokes a hierarchy of descending legitimacy, wherein "Slavs" appear to have legitimacy, even if doubtful, relative to a variety of Asian collectivities, but in which the phrase "no one expected" underlines the utter surprise about and nonlegitimacy of African claims to self-determination of association, as well as the right to judge Washington's leadership, under the guise of praising him. Thus, aggregated, cross-ethnic blackness is deeply disturbing. When people did not stick to their prescribed group, the paper warned, trouble was bound to follow.

The newspaper thus justified the violent clamping down of Black opposition to the aggressive imposition of taxes, stripping of land, property, and political rights, and curtailing of movement underway in southern Africa that mirrored events elsewhere on the continent. By 1910 the act establishing the Union of South Africa transformed two British colonies (Cape Colony, where a limited franchise allowed some Black people to vote, and segregated Natal) into dominions that were now conjoined with the former Afrikaner republics of Transvaal and the Orange Free State. By 1913, the transfer of land and other property from white to Black, and the symbolic and material paralysis of Black movement, was formalized and accelerated under the guise of reducing racial friction by the Native Lands Act, a key legislative plank of the future apartheid state that would not be removed until the early 1990s. Sylvester Williams' Pan-African Association and conference was one dimension of a network of activists situated in southern Africa (including, as Collis-Buthelezi shows, a sizable Caribbean-born resident community), and whose organizations (including the South African Native National Congress, the South African Native Congress, the Indian Congress, and the African People's Organization) participated in the pivotal Kimberley Congress of 1914, objecting to the Native Lands Act.

But I am also interested in another kind of response to events in southern Africa. When members of the "Smart Set" took to the stage in New Orleans one evening in November 1909 to perform *There Never Was and Never Will Be a King Like Me*, we could read the performance in terms of a sort of *ZuluModernism* that was doubtless being played out globally: a rehearsal of an aesthetics of defiance enacted in southern Africa that responded to the local conditions of each global constituency of spectators. At the risk of a perverse ethnic and geographical privileging and erasure (why not "SetswanaModernism," or "Xhosa," or "Natal," or "Cape"?), I take up one community as paradigmatic, in order to suggest that the world incorporates Zulu/*Zulu*, in this moment, but also how it had been looking on for generations as Shaka, Cetshwayo, and other Zulu sovereigns quelled factions within the kingdom, resisted or engaged Boers and British, and celebrated and mourned in 1879, a year of January victory and July defeat for Zulus in the Anglo-Zulu war. Even as white, English-speaking self-fashioning worked itself out as adventurous and ironic in fiction from H. Rider Haggard to Joseph Conrad in response to these developments, I am thinking of a theater troupe in New Orleans in 1909 working out and working through Zulu dissent, in a process of recycling and recreation.[60] How did the performance of Zulu sovereignty allow a community to reimagine itself in early twentieth-century New Orleans?

The skit *There Never Was and Never Will Be a King Like Me* was part of a vaudeville show on the Black theater circuit in New Orleans performed in the theater of Sam Greene's new Pythian Temple building, marking a triumphant return to the city of the Smart Set, after this company's performances had been banned six years earlier because it refused to reproduce racist minstrel tropes beloved by white audiences.[61] So inspired were some theatergoers by the rendering of "Zulus" on the stage, the legend goes, that they renamed their Carnival Krewe the Zulu Social Aid and Pleasure Club. Here my point is not so much to *prove* Zulu influences, or southern African ones more broadly, but to suggest that "Zulu" is particularly available in this decade and a half for this modernist makeover, as postures and signs circulate globally. Generations earlier, as Zine Magubane has shown, African men working in Kimberley's diamond mines were mocked and criminalized for their monetary accumulation and sartorial attire by anxious whites who, schooled on singing "Old Virginny" from the minstrel shows that were all the rage across South Africa, called them "Jim," "Jim Crow," "Nigger Dandy," or "Nigger Swell."[62]

When I see images of Louis Armstrong in his masquerade as the King of the Zulus all I see is a retrograde performance of minstrelsy, but in spurning what I am coding as "blackface" am I really showing my discomfort with *Black* performances that ironize whites' predilection for particular renderings of blackness? I am trying to understand Zulu masquerade when performed annually by Black New Orleanians as (or as also) the rejuvenating rehearsal of a 1909 performance of dissent, by a theatrical group that had been banned by white theatergoers who objected to the group's refusal to play minstrelsy the old way, and in a building, moreover, that had just been bought and refurbished by a wealthy Black man. Refusing to be minstrels (except on their own terms?) they drew on a performance of African sovereignty that was readily available, just as Prince Mackarooroo was doing in the same historical moment as he made his way around the world. Here I am put in mind of Michael North's discussion of the consequences for differently racialized artists of using the same artistic strategies that are coded as modernist: "Linguistic imitation and racial masquerade are so important to transatlantic modernism because they allow the writer to play at self-fashioning," in part because it is not "ancestrally" connected to the white body, whereas for African American artists "the version created by the white minstrel tradition" is a "chain," a "constant reminder of the literal unfreedom of slavery," that is not granted the capacity for ironizing distance and transformation.[63] I am also thinking of Daphne Brooks's discussion of London audiences' dissatisfaction with George Walker's and Bert Williams's 1903 performances in the musical *In Dahomey*: two African American performers noted for donning blackface use a play about imperial exploitation, displacement, and the United States' relationship to the African continent as "a platform to enact and interrogate the possibility of black economic autonomy in a transnational context," that constitutes "a departure from conventional minstrelsy plot machination."[64] A few years later in New Orleans, Zulu performance is a modernist rehearsal of the refusal to accept poll taxes across the African continent, and it is a testing of the waters for theater and masquerade traditions in a southern US (and northern Caribbean) city.

We can track how *Zulu* works itself into a way to style the self by paying attention to its appearance in newspapers: the shocked tones of a newspaper editorial when James Keir Hardie (the same British MP named by Olivier as providing one of Sylvester Williams's letters of reference) apologizes to one of his Zulu constituents in Edinburgh for a "massacre" that "fills one with shame and horror"; Prince Pixley ka Isaka Seme's winning of the Curtis Medal for oratory at Columbia University, on his way to Oxford for postgraduate studies; advertisements for performances, for *Zulu* soap, and for the return of a "large curly-haired black dog answering to the name of Zulu"; and the reference to at least one racehorse: "I named him 'Zulu King' because he was black and the Zulu war was in progress."[65] Many more news accounts mobilized the discourse of "hordes of blacks" and "rebel fanatics" fighting to "blood" their spears in adult initiation rather than pay the poll tax. Thus, *Zulu* also signals Black savagery and recalcitrance, and white bravery and martyrdom, as this or that colonial administrator is described as having won the "Zulu medal and clasp" for bravery in battle.

Zulu seizes the imagination with white men with safari hats and guns, and also with references to Black resistance and sovereignty. It is as a way to signal *Africa*, and it is also a third term that is neither *English* nor *Boer*. It stands for Black dissent and also for the violent curtailment of this dissent that is required by imperial order. But these are not *either/or* options, and both the continuing representations of and responses to "Shaka" in popular culture today can attest to this.[66] When Tsitsi Ella Jaji discusses stereo in terms of sound repeating as an echo that augments and distorts; and when Mary Lou Emery analyzes an argument between characters about the banjo in Claude McKay's 1929 novel of that title in terms of the tension between this musical instrument's connection to "the plantation nostalgia of black-face minstrelsy" and a revived creativity in blues and jazz idioms, in which a "new black masculine agency" displaced the instrument's associations with white women and with "disabling" minstrel masculinity, these critics help us name repetitions and resignifications across time and space.[67] Discussions of blackface in Caribbean masquerade traditions, including Trinidad's, interpret Black masqueraders' darkening of their skin with molasses as a commentary on the exploited labor that white, élite Carnival masqueraders blithely mimicked when they blackened their skin to *play* their "gardeners and servants"; as claiming the freedom of ancestral associations of blackness; and in terms of an "improvisational agency" that may not necessarily generate or seek social transformation.[68]

In 1900, Trinidad's residents joined others around the world in following the progress of events in southern Africa through the mediation of a so-called yellow journalism utilizing new resources of visual technology. In the United States this had just been put to the service of impugning Spain in the coverage of the Spanish American War, and now readers were encouraged to support either the British or the Boers.[69] Across the United States, citizens, immigrants, newspapers, schools, churches, and civic associations showed their support for the Boer or the British side, many by rushing over to southern African battlefields. The promise of mineral wealth, stories of prisoners of war on both sides, and the spectacle of the battlefield itself would have stirred powerful memories of conquest and defeat, in the wake of fresh memories of the Civil War; of constitutional and populist attacks on African American citizenship and citizens; and of recent and ongoing political and military maneuvers in Cuba, Puerto Rico, and the Philippines. Scenes of escape, defeat, and victory in southern Africa were rehearsed, as when General Cronje found himself on Coney Island playing himself, or when hundreds of participants in reenactments of battles, including soldiers who had fought on both sides of the Boer War, captivated attendees at the World's Fair in St. Louis, Missouri a few years later.

The media's coverage of war demonstrates the conjoined rather than oppositional processes of print culture and "commodity spectacle" as "mass management" in marshaling national and imperial loyalty on a grand scale.[70] Bill Schwarz's analysis of how events in 1899–1902 in South Africa were "a test case for assessing the future of white civilization," in which England and Englishness "came actively to be re-imagined through the lens of South Africa," concludes that the Boer War "*produced* a new popular culture," shrinking the distance between and energizing "high politics and low culture."[71] Schwarz examines the new "ventriloquist vernacular" used by the *Daily Mail* (London) and other newspapers to create in the newsroom and disseminate to its readership "real" registers of shock, horror, and amusement—in tandem with the ramped-up pace of "more images of faraway places" that reached English consumers from the battlefield of this thoroughly photographed and filmed war—a war that was also marketed with board games, postcards, and other memorabilia. Crucially, for Schwarz, this kind of highly mediated experience produces for and in a consuming public a collective identity and a collective memory; readers and spectators would *remember* something that they had never actually experienced because of the vivid images of media—the hundreds of thousands of stereoscopic images of the battles in southern Africa that were sometimes restaged on London's Hampstead Heath, for instance.

To inquire into how the Boer War fashioned desires is to see how Trinidadians are interpolated differently by the same events, whether these events are just across town or across the world. Each allows the other to be seen in a dissonant register, rather than as exotic or as mimetic. The global-imperial struggle has local dimensions—"which city, which hillside, which seat on the train, which new nation or colony, and before, after, or during which war"—and one cannot be fully appreciated without the other.[72] We are trying to register Caribbean people's investment in the Boer War without tacking it on as a minor instance of the war's impact on a global English-speaking readership, or as an imperial dimension of a *national* experience in Britain, a reverberation of something felt at the *center*. This is what Trinidad's Carnival masqueraders in February 1900 allow us to do, as we think of their performances in tandem with reenactments on London's Hampstead Heath, or on the fairgrounds of St. Louis in 1904. These performances in 1900 provide insight into "meanings and values as they are actively lived and felt," but not in the reductive sense of a colony being forced to cheer for empire from the periphery as it goes to war somewhere far away on some other periphery.[73] Nor is cheering for the Boers a pure form of dissent which can be cleanly separated from *tainting* colonial and imperial discourses of accommodation, since these are part of the deep reservoir from which language, feelings, and beliefs emerge; they work their way into how daily life is lived and we cannot say for sure how they are absorbed or remembered.

As keen readers of imperial and colonial power for generations, Trinidadians and their postures, lyrics, and skirmishes with the law constitute a theater of their theorization of this ongoing war. Newspaper reports can draw our attention to what people say and what their bodies do, as one way of tracking what it means to endure this wielding of power or the processes of making "Pretoria" and "Majuba" reverberate, of committing them to memory/*memory*. Mesmerized by "more images of faraway places," as they watched alongside others around the world, they must also have been desirous of performing and consuming gestures and products, stimulated by images of this and other wars. Descriptions of commodities mobilized the language of war and assumed allegiances: bicycles fitted with equipment to develop photographic plates in seven minutes, and with better maps that would mean less dependence on guides, and lessen the chance for *our side* to get lost (endorsed by someone who had used the bicycles while in Sierra Leone on the Hut-Tax Expedition); Finzi's Old Rum ("We are marching on to Pretoria / Which will soon belong to Queen Victoria / When we get there won't we have fun / And drink her health with Finzi's Old Rum"); the "Wonder Automatic Photo Button Machine" that looked like an American field gun and "rattle[d] off" 120 "photos" in an hour.[74]

When Victoria Lazaro caused a ruckus on Pretoria Day on Princes Street, perhaps it was partly because its businesses contained commodities that marked the limits of what she could possess, if not desire. "Armed with sticks and fighting attitude," she and others violated the required postures of loyalty, such as the one shown in figure 1.2. The photograph asserts the colony's order, and its loyalty to the British Crown, in a moment of collective and mandated celebration of an imperial victory. *Playing mas* a few months earlier in the exact spot, Carnival revelers produced poses of power and surrender that were also keenly observed and rehearsed, in the body. If not "orderly," February's movements and lyrics are variously interpretable as loyal, grudging, or otherwise ambivalent. If there is similar ambivalence in feeling in such

FIGURE 1.2. "Three Cheers for the Queen." Pretoria Day in Trinidad. From *Black and White* magazine, July 14, 1900, 52.

photographs, the *posture* of rehearsing triumph and defeat, and the public and collective nature of such postures, appears to be obligatory. Newspaper descriptions of such events stressed that they were "orderly." Trinidad's *Port of Spain Gazette* proudly reported that the London periodical *Black and White* carried a flattering account of the colony's celebration of Pretoria Day in its July issue, with this photograph ("taken when three cheers were being given for the Queen") capturing the orderly formation of dignitaries, spectators, and uniformed groups.[75] "Nowhere more enthusiastically than in Iere, the Land of the Humming Bird which is more commonly called Trinidad was the commemoration celebrated," the London publication was quoted as saying. The photograph, reproduced here, shows the Savannah, in the heart of Port of Spain, to be a tableau of civilian and military order, with humans and animals in precise formation. Against the backdrop of magnificent palms and other trees, and beyond them mountain ranges, the tropicality displayed here reflects a different register of power than the staging of the region's people for the postcards that, as Krista Thompson has shown, were increasingly dominating the visual culture of the region: persons posed against the trees of the nearby botanical gardens to demonstrate the height of the trees or inundated with bananas and other agricultural products to suggest the awkward, quaint efficiency of a properly managed labor force.[76]

The postures elicited by such public events assert the power and assuage the fears of imperial whiteness, including the importance of *being seen* to have been victorious, or to have elicited defeat and humiliation, as shown in the insistence of the British forces on sitting on the Asantehene's Golden Stool, in Ashantiland in 1897; in the smug poses of the members of the British "Punitive Expedition" sitting on the ivory and bronzes they have just looted from the Benin royal court in 1897; or in Lydia Liu's proposal that British obsession with the throne of Emperor Quianlong in late eighteenth-century China reflected deep psychic investment in reciprocal registers of sovereignty believed to have been jeopardized by decades of war with China.[77] And is it too farfetched to suggest that this era's spectacle of orderly formation in parade after parade (whether in this year of tributes to British successes in southern Africa, or in the sensory extravaganza of the Odd Fellows Parade in Atlanta in October 1912, with its seven-mile procession) likely inspired future parades and reenactments as ideologically divergent as D. W. Griffith's battle scenes in *Birth of a Nation*, or Marcus Garvey's New York City parades in the 1920s?[78]

Imperial loyalty is inculcated (which is not to imply that it is not genuine) and it must also compete for attention when someone other than the prescribed figure of adulation and respect holds the crowd's attention, as with those gathered on the docks to see "De Vine" being deported to Colombia a few months after Pretoria Day. The steamer transporting the "notorious burglar," whom Trinidad's newspaper readers were informed they were lucky to have been spared, stopped briefly in Trinidad on its trip from Barbados to Cartagena.[79] The reputed arsonist and thief, who had served several prison terms in his native Barbados as well as in British Guiana, and who had been flogged so brutally as part of his multiple sentences that he had ruptured an artery, was "mobbed by the unwashed" in the period between ending his most recent term of imprisonment and boarding the ship that would facilitate the emigration to the Republic of Colombia (and a five-pound stipend) that he had negotiated with the authorities in Barbados. The "one thousand men and women" assembled for his departure, and the reported cries of "what deah goin do wid de poor man!" suggest that the crowd's assessment of him differed markedly from that of the authorities.

Returning, finally, to a queen and her band, we could consider that in playing out class, ethnic, and racial tensions in Trinidad, February's Boer War masqueraders used that moment's imperial vocabulary. But the war cannot wholly account for these tensions. The repeated embodiments of the gestures of Pretoria and Mafeking throughout 1900 were also part of an annual cycle of public performance in Trinidad, in which old grievances and newer ones were both played out and ritually exorcised in a socially sanctioned and often disruptive Carnival season, and in other annual commemorations such as Hosay/Muhurram. These yearly events tested the limits of the authorities and other moral gatekeepers who nevertheless congratulated themselves on their magnanimity in allowing working-class people to perform the gestures (torch carrying, stick fighting, chantwell singing, drumming, as well as the construction, procession, and watery disposal of tazias) associated with these celebrations.[80] Commenting on the annual John Canoe/*Junkanoo* celebrations in the Bahamas, Krista Thompson notes that it was not just a reprieve from "everyday forms of work but it provided a platform, a form, though which [participants'] labor could be made into something else, which lay outside the capture of local and global economies—industries often tied to the freedom or repression of blacks."[81]

"Armed with sticks and fighting attitude," Victoria Lazaro and her brigade band drew on *Kalinda* and *Gatka* stick-fighting traditions brought to Trinidad and Tobago from Africa and Asia. In this colony and across the Americas, people practiced and performed for hours, accompanied by the beating of drums, bottles, and spoons, for the athletic training, competitions between villages, or fighting between rival factions that were modeled on Old World battle dances and war drills. Though it seems clear that, besides carrying spare sticks, bottles, and stones, as well as food and liquor, women also wielded sticks, and though they participated in the sexually suggestive singing and jeering between rounds of drum dancing and stick fighting, as *chantwells/chantuel(le)s* or combative chanters performing the *carisos* that were the precursors of calypsos, by the turn of the century stick fighting and calypso singing, still heavily scrutinized and penalized, were reemerging as male-dominated activities.[82] A tribute to a notorious police captain in Trinidad mentioned confrontations with working-class Black women in the later nineteenth century (multiply "what we call the Demerara centipede" by ten and you have the Trinidad *jamette*, it declared), as during Carnival season he and his men confronted "gangs" of these women "armed with sticks" night after night, "with blows on both sides."[83] In 1903 during the Water Riot (the populist cross-class protest against increased water rates organized by activists of the Trinidad Ratepayers' Association who had earlier been members of the Trinidad chapters of Sylvester Williams' Pan-African Association), the participation of "women and girls" stood out, as both particularly lawless (or shocking in their lawlessness because of their youth and gender) and vulnerable: women and children were "dancing and singing [and] throwing stones," and it was a young woman and a twelve-year-old girl who were victims of the day's bayonetting by the authorities.[84] When a fictional character assures a visiting countess that reports of disorder during the Water Riot are exaggerated, and that the colony stands for the kind of law and order displayed in the *Black and White* magazine photograph, then we could read this at least partially as the recognition that, whether "armed with sticks" or "dancing and singing [and] throwing stones," lawless "centipedes" are both a social problem and a particular target of surveillance.[85]

In a year and on a day of particularly fervent demonstration of sovereign loyalty, Queen Victoria Lazaro marshaled her brigade band, activating dissenting postures and allegiances on Pretoria Day in June 1900. Two turn-of-the-century wars, then, became vehicles for performances of celebration and dissent, and for accumulating bodily postures and other resources for a future opportunity. Narrated retrospectively, or in *real time* at the turn of the century, these wars facilitated a rehearsal of imperial might or dishonor, white rejuvenation and kinship, and new articulations of imaginative defiance fashioned out of distasteful or antiquated performances. Looking on from *home* or from multiple locations across the globe, British Caribbean-connected people joined others in figuring out these wars' relationship to the capacity for movement and accumulation.

2

RUINATION'S INTIMATE ARCHITECTURE

When the earth shook on Monday afternoon, January 14, 1907, it destroyed Jamaica's capital city, with fires compounding the earthquake's damage. Writing six years later, (and activating a discursive temporal break that still exists today in discussions about Kingston's built environment (*before the earthquake, after the earthquake*), the Jamaican journalist Herbert De Lisser noted that with each catastrophe Kingston had "improved itself," and the recent earthquake was no exception: King Street, the hub of its commerce, was "the finest in all the West Indies. It is well paved, well served by electric cars, taxi-motors, and horse-cabs."[1] Flanked by strong, earthquake-proof buildings that were no higher than two stories, the colonnades of businesses protected pedestrians from the sun. Visitors from cities with tall structures would conclude that they were surrounded by "dwarf buildings," and that the pace was slower than normal, but King Street was "Jamaica's Broadway, Oxford Street, Boulevard des Italiens, too, if you like."[2] Converting the familiar into dispassionate observation, and translating the city's experiences into a pleasurable narrative, De Lisser wrote for his local readers, but also with an eye to a tourist market developing since the 1890s around the steamers and hotels operated and built by the United Fruit Company. Was measured walking too slow, or just right? Since tall buildings were of no use in an earthquake zone, and a rapid pace would be foolish in the heat, the discerning visitor would come to appreciate local architecture and strolling as appropriate to Kingston's needs, rather than as somehow less modern than Europe and North America. De Lisser echoes earlier accounts of Kingston's resilience in the face of disasters, such as the 1843 fire that destroyed Mary Seacole's home and almost took her life, part of her narration of her travels and medical expertise in Jamaica, the Panamanian Isthmus, Sebastopol during the Crimean War, and England. In such accounts Caribbean writers are keenly aware of a tradition of hostile metropolitan travel writing in which their societies are used as proof of the absence of modernity, and their accounts make vindicating comparison that reach forward to our present: "Ours are not cities in the accepted sense, but no one wants them to be."[3]

Continuing his city tour, De Lisser declared, "Here [the visitor] will see every shade of complexion to be found in the island. The buggies and motor cars drawn up by the sidewalks contain dames of fair or olive hue; on their heads the hats of 'the latest fashion,' on their bodies simple white dresses that look cool in the heat of the day. Girls of chocolate color, with dresses fitting them 'like gloves' step briskly along, almost as briskly as they would in a northern city. Swarthy men, black men, brown men, fair men move up and down, not rapidly but with what after a while the visitor would come to consider a good pace, the heat considered." Here he claims an apparent belatedness for a different, parallel cosmopolitanism from the one he imagines for his nonlocal readers, appealing to what Jamaica's residents *share*—the way they march in multiracial step from shared past to shared future—even while he carefully distinguishes dark-skinned pedestrians from light-skinned carriage riders. The narration of Kingston strolling inevitably becomes a story about racial mixture, confirming metropolitan visitors' sense of a pace and space that are spectacularly different but, he assures them, comfortingly so, and with their own rationality.

Kingston was devastated by the earthquake and its accompanying tremors and fires, with hundreds dying, and many more left homeless and wondering if they were, in fact, alive.[4] The ensuing financial ruin was compounded by the unwillingness of insurance companies to accept liability, since they claimed that it could not be proved that the fires that caused much of the property damage had *preceded* the earthquake (properties were insured for fire and not for earthquake). Some fifteen years later, Marcus Garvey recalled the devastation and framed the attempt to recover insurance claims in terms of "love of country," criticizing those who testified that they had not seen any fires for supporting "foreign" insurance companies and insisting that he had seen fire on the day of the earthquake, in his capacity as manager of the Benjamin Printing Department on King Street.[5] In the wake of the earthquake a major diplomatic row ensued when Governor Swettenham objected to the circumstances of the arrival of military assistance from the US naval base at Guantánamo Bay (Cuban land that had been recently formalized as US-controlled by the Platt Amendment and lease agreements at the close of the Spanish American War), and he was eventually forced by the British war and foreign secretaries to apologize to US naval authorities, in an exchange of correspondence that was published in the US and UK media. Swettenham apologized and then resigned.[6] This demonstrates the extent to which considerations of official US actions and inclinations shaped both British diplomacy and colonial governance within Jamaica and other British territories, but also overshadows the assistance offered by other territories. The HMS *Indefatigable* brought relief supplies from Trinidad, a steamer arrived from Martinique, and Haitian president Nord Alexis sent health personnel in addition to supplies.[7] What is the real disaster in such moments and thus the most effective relief, and whose diagnosis or intervention is the most compelling, or consequential? To the consternation of some, the preaching and prophecy of Bishop Alexander Bedward's congregation in August Town, St. Andrew inspired many to get baptized and to marry in the wake of the earthquake, in this way identifying him as an important locus of cultural authority.[8] This chapter tracks what ruins besides an earthquake's rubble are evident in the century's first decade, but also how commentators attempt to escape, deflect, or endure ruination in their narration of catastrophe.

Narrating Kingston's devastation in real time, the English surgeon Sir Frederick Treves recounted his visit to Kingston weeks after the earthquake.[9] Riding in a buggy from a bustling train station through a scene of what he called "deathlike silence" and "blank desolation," with "hardly a living soul in sight," Treves asks his readers to imagine themselves standing at the intersection of London's Regent and Oxford Streets, seeing silent desolation where there had once been bustling streets.[10] He discerns and reproduces social distinctions even in catastrophe when, on the one hand, "Negroes blubbering with panic were filling the waste with howls and groans," or "[shunning] the gaunt city after the sun has set—[fearing] to see spectral women grubbing for their dead among the stones"; and on the other, "gentlemen" in a meeting escape heaving floor and falling ceiling, one of them returning "quietly" for his hat and umbrella—"such is the force of habit."[11] In less public spaces, the officer dressing for tennis, thrown downstairs and outside, looked up to see the front wall of the house removed to reveal his shaken wife in her bedroom by her dressing-table; at another residence, amidst the wreckage, the dining room's tablecloth was "just as the neat hands of the housewife left it."[12] Sometimes, Treves noted, a destroyed side or front wall was even more revealing: "Here every intimate corner from the attic to the cellar, from the drawing-room to the black cook's bedroom, is open to the eyes of inquisitive neighbors."[13] Labor is registered differently if we read the housewife as the marital partner of the patriarch, capable of a certain kind of feeling, like the "shaken wife" earlier; her "neat hands" betoken domesticity and femininity, even when exposed by catastrophe to the neighbors' eyes. This is very different from the cook's bedroom, and the cook herself (and in what follows I gender this figure female).

One site of what we could call the city's intimate architecture, the "black cook's" exposed bedroom, presses us to ask which bedrooms are or are not accessible; who floats above certain kinds of labor; and what are the ruins that cannot be seen, or that are not seen *as ruinous*. Nancy Rose Hunt analyzes the circulation of images of severed limbs in the Belgian Congo in photographs and lantern lectures of the same era. For Hunt, the concentration by European and Congolese commentators on *visual* evidence by way of the heavily circulated, shocking photographs has deflected attention "from the more hidden, tactile, and out of sight, away from another modality of violence, the sexual. And this modality of violence was intrinsically more reproductive and transgressive in its nature."[14] The ruination that is less visible would include sexual violence, or sexual and social relations scripted as transgressive. This "black cook's bedroom," is, in the US context that Jasmine Cobb discusses, the Black woman's chaotic boudoir offering the Black female body as "always already available to the needs and desires of White society" during slavery, and still "implicitly public" after abolition.[15] Cobb examines the portrayal of an "untamed Black interiority" in an 1834 caricature that justifies the denial of rights to nonwhite people whose "chaotic" morality and social relations (rather than, say, low wages, precarious living conditions, or sexual violence) prevent them from handling the moral responsibilities of respectable citizenship, including marriage or motherhood. Cobb's analysis of the aesthetic rendering of freedom—or rather of the absurdity of granting freedom—in the print caricature suggests that the hostility to Black freedom is depicted even in the inability of the boudoir's occupant to see the chaos, when her bedroom mirror tells the story that she fails to apprehend, and when even the startled cat who shares the image with her sees what she cannot. This is a reminder that long before the kodaking which is the next chapter's focus, these cartoons and other images give life to hostile visual conceptions of the Black subject.

If it could be argued that in Treves's account the cook's bedroom is rendered as chaotic *alongside* the employer's bedroom because of the traumatic event of the earthquake, with no necessary racial difference, we will still suggest that its ongoing connection to salaciousness renders it an ongoing site of the production of knowledge about Black women as available for public speculation, and as undeserving of privacy relative to employers assured of privacy. Not only visitors such as Treves, but local men narrate the earthquake and other events in this historical moment, and we are interested in their narration of the catastrophe of social mobility in terms of the bedrooms of working-class Black women, since the right to look into her bedroom is closely tied, as we will see, to the political ascendancy of Black Jamaican men. *That* we can see into her bedroom is a sign of her promiscuity and of the colony's moral diminishment. This is what Marcus Garvey tells the president of Tuskegee Institute, Major Moton, eight years after the earthquake: that to walk Kingston's streets is to be mired in an abjection made palpable in Black Jamaican women's appearance and behavior.[16] Garvey identifies her preference for nondark-skinned élite men as proof of her degeneracy, even as he struggles to script his own bid for social mobility in the British colony as other than intrusive or uncouth, and even as he and other men promote and benefit from the political activism of Amy Ashwood, Catherine McKenzie, and other Black women activists.[17] In what follows we will pay attention to this keen interest in Black women's relations—in seeing through to her room.

In a 1901 article in the *Jamaica Advocate* Catherine McKenzie uses an image of women occupying space to illustrate the convergence of the burden of taxation, the denial of political participation, and the gendering of labor. "Whether she be maiden or widow," the working woman could not participate in deciding how her taxes were spent, or in electing the people who would make those decisions, yet she was held to a higher moral standard, and had to "contribute equally" to the tax base with men, including "heavy 'surcharges' on tax bills": "Whether in the shop, with the needle, at the wash-tub, in the schoolroom, in the provision ground, on the hill-side, or plain, breaking stones on the open road, or carrying coal on the public wharves, she fills up the measure of her life, and meets the responsibilities of her station."[18] In a striking reformulation of an era claimed for empire, for "the color line," and for metropolitan suffragettes, McKenzie claims the age for heavily taxed and undervalued working women, an issue of equity and justice that she casts in terms of occupying space.[19] What could it mean to "fill up the measure of her life" differently? Can her right to stroll be valued as being as ruminative and engaging as the newspaper editor, or the poet-policeman, or the visiting tourist-photographer who might share the road with her? From another vantage point, can she credibly share with her male partner an "exclusive claim to be able to look" (or a claim to the mutuality of "the right to look") at miles and miles of estate land successfully acquired (or recovered)?[20] How does she claim space? What are the various ways in which she is *taxed*?

Decades earlier the enslaved narrator and antislavery activist Harriet Jacobs theorized the political implications of race, intimacy, and the right to look at (and to look out for) her children in the US South in the context of her own confinement for several years in a tiny attic that she termed her "loophole of retreat."[21] Theorizing Jacobs's precarious position as paradoxically cooped up but also "protected"—a "terrain of struggle" in which her "body [is] painfully protected deep within the crevices of power"—Catherine McKittrick registers an impatience with the theorization of the *margin* as a place to which Black women are consigned when we theorize carelessly: a sort of placeholder that forecloses deep inquiry.[22] For Tina Campt, this attic "is a site Jacobs claimed as simultaneously an enclosure and a space for enacting practices of freedom—practices of thinking, planning, writing, and imagining new forms of freedom. It is a place we mobilize in an effort to revalue black women's intellectual labor."[23] We are trying to track Jacobs's Jamaican counterpart generations later, whether in her room as it is turned inside out, or in the public domain as she negotiates her propensity to be surveilled. We are tracking her, usually through the lens of a mediating male commentator, and noting how my regard further deprives her of relief from scrutiny, while we are marking how various social actors position themselves in relation to her, whether white, or upper-, middle-, or lower-middle-class Black people who are her employers, for instance, or the single women moving between country and town who help her, and whom she assists in navigating the geopolitical terrain. She is dressed and turbaned in "spotless white" like Mary Jane Robinson, arrested for standing at dawn outside of the home of the beadle of the Halfway Tree Parish church and accusing him of killing the church's gardener; though her fearlessness could not prevent (indeed, it precipitated) her arrest, she is emboldened by prophetic insight as "a member of Bedward's flock."[24] She is also one of Erna Brodber's interviewees who, in the late 1970s, notes that her family's migration to Cuba early in the century left her vulnerable to neighborhood predation:

> Trap man, trap, you don't understand when a girl mash up? You don't understand, I just get mash up with him because I was unprotected. I didn't

have me mother to stand by me to open her eyes.... from I was about 13 [the fellow] been worrying around me and trying to... you know, to see if he can calm me down that I can love him, but I never did.... and Daddy not there to beat me, and mother not there to stand against me, and so on, I just fall in love with him. That was the way it is that I get to marry him and have 5 children.... Because when I have the first baby I love the child to my heart.... And that's why I have the second and so on. So, I was just a prisoner to feed them now so I couldn't go nowhere.[25]

Here parental, marital, and maternal affection are narrated as a tethering, as an entanglement of the consensual and the forced, the liberatory and the confining. Her future seems stymied by her intimate choices, represented here as a coercion that she must learn to live with. What does it mean to "just get mash up" and how is this related to someone else's capacity to move? In a body that did not often elicit sympathy, particularly relative to female subjects who were neither working class nor Black, who noticed her ruination, and on what terms?

Anxieties about the shifting gender roles of middle- and upper-class women, as demonstrated by their earning power and their "mannish" ways, are captured in letters to the editor that appear to be both élite debates between the sexes, and cross-class (élite and lower middle-class) dialogues. Women who left the home to work had "a mannish character [very different] from the womanly dignity which they ought always to preserve," complained one letter writer; they were "bent on pleasure at any cost... the subject of marriage as distant from their ideals as the North is from the South pole"; furthermore, this letter scoffed at the gender discrimination in the labor market, and mocked women's agency with a reference to "the earning of wages even less than that for which men could live on."[26] "Young Woman" in another letter asked why "we never hear of men being educated so as to be *our* companions."[27] Countering De Lisser's narrative of multiracial strolling in downtown Kingston, "Working Girl in Jamaica" questions her respectable prospects in the context of being snubbed by women of a higher class when they "happen to meet downtown," even though they had been introduced several times. She felt "dismissed" as a marital contender by Jamaican gentlemen, despite her "unsullied" purity and "untarnished" name, and warned that this social snobbery, as well as giving the best jobs to foreigners, would continue to result in Jamaica's loss of "the flower of her young men" and "the best of our women" to migration.[28]

Here migration is connected to cramped opportunities in Jamaica, another side of a relentless media focus on Jamaicans migrating to work in Cuba, Panama, the United States, and elsewhere. Expatriates, presumably British and North American whites, have access to jobs that this "working girl" sees as an additional affront. Downtown strolling is portrayed as fraught with class and probably also racial prejudice, and the writer alludes to an expectation about public social interaction leading to cross-class intimacy, or at least its possibility—at once an affirmation of De Lisser's celebration of King Street's cosmopolitan strolling and a challenge to his implicit social divisions. In making transparent assumptions about women such as herself (lower middle-class? Black?) as morally compromised, and in critiquing the connection that men make between women's purity and marriage, "Working Girl" also affirms the validity of these assumptions by distancing herself from the idea of being tarnished.

Letters to the editor complained about Black female servants, comparing them unfavorably to their counterparts in the past: "Jamaican" noted that while the recent formation of Garvey's Universal Negro Improvement Association (UNIA) and other institutions "for the uplifting of the colored inhabitants of the island" might have been commendable, "they all seem to aim too high to be of any practical help to the unfortunate class who act as our house-servants . . . Times have indeed changed from when we loved and respected our nurses. (I speak from experience, and will ever love and reverence the memory of my Nana) and are there not many families in Jamaica today who will bear me out in this? Who does not long for the old days when we loved to see our maids first thing in the mornings bustling around, with a cheery 'Morning Missus?'" Very different, complained the writer, from today's sour and ill-mannered housemaid threatening to quit if she was ever admonished. "When I read of Mr. Marcus Garvey, Jr.," the letter concluded, "I wonder if he could not be prevailed upon to sacrifice, for the present at any rate, his ambitious scheme of touring the US. . . . and persuade him to have a branch of his society equipped to help better the women folk who depend for self-support as House servants."[29] Here the surliness and insubordination of a new age is linked to new and questionable local and migratory projects associated with a rising Black middle class. The UNIA's investment in Black uplift comes at the expense of *getting good help*. "Aiming high" comes at the expense of old-fashioned, paternalistic social relations that favor the Jamaican élite.

Middle- and upper-class Jamaican male writers introduced their newspaper readers to the lives of working-class people, including women, as when

De Lisser noted the unfairness of their wages and cast this in moral terms: "Many earn only 4s. a week. So [they] are obliged from sheer poverty to drift into a loose manner of living."[30] They also penned novels and poetry with Black female working-class protagonists, migrants to Kingston from a rural location whose resilience cast the desire for legal marriage as either the staid and moralistic provenance of the élite, or the affectedness of members of her own class forcing their way into a higher social rung. Such portraits of the working-class single woman in the city approve of and are troubled by her modernity. Working-class women thus become part of the way that Jamaican men across class and race work out their own capacity to record her ruination and thus displace and reframe their own. For the middle- and upper-class *woman* writer this would have been more fraught, for her very familiarity with the proclivities of the rural or urban Black lower class would risk tarnishing her femininity.[31] In fiction such as *Jane's Career*, De Lisser's characters eventually assume these norms of respectability. McKay's poetry and shorter narrative fiction and nonfiction shows the high price for Black women *and men* for attempting to achieve (but also, conversely, for ignoring) this respectability. In pairing McKay, a Black middle-class writer and also a policeman during this period, with two other Jamaican writers—De Lisser, a journalist and novelist from a middling light-skinned class, who was already demonstrating the inclination to champion local and imperial white élite orders that he would come to be identified with over a long career, and Herbert Thomas, a white Jamaican officer—I want to press on the presumed borders between fiction and the law; between disinterested strolling and the cop on the beat; between surveillance and aesthetic observation; between the salvific nationalist whose local knowledge heals the colonial territory from the onslaught of hostile metropolitan and imperial words and action, and the local writer whose words and actions (rooted in local knowledge or not) are continuous with the violent wielding of the law. This is how the paths of the policeman and flâneur come to merge.

Caribbean Flânerie: Surviving Catastrophe

Proposing that it is "the Caribbean flâneur's fate to document catastrophe," Marla Zubel claims for the Caribbean chronicler a particular relation to ruination; and Julio Ramos draws on mid-nineteenth-century theorizing of the 1851 earthquake in Chile (such as Domingo Sarmiento's proposal that "tremors come to life at the precise moment that an extraneous revolution is at work in our lives") in his discussion of the role of the Latin American narrator who "transforms the event into a convergence of different signifieds that chaos—danger, disorder—may bring about a given conjuncture."[32] For Ramos, the Cuban intellectual José Martí, as a narrator-journalist in this tradition, exploits the capacity of the newspaper to "articulate the fragmentation" of the city, using the form of the chronicle. Martí's essays in New York were based on his culling together of several news bulletins from North and Latin America, and Ramos notes that Martí's question, "How can one put together such varied scenes" is both his practice and his reflection on his practice. "The stroll orders for the subject the chaos of the city, establishing articulations, junctures, and bridges between disjointed spaces (and events)."[33]

Generations later in *Notebooks of a Return to My Native Land*, first published in 1939, Aimé Césaire utilized Martinique's May 1902 volcanic eruption, which destroyed the city of Saint-Pierre, to chart the as yet inert potential of a small-pox-pitted, hungry, and inert Antillean landscape.[34] In this text Martinique's anomie and desolation are directly connected ("my filth in the glitter of gems") to the civilization and prosperity of "that other dawn in Europe" and North America.[35] The volcano also represents the ongoing potential of the earth in the face of the inhabitants' inertia: "*fumerolles d'angoisse*" (gas from a sleeping volcano; anguished volcanos); a landscape where "the volcanoes will explode"; "mountains uprooted at the hour when no one expects it/the islands linked for a thousand years!"[36] Césaire reaches back to the historical moment that marks the present tense of this chapter, bringing into view a catastrophe that precedes Kingston's by five years. In 1939, in the heat of explicit contestation of imperial rule and in the register of surrealism he joins Caribbean commentators before him in explaining the unevenness of modernization as devastating, but subject to the interrogation of historical and political analysis, rather than as innate, or as somehow indicative of Caribbean pathology. Crucially, he keeps in view *fumerolles d'angoisse* as the source of an energy as yet untapped, tamped down, brushed aside—a reminder of what is rumbling beneath, waiting to erupt. This is a *something* that insists on hanging around: a *trace*, in Lisa Lowe's sense of racial and geopolitical hierarchies of underdeveloped and developed that haunt liberal humanism's claim to guarantee freedom—"*traces* of liberal forgetting" that are read as "contradictions" to be "overcome."[37]

These reflections on the Caribbean city are often grounded in the travel (sometimes in the context of political exile) that gives these commentators the capacity to make regional and global comparisons that European travel writers claim as their prerogative. Thoroughly familiar with local and regional Caribbean and Latin American contexts, as well as with Europe or North America, though with divergent ideological conceptions of the region's history and future, they share a fascination for the pleasures and anxieties of walking in the city.[38] Writing in the wake of another catastrophe, Hurricane Hugo in 1989, Guadeloupe intellectual Maryse Condé proposes that Caribbean people's alienation from a Creole worldview embedded in names for the landscape is more disastrous than hurricanes, and implicates the region in ecological devastation culminating in events such as Hugo.[39] Returning writers such as herself have to reacquaint themselves with the landscape and with these names—in her case after living in an arid ecological belt of the African continent (*"j'étais dans ces pays du Sahel"*) where there was a spiritual system in place for theorizing and propitiating a hostile climate.[40] Visitors to the Caribbean ask us if we once thought of our volcano [Guadeloupe's La Soufrrière] as a god, Condé notes; they are eager to know our myths about it and maybe we answer too quickly that we don't have any.[41] Our rapport with the environment is impoverished. There is a way of speaking about nature (*parler de la nature*) that has been severed. For Condé as a returning writer in the 1980s this became connected to learning that the trees in her memory of her childhood had Creole names, not just Latin ones. Learning these names as an adult returning to live in Guadeloupe means that the trees now became integrated into her understanding of herself, of how she is placed in relation to the region, including its ecology.

Earthquakes, hurricanes, volcanic eruptions: even with the consideration that the narration of Caribbean observers is inevitably tied to observing these disasters and parsing their relationship to catastrophes of underdevelopment and the amnesia of Creole epistemologies, it is still possible to overlook the fact that what ought to be the mundane act of walking can be catastrophic— that there is a history of being mutilated, tortured, or killed by the colonial state for walking outside of the context of the plantation, or that recent vivid accounts suggest that in the twenty-first century walking can incur disaster (since some walkers are perceived to be contagions of disaster).[42] The stroller-narrator as journalist, memoirist, poet, and novelist seeks to observe and narrate without being made vulnerable by proximity to the nonrespectable body of the object of narration: the "black cook" must be consumed without jeopardizing the self-possession of the one who consumes her, or with whom she consumes. When she is absent, or when we do not have a record of the *flâneuse/passant/female flâneur* in her own words, we understand her to be present implicitly, as an observing and reflective stroller and interlocutor, and we also understand Jamaican male flânerie as in large part the keen awareness of this figure—the Black cook, the midnight woman, "Jane"—as a modern subject.

As perverse as it may seem to claim the figure of the flâneur for the early twentieth-century Caribbean city (so thoroughly identified is the figure with the nineteenth-century European city, with masculine narrative authority, and with a disinterested gaze), it allows us to consider masculine anxiety on Caribbean roads, and walking itself, in terms of the capacity for narration that is vindicating and recuperative. One of the paradigmatic figures of Paris in particular, the flâneur gains access to fragments of conversations and stories, as a stroller mingling with but not subsumed by the crowd, as a window-shopper observing others' consumption, as a solitary figure congregating with others like himself in the city's cafés. For some theorists the flâneur had been the perfect figure, emerging from the city's very sinews, to document the nineteenth-century city's sense of its modernity. Critics of this view note that this concedes too much power and coherence to the flâneur's narration, that the figure is insufficiently recognized as deeply gendered: a strolling recorder of urban life who projects a male gaze that exerts power *vis á vis* other, less privileged strollers such as women (the prostitute, the actress, or some other example of perceived female moral transgression), whom he narrates as the very embodiment of the troubling commodification of urban life.[43] He is both drawn to and terrified of the figure of the prostitute, whose body represents the promise and danger of commodification, and who thus reminds him of his own vulnerability. The flâneur's reputation as an intellectual who is not beholden to commercial interests because he does not receive a steady income, mystifies the poor writer-artist of limited means who needs to eat. If this is indeed a man who can wander unmolested, resisting the soullessness of employment in the professions or the military for a life of marginality and rootlessness, does he not also have to offer his essays for publication? How would he live otherwise? Looking and consuming, he is also being looked at and consumed. Both flâneur and (uncredited) flâneuse, walking these nineteenth-century Paris streets, create meaning out of the disorienting anonymity of urban life.

Flâneurs or commentators on flânerie were pursuing an "afterimage" of the working-class women who, as their nursemaids, were their initial guides through the European city.[44] Since they sought her "afterimage . . . in the prostitutes, servants and actresses who served as their mistresses, muses and models," we must read the modern city as both imagined through her and as "a feminine space" that has to be disavowed as a site of her agency; the city must be transformed into the spectacle which can be documented, tamed, made safe for the male observer's authority. If, for these intellectuals, "the city, as the first space of modern self-knowledge, was mapped as a feminine space," we want to pay attention to the gendered maneuvers of simultaneous confidence and destabilization in male narratives of the city (she can be a mentor, theorist, and guide but cannot be claimed as such). But we also want to keep in mind that colonial space, as itself gendered and raced, therefore implies a difference between the "modern self-knowledge" in the European or North American city and the Caribbean. Recall Césaire's reminder that Martinique's abjection guarantees the Parisian modernity that is documented by the Parisian flâneur. This is an insistence on keeping in view the colonial conditions that connect the underdevelopment of one space to what gets named as the modernity of the other. In this space of dissonance, we want to note the gendered difference that marks the female stroller as too contaminating (in the specific or vague nature of the sensuality that attends her) to be taken seriously as a bearer of knowledge.

I want the figure of the flâneur to hover, however loosely or imperfectly, over the Caribbean scapes that I discuss here: male stroller-writers who have (or who seek) the authority to craft their theorizations of public life into a narrative that is commercially viable; strollers who know themselves to be the objects of such gazes and narratives and who offer up competing narratives or other services for consumption; narratives that use observations gleaned from strolling to speak for, vindicate, castigate, or inspire a community of readers. If it is "the Caribbean flâneur's fate to document catastrophe," to return to Zubel's formulation, then we could also note that Caribbean streets will also have the hazards and opportunities presented by uneven or hilly surfaces, carts and animals; visiting amateur photographers, who, "reconnoitering, stalking, cruising the urban inferno," feel newly entitled by Spanish American and trans-African wars and land grabs in this turn-of-the-century moment; and the quotidian social relations of a hierarchical postabolition society.[45]

The Caribbean flâneur does this parallel documentation but must also avoid the unsettling feeling of being "feminized," either by the patriarchal colonizing machine, or by the feminized subjects in his vicinity. Much as De Lisser does at the head of this chapter, the flâneur strives to demonstrate that the Caribbean space is as modern as anywhere else, showing that any difference from the metropolitan arena makes sense in *this* space. The Caribbean stroller-narrator might do so by making a spectacle of others, whether the Afro- and Indo-Caribbean subjects comically burdened with bananas, in photographs in which their apparent submissive, quaint nonmodernity can attract tourists, or the working-class woman whose apparent excess is identified as the source of perceived colonial shortcomings. Stroller-narrators are writing in a moment of not just earthquakes, but of *social* cataclysms, as a middle sector of mostly lower-to-middle-middle-class teachers, clerks, parsons, journalists, and professionals use newspapers, churches, and civic organizations to pressure an upper sector of merchants, planters, and colonial authorities to loosen their tight grip on the political and economic domains of the colony. Each faction claims moral superiority, and the right to interpret and wield control over the rural and urban constituencies who form the lowest social echelon. The accumulated wealth of returning migrants, alongside that of generations of indentured migrant laborers, represent new, nonelite sources of wealth, new ways of dissociating wealth from the performance of respectability, new political demands, and changing social relations. Perceived upstarts are narrated as vagrants who need to be returned to their proper place, by strolling, documenting, interpreting commentators who claim the cultural mastery to document and to interpret what is authentic, fake, or borrowed, with attendant notions of purity, ancestry, reversion, and inheritance.

When the Jamaica League, formerly the Patriotic League, an organization which I assume was composed of brown and Black men, objected to the display of postcards of "native scenes," including working-class Black women in head ties, to the Bee Hive store's advertising campaign as caricaturing Black Jamaicans, and to a new literary anthology *Pepperpot*, that appears to have included a short piece by De Lisser entitled "Jane," and when the league underscored its objection by passing a resolution banning dialect in material representing the colony, it set off a flurry of editorials and letters to the editor, at least for the month of January 1915.[46] This is a period on the cusp of the moment where this book leaves off, when the papers were full of news of war between European powers, including a British attack on Dar es Salaam, the capital of German East Africa, yet another earthquake in Italy, political tensions in Haiti, and a US immigration bill that was perceived to be targeted at aligning "coloured people" with anarchists and curtailing their entry into the United States. Letters in the *Jamaica Times* and the *Daily Gleaner* supported the league, concerned that people in England would think that all Jamaicans spoke dialect, and expressing disappointment that train conductors and policemen spoke Creole in public. But other letter writers chastised the league for overreacting, as Claude McKay's older brother, the prominent educator U. Theo McKay, did when he reminded the league that Albert Tennyson, Paul Lawrence Dunbar, and his brother used dialect: Dunbar's poetry "didn't prevent the existence" of a Booker T. Washington or a W. E. B. Du Bois, and "our sons and daughters, who know our manners and customs" and "translate them" with the "insight and sympathy, which no stranger can emulate . . . should receive every encouragement, for a people can only come into its own when from its ranks, there come its novelists, its historians, its poets and its prophets."[47] Here references to "translation" and to Du Bois and Washington keep Creole speech firmly in place as an auxiliary language, which finds its proper endpoint elsewhere. Indeed, U. Theo agreed that while dialect was the obvious choice for "Jane" (meaning De Lisser's working-class heroine), it would be libelous in the mouths of "native ministers, native school teachers, native doctors, and native lawyers."

De Lisser used an editorial to scoff at the league's objections, thanking it for "supplying us with something to consider besides a disastrous war."[48] He expressed puzzlement at its position, declaring that "Jamaica dialect is the spoken language of the vast majority of the people," and "We are not ashamed of the working classes." De Lisser proceeded to spin a hypothetical tale of two working-class Black women, a milk seller supplying Kingston's households with "matitutinal milk" and the housekeeper of one of the households, receiving the milk on behalf of her white employer. Their unlikely dialogue ("a well-modulated tone of voice enquired, 'Pray, who is there?' 'It is I,' was the answer") is intentional in its use of the wrong linguistic register, and therefore also ridiculing. In choosing milk sellers, we could read De Lisser as punning on current print advertisements for "Milkmaid" condensed milk carried in the paper, but also riffing on the iconic "Milkwoman," part of Isaac Mendes Belisario's 1837–1838 *Sketches of Character* series of lithographs appearing just at the moment of the official abolition of slavery.[49] The commentary that forms the caption marks her as a "sable sister" of "striking difference" to her "rosy-cheeked" counterpart in London, making the inevitable comparison to England, but also tying the image to the tradition of painting itinerant street traders in "Cries of London" and other series of images of the condition of England's working classes. The commentary notes that unlike her corrupt counterpart in England, her "adulteration" of the milk she carried was judiciously done, and necessary, since goat milk was so rich. "Milkwoman" was part of a Black Jamaican typology, the tin pans of milk on her head used to reference the "erect" posture of Negroes, who were "trained to sustain weights" from a young age, and her singing on her journey into Kingston as part of the city's soundscape.

The *joke* of De Lisser's anecdote turns on pure and impure, counterfeit and authentic—counterfeit money, the corrupt dilution of milk, the visual pun of Black women selling white milk, and the implied sonic dissonance of elevated prose and the Black laboring body, a perceived incongruity that would have stung the league's members as revivifying a long-standing idea about the English language and Black pretentiousness, and as magnifying the insult by connecting them to an undignified and feminizing spectacle.[50] Faced with the common critique that they were hysterical mimic men who were ashamed of working-class speech, these Jamaican middle-class men would have seen the editorial as the disingenuous scolding by a light-skinned man with white patronage who had a lot to gain from exoticizing a particular rendering of dark-skinned Jamaicans for tourist consumption, and who had the social distance that allowed him (De Lisser) and others to utilize Creole speech without fear of being identified negatively with it. [51]

In such discussions, working-class women were a useful point of reference for the authenticity or misrepresentation of a constituency, their materiality filling in and speaking for those not directly invoked. In De Lisser's anecdote this included their employers, presumably upper-middle-class or upper-class women who were marked off from the direct *kass-kass*, as they sold and purchased milk with Black women as the public mediators who crossed the liminal space between public and private in order to protect their mistress's privacy. For a rising Black professional class, a working-class woman could not be used to represent Black people as modern, since such images drew on old ideas of the (racial) group in stasis, and they understood the circulation of images of her on postcards washing clothes to be used in the service of a tourist industry that wished to characterize dark-skinned Jamaicans as a quaint and pliable community of laborers. The postcards were the era's photographic update of Belisario's mid-century lithographs. In their objections, they cast Creole speech as part of the problem, explicitly or implicitly faulting De Lisser, the defender of the status quo, and McKay, the poet whose poetry in Creole had propelled his migration to the United States. Ideologically different these two may have been, but in being identified with the use of Creole speech in fiction and poetry, they were irresponsible bohemians who misread (or dismissed) the consequences for foreign perceptions of nonwhite Jamaicans' aspirations in a world that was changing.

De Lisser cut his journalistic teeth sharing the discoveries of his strolling with Jamaican newspaper readers. As a cub reporter he introduced them to lunchtime diners along Tower Street who, discussing the Boer War, knew "all about the movements of the troops. They speak of 'our war in the Transvaal,'" criticizing Kruger and saying that they still had confidence in General Buller; and to a "moving stream" of mainly women negotiating crowds and tramcars as they walked into Kingston with their produce on their heads or steered donkeys carrying full hampers, teasing De Lisser about his presence on the road with them—"'You mean you leave you nice house a Kingston to come up yah fe walk? Cho massa, you making fun'"—and sleeping overnight in the market to get the best spot to sell their produce the next day.[52] This is a sympathetic stroller, recording the living conditions and meager income of working-class residents of the city and its suburbs, especially women; an astute stroller, who uses the diners on Tower Street to show the intricately stratified hierarchies within working-class communities in Kingston, as demonstrated by their choice of restaurant and menu. This is intimate strolling, as he appears to accompany women crossing the border between *country* and *town* for hours. A careful listener, who is still in the market late in the evening, this "gentleman" flâneur resolves to "do in Rome what is expected of us," and has to suffer hearing his own social acquaintances cut down to size: "De gentleman dat keep a shop out a de new Cross Roads.... Him pupa used to keep a rum-shop where Missa Perry live now."

This is not the disinterested flâneur who records from a distance, but one who gently prods a readership perceived to be property owning and residing above Halfway Tree to be more sympathetic, to see that Kingston's streets are cosmopolitan in their teeming variety. But this cosmopolitanism really redounds to De Lisser, who as narrator can read faces, accessories, emotions, and match them up with appropriate histories and contexts. De Lisser says he is present at the market "as an intruder—a stranger in a strange land," but he is there because he chooses to be, and his interlocutors cannot ask him to leave.[53] They must answer his questions, humor him, marvel at his willingness to speak Creole, as when he says they respond with delight to his "yes, me dear," with "Weh de gentleman sey." If this is an ironic rejoinder on their part, as well as De Lisser's wry recognition of his own linguistic shortcomings, they still have to pause and engage him.

This trafficking back and forth of women transporting produce in heavy containers from their families' rural plots to markets in Kingston and its environs renders the line between *country* and *town* very porous. They join a multiply originating crowd and help to make it a space of sociality, as they greet passersby—even, to De Lisser's consternation, in the dark. But this is turned into something else when travel writers, increasingly equipped with cameras, or studios such as Duperly and Sons or the Scottish firm Valentine and Sons hired to produce photographs that would attract investment and tourism, make them wait in poses that must be held for the duration of the desired exposure. Their own schedules disrupted (including plans to get to the market in time to reserve a favored spot), they are transformed into images of industry, of supervised labor, of a stultifying postcard quaintness as far as annoyed league members are concerned, and also an archive of agency and endurance. They are arrested, for the duration of the shot, even as we can imagine them staring back, grumbling, or asking questions, in a *tense* negotiation of what is imposed and what they manage to assert.[54]

Although most of De Lisser's 1913 novel, *Jane's Career*, is closely focalized around a young working-class woman who moves to Kingston from a rural village, in the first two pages or so of the third chapter, a second-person *you* engages a reader imagined as an élite tourist, whose gaze merges with the élite omniscient narrator to share an aerial view of Kingston, framed by the narration of a history of colonial conquest.[55] This is a history as well as an exercise of visuality, in which Jane, as the object of De Lisser's social meditations rather than as a full-fledged political subject, is not allowed to participate. As she moves into the city to make a life that is different from her family's, then, she is kept unaware of a narration that links a particular past to the ongoing present and future, even as her desires and aspiration are the chief engine of the novel's plotting of modernity. On my reading markets and their moving vendors also feel marked off from Jane's new life in Kingston, and this has spatial, not just temporal implications. Kingston and *country* feel more marked off from each other, as the crossing back and forth of the border between them now becomes more closely identified with Jane, as she stakes her claim on alternative experiences of Kingston. Spaces of modernity for centuries—as part of a cycle of moving produce from plantation provisions grounds to points of sale, feeding the colony, and generating proceeds used to buy land and the education of a rising professional class—markets and the physical, socioeconomic, and symbolic movement that they make possible are not represented in the novel or elsewhere as the analogue to, say, the department store. Similarly, the agency of the women who are these markets' most powerful visual representation become the quaint core (reviled or humored) of the era's postcard culture.

Jane's familiarization with the city is partly realized through her interaction with mediating figures: Syrian merchants who sell her clothing on credit, and Chinese shopkeepers whose stores are a proving ground for a Black feminine practice of haggling and commerce, and thus the honing and acquisition of voice, social networking, and taste. Parallel metropolitan and colonial contexts are interesting here, as when Enda Duffy compares James Joyce's Dublin strollers to their counterparts in London and Paris: the Londoner and Parisian see luxurious commodities through the shop window, dazzled by the "delights of consumption" of the advertisement, while the Dubliner, more alert, and inured to such seductions of colonial space, sees symbols of colonial power.[56] Rita Felski discusses the way in which a deep discomfort about consumerism is dramatized in the depiction of the department store in nineteenth-century French fiction: women's attraction to the allure of the department store's textures and colors, available for touching "without any obligation to buy," and thus the store's facilitation of shopping as both sensuous and a site of cross-class mingling and aspiration, contributed to a deep disquiet about the "feminization of modernity," read as its "demonization."[57]

On the one hand such examples would apply more precisely to the middle- and upper-class women discussed earlier in connection to letters to the editor, some of whom presumably had the leisure and means to shop in Jamaica's finest stores. On the other hand, the juxtaposition allows us to highlight the shop as a key site of Jane's desire and consumption. Unlike the Kingston firms whose advertisements in the newspapers seem targeted to more élite tastes, the Syrian shops patronized by Jane and her companions (and which I assume would be beneath the notice of upper-class women, until a later period when such merchants had moved up the social and commercial ladder) deliberately use lights to "capture the fancy of servant-girls and women from the country."[58] Thus (possibly) immigrant merchants center the working-class woman as a desiring subject whose tastes are taken seriously. Her consumption of fabric and other goods drives their emerging businesses and offers her opportunities for self-fashioning, which, in enabling her sartorial confidence in a new location, casts both merchant and consumer as sharing a register of modernity that we must learn to track.

This novel employs tropes of Black femininity that would be taken up in fiction of subsequent decades: rape, framed as both a necessary experience of social mobility for young Black women, and a critique of priggish middle-class obsession with sexual dishonor; the representation of Black men as foolishly tied to the immature performance of rebellion through misguided labor strikes, in contrast to Black women's realization that Black political solidarity is a waste of time; Black mating as at once unattached to formal marriage before childbirth, and deeply attached to expensive wedding rituals. The novel's barely visible cast of white characters consists of legally married couples, inhabitants of faraway suburbs, and quietly scrupulous employers, who render an aspiring nonwhite middle class as affected, pompous, and hopelessly doomed to ludicrous imitation by comparison. The police, and Black constables, specifically, are mocked, and Jane's vulnerability to the law's arresting gaze and to the accusation of immorality on the streets at night is transformed into her capacity to reduce the figure of the constable to a "cartman." Jane's fate—her unfortunate teleology, in De Lisser's logic—is to become the upper-working- and lower-middle class woman who treats her inferiors badly, just as she herself had been treated badly by them at the beginning of the novel. *This*, De Lisser implies (not their limited economic and political prospects in urban and rural life, or Jamaican élites' contempt for them), is the problem with a socially mobile class of Black and brown Jamaicans.

By the 1930s when Claude McKay writes a novel about Jamaica, he will locate the Black woman protagonist and other characters firmly in a rural pastoral setting, bypassing Kingston as he moves them between rural Jamaica on the one hand, and English boarding schools or Panama on the other, in order to show that far from exotic folk props in the modernist repertoire these social actors are thoughtful, ironic participants in and critics of modernism.[59] They do not exist outside of the time marked by *real* cosmopolitans in Kingston, or of another class or territory. They make time. They beat time. They are in time. "Jane," "Bita," "black cooks" thus become a sort of origin story, a paradigmatic life lesson, the linchpin of the self-narration of Jamaican male narrators who locate their capacity for self-possession at least partly in relation to them.

Policing the Crisis

When De Lisser's Jane calls a policeman a "cartman," her contempt is part of a long-running discussion about whether law wielding can credibly inhere in the personhood of the Black man. If I want Claude McKay's poetry and short stories to count as flânerie, since they document Kingston strolling in a period in which he is strolling in his capacity as a policeman, just before he leaves Jamaica for good in 1912, is it not as ludicrous to think of the policeman as synonymous with the (disinterested or politically aware) flâneur, who would be expected to be critical of law enforcement, as it is to think of Jane and others taking his Black law-wielding capacity seriously? For how can the flâneur wield the law? In the bleakest accounts of law, violence, and policing, the law itself (rather than, say, the person tagged as the criminal) is violent, and violence upholds the law; we obey the law because it has authority over us rather than because it is just; modern law and the police are just as violently impulsive and inescapable as the gods; and even our *anticipation* of the law already brings us into relation with the law and its violence, for our patient expectation of justice becomes the very work of law itself.[60]

The police narrator claims the right to be understood as fragile, as vulnerable to the harm of others, and also the right to hail others violently in the name of the law. We could think of sovereignty as the violent arm of the state; sovereignty is discernible in acts of violence, and policing is the state performing its violence.[61] Thinking about what it means to be hailed by the law, in a twenty-first-century context that refocused attention to the threat posed by the *terrorist*, or when the armed forces in at least two national contexts that are close to me wield this so violently and insistently against Black people in the era of Black Lives Matter activism and in the wake of Jamaica's Tivoli Incursion of May 2010, feels at once surreal and all too real. In *Policing the Crisis: Mugging, the State and Law and Order*, the authors urge that rather than yielding to a moral panic about crime, in the context of 1970s British media reports about the "crisis" of mugging, particular cases of mugging have to be analyzed in relation to societal anxieties, so that we can see that criminality is produced.[62] For Angela Davis, Critical Prison Studies presses us to attend to those "circuits leading from intimate to institutional" that would allow us to apply the insights of *Policing the Crisis* to Black women's entrapment in the carceral system in the United States.[63]

Jamaican policemen have given us two retrospective accounts of policing in the late nineteenth and early twentieth centuries: Herbert Thomas's *Story of a West Indian Policeman* was published in the 1920s, and Claude McKay published two books of poetry on desk duty as a constable in 1912, the year he left Jamaica, as well as short fiction and nonfiction that he published later about this period.[64] These two men, white officer and Black constable, wield the law (or attempt to) in early twentieth-century Jamaica, and they give an account of themselves through their writing. What interests us here is a pressing on the terms, the affect, the gendering of flânerie and its claim to knowledge, through a simultaneous proximity and fear of proximity that is managed by the ability to produce a retrospective and recuperative narrative. Thomas demonstrates white Jamaican resentment of both Black social mobility and white expatriate contempt. McKay conveys Black lower-middle-class reluctance to wield the law, a suspicion that his performance of law-wielding is a farce that is seen through by working-class women in particular, and thus a masculinity that he seeks to manage and recover. Thomas, I assume, does most of his patrolling on horseback, unlike constables such as McKay, who patrol on foot as a sign of their social power when they "beat de eight" relative to working-class walkers, but genuflect to élite walkers and riders.[65] Constables were generally Black men serving under white officers. In Trinidad, Black constables tended to be Barbadian migrants used as an English-speaking and anglophone Creole-speaking wedge between the police force and the francophone Creole-speaking population of Trinidadians and migrants from francophone Creole-speaking Caribbean territories.[66]

Thomas's and McKay's police musings, often accounts of their familiarity with the social landscape attained through strolling, gain another layer of significance when we keep in mind that colonial policemen—indeed, any Black man in police or army uniform—are coveted *visual* objects for strolling photographers.[67] I read such images as indicative of both an ordered territory appeasing the traveler who might be apprehensive about a majority-Black space, and of a quaint attempt at *play-play cops* that mimics real law and order in the modern space of the tourist imagined as European or North American. We can hear this in the white US visitor who refers to "the constabulary, or policemen, who match the color of the darkness very well, and who wear their uniforms with great dignity, are extremely polite, and never think of using a word of one syllable, when a longer one can be employed. While we stood watching the merry-go-round, one of these dusky constables approached us, and with a pompous, but friendly air, offered to 'rush in and secure seats' for us."[68] Here "great dignity" parses pride as comical excess and buffoonery, as a connection is drawn between the incongruity of Black police and that key marker of Black/brown transgression—too much learning. This is a Trollope moment, applied to Black Jamaican police.

Both Thomas's and McKay's texts make it clear that good police work requires a violent assault on Black life to uphold colonial order and the myth of racial impartiality. As Patrick Bryan points out about the use of force in 1902 in Montego Bay in western Jamaica: "The Mobay Riots demonstrated that the [Black] paramilitary constabulary could be relied up on to defend the white dominated status quo. More could not have been expected, or more demanded."[69] This is why the observations of two of the most well-known US

African American figures, W. E. B. Du Bois and Booker T. Washington, bring me up short. For if McKay is suspicious of the law's anti-Black intent, as well as his own incapacity to inhabit the role with authority, and if Thomas craves a Black police force that will affirm white supremacy, Du Bois and Washington cannot get enough of these "smart, dark" Caribbean men in uniform. They see a parallel empire in which Black people seem to be in charge, and that might, therefore—European colony notwithstanding—affirm Black life. Since we know that wielding the law is in and of itself violent, this is a diasporic fantasy, but the idea that blackness in uniform could guarantee peace poignantly conveys the violence of the US landscape, in this historical era of unprecedented lynchings.

"I think if there were throughout our Southland a system of Negro policing somewhat after the fashion of the Negro constabulary in the West Indies, that this would go a long way toward increasing the Negroes' respect for the law and tend to decrease our crime rate."[70] In his review of Harry Johnston's *The Negro in the New World*, Washington attributes a low crime rate "among the West Indian Negroes," relative to "Negroes in the United States," to a sense that the law protects them, and that this sense is conveyed by the fact "that policing and the administration of justice in the petty courts is to a large extent in the hands of the Negroes themselves." In the United States, he says, it is not yet possible "to dis-associate [*sic*] law from slavery." Attributing law and order to the Caribbean, Washington confines "crime" to what African Americans do, without a consideration of what the latter endure under the auspices of white savagery, whether legal or not (that is, unless we can parse an inability to disentangle law from slavery as a quiet admonition of a *status quo* that is the agent of this refusal).

"The smart, dark Constables in their gleaming white hats and coats gave me a double sense of security."[71] For Du Bois, visiting Jamaica on holiday in 1915, it is precisely the blackness of Jamaica's constables that makes them noticeable and desirable; they are part of a phalanx of dusky civil servants who model for him what it would mean to live "beyond the color line": "In Jamaica for the first time in my life I lived beyond the color line—not on one side of it but beyond its end. There in strange places I could sense its curious paths stopping and wavering and fading into uncertain threads. Of course, I was ever looking for it. That is my inborn nature." Here, he makes clear that it is his own protocols of reading that produce this as noteworthy, but this does not diminish the pleasure of discovering that the Lord Mayor "was colored," or the "strange sort of luxury" of a train ride wherein all the personnel are Black; or "a curl or a tint" in clerks in post offices and stores intimating "the most ancient of blood."[72] This is a social world that generously opens out to him as fully human and deserving, and in which his *hesitation* at the expectation of their hesitation is blissfully misplaced: "I almost hesitated at the barber shops but the barbers did not hesitate." In Jamaica Du Bois feels fully protected, since Black constables give him "a double sense of security"—we imagine because his personhood is not assaulted by the law as it would be in the United States. This state of being "*beyond* the color line" weaves in and out of race, since he says, in effect, that when blackness becomes normative, regularized, it seems to wither away or to mean something different.

But how might McKay, living in New York for three years in the summer of 1915 when this essay appeared, have read this? With pride at the ordered world Du Bois describes? We know how Marcus Garvey read it, because he condemned the article as part of an embittered response to what he experienced as social ostracism from Jamaica's professional middle class even more keenly than from white élites. That is, Garvey, born in Jamaica and not yet living in the United States, was never toasted by the Lord Mayor of Kingston at a dinner in his honor, as Du Bois was.[73] Du Bois makes us wonder about the difference between "smart and dark Constables" and the "tint and curl" of clerks, since dark-skinned Jamaicans complained about hiring preferences for light-skinned applicants. Perhaps in the accounts of two Jamaican policemen we can discern, less the *actual* condition of policemen, than their discursive production, and the social tussle of which Thomas's and McKay's contiguous portraits are an effect. If Thomas presents blackness as exceeding its proper place, as a dangerous excess that gives particular injury to him as a Jamaican, then McKay cautions that the smart darkness which Du Bois finds so appealing is an enormous burden, and that it conceals a violence that he and Washington fail to discern when they look south of South.

The Story of a West Indian Policeman is as obsessed with Thomas's sense of being disrespected by colonial authorities (the Jamaican governor and other colonial administrators fail to pay him enough to allow him to have his family live with him in Jamaica, and he is obliged to house them in England, or his knowledge of Jamaican topography is never recognized by publishers), as it is with social fraudulence, as practiced by powerful female obeah practitioners or overreaching lower-ranked policemen. Clothing and language in particular powerfully encapsulate this difference between impostor and professional, as when a white colleague wears a medal inappropriately, or as evidenced in his own photograph on the book's frontispiece, garbed in full ceremonial police dress, complete with sword.

Black male social mobility is deeply unsettling to Thomas, and much of the text is devoted to railing against Black promotion in the police force. As a white Jamaican invested in the mystification of Jamaican whiteness and also conscious of its inferiority to metropolitan whiteness, he senses that the elevation of Black men, who were permitted to occupy only the lowest echelons, would undo him. In example after example, he shows that Black promotion is bad, so that giving commissions to "native sub-officers," for instance, would be a mistake, since it is based "on the utterly fallacious theory that all men are born equal."[74] Promotion, he advises Black men, would cause them to be "cut loose" from their peers but "boycotted by the upper classes" and therefore they would "[hover] between heaven and earth, like Mahomet's coffin." The custos and resident magistrate would not invite them to tea—and if they did, "how you would feel in their drawing-rooms?" He persuades his own "friends" who are "clear brown" and "as near black as could be although [their] hair was fine in texture and only slightly curly," that "deserving black and coloured" policemen should not be promoted, pointing out that Black officers under them would resent their authority, and say, are you not the "same damn naygur like myself?" If he, as a white officer, could be subject to "tracing, that is making uncomplimentary allusions to one's ancestry and antecedents," as he was by disreputable (and presumably Black) policemen in his early days on the force, how much more would they be, as Black men?

Thomas's anxieties show that he is deeply cognizant of a general social disregard for the police force in general—it is socially undervalued and élites' deep sense of unease about the majority Black population feeds a worry about whether they are to be trusted in a crisis (trusted to be brutal enough, and also not to be brutal, depending on the particular constituency). Should not the police just carry handcuffs and batons, instead of firearms? Why are they in spurs, or on horseback? Should the red stripe be removed from police trousers? Should English troops be sent in from their Newcastle encampment to supplement the police? He notes that he is "the first officer to cause the men of the Jamaica Constabulary force to use their weapons on a riotous mob," during the Montego Bay disturbances in 1902; at that time Black policemen were prepared to "use their weapons against their kith and kin. I am proud to have had the honor of thus 'blooding' the Jamaica Constabulary, especially in such trying circumstances. . . . They proved their loyalty to the hilt on the night of 6 April, 1902; and they have done so repeatedly since then."[75] Good policing is Black-on-Black violence. This is what Du Bois and Washington cannot or will not see. Thomas lays bare here what whiteness requires to counter the dread of feeling unhinged.

In an extraordinary passage, Thomas relates an incident ("forty years ago" in this 1927 publication) when in the course of his constant travels across the island he encounters "a very well dressed and well groomed black man, evidently on very good terms with himself" distributing medicine to a gathering of "honest country people" from his "two-wheeled vehicle."[76] Disliking the man's demeanor, which Thomas interprets as explicitly anti-white, he proceeds to question him on every aspect of his clothing and his dental fillings, follows him home to ask about his furnishings, and then forces him to accompany him to the railway, the telegraph office, "and every other appliance of civilization that I could remember." Asking him, in each case, "Who mek it, naygur, else buckra?" Thomas displays his facility in Jamaican Creole, as well as the utter thrill he feels when in each case his interlocutor responds that the inventor was probably white. "Yes, you impudent and ungrateful nigger," he says that he tells the man, warning him that instead of "abusing" the things he wears and uses he should be thankful that his ancestors were "brought to Jamaica as slaves," since otherwise he would be "a naked cannibal." Thomas notes that rural Black onlookers, "honest country folk," express delight, and one woman says to her companion, "Lard! Missis, Inspector mash up de man fe true."[77]

In this public tracing, in which Thomas turns the Black professional and gentleman inside out, as if to undo the possibility of *Black-as-middle-class*, Thomas wields the Creole speech that is often erroneously perceived to be linked exclusively to blackness, while stripping his interlocutor of the right to claim Africanness as other than uncivilized, and Jamaicanness and any other material or symbolic property as anything but borrowed, under the auspices of whiteness. I read Thomas's hysteria as occupational, "Irish" and "Negro" underlings in the force notwithstanding, but also as a desperate holding on to a white supremacy that he registers as either slipping from his grasp or as something that he has never felt securely. In this sense his performance of whiteness differs from that of the Clarke family, whom we will meet shortly, even as the latter also worries constantly about children left behind in England. Thomas wants to point out and consolidate a trace that asserts white imagination and prior ownership. The laughter of Black bystanders does a further violence to Thomas's interlocutor, whom we can surmise is a physician or pharmacist. These bystanders' "honesty" invites us to interpret this carriage-driving Black man's distribution of medicine as quackery. We can surmise that Thomas imagines their enthusiastic support because it suits him to do so, or that their laughter is elicited by Thomas's presence as a powerful police officer. But this would be to assume that the Black middle-class figure would not be ridiculed by Black people.

Turning to Claude McKay's work we will see how his poetic and narrative personae are constantly aware of being scorned by élite and nonelite alike. Like Thomas, McKay is caught between the violent order-management required by his profession (not, like Thomas, a vocation) and the desire to be a stroller-narrator. Refusing to produce the redemptive heroic constable who would vindicate Thomas's vitriol or satisfy Washington and Du Bois, he also shows that violence is located within and outside of the police force. Unlike Thomas, McKay critiques this surveillance with the shared solidarity of a member of the Black nonelite classes (though a property-owning, rural, and socially mobile lower-middle-class child of the peasantry, in his case), but he also affirms the cross-class and cross-racial assumption that access to "the cook's bedroom" is everyone's right.

McKay's poetry and fiction are often read in conjunction with US literary histories, including those of the Harlem Renaissance. Here I focus on a collection of short stories published in 1932, based on life in Jamaica in the late nineteenth and early twentieth centuries, and apparently connected to a memoir of his early life that he was working on when he died in the mid-1940s. Five of those stories together with the draft of the memoir exist as an anthology called *My Green Hills of Jamaica* (1979), edited by Mervyn Morris. It is a fascinating archive of the themes that inform his more well-known poetry and fiction. Characters and incidents from the novels of the late twenties and thirties are recognizable here, as McKay accounts for his life up to 1912, when he leaves Jamaica, never to return. But even before leaving his home in Clarendon, in the rural heartland, to go to Kingston, just before the 1907 earthquake, the various narrators identified with McKay's I/eye have been shaped profoundly by island-wide and global migrations, in the context of a stable, land-owning family entering the Black professional lower middle class. His schoolteacher brother U. Theo McKay directs choral renditions of Handel's *Messiah* and encourages his young brother and ward to follow in his atheist footsteps, contrary to both their "Presbyterian Calvinist" father and their evangelical fellow villagers. Neighbors are returning from the Panama Canal zone or departing for Cuba and Costa Rica. The Baptist missionary

William Hathaway is a descendant of William Shakespeare's wife. Neighbors include white descendants of migrants from the US Civil War, and an African American African Methodist Episcopal (AME) minister and his wife.

In account after account, McKay registers formal education and social mobility as necessarily accompanied by public humiliation, sexual spectacle, and loss. Women in educational institutions hide their lovers under their beds and identify them as interlopers when discovered. The English-educated children of "one of our village women," a "pretty" and "illiterate quadroon," beg their white father to abandon his plans to marry her on his deathbed, because they are ashamed of her, so they live in the city, while the broken-hearted mother returns to her village. Clearly, these children have determined that to stand beside their mother publicly is to be reduced to "naked-'kin," but for McKay such stories prove that local and foreign social reformers are too heavily invested in formal marriage. This anecdote, for instance, proves that "bastardy is no social stigma in Jamaica," since the children can become professionals. "Only" mothers are stigmatized, and their partners treat them well.[78]

Another story shows the casualties of the monumental shifts in social status in this era of migration, as we witness Miss Mary's reaction to a schoolmaster who has just returned—"dapper," married, and walking with a "Yankee strut"—to his village from Panama. She throws a bouquet of flowers at his feet and then, screaming deliriously, runs toward and then beyond the graveyard, heading for a waterfall "that from the churchyard looked like a gorgeous flowing of gold."[79] Miss Mary drowns herself in gold, the very element that adorns bejeweled Cuban and Panamanian returnees, mocked as crass for their big gold watches and as insubordinate for what they will no longer tolerate in their colony of origin. If Césaire uses jewelry to suggest the exploitation of Caribbean and other proletarian constituencies in the process of making Europe wealthy, McKay's story shows that the rerouting of gems into the Caribbean colony is both a triumph of nonwhite migrant prosperity and the intimately felt devastation of the one left behind; a ruination, transmuted into bling, that is one trace of the accumulation on offer at this historical moment.

McKay moved to Kingston to be close to one of his mentors, Walter Jekyll, who had relocated to Jamaica from England about a decade earlier.[80] Jekyll encouraged McKay to write poetry in Jamaican Creole, and McKay published two volumes before he left in 1912. Critics have rightly attended to the homosocial friendship and racial and class patronage that shaped their relationship. This is evident when McKay's narrators express anxiety about spending weekends with Jekyll and concealing this from family members and friends, or in Jekyll's encouragement of the young man's Creole voice that was both an important affirmation of a language that had no respectable currency and the advice of an upper-class Englishman who was invested in his Black charge's "natural" and "essential" voice. They see a poem such as "A Midnight Woman to the Bobby" as precisely the admonishing of the pretentious lower orders that Jekyll would have encouraged, as opposed to a poem that McKay wrote in tribute to the rebels who challenged the planter class in the 1865 Morant Bay Rebellion and were brutally punished by the colonial state, and which Jekyll did not allow to be included in either of the 1912 publications.[81] I am interested in the staging of gendered and class anxieties in this confrontation between the "midnight woman" and the *constable*, the nonofficer rank beyond which level Black men in the police force could not aspire, and a position that McKay occupied for much of his time in Kingston.

In his retrospective narration of his life before he leaves Jamaica—an account that includes his firsthand experience of the afternoon of January 14, 1907 when the earthquake occurred, when he had just left his rural homestead to live in Kingston—Claude McKay notes that his father had been a head deacon of a Baptist church in their rural community, and who left because of the hypocrisy of the missionary who supervised the church.[82] A smallholder who had sufficient property to allow him to vote, he "[resolved] boundary and livestock disputes in the community [and] would do nothing on behalf of a thief caught in the act or a rapist, which was rare among the peasantry; or carnal knowledge of animals, which occurred pretty often."[83] It is this violence that McKay stamps on the body of his work, a violence that must be borne and recoded so that one survives and moves on. His father is a local informal community magistrate, in effect, and ignoring "carnal knowledge of animals" means protecting someone from the colonial court system, from the violence of the law. But if this means contesting what the law has adjudged to be bestial, monstrous, queer, it also means that someone must endure, and make peace with, a violation that the community, if not the law, has condoned. For these acts are both "rare" (so that the Black person, so reviled and deemed monstrous in the letter of the law, is not thereby inherently criminal) and actual, material.

Who, then, bears the brunt of this materiality, of this making peace with violation in order to protect another from the violence of the law? An animal is abused. A violated person's rape goes unpunished. In *Banana Bottom* (1933), the fictional social world McKay creates some two decades after his departure from the colony, all of these violations are rehearsed, as when the learned teacher or parson, or the sensitive musician—that is, the lower-middle-class man who should properly take his place with a rising and future political class—violates a little girl or a goat because he has not found the right calibration between what to accept and what to reject of an Englishness that is at once enforced, out of reach, and a repudiation of Jamaican blackness. The narration of the childhood rape of the Black female protagonist, Bita, is heavily aestheticized, as she succumbs to the violin playing of a mentally ill and musically proficient neighbor.[84] *Both* rapist and victim are shown to have been unsuccessful in reining in their passions, and thus the rapist's transgression, rooted in the sublime, is rendered excusable. The community marks Bita's violation in song, indelibly and eternally connecting her to this violation, and freeing its narration to be appropriated by everyone, as a parable of fortunate misfortune leading to upward social mobility, including her English boarding school education. The song narrates this series of events as success, even if we might hear in its repetition a recognition of a violence that has to be resignified. This is how pastoral is culled out of rape. In the case of the goat, the teacher-violator is shamed, not by a withering white policeman, but by his Black peasant community; publicly shamed, he is not allowed near Bita, whom he has been courting, and he is banished to Kingston. McKay's work is an archive of these violations. In his discussion of down low genealogy, C. Riley Snorton notes of Frederick Douglass's testimony that the "depiction of blackness as abnormally licentious obfuscates the fact that even under the brutal system of slavery, black people's sexuality was still something that could not be fully controlled. . . . The down low is about the inevitable discovery of forbidden intimacy, which once found out is made to serve as an example of the unforeseeable consequences that occur when black sexualities are apprehended."[85] McKay's work exposes this figure both to censure and to the horror of censure; we see what it means to keep order and to be traumatized in so doing.

McKay's work shows us that there may not be public lynchings in Jamaica, as in the US South, but that there is constant humiliation and violence that requires the labor to distill this into manageable beauty or laughter, in order to live to see another day. His work shows us what it means to feel this, to endure it, and it also shines a lens on those who bear the brunt of it. On my reading, the Black male class poised to be the potential inheritors of political leadership, should the British authorities and the Jamaican élite choose to share this, are shown to bear the brunt of this violence (even as they also wield it, as a consequence of trauma). Bitas, Janes, and Black cooks emerge in

McKay's work as violated, but also as capable of being able to withstand this, and therefore as a reminder to sidestep the bourgeois sentimentalism that would call for romanticizing or unduly dramatizing their violation as tragic. This inclination on McKay's part enacts further violence on her, by casting Black women with a sort of good-humored inviolability and insentience.

Here we could ask if the community's differing reactions to the goat's violation and Bita's rape tells us what is both present and most highly feared and repudiated: the rape of a Black female is natural, even if it is unfortunate or unseemly. My reading of McKay's rendering of gendered vulnerability in what follows is intensified rather than undermined by his rendering of a queer Black masculinity in his oeuvre. That the Black woman is available to McKay and his colleagues in the police force, as well as to the figures who populate his fictional and nonfictional narratives, is a function of the state's casually violent dismissal of her right to be free from harm, whether in the streets or in her bedroom; of a general understanding that policing includes privileged access to her body, or that it ought to; of the pact *between men* that her presence solidifies homosocial desire, and also rescues men from the charge of bestiality; and also sometimes possibly of her own desire, though this seems most hidden from view.[86]

The January 1907 day of the earthquake that opens this chapter finds McKay lounging without a shirt on in a Kingston home. Indeed, he has moved away from his respectable family home in the country so that he can be free to lounge shirtless. Like De Lisser's fictional Jane, he abandons the country for more interesting prospects in the city, though unlike Jane he is trying to shed the confining respectability of a lower middle-class life founded on an independent and prosperous Clarendon peasantry. Kingston offers De Lisser's fictional Jane the opportunity to try to acquire the mahogany dressers that have furnished McKay's rural homestead for generations. That Claude has psychically cut his ties already makes the catastrophe that sends him trudging back home with other survivors in the days following the earthquake all the more poignant—he has a home to return to and this makes it possible to survive Kingston's tragedy, but the rural kinship and social life that enables this is stifling. His father joins other rural residents in calling out to streams of weary travelers fleeing the ravaged capital, walking or traveling in carts, and he is overjoyed when he recognizes his son, hugging him so that Claude can feel the sensation of his beard. This strikes me as already an expanded possibility of having lived, even for a short time, away from home—touching a father intimately after being able to read shirtless if one chooses—for in his childhood and adolescence it had been his mother rather than his father with whom he could share such tenderness.

This crossing of the border between country and town, as Claude does on the day of the earthquake, as Jane does in De Lisser's fiction, and as De Lisser's market women interlocutors do on a weekly basis in his early journalistic reporting, reminds us to keep track of the possibilities and the limitations of performing social roles in a colonial society that questions the physical and social mobility of people who are not upper class or upper-middle class: recall the physician who is stopped by Herbert Thomas and, in effect, forced to show rhetorical papers of identification in the process of being forced to rescript his genealogy of himself. McKay is in the position of wanting to step down from the comfortable rural respectability that his family has made possible for him, to escape a confining heterosexual project, and also to mitigate the surveillance of Black male sexuality that his work shows us is part of daily colonial life: his work documents the threat of being traced, outed in the streets (though sometimes by a Black working-class woman rather than a white man), or of junior teachers being discovered under the beds of their sexual partners.

Before getting to Kingston the first time he leaves home, McKay spends time in Spanish Town, the colony's earlier capital city, and a space that we can read as a sort of paradisiacal time lag. Time spent here cannot be sustained, and yet it shows him what marking time differently could mean. He befriends another man, whom he soon finds out is being kept by a wealthy female prostitute. This is a *kept* friend who presumably, then, has the time and resources to show him what spending time off the clock could mean. It is here that the possibility of police work is presented as an option for both of them. As they settle into jobs as police constables in Kingston, Claude does desk duty and his friend does postal duty, and they are constantly being called out by the precinct officer for failing to show evidence of sufficient or proper police work. Their performance—as ambitious policemen and perhaps also as straight men—is found wanting. The sympatico of patrolling together, hearing tattoos or final bugle call together, is a marking of queer time that McKay's persona grieves when his policeman friend "Bennie" leaves the force, in the poems "Bennie's Departure" and "Consolation."[87]

I read this as an attempt by Claude and his colleague to be in but not of law-wielding time. This is just one of a series of occasions in which Claude is called out for failing to produce the proper postures: a credible policeman who visually fits the bill of the profession, for instance, or who can sit up to catch a suspect without falling asleep, who can "pound the pavement" and make his quota of arrests instead of writing poetry at his desk, or who attends the mandatory lectures on police training in the precinct house. We could surmise that his performances, whether as a Black constable who is sufficiently subordinate or willing to terrorize working-class people, or as sufficiently respectable or heterosexual, seem doomed to disappoint because of his reluctance to harm Black civilians, his Spanish Town and precinct friendships, and the strange man who comes to the police station to check him every weekend, Walter Jekyll, his English friend and patron.

"Think of ephemera as trace. The remains. The things that are left. Hanging in the air like a rumor."[88] José Estéban Muñoz's proposition that we seize the opportunity to "read queerness" in what is never held to count as reliable documentation is useful here. For Muñoz the ephemeral fails the test of presence, when "the gatekeeper, representing a straight present," refutes the coherence of the evidence presented to prove queerness; at the same time, the ephemeral gestures toward a disinvestment in the *tyranny* of foolproof evidence. Though the logical step would be to put Muñoz's proposition to the service of an accommodating queerness, one that could mark colonial Jamaica as other than (only) the abject past for which a liberatory future in the United States and Europe is necessary and emancipatory, we want to see how McKay reads colonial subjectivity as layers of racial, sexual, gendered, and classed gestures that are sometimes barely perceptible: that is, as traces. This means that what queers is not only sexual, but it also means that what is taken to be queer can be anything but emancipatory, as when the woman produced to straighten men's desire for each other is rendered invisible or is casually annihilated, her presence "a perverse consecration of the space, ritualistically doing away with 'homosexuality' as such and creating a contract of disavowal such that nothing in the area was gay because nothing *could* be gay"; policing, and policing her in particular, becomes a front.[89] A poem by McKay, as well as a court case involving the police, can help us to tease this out further.

In "A Midnight Woman to the Bobby," written on desk duty as a constable in Kingston, McKay depicts a policeman confronted by the first-person persona, a "midnight woman" on a Kingston street: "No palm me up you dutty brute / You jama mout mash like ripe bread-fruit / You fasn now but wait leeya / I'll see you grunt under de law."[90] Her rhetorical facility and confidence, familiarity with the law, and withering critique of men of his class enable her to reduce him to a mass of unprepossessing parts: "You come from mountain naked kin / And Lawd a mussy! You be'n thin / For all de bread-fruit dem be-n done / Being 'poil up by de tearing sun." If he thinks he can pretend that he is a city slicker she links him not just to the country, but to a drought-ridden devastation that has driven him to the city, and that has ravaged his body. In effect, much like Inspector Thomas's unfortunate interlocutor, he is undressed by her.

Patrolling the border between rural and urban she tells him that she is not a "come-aroun" or day laborer, implying that while she is not transient labor, tied to a space because of labor, she can measure his and other policemen's transience; they think they have moved up in the world, but in fact they have not, and she can tell this *externally*. With "naked kin," '*kin*/*skin* bared to the elements, visible because of torn clothing disclosing the scrawniness brought on by hard times in unasphalted rural areas ("where de groun is pure white marl"), she *traces* him—Who are your people? What is your past?—transforming him into someone who is naked, stripped of kin and kin(ship). His ill-fitting police uniform, which should have been the visible sign of not being a *come-aroun*, only reinforces the fact that he is unsuited for his profession. Her assessment is corroborated by Herbert Thomas's description of the conceited Black Jamaican policeman, a "raw and rustic youth" who "knows nothing of town life," is not of the "highest order" of intelligence.[91] In McKay's poem the constable's very physical features, probably mirroring hers, will always mark him as unsuitable, as ill-suited to whatever he thought that this new position on the force offered. The trumped-up, put-together clothing goes with this unpleasing physiognomy. His attempt to put himself together in order to pull himself up has been thwarted: her atomizing gaze and loud narrative have reduced him to a spectacle of unpleasing body parts, a failed project of self-invention. Du Bois's smart, dark constables are, in the end, at the mercy of boisterously eloquent midnight women who walk Kingston's streets and reduce constables to rhetorical rags.

When she taunts him that the police force belongs to "*buccra*" (whites), and that he will not be able to convince a judge that he has a credible case against her to justify arrest, she is both cynic and believer as she prepares herself and her uniformed interlocutor to wait patiently for justice that is inaccessible. As both wait "before the law," does she believe that a judge will bypass his word to come to her rescue, or does she understand the law to be a charade that must still be appeased by going through the motions; and does she mistake his sartorial performance of credibility for *his* faith in the law and its promise of justice? I read this poem as a process of mapping the Black masculine subject's vulnerability onto the Black female body—a mapping that is a response to and is itself a catastrophe. If it is the Caribbean flâneur's fate to document catastrophe, then here the poet-policeman indicates that this includes the threat of being turned inside out like a woman and maybe by a woman, when women ought to have been the natural *object* of a public exposure properly culminating either in a sexual transaction, or the commercially successful writing that yields fiction with a Black female protagonist, or both. What is displayed but also disavowed in the poem is the body that allows everyone to manage the toll, the bedroom of the cook or the nightwoman that facilitates sexual labor, and here I have in mind Christina Sharpe's theorization of the domestic worker in white households of the US South in terms of African American women's sexual labor "[securing] everyone in their place."[92]

Jamaican readers were introduced to this poem in October 1911, in a period when the papers carried news of Italy's conflict with the Ottoman Empire—including the novelty of aerial bombing, and the bombardment of Tripoli by November—and news of the demise of the Quing dynasty in China, with the fall of the Imperial Court. In the October 7 edition of the *Daily Gleaner*, McKay's photograph in his police uniform shares a page with an announcement that a "celestial" shopkeeper, Yap Sam, had fifteen shillings of stock stolen from his Cross Roads shop, and that the King Edward Memorial Committee planned to erect a memorial clock and tower at the junction of Half Way Tree and Hope Roads.[93] Readers learned of Jekyll's "discovery" of "an infant prodigy," a "boy," a "promising young Jamaican" stationed at the Half Way Tree police barracks, whose poetry, which had caught the interest of the governor, would soon be published. Readers were assured that they would like the "directness and vigor" (citing McKay's patron Jekyll) of "A Midnight Woman to the Bobby." McKay's right to trace in Creole was being authorized by his expatriate sponsor and the newspaper.

In "Pounding the Pavement," the narrator does his stint as a policeman in Kingston, trying to avoid patrol duty so he can avoid arresting anyone: "As a son of peasants, I also had in my blood the peasant's instinctive hostility for police people."[94] As his supervisor threatens to take away the office duty that facilitates his writing if he does not make his quota of arrests, he takes his cues from his patrol partner: "While he was on his beat he was accosted by a street girl that we both used to visit in common. She teased him a little for doing patrol duty, and he arrested her for 'obstructing a constable on his duty.' The girl had thought it was all a joke. But when the court fined her ten shillings [with] 21 days imprisonment, her smiling turned to a terrible howl-ing."[95] Her sexual labor is and has been made available to both policemen, plausibly but not necessarily consensually (for is she free to say no to the police?): "a street girl that we both used to visit in common" means that this is a perquisite of their uniformed masculinity. The narrating *I* of "Pounding the Pavement" informs us that Kingston's servant girls, barmaids and other working-class women were the "chief lovers" of the Black and brown clerks, schoolmasters, police, and other members of an emergent male lower-middle class. These are the very men who were beginning to run for office when the all-nominated legislative council made a few elected seats available. A court case that riveted courthouse spectators and newspaper readers returns us to what ought to be a sanctuary from the streets, but that is a site that is liable to be turned inside out—the "cook's bedroom"—and underlines the related and differential positioning of Black men and women.

Late one August evening in 1910, Catherine Stewart, a butler employed to one of the most prominent families in Savanna la Mar, the capital of the western parish of Westmoreland, let pharmacist Fred Evans into her bed-room.[96] Within a month, the town was riveted by a case that "turned the Court House into a sort of theatre."[97] Through coverage of the "spicy" events in the *Daily Gleaner* in particular, the crowded courtroom, and by extension the whole colony collectively leaned forward to revel in all the salacious details of the case. Stewart was employed as a caretaker in addition to her duties as butler, and she lived in the outbuildings of her employers' property, while Evans operated a dispensary in the town, had chaired and was still a mem-ber of the town's parochial board, and was one of the trustees of the parish's high school (Manning's). Being found in the outbuildings at midnight placed them in specific violation of a harsher version of the Vagrancy Law that came into effect in 1902, partly as a response to that year's unrest in Montego Bay.

Indeed, the law was designed to make that part of the premises (desig-nated as the "outhouse" in the legislation), and her room within it, a weapon of criminalization of the men who were likely to visit her. Recall that McKay's sociological parsing of "chief lovers" fits the occupational descriptions of Stewart and Evans. Section 7 of the Vagrancy Law stated: "Every person found by night without any lawful excuse (the proof of which excuse shall be on such person) in or upon any dwelling house, warehouse, coachhouse, stable, or outhouse, or in any enclosed garden, yard, or area, or in, or on board any ship, or other vessel when lying, or being in any port or place within the Colony shall be deemed a rogue and a vagabond." The law characterized a "vagrant" as someone without visible or lawful means of subsistence—able to work but abstaining from doing so. Moreover, the prosecutor did not have to prove the absence of this; the onus was on defendants to prove that they had such means of subsistence, or employment. Letters to the press noted that the 1902 amendment unfairly penalized people whose straitened economic circumstances forced them to wear tattered clothing, to walk the streets in search of work, or who had a trade but no regular employment. Jamaica might have its share of "the idle, the dissolute, the rogue and the vagabond," as in other countries, but it was *Jamaican* labor that was responsible for the construction of the railroad and Canal in Panama, commentators argued.[98] In this case Jamaicans working hard abroad were used to counter the perceived or actual existence of "vagrancy" at home. What about those, another letter to the editor asked, who were willing to work but could not find employment? There were clearly lazy people out and about, but surely these were already known to the constables: why was it necessary to have new legislation to manage them?[99] Here commentators were coming to the defense of the "deserving" who were willing to work.

Another section of the law, Section 5, covered "Idle and Disorderly Persons," including those dealing in "obeah, myalism, duppy-catching or witchcraft," fortune-tellers, and the use of palmistry or "such like superstitious means" to deceive; as well as subsection 2, the "common prostitute . . . found wandering in any public place," behaving riotously or indecently, annoying by soliciting passersby. Actual arrests could also function as a sort of debate, alongside editorials, about the function and limits of the law, as when Mabel Heron was charged with solicitation for annoying a sailor in a tavern at the corner of Kingston's Princess Street and Water Lane in March 1903. The judge dismissed the case "with regret," conceding that her solicitor's defense was sound: Heron could not be charged with public wandering, if she herself was drinking *inside* the tavern.[100] What critics of the amendment found particularly objectionable was the harshness in the Jamaican law that exceeded its English counterpart; Section 16 stated that it would not be necessary to prove that someone was actually guilty of committing what constituted a crime, but only the presence of the "purpose or intent" based on "the circumstances of the case, and from his known character" as "it appears to the Resident Magistrate or the Court that his intent was as alleged."[101] The combustible intersection of "lawful excuse" "purpose or intent," and "outhouse" in the language of the legislation doomed the Westmoreland couple to incriminating exposure.

Catherine Stewart's employers, Mr. Hugh and Mrs. (Lee Morris) Clarke, were a prominent white family in a parish with a long history of wealthy land-holding families.[102] Westmoreland was the parish in which many branches of the Beckford family owned property, for instance, including William "Alderman" Beckford, a member of the British Parliament for Shaftesbury from 1747 to 1754, who served two stints as Lord Mayor of London; his son (and the person usually signified by "William Beckford") William Thomas Beckford, the author of the Gothic novel *Vatek*, and one of Europe's most well-known art collectors; and William Beckford ("Beckford of Somerly," a nephew of "Alderman" and cousin of William Thomas), who spent time in debtor's prison in England.[103] One of "Alderman" Beckford's neighbors in Westmoreland was Thomas Thistlewood, who kept a meticulous record of his abuse of his enslaved human property on any and every corner of his properties, and of his particular delight in forcing them to abuse each other or to prepare each other to be abused by him and his neighbors. Thistlewood recorded his delight when he dined with the Beckfords and perused "Folio Volumes of Excellent plates of the Ruins of Rome, Etc," and again when Beckford sent over six *views* of his Roaring River estate and of the bridges crossing the Cabaritta and Cobre rivers.[104]

Two neighbors perused the artistic renderings of the Westmoreland land-scape as picturesque, but as they enjoyed the representation of enslavement's violations as beautiful, as pastoral, we have to imagine the enslaved people on their estates as surviving in the face of this, followed by their descen-dants and by the indentured populations from Africa and Asia who joined them from the middle of the nineteenth century. How did they reclaim the landscape, how did they search for their mothers' gardens, in the context of this history of befoulment?[105] What were the gestures of recovery and replenishment? When Stewart and Evans entered the crowded Sav-la-Mar courthouse in August 1910 for the beginning of the case, it had been several generations since the heads of executed enslaved persons were "displayed on poles" in its vicinity, but daily interactions were possibly sometimes still shaped by, or bore the traces of social relations of enslavement; no doubt many African- and Asian-descended people bore the physical features and the name of the Westmoreland Beckfords, for example.[106] Ten years earlier, within hours of hearing the news about British success in Pretoria, southern Africa, "prominent men" in Little London, another town in Westmoreland, dressed and acted as Boer generals in postures of submission, and as Brit-ish generals on horseback, as the Union Jack was hoisted and a "large crowd headed by a fife and drum band formed a procession [and] marched up to the main street for a about a mile and back again."[107] In this latest instantiation of imperial power, a year in which celebrations of British victories in southern Africa were celebrated throughout Jamaica, did estate time recede or become more deeply embedded? It is tempting to speculate whether, like that year's Trinidad Carnival, Jamaican *Jonkannu* and *Hosay* celebrations for 1900 reflected any allusions to events in southern Africa.

Sav-la-Mar's main thoroughfare, Great George Street, led (and leads) right down to the water's edge, a convenient setting for the procession and then setting afloat of tazias that marked the end of annual *Hosay* celebrations. In 1911 when this festival was banned across the colony because of reports of disorder, the custos of Westmoreland rescinded the order for the parish, noting the width of Great George's Street, but also the law-abiding nature of "our" Indians; it was the Black people who attached themselves to such processions who were responsible for the rowdiness, he said.[108] No doubt viewed as generous, the ability to grant or rescind the right to celebrate *Hosay* was continuous with a long and deep affiliation with the rhythms of the plantation. Giving Indian migrants and Indo-Jamaicans (and clearly also, given the custos's remarks, Afro-descended participants) the time to celebrate *Hosay* also meant ensuring that as soon as the tazias floated in the sea the celebration was at an end and it was time to return to work. How did the courtroom proceedings reflect Westmoreland's histories and continuing rhythms of estate time, and the most recent rhythms of the imperial twentieth century?

The publicity surrounding the case stemmed in part from the prominence of the extended Clarke family. Biographical descriptions are at pains to separate the family from histories of Jamaican slaveholders' moral dissolution and even prosperity.[109] On the one hand, its patriarch, Rev. Henry Clarke, did not arrive in Jamaica from England until after the postabolition period, and thus the story of his striving, his head-butting with the planter interests that dominated lawmaking and other sectors, his advocacy on behalf of indentured immigrants, and of Black working-class women struggling to get delinquent fathers to pay their share, frame him as liberal and beneficent, as someone at odds with an older performance of slaveholding whiteness in Jamaica. Joy Lumsden calls him a "maverick" white member of a group of "moderate, liberal" white and brown politicians on the Jamaican political scene from the 1890s, and he had the support of the prominent pro-Black, Black intellectual Robert Love.[110] On the other hand, the ability to accumulate property and status, and the speed with which he was able to do so would have been a function of his whiteness, whether or not he thought of himself as differently committed to accumulating wealth than his peers. By the turn of the century he and his children managed and owned estates within and beyond Westmoreland, and through the building society they managed the savings of laborers. In 1910, Catherine Stewart's employer, Hugh, a son of Rev. Clarke, managed the Westmoreland Building Society and a decade later he became custos of Westmoreland. The daughter of Hugh and Mrs. Clarke, a teenager who was possibly away at school in England during the time of this court case, would write one of the most well-known studies of working-class Jamaican family life and inheritance, and it is tempting to speculate what impact events at Hendon House, where Catherine Stewart was employed to her family, would have on the trajectory of her research.[111]

Stewart let Evans into her room after 9 p.m. on August 17, and he was there around midnight when a party of men including her employer, obviously assuming previously assigned roles, listened outside her window; knocked on her door and asked for the keys to the Building Society; broke into her room when she refused entry; waited outside on the veranda for Evans to be brought out in his undervest and socks where they refused him permission to put on the rest of his clothing; and sent for the police. Both Stewart and Evans said that he had come to dress a boil under her arm, and the prosecution asked why she did not visit him at his dispensary to get the medication, and why it had been necessary for him to be in her room for several hours, and to be there in a state of undress. She was questioned closely about allowing her visitor into her quarters after locking the gate at 9 p.m. after family prayers, about how long they had been conducting a relationship, whether he had offered marriage, and whether another man to whom she had been linked had offered marriage. (Another man had received permission from her employers to visit her because of his alleged matrimonial intentions, as long as he left by 9 p.m.) A letter found in a trunk in her room, addressed to "my darling Kittle" and promising something for her boil, was read aloud in court.

While Stewart was arrested but not prosecuted for stealing a knife and corn, one of her coworkers, the cook Julia Clarke, was prosecuted and jailed for stealing the corn and the knife from the main house, because she and others refused to say anything incriminating about Stewart (about her relationship to Evans, about whether or not she had a child on the premises, and about asking her coworkers to help her to conceal her alleged theft of the corn and the knife) but possibly also because arresting her instead of Stewart would not require their female employer, Mrs. Hugh Clarke, to appear in court.

Julia Clarke said that Hugh Clarke and others searched her room in the days following the initial incident, forced her and the housemaid to swear on the bible in the dining room, removed money from her room, and did not give her that week's wages. Julia Clarke and her husband, Richard Clarke, also employed to the household, sued to recover 100 pounds for false imprisonment and "malicious persecution" in a case heard a year later that forced their other employer to come to court and testify.

The tenor of social relations was evident not only in the details of the incident and of daily life in the Clarke household, but in tensions in the courtroom. Besides distinctions between barristers and solicitors or irritation about being addressed as "Mister" rather than "Counsel," the prosecution and defense reflected factions of men who held power and those who sought to acquire it. I am assuming that Hugh Clarke, his defense team (including a relative) and the resident magistrate, C. M. Calder, were white; while the legal team defending Evans and Julia Clarke included S. A. G. Cox, Hector Joseph, J. A. G. Smith, and H. A. L. Simpson, some of the most prominent figures in the colony involved in organizations that were incubators of Black political participation, such as the Citizens Association and the National Club. These were organizations that succeeded Love's People's Convention and the Jamaican branches of Henry Sylvester Williams's Pan-African Association, and they preceded the Jamaica League and Garvey's Negro Improvement Society (an earlier incarnation of the UNIA) before he left Jamaica to live in the United States. Both Simpson and Evans would run for electoral office later in 1910.[112] Spectators and readers could decide if they thought that the judge was being ironic when he declared that he would not allow matters of "color" in his court; if Cox's bristling was the typically thin-skinned response of his social group; and if Hugh Clarke was a reasonable defender of his family's property and safety, or the petty and cruel employer who maintained close scrutiny of his kitchen knives, claimed that the corn in his buttery was of so distinctive a red color that it had obviously been stolen, and called an employee who had been present at his parents' deathbeds a "brute."

Ideologically at loggerheads these men might have been in relation to each other, but they colluded in racist slurs and sexually suggestive speech that confirmed their status as socially elevated men. Cox asked Clarke if he was an expert on matching corn and when Clarke replied that he could tell the differences by sight, Cox asked if it was "a case of 'any coolie is a coolie'"; and in ascertaining how long Julia Clarke had worked for Clarke's parents' household, Clarke answered that he would have been "a bit of a boy," and

Cox asked if that meant that she had "probably nursed" him.[113] The latter comment underlined the prurient courtroom and media interest in the case and the way in which it attached the Black female employee to salacious speculation—breast-feeding and who-knew-what activities when her current employer was a boy, extra-marital sex, multiple sexual partners. Hugh Clarke insisted that his determination to search Stewart's room was rooted in the fact that she was in charge of the keys to both his home and the Westmoreland Building Society's office, and that Evans was "very evilly disposed towards me."[114] As the prosecution noted, the "privacy of a gentleman's house should be maintained and not every dirty scoundrel should be allowed to come in and make it a brothel." Or as Clarke put it, as soon as he heard that Evans had been caught in Stewart's room (as if he had had nothing to do with engineering this), "I felt that the position was a most serious one as it was impossible to think that a man in his position would put himself in my power by coming on my premises for the mere sake of the company of a woman like that."

Here visiting Stewart is framed as a way for the middle-class Black man to compete with the upper-class white man (whether successfully, or as in this case to make himself vulnerable in relation to Clarke) and Stewart is a pawn in the classed, raced, and professional struggle between two men. Evans's desire to be in her company demeans *him*, because she is *a woman like that*. Even if the Vagrancy Law could be understood here to be punitive to Black people, political advancement and social mobility for Black people was demonstrated, at least in this case, to be gendered male. The Black woman butler and caretaker is at the center of the case but visible in a particular way—as a source of pleasure and libidinal energy for a particular class of men, as a source of shame, and of having the capacity to taint with her shame. She let him in, and her permeability put the morality of her social group, and arguably the colony, at risk. Even as Stewart indicates what it feels like to be "palmed up" by the law, to have the cook's or butler's door propped wide open, to have a visitor turn her bedroom into a place of ill repute, it is also the case that her own personhood, her own desire, has already marked it as at least potentially so.[115]

Rather than focusing on a wronged employee who was deserving of intimacy, privacy, and professional courtesy, the case centered on two wronged parties, depending on public sympathy: a white family with untrustworthy employees who left them vulnerable to an infiltrating and sinister middle-class Black masculinity desirous of premature political participation; and a Black male class penalized salaciously for being sexual, its professional and political ambitions thwarted at every turn. The judge's summation made it clear that neither older nor newer imperial orders of accumulation and success would allow this rising class to slip past colonial barricades, or at least not without public humiliation. In finding Evans guilty of being "a rogue and a vagabond" the judge dismissed his defense team's argument that Evans's occupation and "means" exempted him from the category of the "vagrant" with "no visible lawful means of subsistence . . . [abstaining] from working at any trade, profession or calling" (the originating condition from which the "rogue and vagabond" emerged): "You might have the wealth of a Rockefeller or of the richest man in the British Empire. It does not matter!"[116] Evans's appeal on the same grounds was similarly unsuccessful: when the law said "every person found by night," that did not mean *every person who is a vagrant* found by night. Moreover, Catherine Stewart did not have the authority to invite someone into her quarters who had not received permission from her employer, and Evans could not assume that she had that authority. While English law would require proof that he went to her room with the purpose of breaking a law, in Jamaica it was sufficient that he was "found by night on the premises without lawful excuse."[117]

Evans was sentenced to seven days in the parish lockup. He served his sentence, and then ran successfully a few months later for a seat on the legislative council, newly opened to elected representatives. On the day of the election it was reported that huge crowds turned out, and that "The cry frequently heard [was]; 'I am backing the black horse.'"[118] Evans won by a wide margin, beating a white opponent and joining a growing number of Black male elected representatives on the council. When the legislative session opened, his photograph appeared in the papers, with the commentary: "The Hon Member for Westmoreland: that tall gentleman in white helmet and morning coat who wears glasses."[119] Arguably, the photograph indicated a continued interest in the whiff of scandal, but it is also probably the case that the scandal garnered him votes, as onlookers perceived an élite class attempting to squash the political aspirations of a Black man by throwing him into prison for visiting a friend. This battle between two differently classed and raced male opponents for the future of the colony perfectly captured the wielding of the law by legislators and their élite peers to racialize and penalize sexual congress in the colony in order to limit the political fortunes and upward social mobility of Black men. Over the life of the publicity of the case, Stewart shared with Evans the risk of being rounded up by the law, though he was its particular object because of his political interests, and it was he who spent time in jail. Ultimately his political ascendancy occluded her; the case marked them differently.

I stumbled onto this case when, in reading Claude McKay's account of his time as a police constable in "When I Pounded the Pavement," I checked the newspapers to verify my assumption that McKay himself was the constable called by a white family to break into their female employee's bedroom in Kingston. I realized that he used the details of the 1910 case in western Jamaica to craft a first-person narrative about a policeman in Kingston. The story expresses the Black constable's revulsion for policing Black Jamaicans, as we have seen, and it maps his general experiences—including the resentment directed at him by white superiors and Black peers in the precinct house—on to details that we can connect to the Sav-la-Mar case, and that explain its social significance. He is assigned the case because of the perception that band members, clerks on desk duty such as himself, and others on the force occupy the "special little posts" that allow them the time to spend their evenings as they choose; these men fail to "mark time regularly on the beat."[120] Indeed, it is because of this perception that his friend on the force arrests the "street girl that we both used to visit in common," since it is an easy way to make his quota. Having "boasted that I had never made a case since my enlistment and did not intend to make any," the narrator is forced to demonstrate compliance, and on his initial foray the superior officer who is his patrol partner wants him to arrest a sleeping man for being "drunk and disorderly"; when the narrator refuses, they quarrel, and the man is able to flee. Responding to the white couple's request is another chance to prove himself, but his individual opportunity to exercise proper policing instead of spending Saturday evening in the way he prefers, with his friend at a favored bar, is also part of a long-standing social debate about "intruders at night on the properties of the wealthy and respectable."[121] In McKay's rendering the amendment to the Vagrancy Law is the long-awaited solution, and the Black men who are its targets are not only the political opponents of the class represented by the white legislators who pass the law, but part of the intraclass wrangling between Black teachers entrapped by the law and the Black pastors who, snubbed by the teachers as their intellectual inferiors, employ these teachers in their church schools.

In "Pounded," the woman whose employers are spying on her is someone known to the first-person narrator, part of the pleasure of daily social relations that redeems police work—"I used to tease her when she passed under the window of the constabulary station"—and this intensifies the trauma of being forced to break into her room. Her partner is the popular Black candidate of an upcoming election, and her employers are friends ("some said he was even a relative") of the white man who is to be his opponent at the polls. "Pounded" indicts both employers—husband and wife—as initiators and perpetrators of the plan to break in on their employee; there are no conscripted intermediaries. The constable is their reluctant accomplice, a guest (rather than an "intruder" on the "wealthy and respectable") who sits on their veranda and, lulled by a comfortable wicker chair and an Edenic garden, keeps falling asleep. His lush surroundings support his body's unwillingness to invade the woman's privacy, as he exercises a refusal that accords with the details reported in the case at Sav-la-Mar: when the police were first called, they "refused to arrest" Evans.[122] After the fictional husband has gone over to her room to listen at the window, the couple decide it is time, and rouse the narrator (who has fallen asleep a second time); accompanying them he treads heavily in a futile attempt to warn the lovers. Once inside the room, the employers rip the sheets from the sleeping pair, both crying, "look at them!" This marks their interest in their employee and her guest as intentional, excessive, and sexual in its intrusiveness. McKay shows how this violent invasion is legal and supported by the Black constable's surveillance work on his own class.

It is tantalizing to speculate why, writing decades later in another part of the world, McKay represents the story in the first person, and in Kingston rather than Sav-la-Mar. His *I* throughout *My Green Hills* is a complex aggregation of the fictional, the historical, and the purportedly autobiographical and perhaps this is an attempt to disperse a feeling of vulnerability across different registers, to displace his own experiences or his reactions to the experiences of others in order to reckon with this violence without being eviscerated. That he tells the story at all might indicate that he remained haunted by it, and wished to work through it, imagining and inhabiting the various roles: was he the surveilled employee, the reluctant constable, or the nighttime visitor-"intruder"?

Evans's photograph marks his electoral triumph, but in "When I Pounded the Pavement" a photograph in the newspaper records the shame of a man who has been sentenced to six months in prison. Moreover, in McKay's story the man caught in the bedroom is sentenced to be flogged with a tamarind switch, in addition to six months hard labor: "But I think what broke him most of all was the switch. Policemen holding him down on a block and taking down his pants and whipping him for sleeping with a girl."[123] This is a punishment for sexual violation that is itself suggestive of sexual violation by the police in the jailhouse, and that takes the rhetorical undoing of the Black constables' personhood to another level. That is, if the (fictional) constable's reluctance to break into the woman's room is due to class identification with the woman and her partner, then her partner's flogging-narrated-as-sexual-assault signifies the vulnerability of their entire class to such treatment as punishment for the crime of claiming time for private intimacy—a time that should have been their employers'.

Both social actors (Evans and Stewart but also their fictional counterparts) are refused access to intimate relations that are private. But McKay locates the intensity of the punishment both on the body of the Black man—to suggest that he and not she must suffer this physical consequence in particular—and on *flogging*, a detail that does not appear in the newspaper coverage of the court case in Sav-la-Mar. Diana Paton's research on a much earlier moment in Jamaican history suggests that flogging itself gave Jamaican court cases a whiff of sexuality, where "unruly passions" specifically and men in particular were targeted: "The exclusive concern with men reinforces the point that the reintroduction of flogging [in Jamaica in the 1850s] was connected more with anxiety about sexuality than with anxiety about property crime. Bestiality, sodomy, and rape, for which flogging was most commonly used, were, by custom or legal definition, strongly associated with men. Women's withdrawal from the paid labor force perhaps also meant that planters were less concerned with controlling their behavior than that of men."[124] McKay's addition of flogging to the sentence of the man caught in a woman's bedroom reinforces Black men's vulnerability to being turned inside out, in terms of reputation and in terms of their bodily violability. In McKay's story the court case and its traumatic outcome marks the constable-narrator's limit; he resigns from the police force.

Thus "Pounded" is an archive of the racialized use of the Vagrancy Law to stall the political participation of Black Jamaican men, a law that intensifies already existing indignities. Midnight women might undress constables rhetorically, but Fred Evans and his fictional counterpart are publicly undressed and imprisoned; elsewhere in *My Green Hills* men are caught under partners' beds and lose social standing, and here the bedroom of the outbuilding of the white couple's property is the site of scandal, trial, and arrest. The story narrates, or renarrates, the period's relations of power—a struggle that is deeply gendered, and in which men confront each other across racial and class divides in a tussle for social power, with working-class women often serving as the symbolic and physical means by which they win or lose these battles.

McKay's work *critiques* the surveillance of the Black cook's bedroom with the shared solidarity of a member of the Black nonelite (though in his case as the child of a propertied and professional rural middle class), but he also *affirms* the cross-class and cross-racial assessment that access to *her* room is everyone's right: "For it had become something like common right to us to visit the pretty servant girls of our own class who roomed in where they worked."[125]

Herbert Thomas shows how policing means being on constant alert for the uppity men who threaten Caribbean-born white personhood and authority. For McKay Black policemen are reluctant accomplices of this authority and also its target; they are survivors of a concerted attempt to break their will. Fred Evans in Sav-la-Mar, the corresponding fictional figure in Kingston in "Pounded," and their intimate partners are publicly shamed, as they are made to understand that they are not entitled to the intimacy—the "[private] conjugal and familial relations in the bourgeois home"—that Catherine Stewart's employers enjoy.[126] McKay shows us how to connect the Black woman's bedroom to Black men's participation in political life. His work is also a repository for particular kinds of otherwise indiscernible violence in a British colony; for how bodies produce the poses and postures for succumbing to or enduring such violence. Keeping in view Muñoz's proposal to attend to what "remains," what "hangs in the air," we could read McKay as inviting us to see the Black male body as an archive of the promise and limits of both colonial life and Black futurity.

But we cannot always see *her* as enduring this violence. Women such as Stewart willingly or unwillingly service a class of upwardly mobile men who consort with her at their peril, and who sometimes go on to win the day socially and politically. In the wake of his advancement, she is stalled, or viewed another way she entangles him in scandal, so that congress with her is retarding; her single status, mobility, and location on the premises of "the wealthy and respectable" lure men to an unsavory end. Certainly McKay encourages us to see her as sharing something with her male counterpart. Both are at least potential vagrants according to different sections of the Vagrancy Law. Both are vulnerable to the policing of the colonial state, and in this sense Marcus Garvey's warning about Black women's tainting sexuality can be read as a fear of the consequences of this conjoined criminality.[127] McKay registers this as a vulnerability to the thin line between criminal and noncriminal, since fully employed desiring subjects having sex while Black was enough to pitch this couple into the headlines. McKay's "Midnight Woman and the Bobby" and "When I Pounded the Pavement" highlight Black women's vulnerability to abuse but also her power to make Black men vulnerable. McKay's (or "McKay's") friend in Spanish Town who is kept by a prostitute reminds us of an alternate narration of women's social power that also troubles McKay. For does not her ability to keep a man, or to humiliate him with her rhetorical facility, limit his capacity for flânerie? Such women haunt his fiction; their financial acuity and stability support and also stifle men's social power, and their ugly verbal sparring wounds men's sensibilities.[128] Where we agree with McKay that Black men's social mobility and emotional equanimity are profoundly destabilized, we also discern an exaggeration of her social power.

Assessing the implications of policing for the intimate architecture of Stewart's place of employment, we can imagine her in her room: "*a space for enacting practices of freedom—practices of thinking, planning, writing, and imagining new forms of freedom,*" to quote Campt again. Arguably, as the holder of the keys to both her employers' home and to the important civic institution of the Building Society, she holds a position of responsibility that grants her full access to "the most secret aspects of their lives," as Michelle Johnson puts it in her study of household workers in Jamaica.[129] Even as she pays dearly, she drags these employees through the publicity of a trial, when her laboring body ought to have been the public wedge that shielded them from scrutiny. Does having the keys to the Building Society make her both appealing and ultimately expendable to ambitious men, once they have used her to secure the access that they need; and does she think that this compromises their professed interest in her, or that it clarifies it? If this court case ends the relationship between Stewart and Evans, does each feel bereft, or are they both clearheaded about the parameters of their relationship (or both)? Does Evans challenge the Vagrancy Law when he takes his place on the council, or does he understand that upholding it is the price of admission?

Looking across from her room to the veranda of the main house, the "architectural threshold" that demarcates visitor from intruder, server of lemonade from employer, Stewart can see a space of both conspicuous leisure and of "violence . . . directed outwards towards intruders."[130] What other kinds of physical or emotional labor are required from her and her coworkers by the main house? What is the tenor of her relationship with other staff on the premises, including Julia and Richard Clarke, who had been dragged into court, or the woman who stood in for her during the illness that had brought Evans to her room? In supporting her even at great cost to themselves, do these coworkers also despair, or disapprove of her visitors, of her motherhood (if she did "have a child in the yard"), or of her perverse exercise of her right to her own time, when her employers claim all her time as theirs?

Strategizing, perhaps from her first day on the job, Stewart weighs the costs and gains of an upper-class outbuilding and its alternatives (De Lisser's fictional Jane moves from a room in a Black middle-class home to a home in a communal working-class yard). The narrator of "When I Pounded the Pavement" says that persons in Stewart's situation were "chiefly the girls fresh from the mountains. The free room was a part of their wages."[131] Relatively safe from police "palming" in the streets, Stewart has no privacy in her room on the premises of a prominent couple. "When I got to the room I heard blows firing on all sides," testified the first man who entered Stewart's bedroom that August night: "The woman was hammering at me while I held Evans and I struck her."[132] This is a violent entry that Stewart does not passively endure, and which we can assume that she expects, as a condition of her employment. The price of getting a job in which she could have a room to herself is that the room, her trunk and its possessions, her life, are all open to scrutiny.

Providing relief from travel and lodging expenses, live-in domestic work was coveted as less strenuous and better paid than other employment options. Employees worked from 6 a.m. to 9 p.m., with every Saturday off, and with the option of sick leave at the employer's discretion.[133] We can get a sense of how Stewart and others may have strategized from the analyses of Black women charged under the 1861 Offenses of Persons Act for concealment of birth or child murder, as part of the turn-of-the-century discussion about low birth rates, children born outside of marriage, and the moral fitness of working-class people to be responsible parents in the Caribbean as well as in Britain.[134] What might a woman who threw her child into a river and testified that "she could have got employment as a servant but for this child," tell us about live-in domestic service as a desired option among other options?[135]

In postcolonial Jamaica this bedroom is still a space of sexual exploitation, and of poorly compensated labor and time—the price, for instance, of the advancement of the professional (feminist) woman in whose home she labors. In unearthing such stories from the archives I am cognizant of my will to critique this propping up of the postcolonial middle-class project, or to redeem: to celebrate a job without children, for instance, as the refusal of compulsory maternity by women such as Stewart, even as Altinck documents the fear of tarnishing their families' reputation with nonmarital pregnancy as a reason for women to commit infanticide; not shame, that is, because of the disapproval of material or abstract reformers, or onlookers in court, or employers, but because of their own families' disapproval. I am mindful here of the invitation to resist either/or conclusions about respectability, agency, or resistance: to think in terms of what is "fluid and shifting . . . along a continuum" rather than "[compensatory] postures in the face of powerlessness; and in terms of a "continuous series of maneuvers to be enacted and reenacted" rather than a "singular moment of resistance."[136]

For what if Catherine Stewart is neither the tough, exuberant protagonist of McKay's and De Lisser's fictional universe, nor the silenced subject imprisoned by discourse, law, or photography? What if she is "wayward," snatching her pleasure where she can—inviting us to attend to "a history as wayward as its subjects, with waywardness being a register of the non-reproductive, of that which traffics in wild visions of other worlds; a waywardness that is concerned with neither progress nor decline"?[137] Receiving and returning blows as she fights intruders in her bedroom; the contents of her chest made available for a titillating audience: this literalizes the politics of intimacy for Catherine Stewart and her fictional counterpart. Her labor ought to guarantee the privacy of others, but she is not entitled to it. Yet her room is not only a scene of ruin, destined to be propped open as a symbol of disaster. This room is also chosen strategically from a range of bad options.

3

PHOTOGRAPHY'S "TYPICAL NEGRO"

When the Countess of Rothberry strides across Port of Spain's Savannah and enters the Trinidad Botanic Gardens with her Kodak in Stephen Cobham's 1907 novel *Rupert Gray: A Tale in Black and White*, she snaps a photograph of a man under a hog plum tree, mistaking the novel's eponymous protagonist for what the omniscient narration terms "a typical Negro."[1] Rupert Gray's immediate response and subsequent friendship notwithstanding, the scene clarifies the dangers of misrecognition for an emerging Black male leadership class within the Caribbean but also globally, as many of the era's commentators take up various permutations of the term. "What do you think of the Jamaica negro after so many generations of British rule?" asks H. G. De Lisser of a visiting colonial administrator.[2] I read this as a question about Black civilizational capacity, with implications for white futurity, that frames the region's nonwhites as laborers who follow orders rather than as political subjects who have a robust part to play in the region's future.

This chapter takes its cues from *Rupert Gray*'s insistence that De Lisser's question requires urgent attention from colonial subjects in the imperial Caribbean and across the world. The fictional snapshot in the botanical gardens underscores the recognition that the era's negotiation of power must of necessity take into account the register of *visuality*: the array of resources and effects through which the ability to look is organized, but also the ways in which those who are typically the disempowered object of the gaze are contesting and attempting to redirect this gaze or are otherwise participating in the protocols of looking. The novel's encounter in Trinidad's botanical gardens convenes multiple events, geographies, temporalities: London and Port of Spain; Port of Spain as the site of both celebrations of British victories in southern Africa and the 1903 Water Riot; a past of enslavement and abolition that cannot even be enunciated; and a relationship between the African continent and the Americas imagined as evolutionary and static, or as contemporary and dynamic.

In his review of the travelogue of Sir Harry Johnston (the British colonial administrator to whom De Lisser directs his question), Booker T. Washington worries about a photograph captioned "A Typical Negro," and thus concedes the perceived truth-telling capacity of photography.[3] He expresses reservations about the photograph of a muscular and bare-chested man from Liberia in the opening pages of Johnston's *The Negro in the New World*: "[The photograph] as representing the typical Negro will, I am afraid, be misleading to the average reader, in that the type here shown does not represent that to which the present Negro race is tending, but rather that away from which it is tending."[4] Here Washington anticipates a question that would exercise the members of the Jamaica League a few years later: given that visual representations of blackness were assumed to correspond to racial types rather than to individuals, how could images of seminude men or of women washing clothes properly represent "us"? Washington's concerns are aligned with the vindicating efforts of his and W. E. B. DuBois's commissioned photographs for the Paris Exposition in 1900, and Marcus Garvey's carefully photographed parades later on in the 1920s. Rather than a critique (even one as cautiously framed as Washington's) Cobham's novel has faith in the power of imperial, cross-racial friendship and wants to intervene in such questions in another way.[5]

As Marlon Ross notes, Washington is alert to the commodification of *images* of *the Negro*, recognizing that "[increasing] the value of the race through savvy marketing would be far easier than gaining access to capital and fair wages."[6] Washington's book review and Cobham's novel remind us that shadowing the *Typical Negro*'s presumed identity as good or bad labor is the *New Negro*, who is being recuperated in different discussions for different ends: updated, modern, autonomous, sartorially and sonically interesting. If we understand the New Negro to be a major trope of this historical moment, often if not solely aligned with the United States, I draw our attention here to its *global* contours; that is, the New Negro in this first decade of the twentieth century has multiple and sometimes overlapping itineraries in Port of Spain, Port au Prince, Oriente, Lagos, Natal, Tuskegee, Colón. Cobham's *Rupert Gray* understands that the *typical* Negro is a nodal point, a type, one image in an endless vortex of image making in this age of high imperialism, and the novel seeks to intervene in and recalibrate that process. Each image of distinguished *atypicality* also contains the seeds of its own undoing, since it can hew so closely to the racial, gendered, or working-class *type* that ought to appear debased by comparison. This visual system requires more and more images to adequately shore up the system of distinctive and coherent élite selfhood, and inevitably the endless proliferation confounds distinctions and categories that ought to have been obvious. As much as it creates anxieties for those nonwhites whose pictures are taken, photography both stokes and assuages the anxieties of middle- and upper-class whites who tote a camera as they move around Caribbean streets. Rupert Gray struggles, like the rest of a global cohort of the Talented Tenth, against being typecast, and to be seen as the *atypical* leader of an international Black working class imagined precisely as *typical*, and if we look keenly we can see him participating in the objectification of his working-class counterparts.

I am wrestling in what follows with the legacy of this archive of images, but also with the scene of the taking of the photograph itself: the ways in which daily life in the Caribbean colony entails the risk of being assaulted by the inquisitive and entitled European and North American tourist who is granted more space to move about freely in Caribbean streets than native-born and migrant nonwhite residents. Caribbean people understand that, given the region's long-standing engagement with protocols of looking that demean, the early twentieth-century photography of tourists is a particular nodal point in rather than the inaugural moment of visuality in the region.[7] Furthermore, though photography does not *create* the conditions for the shaming of the presumed social upstart, it has the power to *amplify* the spectacle of such shaming, in part by preserving these moments of degradation for prosperity. A phalanx of kodaking tourists, sometimes traveling in the United Fruit Company's vessels and staying in its hotels, update and intensify the cultural work of the nineteenth-century travelogue and of sensational journalism, as they capture nonwhite Caribbean people inundated by fruit or posed alongside giant trees to demonstrate their scale. These are poses of arrested development, when these constituencies struggle to *move*. The staging of their purported lack of modernity, quaint and submissive, is visually commandeered at the very moment when the Caribbean's nonwhite lower and middle classes struggle for economic autonomy and political participation; but at the moment, too, when visual technologies promise to reduce the long periods of stillness required in earlier times to capture the image. It is the photographer rather than these sitters who benefits from greater ease of movement afforded by technological advances and less onerous equipment.

Cobham's fictional countess in *Rupert Gray: A Tale in Black and White* already *knows* Trinidad on this, her first visit to the British colony, because of her own imperial travels, and because members of her family have participated in imperial wars all over the world, most recently the Boer War. What interests me in this chapter is how this claim to knowledge bears on photography. Standing in Port of Spain's botanical gardens, the countess has the power, and is willing to read Rupert Gray as a specimen, her camera freezing him into a scrapbook image of mementoes, even as her own aristocratic entitlement to move around Port of Spain and other cities of the British empire is affirmed. If her camera is not synonymous with the military weaponry of the soldiers in her family, the invocation of this ancestral plunder at the scene of her snapshot taking allows us to see that the countess has both the noble moral inheritance of her class and the sentimental ones of her classed gender, and that the violence inheres precisely in this inheritance. The novel's very quest for a way to redeem or escape violence, its faith in the capacity to believe that this is possible, interests us here. Cautioning against nostalgic or otherwise celebratory analyses of turn-of-the-century New Women photographers in the United States by late twentieth-century feminism, Laura Wexler proposes that they updated enslavement for a new imperial age: "Acting as the visual equivalent of ventriloquists, turn-of-the-century white women photographers in the United States found they could have satisfying careers if they used their photographs to mirror and enlarge the whiteman's image of himself as custodian of civilization just as the white mistresses of their mothers' generation had used softened tones to amplify his voice."[8] Where Wexler shows us the "tender violence" of North American white women's sentimentalizing photographs of US imperial power, Cobham's novel shines a light on white female European kodaking in the Caribbean. Tourists on the United Fruit Company's "fruiter" boats who board at Boston or New York are thus aligned with older histories of imperial travel and power. Aristocratic and middle-class modes of looking are brought into proximity with each other, when the supposedly crass North American tourist for whom both British *and* North American tourists express contempt in the era's travel writing is engaged in the same imperializing projects as the well-heeled, liberal countess making her way through Port of Spain's botanical gardens.

One of the era's US New Women photographers, Frances B. Johnston, was commissioned by Hampton Normal and Agricultural Institute to take photographs of the Virginia campus for the American Negro exhibit at the Paris Exposition in 1900. Johnston's camera captures students in classes, faculty at dinner, as well as those images of homes on the margins of the school's premises, and of students dressed in the clothing identified with their Native American nations that were supposed to represent what both Hampton and Tuskegee were teaching them to transcend.[9] Johnston took photographs of US naval forces on board the *Olympia* heading out to the Philippines under the command of Admiral George Dewey, in what Wexler reads as "a new kind of theater of force . . . the production of domestic images in an age of American imperialism."[10] Photographed at rest doing chores on board together, Johnston's photographs of soldiers headed to war had the potential to allay concerns by the newly formed Anti-Imperialist League and the general public about the water cure and other forms of torture reportedly being used on Filipinos by US armed forces, and about US activities in the Caribbean and the Pacific in general; her photographs transformed military aggression into wholesome masculine camaraderie.

Emme and Mayme Gerhard, professional photographers in St. Louis, Missouri, were commissioned (as Frances B. Johnston was as well) to produce images for the 1904 Louisiana Purchase Exposition or the St. Louis World's Fair, and they photographed members of groups including Inuit, Navajo, Chinese, and Igorot- and Moro-nation Filipinos.[11] In one of the era's important sites for displaying the products of empire (Chicago's 1893 Columbian Exposition and the 1900 Exposition Universelle in Paris were recent earlier examples), organizers of the exposition in St. Louis *acquired* (by purchase? from kidnappers, expeditions, missionaries?) and exhibited these captives in booths purporting to re-create their authentic living conditions in their alleged sites of origin. The violence of the visual project represented by such photographs is suggested by the Gerhards' captions, such as "Missing Link #1" for a Filipino man, suggesting the evolutionary chain that designates the fairgoer and viewer of the photograph as normative, modern, future-oriented. Whether the penned-in human beings and their images were held to represent *authentic* traditions disappearing with the onslaught of the modern world or intransigent communities who refused to embrace *civilization*, their presumed stasis was produced and enforced at the exposition, and the fair's attendees were supposed to understand that the human subjects on display did not share the same time with them.

When the social scientist Jean Price-Mars visited the St. Louis fairgrounds that summer as one of Haiti's official representatives, he encountered, in the description of his biographer drawing from his account, "ridicule and rejection" from "a group of Black Filipinos dressed in loincloths, who had been brought to the Exposition and penned in an enclosure."[12] He assumed they felt he was "'one of their own who had rejected the faith of the ancestors,'" or that they "'found me extremely ridiculous in my costume.'" Did he expect, from interlocutors that he referred to as "primitive," *recognition*—whether as diasporic subjects together, as ostensible colonial subjects, or because both he and they knew that their encounter was being closely scrutinized by others for signs of mutual recognition? At the very least this is a reminder that if the era's expositions are curated for an implied white gaze, there are also non-white spectators who must presumably assume that they are situated *within* the implied "magic circle of domesticity" rather than outside of it, marking its limit.[13] Besides Price-Mars we could also include those African Americans who visited the fairground that summer and discussed their experiences there in letters to the *Baltimore Afro-American* and other newspapers. If the Sorbonne-trained Haitian simply assumes his place within this magic circle, it is possible to interpret his feelings of "rejection" as his sense that he is not given the proper recognition due to a privileged Westerner by his Filipino interlocutors. Conversely, *they* may rebuke this World's Fair attendee for forgetting that his freedom to stand outside of their booth did not free him from the ignominy of the segregated travel and lodging he experienced that summer in the United States; that it had not freed Haitians from the grip of financial and political constraints, even as an independent republic; no more than it could free Filipinos currently locked in a death grip with the US naval forces seeking to supplant Spain as their new imperial power.

When Price-Mars headed to Tuskegee after his visit to the exposition, he may have been shown Frances B. Johnston's Hampton photographs.[14] Such photographs, exhibited in Paris alongside photographs of Georgia's African American middle class commissioned by W. E. B. Du Bois, are meant to contest the power of postcards of watermelon eaters or of police precincts' file of images of criminals that constitute what Allan Sekula calls the "shadow archive," a power that shapes Washington's misgivings about Harry Johnston's caption of a Liberian Kru-man.[15] But the danger is that contestation risks replication; the cropped portraits in the photographs commissioned by Du Bois are *haunted* by the mug shots of forensics and phrenology that they are being used to contest.[16] This is the dilemma of a global Talented Tenth, then—to confront and try to thwart the catastrophe of evolutionary calculation regarded as *scientific* that consigned them (or at least their untalented counterparts) to the "missing link" of humanity.

Being photographed against a tree, as Rupert Gray is, invites comparisons with another photographic opportunity of the era. The lynching of African Americans in the United States generates an industry of snapshots and postcards that, when circulated through the national postal service, in addition to giving public annihilation additional publicity, cements ties of white intimacy. The photograph of the lynched Black body in the context of the cheery note to Aunty Sue on the back of the postcard intensifies affective bonds founded on shattered, broken blackness. No doubt long after it stops being publicly permissible to circulate such images, they are wistfully pulled out of desk drawers across the United States and perused and fondled before being secreted away again.[17] In the previous chapter Claude McKay suggests that being discovered under beds and shamed—the public sense of being turned inside out, anticipating Frantz Fanon's evocative description—is on a continuum with the terror of this literal evisceration in the US South. Cobham's Trinidad protagonist, eager to retrieve romance from racial terror, suggests that only a paranoid reading could imagine him standing under a lynching tree in the botanical gardens, though later in the novel the father of the white belle he attempts to woo uses the word "lynch" when he shoots Rupert Gray in order to sever him from the estate that he stands to inherit through marriage.

Rupert Gray is caught between the tender violence of polite kodaking countesses and the ire of murderous cocoa planters. What the novel suggests is that increasingly this violence will be recorded, as well as wielded, by a camera. I read Cobham's (or, at least, Rupert Gray's) faith in the power of the charismatic Black sitter to disrupt the disabling power of the imperial photographic gaze as more than simply misguided, tragic, naïve, sycophantic, egotistical. If it is not possible to stop the picture from being taken or to take the demeaning postcard out of circulation, the novel proposes that the scene of a powerful camera-wielder and degraded sitter can at least be revised. What can we see when we consider Rupert Gray as not only the victim of an imperial gaze, and this scene in the botanical gardens as not only a wounding, but as his exercise of the right to look and talk back, as well—and also, crucially, the exercise of his right to stand or sit still under a tree in his own territory, albeit as a colonial subject? This is what he was doing, after all, when the countess disturbed his solitude.[18]

I am inclined to privilege the violence of the photographic encounter and gaze; to dismiss the *good intentions* of the photographer who is courteous to the *natives*, and whose respect for protocols of preservation and aesthetics will redeem whatever bad faith ensues from the original scene of the photograph; or the good intentions of modernism's (and the museum's) consecration of the aesthetic worth of the *primitive* as continuous with the well-meaning tenderness of a countess with a camera. At the same time, the involuntary sitter has a right to a complex reading that exceeds my readings of abjection or my advocacy. Here *uncertainty* "about exactly what photographs seek to represent," and a *curiosity* that "opens up multiple relationships [that can] spread the concept of the gaze across a range of encounters and effects," are useful to think with.[19] When Rupert Gray shows the countess that the photographed colonial subject sometimes talks back, he does so to distinguish himself from the mass of working-class Trinidadians but he also reminds me to adopt a posture of curiosity about them, and about him.

I tend to ascribe *private* circuits of intimacy animated by photography only to the era's white middle- or upper-class subjects, as when two white women characters in *Rupert Gray* use photographs as the means by which one will assure the other that she is recovering satisfactorily. Gwendolen can afford to hire a photographer to come to her home (or to patronize Port of Spain establishments such as those that advertised "high-class Portraiture" available at Photo Gallery, 54 Charlotte Street, or "One Eastman Kodak No. 3—fitted for films. Dark room unnecessary. Just the thing for an amateur. Apply to 32 Dundonald Street") and to mail daily photographs of herself to Florence in Scotland.[20] But while this exchange affirms the privacy of bourgeois intimacy, albeit accompanied by the anxiety of illness, it does not mean that photographic exchanges and the care that animates them is limited to élites. When Paula Reyes instructs Tuskegee Normal Institute in Alabama to see to it that her son, a student at the school, gets the money that she sent the previous month, so that he can take photographs of himself, I take this to mean that, like fictional Florence, she wants visual proof that her son is being properly taken care of.[21] But of course she also wants a keepsake for herself, and I imagine that this photograph, when it arrives in Havana, will have pride of place in her home, and as it is passed proudly around to neighbors and family members.

My assumption that fictional Rupert Gray is demeaned by the snapshot that an English tourist takes of him; my investment in retrieving respectability and racial virtue; my nostalgia and pride in the endurance that I discern in many of these historical images; or my irritation when a Black person smiles into the camera, and thus colludes, as I see it, in his or her own debasement— these feelings may well be an affective postcolonial response, in my search for a recuperable nationalist self in colonial-era photographs.[22] But images taken by local and visiting photographers that I am inclined to read as dehumanizing because they are posed on donkeys or inundated by bananas must also have recalled the day that the photographer visited a neighborhood, or they must have been treasured because the person pictured was a loved one or someone who assumed that others would know that the donkey signified hard-won prosperity.[23] The photograph may "trigger emotions and elicit feelings" in part as an object to be held, stroked, fingered.[24] My students remind me of the photograph's affirmation of presence where I am inclined to see indignity, pointing out that the image is rare proof that these communities existed. When the Seminole-Muscogee-Diné artist and theorist Hulleah J. Tsinhnahjinnie discusses the experience of recognizing relatives in the dehumanizing trading of images of Native Americans on eBay, she demonstrates that there is no option but to locate oneself within, rather that cleanly separated from, the ongoing violence of the consumption and objectification of her community, and in her art practice she endows these retrieved images with First Nation iconography and intense color.[25] In another kind of wrestling with presence and repair, Jamaican-American artist Albert Chong discusses his realization that a "torn and yellowing" photograph that his mother asked him to restore was a rare image of herself and her sisters "as they poised themselves for history" in the context of a childhood marked by their traumatic loss of both parents, and his own limited experience of a historical visual record of any nonwhite subjects, let alone these African-Chinese Jamaican sisters.[26]

The impulse to map presence can be in tension with a problematic will to *certainty* and here I am aware that I participate in the visual taxonomies of race that I share with the early twentieth-century white photographers I am condemning. Tina Campt critiques her own practice of "coaxing" in the process of interpreting discarded plates of a Birmingham photographic studio serving Black communities in Europe in the 1950s, communities whom, she points out, "were neither lost nor forgotten."[27] If we regard travel writers' written commentary on the moral pasts and futures of the people they photograph as they roam the Caribbean and the world, as an extended and violent caption of their images, then the film practice of John Akomfrah is instructive, because in diminishing or excising the specific visual and aural descriptive markers of archival photographs and other footage, he releases these images from the spell of the caption to vibrate with a new relationship to each other, and with the viewer.[28]

Inserting *Rupert Gray* into a contemporary matrix of photographer-travelers and discussions of photography's aesthetic and social consequences reveals concerns about the value of the photograph, relative to other aesthetic objects, and of the social subject who is being assessed to have the moral and genealogical ability to keep or assume social power, or to obey those who have this. In order not to be valued as manual labor Rupert befriends a mischief-making photographer to try and argue for an adjustment of the standards for assessing moral and intellectual worth. This in itself is strenuous labor, especially because (as with questions of the African continent's *value* as contemporaneous and coeval, as more than the object of violent extraction) there can be no explicit rebuke by Rupert himself—only a polite response to imperial moralizing.

As commodities from Africa and Asia enter North American and British living rooms at an accelerated pace in this era, Rupert Gray reminds Britons, at least, that even if now saddled in debt, or passed over for greener imperial pastures of rubber and diamonds, Caribbean estates had facilitated the accumulation of the wealth that made possible an earlier generation's valuable oil portraits and other objects of the art collection that "would become an important conduit for laundering a self produced by slave money into a civic, virtuous subject . . . [and] a site for displacing or representing the culture of slavery."[29] Chapter 4 explores questions of value for members of Rupert Gray's social group, which is invested in the protocols of prestige and taste connected to the plantation great house: a process that potentially both *threatens* the status quo, since they are defying the lily-white provenance of this transatlantic wealth, and also *rejuvenates* it, since they are attempting to join or supplant rather than destroy the current or traditional propertied class. But in the present chapter we have to tackle residual questions of genealogy, value, and posterity that bear on visuality and that help to tease out the implications of the fictional encounter in the Trinidad Botanic Gardens—among them visiting photographers' racial portraits, photography's capacity to reserve gleam for the upper orders in a democratizing age, and the multiple resonances of discarded photographs in southern and western Africa.

Visuality as Time-Keeping and Kin-Making

When a camera-toting British colonial administrator Harry Johnston, a veteran of multiple postings across the African continent, is invited to the White House to give advice about safaris to President Theodore Roosevelt, and is in turn urged to use his expertise to study and surveil African-descended people in the Americas, it allows us to see how US imperial projects are continuous with European ones in this historical moment—in the Americas and in Africa.[30] If official British imperial attention was shifting from the Caribbean to Africa and Asia, Johnston could draw on his extensive experience of travel across the African continent to address a subject that had long intrigued him: "the great question of the eleven millions of Negroes and Negroids in North America and the West Indies."[31] As a British colonial administrator, author, photographer, and botanical artist, he had acquired a reputation as an expert on the politics and society of central Africa, Uganda, and (with a recent two-volume study) Liberia.[32] Theodore Roosevelt invited Johnston to the White House to discuss Liberia as well as his own plans for a trip to East Africa after he stepped down as president—a media-saturated safari, in which he stayed in ranches and homesteads owned by European and US officials and traders, whose conquest of African people and land (at least) a generation earlier smoothed the way for him.[33] These two men's collaboration is a reminder of the ways in which transimperial ties are being strengthened in this era.

Johnston, in turn, travels through the Americas with the full support of the region's officials: "From Cuba I passed to Haiti . . . with the potent assistance of the American Minister and Consul-General; Governor Sir Sidney Olivier, previously a clerk and undersecretary at the Colonial Office . . . gave me all the facilities which could be afforded for studying the Negro question in this island"; "I decided to go on to Panamá with a latent commission from Mr. Roosevelt to join Mr. Taft's mission of inspection of the Canal, in course of construction across the Isthmus."[34] Johnston is a custodian of Black futurity, alongside Olivier and Roosevelt in their different and sometimes overlapping domains. As he travels through the US South, the Caribbean, and South America, he is at once deeply imbricated in official US and British imperial circles, and free to claim to float above them, as someone who is not formally appointed by any political administration.

Johnston's observations were steeped in his own years of research, melding ethnography, linguistics, physiognomy, exploration, and conquest. As he travels across the Americas he draws on his own experiences to make transatlantic comparisons about Black life. An intense interest in his travels and opinions, generated by articles he himself had been commissioned to write on the places he was visiting, and as implied by De Lisser's gushing interview with him, suggests that even those who disagreed with him would have had to acknowledge his authority.[35] Simon Gikandi draws attention to the process by which an anxiety-producing sameness was transmuted into a manageable otherness by what he terms "minor figures": the soldiers, merchants, administrators, ethnographers on all those *expeditions* to the African continent. In "[bringing] the other home to us" (here I take Gikandi to mean *us, in a space marked as Western*), these turn-of-the-century travelers "institute the crucial separation between the African aesthetic and African bodies and cultures," in order to respond to this fearsome question with an answer they could live with: "how could a culture of barbarism produce such great objects of art?"[36] Johnston is just such a "minor figure" and we should thus see him as intimately involved in the process of dislodging African imagination and creativity from African *people,* as a crucial figure in the adjudication of the value of both the masks and other artifacts he is pilfering for museums, and of the societies who must yield them to him. But he also makes comparative assessments of labor, capacity for *civilization,* and diasporic *origin* on both sides of the Atlantic, as he travels from the campuses of Tuskegee and Hampton in the southern United States, and through the Caribbean and South America, from 1908 to 1910.

His title, *The Negro in the New World,* reverberates backward and forward in time with titles and preoccupations in the decade or so before and after his text: "Negro," "New," "New Negro," "Negro World," "New World Negro"; *A New Negro for a New Century* (1900), edited by Booker T. Washington, Fannie Barrier Williams, and N. B. Wood; *The New Negro* (1916) by William Pickens; *The New Negro* (1925) by Alain Locke; Melville Herskovits's "The Negro in the New World: The Statement of a Problem" (1930). Thus colonial administrators, Black modernists, and anthropologists train their eyes on transatlantic Black life (whether masks, the performance of kinship, or their photographic reproduction), conceptualizing racial soul and origin, and suggesting how closely diasporic intimacy and imperial power hued together, even as these photographs and masks become the inspiration for canonical Anglo-American modernism. A British colonial administrator-photographer stands at the nexus of modernism, colonial ethnography, and military rule, and demonstrates the era's immediate connections between imperial Africa and the US state, imperial Africa and the imperial Caribbean, the Caribbean and the US South, and the Caribbean, United States, and Africa.

Johnston's description of his time in Cuba, in the three-year period of heightened tension over Black citizenship before the terrible violence unleashed on Black Cubans in 1912, exemplifies this sense of the disinterested observer and helps explain why some US reviewers were irritated by his book's critiques of US slavery. Johnston veers between criticizing racist hysteria and decreasing opportunities for Black Cubans "who fought so [bravely] to establish Cuban independence," on the one hand, and affirming the inevitability of white rule, on the other.[37] All of "Tropical America," Johnston declares, should be grateful for 1898; Spain's misuse of "a splendid property" had thankfully given way to "twentieth-century Anglo-Saxondom." The United States had put in place a strong infrastructure, which was thankfully encouraging white migration into Cuba. It was left to a multiracial Cuba to work together and prove itself worthy of its new imperial power.[38]

We are most likely to encounter Johnston's photographs of the Caribbean today in the wake of a 1998 exhibition that toured the region accompanied by the catalog *Photos and Phantasms: Harry Johnston's Photos of the Caribbean*, introduced by Petrina Archer-Straw.[39] I experience these photographs very differently from viewing them in Johnston's *The Negro in the New World*. The seventy prints in *Photos and Phantasms* were culled, for the exhibition, from the original glass plate negatives that are part of the collection of over one thousand donated to the Royal Geographical Society by Johnston's family in the 1930s. In *Photos and Phantasms* the photographs fill the page, rather than, as in Johnston's book, sharing the page with his written text. They are beautiful. On heavy cream paper, they manage to breathe, defying their original confinement in the pages of *The Negro in the New World*.

Thus I have to concede what he and his assistant, Mr. Greaves, aspired to and achieved in their interaction with the sitters. For if those "Negroes at Work in a Cuban Sugar Plantation" are smiling, it is surely because one or both of the men behind the camera culled this smile from them.[40] On the opposite page, in an image captioned "A Cuban Negro," a slim, muscled man wears a thin, stained short-sleeved cotton shirt, and his trousers are secured by a leather belt with silver studs. His face is framed by a hat that is turned up, and there is a knife or other implement sticking out of the belt.[41] Against my will, he is smiling, fully and unironically, which I find breathtaking and discomfiting. Behind him is a grove of bamboo that, blown up in the 1998 text, anticipates Wilfredo Lam's *La Jungla*. This is the domain of the *yerbero*/herbalist, the space of cultivation, experimentation, and reflection, as shown in "A Jamaican Negro Farmer or Beekeeper."[42] In Johnston's text, the captions of these two Cuban photographs tie them to that territory (albeit precariously: *Negroes at work in*), so that "Cuban" risks erasing histories of migrant labor; but their identification as possible migrants from Haiti or

Jamaica in *Photos and Phantasms* potentially undermines the normativity of dark-skinned Black Cubanidad. The figures in these images embody but also exceed their captions' narratives of Afro-Cuban citizenship and the place of the migrant laborer in accounts of *Cubanness*, *Haitianness*, and *Jamaicanness*.

Responding to the proposition that "the Jamaica negro has advanced considerably on the West African negro from whom he is directly descended," Johnston agrees, noting his encounters with "Jamaica negroes with real savage features and looking like pure savages. But the moment I spoke to them there was a smile on their faces and a civility of manner that spoke of civilization"; central to Jamaica's future, Black Jamaicans would "develop under Anglo-Saxon influence. From the earliest times the white man has never left the negro alone, and he never will leave him alone."[43] Johnston is an arbiter of Black kinship, juxtaposing photographs from the African continent and from the Caribbean on the same page, discerning in Black faces transatlantic ethnicity and Black intimate relations, and the capacity for a thriving future predicated on white presence and authority.

Claiming a similar authority to connect Black pasts and futures, Ella Wheeler Wilcox, traveling in the region over several winter seasons before the publication of *Sailing Sunny Seas* in 1909, notes that the "recent discovery of a buried city in Absynnia, of artistic and architectural beauty, shows that the ancient race of Negroes possessed originality and constructive ability, and culture."[44] Wilcox regrets the moral failings of "the white man who took his black slave to concubinage," but insists that this lack of morality from that time to the present ultimately redounds to Black people.[45] Wilcox keeps her eyes trained on the physiognomical legacy of this history, repeatedly pointing out the presence or absence of African ancestry, as revealed on the body—the happiest Trinidadians are those whose dark skin makes it impossible for them to deny African ancestry—and comparing women across racialized categories: the Indian woman who is "a sketch for a color artist . . . slender and erect" with "a thin gold hoop in her classic nose" and "jewel in her left nostril" that constitute engagement ring and "marriage seal"; a "colossal Juno in ebony" who wears a "gown of screaming scarlet"; and a woman, "beautiful as a dream of old Castile . . . but with the blood of some slave ancestor staining her beauty to unwashable brown."[46] Postures, clothing, and mode of travel and labor help to frame a sort of moral postcard, in which we are directed to be charmed or pained by the kinds of femininity on display in Port of Spain, and to mourn the capacity of enslaved forbears (not enslavers) to "stain" otherwise beautiful white descendants.

Such Caribbean women are part of a global intimate history that includes "deserted wives in Hawai'i" whose US partners never fulfill their promise to send for them, and "abandoned women" in Havana, and compiled as she accompanies her husband, referred to as "Himself," on his business trips. In wondering aloud about whether Cuban sex workers are better housed together or dispersed over Havana, or about differences between women in Hawai'i and Black Caribbean women, Wilcox reveals a fascination if not obsession with the sexual relations of the "others" she encounters abroad. If they confirm her and her social group as respectable, they also suggest the threat to the white male business traveler of sexually loose brown women at every port of call, while the good wife, marked as white and North American, waits at home. "Business, my only rival," Wilcox sighs, lamenting that her husband and other men like him are "weary with that incessant battle which our competitive system forces upon men of business."[47] If we can assume that her husband is part of the phalanx of US business interests extracting resources in the wake of the Spanish American War, Wilcox casts US business as a solicitous and protective husband, and herself as worthy of him, in an expanding empire of morally questionable women who, deserving or undeserving of sympathy, are also her "rivals."

Just as Johnston blames US tourists for Jamaicans' expectation to be paid for taking their photographs, Wilcox complains that Jamaica's "natives," whom I take to mean people of African descent, no longer curtsy and smile: "Today they demand one or two shillings . . . their flowers are no longer offered . . . and where ten gave the pleasant greeting as they passed, one give it now. America's brusque manners, and money standards have been adopted by them."[48] Clearly these Jamaican strollers have had enough. Here Wilcox reads her own US American identity as standing above the fray; she is not a crass American, so that this is in part a classed comment about what she sees as the ill-effects of a lower class of US traveler. "No amount of travel," she declares elsewhere in the text, can transform the "vulgarity" of travelers whom she terms "Mr and Mrs Sudden Rich," or identifies as the "first" family in a small American town but out of their depth elsewhere, people who "never see Newport or Fifth Avenue."[49]

Wilcox's illustrations include a photograph of two women in Trinidad, bodies covered in clothing from top of head to around mid-thigh, where the photograph ends.[50] Both incline their heads right toward the direction of the camera. They are standing in front of the home of the Indo-Trinidadian or Indian migrant woman on the right, part of the wooden façade of which is visible just behind both of them. I would describe her loose layered clothing as a long skirt or *ghungari* and an *orhni* or head covering. Her face, framed by the *orhni*, is uncovered, with the kind of tight-lipped expression which may indicate a polite smile or an irritated grimace. Not knowing her willingness to pose for this picture, we can at least surmise that she does not have the power to refuse to do so. I assume that the woman beside her is Wilcox herself. The hat and attached veil cover her face completely. She wears a high- and cowled-necked dress that is either long-sleeved or accompanied by long gloves. Cinched at the waist, it continues into a pleated skirt. She is holding pince-nez or some other object in her raised right hand. Did Wilcox herself pose with many of those whose images she took (or had taken) or was this a sign that this woman met her moral standards?

Standing beside her companion, then, in the Trinidad photograph, Wilcox draws attention to a pleasing local figure, pressing us to wonder what brown women in close proximity make possible or how they occasion anxiety. She also gives us a glimpse of how women traveled in the region—perhaps élite women including white women, both resident and visiting, perhaps only tourists. We could surmise that Wilcox's covering, including her veiled face, protected her in such a way that she was then free, as an upper-class woman, to be photographed with persons who were not in her party. An élite white North American who counts as her acquaintances Henry Blake, the former governor of Jamaica and of Ceylon, and his wife, who were visiting Jamaica during one of Wilcox's trips, she exercises the freedom to take pictures of the people and places within the bounds of a respectable female traveler (distinct from other classed and raced women, and also from New Women who share her class, and who possibly travel confidently with less protection).

Wilcox's socially powerful eye frames and analogizes what is dimly perceived or not seen at all: "But the morning was as black as a full-blooded young maid of the Jamaican Mountains; and we could see nothing."[51] Black Jamaicans' dark skins provide the literal and metaphorical registers for assessing Jamaica and underlining Wilcox's authority, even as their own reluctance to be photographed or to greet visitors is ascribed to their moral decline and their blind submission to the negative US influence. Traveling at dawn in Jamaica's countryside, Wilcox discerns figures on the road, silhouetted "like negatives on a Kodak film; then like developed prints; and next we saw the mountains appearing from the mist."[52] Photographic technology provides the trope of legibility—images emerge out of the darkness as the day emerges out of night, and as a white female visitor interprets the physical and social landscape. But Wilcox is also mapping whiteness very powerfully and here we could speculate that, like other well-heeled travelers to the Caribbean, her itinerary takes her to exhibitions in the United States and Europe. Though Wilcox could not yet have seen the play of blinding light on stone and marble, of white clothing against white skin in the sunlight, in John Sargent's "Group in the Simplon" and "Bringing Down Marbles from the Quarries to Carrara" before her book's publication, Sargent captures the problem of achieving whiteness, the work of rendering it on canvas, and in the backbreaking labor of retrieving white marble (the element used in the neoclassical architecture of the White City, at Chicago's Colombian Exposition of 1893) to display imperial power.

We could view such paintings, the museum culture which shapes their viewing, and the social milieu which facilitates extensive travel in the United States and to Europe, as the lens through which each Caribbean territory is viewed, and in which the region functions to assure travelers of their place in the order of things. As a veiled Wilcox and her party set out every day from their perch at the Queen's Park Hotel at one edge of the Savannah in Port of Spain, Trinidad, or from the Titchfield Hotel in Portland, Jamaica, their right to go anywhere and to have the region's residents pose for them is facilitated by acquaintances such as former colonial governors, and the US Consul in Jamaica, who tells Wilcox that his job includes making local inquiries about the possible Negro lineages of Jamaican-born women, on behalf of prospective white in-laws in the United States. We are meant to hear this as another example of ancestors who "stain" the present and future, through the body of the woman. Not a professional photographer herself, then, Wilcox's illustrated travel writing is nevertheless continuous with both Harry Johnston's text and the work of professional female photographers in the United States, as it weighs in on the potential for civilization of nonwhite subjects of European and US imperial rule.

As Rupert Gray stands in the botanical gardens against a gigantic hog plum tree, his soul "floating towards the spheres," he demonstrates his entitlement to transcendent solitude, and in this space in particular.[53] It is tempting to speculate that, knowing that he is bound to be disturbed by inquisitive tourists, he has arranged himself in a pose of his own making, hoping for the best, though this implies that he cannot be still for himself.[54] He insists on being in nature *and* being seen as modern, in an era when photographs of nonwhite people and nature are being used to prove Caribbean people's quaint lack of modernity. Rupert is still, not *stilled*. If the countess is moving forward through the space, from the adjoining Savannah to the gardens, to photograph someone who is in turn destabilized and mobilized by the power she represents, we have to see something else as well: a "native" enjoying the gardens in the place where he lives; claiming the gardens as a space of reflection, a way of recollecting the transcendent; insisting that the *sublime* can be *here*, accessible to and through him.

Charged sites of imperial and colonial power, the Savannah (where a political meeting once prompted a prominent Victorian traveler to declare African-descended Trinidadians unfit to share political power), and the botanical gardens (a zone of species identification and hierarchy, and the final resting place of prominent white officials) require recoding in this new imperial phase.[55] In a postcard captioned "Bay Tree Avenue, Royal Botanic Gardens, Trinidad," a man sitting on the left, at the base of, or in the clearing beside one of the giant trees in Trinidad's botanical gardens, is in the shot in order to show context and scale—to demonstrate the height of the trees.[56] Fictional Rupert Gray may well be aware that he is being used to show the immensity of the hog plum tree in any photograph taken by the English tourist who encounters him; where, then, is his own humanity, his own atypicality? Krista Thompson has argued that, "Like the relegated role of black servants in eighteenth-century aristocratic family portraits," Black people posed in turn-of-the-century photographs in Jamaica were "peripheral props to the main photographic subject: bananas and other transplanted crops" that replaced the sugar of an older plantation economy in the "new Jamaica."[57] Cobham's novel shows photography presiding, not over the agricultural contexts that Thompson discusses for Jamaica and the Bahamas, but over the need to recode what it means for nonwhite Trinidadian residents to be posed in nature—for introspection, rather than as "peripheral props" that show the height of trees.

But the novel also highlights another aspect of the traveling photographer's harm: willingness to export slander about the colony. Thus the countess tells Rupert Gray that while traveling in New Zealand she had heard that Trinidad's "natives" were "far behind the Māoris," because during Carnival they had continued to play masquerade on Ash Wednesday and had invaded Government House, forcing the governor to seek shelter.[58] Both the celebrations for British victories in southern Africa in February 1900, and demonstrations in the streets of Port of Spain during the Water Riot of 1903 are reduced to the slander that Trinidadians are rowdies. Recalling the pride taken in a Pretoria Day photograph circulated across the empire by way of

Black and White magazine (in chapter 1), we can see here how the stakes of such pride involve competition between colonies and a ranking of specific constituencies within them—here Māoris and "natives" (which I take to refer to Black people in Trinidad). I assume that not just fictional Rupert would have bristled at the comparison, and not because of a concern for the intended slight to Māori cultural integrity. The countess is implicated because she chooses to believe scurrilous slander about Trinidadians.

Both amateur botanists, the countess and Rupert Gray are experts without the sanction of formal credentials, as the discipline shuts them out from the professionalization open to white men at the same time that it arguably makes different kinds of accommodations for their expertise: she is a member of London's Botanical Society, and his mastery of the Latin names of all the trees in the gardens represents a Black male colonial class that has mastered the imperial canon and also has a deep multidisciplinary sense of his own landscape.[59] Where a previous generation of Black vindicators negotiated the European traveler's authority in *writing* in the early twentieth century, this occurs in the precariousness of the personal encounter; competing with upper-class white English women to identify the correct names of plants, after being subjected to the intrusive Kodak shot. Perhaps this is the fantasy that roaming *female* photographers "in search of specimens, taking notes and snapshots" facilitate a more egalitarian encounter: "West Indian native and English noblewoman meet, face to face, on the common ground of science."[60] But in the gardens, a key site of imperial taxonomy, she is aligned with a bloody lineage, most recently in Pretoria: "a daughter of the Teutons, a blue-eyed, fair-haired Aryan, whose Anglo-Norman ancestry had bequeathed to Great Britain a line of warriors bold. . . . When the folds of dominion were flung out over Pretoria, another son of this historic house joined in the 'tremendous cheering' that echoed far away beyond kopje and veldt."[61] As "a soldier of peace . . . a patroness of letters . . . a friend of subject races" she softens the edges of military might, recalling Wexler's point about professional women photographers tempering or concealing military aggression.[62]

But what of Rupert's lineage, his local coordinates already flagged, for readers in the know?[63] "My name is Gray—Rupert McKinley Gray."[64] This gesture to the US president who oversaw US victory over Spain in the "Spanish American War," and who appointed twice as many African Americans to federal positions than any previous US president, is part of the novel's overlapping imperial, business, and diasporic invocations of the United States: Rupert turns down a US job offer, meets with African American leaders on his world tour, and the novel ends with his creation of an ambitious, Tuskegee-like institute in Trinidad.[65] When Rupert is described as "a gentleman with no ancestry—no history—no past [it] is idle for coloured people to boast of parentage in the West Indies where emancipation is the common stock," this sounds like the incapacity of enslaved people to integrate freely, at their will, "the experience of their ancestors into their lives," if we read the novel's description in terms of an ancestry that has no past preceding enslavement worth mentioning, and with a negativity that redounds to the enslaved, rather than the enslaver.[66] Here Rupert is disencumbered from an ancestry that is delegitimating: *I can't provide a matching genealogy—this is not the basis on which the two of us are equal.* His claim to full equality with a British countess, and to the capacity to accumulate wealth and to share in his colony's political power, comes from his moral, intellectual, and charismatic personhood: *from a past that is a void I have birthed myself, and I am sufficient to be your equal.* This is the preferred outcome of a "typical Negro" captured against a hog plum tree and headed toward a humiliating postcard or Linnaean Society lantern slide: that a visiting aristocrat will come to know that Rupert Gray is her social equal.

With the presence of a world-traveling British countess in this era of greater US entry into the Caribbean, the novel invites us to assess the comparative value of imperial prestige, but also the relationship between greater access and declining value. Issues of mass circulation and the invasion of privacy that partly turn on questions of photography and mass media are convened in the Caribbean novel, which shares these concerns with the UK contexts it delineates. In 1857, at what was by that point the decade-old development of photography, English aristocrat Lady Eastlake weighed in on the cultural debates about its relative merits as artistic, natural, or mechanical, and concluded that photography could never usurp the cultural power of the portrait-as-art, and that in fact photography would actually *increase* the demand for and drive up the value of the real thing, as it were—the portrait.[67] Nancy Armstrong's discussion of photography in the age of realist fiction proves Eastlake both wrong and right.[68] Armstrong discusses the work of Margaret Cameron, a predecessor of the early twentieth-century kodaking tourism of Rupert Gray's aristocratic interlocutor, with parallel photographic sites of London and laborers on her husband's Ceylon tea plantations. In the 1860s Cameron, an upper-middle-class Bloomsbury matron, garnered acclaim for her blurred photographs of members of her circle of London family and friends, but also scorn—her children gave her a camera for Christmas and she set up a studio in her home—as an amateur in an era of aggressive professionalization. With her aspiration to "ennoble Photography and to secure for it the character and uses of High Art by combining the real and Ideal and sacrificing nothing of Truth by all possible devotion to Poetry and beauty" she raises questions of taste and value that photography poses for aesthetics.[69] Armstrong's reading of the translucent women in Cameron's photographs—"Transparency cloaked in literary dress indicates 'soul,' in the Victorian sense of the term, or what might simply be called interiority"—suggests how her images cast the upper-(middle)-class English subject in a heavenly light that added ethereal value and aesthetic radiance at the very moment when the photograph was beginning to offer a middling, interior respectability to *middle*-middle-class Victorians photographed in a domestic interior packed out with things.[70]

That is, far from a democratizing technology, photography facilitates a recalibration of class hierarchies, which is typified, for Armstrong, by a photograph of two young women playing the piano with ornate carvings of candelabra and Chinese ceramic vases representing the *chinoiserie* of the imperial circuit of commodities; images of refined fragility securely ensconced and demarcated from the uncertain outside world. I am struck by the similarities here to Shawn Michelle Smith's discussion of a photograph from *Negro Life in Georgia, USA*, the series commissioned by W. E. B. Du Bois for the 1900 Paris Exposition: a young woman seated at the piano, flanked by a similarly formally attired man, with a photograph of the pianist and an ivory statuette of Lady Justice wearing a toga.[71] While this confirms the demarcating interiority of the parlor-situated piano, Smith points out Black leaders' exasperation, as when Booker T. Washington berated the presence of rented pianos in rented cabins, or a "$300 rosewood piano" in a Black Belt country school, evidence of a misguided population led astray by the impractical tastes of the Du Boisian stream of the Talented Tenth.[72] Washington cautions African Americans to wait: behind the piano in the New England home, he says, are "one hundred years of toil, sacrifice and economy." But Washington's account of Yankee thrift makes no reference to bootlegging or enslaved labor as routes to white accumulation. He gifts white New Englanders a caption, as it were, that grants them radiance, that reads them as naturally entitled to their pianos, while piano-owning African Americans are cast as upstarts.

This era of photography presides over a moment of crisis about social upstarts, about originals and fake copies, even as this technology promises to locate the criminality inhering in foreheads and ears. But if it targets laborers, *Negroes* and *Orientals*, prostitutes, pickpockets, or hysterics, it also poses a crisis for the very élites in whose service these systems of images are supposed to be functioning, and anxieties in British fiction about stolen photographs or oil portraits that can be duplicated register this destabilization of value, this loss of privacy and exclusiveness.[73] When the Victorians and Edwardians worried about a surfeit of images let loose in the world, creating anxieties about copies that undermined what Walter Benjamin would later term the "aura of the original" in the age of mechanical reproduction, this could be read as a crisis of value that Benjamin is also mourning: "that which withers in the age of mechanical reproduction is the aura of the work of art."[74] But Benjamin is signaling a necessary process that is by no means new, and that is deeply political. "In principle," Benjamin proposes, "a work of art has always been reproducible; far from being a crisis, this loss of 'originality' is liberatory, facilitating a release from 'ritual' into 'politics.'"[75]

The photographs in Santu Mofokeng's *The Black Photo Album/Look at Me: 1890–1950*—of Moeti and Lazarus Fume in tennis togs, and of Rozeta Dubula, née Duma, and two other women dressed in their Sunday best, in H. F. Fine's studio in Johannesburg—were taken at a moment of upheaval in the early years of the twentieth century, as the Boer War solidified a process of industrialization that saw South Africa producing a sizable share of the world's diamonds and gold.[76] This process required cheap Black labor, rather than Black property owners and consumers who demanded the right to vote. As Mofokeng points out, the photographs in *Black Photo Album*, commissioned by the sitters themselves, who are dressed in what could be described as *European* or *Victorian* clothing (but might be called simply *formal clothing* if worn by their white English or US middle-class counterparts), were made in the same moment of the production of a more familiar context of ethnographic photographs capturing the *authentic* African in *traditional clothing* who was in danger of disappearing. In this latter context photography records and also helps to produce the process by which, as we saw in chapter 1, Black people in southern Africa were increasingly displaced politically and geographically, removed from voter lists, and subject to legislation on taxes, squatting, and a strengthening of the pass system in the period leading up to the 1913 Natives Land Act.[77]

This evisceration was so successful that Mofokeng's generation had no inkling of the existence of that turn-of-the-century class of Black southern Africans. They were not available to him to integrate into his and his community's ongoing present and future: "These solemn images of middle- and working-class black families . . . portray a class of black people which, according to

my education, did not exist at the time that they were made."[78] It is not just
that these sitters staring back at us, in photographs of themselves that they
have commissioned in the 1890–1910 period, are on the verge of losing their
property and their political rights, but that they are actively disappeared in
order to affirm or enable the capacity of others to be enfolded within the
"circle of domesticity." They cannot become part of a dynamic, living history in which they share time with Harry Johnston or the fictional countess.
But is Rupert Gray attempting to occupy this time alongside these fictional
and actual photographers, or to make transparent the process by which
some become unable to move? How does the novel argue for recognition of
its protagonist as more than the object of the gaze of the implied bourgeois
subject with whom he does not share coevality; furthermore, who falls by
the wayside after Rupert Gray succeeds in achieving this recognition?

   Mofokeng's archive shows the wear and tear of the conditions of retrieval:
family heirlooms preserved or about to be "destroyed as 'rubbish' during
'spring cleans,'" photos rotting in plastic bags. Rather than a spotless process
of recovery or restoration, Mofokeng allows for "the tears, holes, and gaps to
be handed down—even illuminated."[79] A quite different process of "spring
cleaning" involves a loss of photographs-as-artifact, but that is not commen-
surate with straitened circumstances. Because this community's capacity to
accumulate and to remember is not in peril, the destruction of these particular
records appears to be inconsequential. The context is the archival holdings
of West African studio photographers and the élite families who were their
clients in late nineteenth- and early twentieth-century Accra, Cape Coast, and
other West African towns and cities.[80] These photographs, often in private
circulation, record impending marriages, ceremonial installations, and the
portraits of distinguished family members. Some retouched by succeeding
generations with charcoal and other substances, "some images left in tatters
and others taped together," they constitute a "multi-locus and multi-media
collection" that "begs the question: what exactly constitutes a photograph?"[81]
The discussion here of paintings based on and replicating the "monochrome"
"verisimilitude" of black and white photographs; of artists commissioned to
do oil portraits based on daguerreotypes; of photographers who work in tandem with sitters to capture the symbolic resonances of a ceremonial event;
of charcoaled portraits re-created to look like photographs, and photographs
taken of portraits that have obviously been torn—these contexts imply histories of image-making, aesthetics, and *originality* that require alternative
vocabularies of interpretation. In this era when the Oba of Benin's capture

by British forces is recorded by photography, these archives discussed by Haney require another lens, since for this community (or more precisely, this class within a community) the colonial encounter did not appear to signal the sort of devastation experienced in Mofokeng's contexts. What would communities who commissioned photographs of themselves from the Lutterodt photographic studios in the Gold Coast make of Harry Johnston in this era? How would his gaze be returned by such sitters? Even as I am cognizant of appearing to equate African and European capacity to accumulate (mindful of Taiwo Osinubi's reminder that, for Africans, "implication" in the slave trade cannot be disentangled from "colonial conquest" and "cultural mourning"), these stories of turn-of-the-century West African prosperity remind us to be curious about what escapes representation in the age of the European or North American world traveler-as-photographer who dismisses, is troubled by, or has limited or no access to the ongoing scene of Africans who commission images of themselves across the continent at the turn of the century.[82]

At the end of *Rupert Gray* Rupert goes on a world tour with the countess's nephew (consecrating a friendship solidified by the death of the countess on her return to England), a dizzying itinerary that includes visiting the Lake District and the tombs of William Wilberforce and Admiral Nelson in England, dining with Maharajas in India, and, in the United States, meeting "black professors, judges, capitalists and authors . . . the following of Booker Washington."[83] Following in the footsteps of local Trinidadians whose tour of Europe and other parts of the world rounded out their academic and cultural credentialing, Rupert shows his own social group catching up and building its own global networks, even as he possibly also demonstrates his belatedness and lack of privilege relative to some other Trinidadians. Here we could ask if the world tour is a British aristocrat's concession of parallel systems of sovereignty, with Maharajas as his global counterparts, or if this journey maps a global snapshot of extant and emerging locations and constituencies that remain accessible for imperial consumption. When they visit the Penrhyn Quarries, the Welsh slate quarries that were the scene of an important labor strike at the turn of the century, is this a "ritual" stop (to return to Benjamin's distinction) for one aristocrat to salute the accumulation of another or for tourists titillated by reports of unruly behavior, just as the countess repeats reports about a Trinidad mob? Or is it a "political" salute from a veteran of Trinidad's Water Riot?[84]

For the Londoners who will presumably look through the countess's scrapbook on her return to England, this typical-Negro-turned-friend might trigger anxieties about a disquieting proximity to them. Rupert Gray is the collectible Kodak snapshot or postcard, the strange imperial commodity that shores up jingoism, but who speaks back to the photographer on her terms and tries to transform himself from commodity, or "frames for the commodity, valued for *exhibition* alone," into a "historic [agent]."[85] Even the countess's death brings proof of comparative aesthetic value and of prosperity, when she is honored posthumously in London with a bust of her image in bronze *mezzo-rilievo*; her stillness in posterity exceeds Rupert's aesthetic value as a photograph, postcard, or lantern slide of a "typical Negro." But if he can overlook the ignominy, if he can just tough it out, her death and sculptural confinement can facilitate his access to the powerful patrons made possible by their friendship, including the friendship with her nephew solidified by their world tour.

The cigar smoke in a photograph of a Haitian woman who faces Harry Johnston's camera full on, and of her two children, naked, their hands either reaching for her, or marking themselves off from the inevitable, gestures toward a withholding, an elusiveness, something kept back and protecting their full access to Johnston, Greaves, and whoever has assisted these men in waylaying her and her children to pose. (At any rate, I am aware of how much I am invested in such a reading.) It is a reminder to separate the will of the photographer from that of the sitter.[86] Early in *Rupert Gray* the busy efficiency of multiple departments of Rupert Gray's firm unfolds into the frenzy of Port of Spain's harbor district on a normal workday, a concatenation of movements on land and water that is meant to showcase the city's bustling modernity. Two groups of social actors are particularly striking in this "vortex of survival": "industrious Indian matrons—red-spittled Madrassees" and "white-aproned Bimshire wives."[87] These are Indian and Barbadian immigrants (or their Caribbean-born daughters) selling fruit or purchasing goods from wholesale merchants to resell in smaller quantities. The attire, fruit, and buckets of the two groups of women, read as exotic, charm visitors and render them "peripheral props" of both a modern colony and Rupert's class. These are snapshots of a sort, of minor characters who are there to convey both the scale of the city's industry, and the social polity over which Rupert Gray and his class are poised to share power with (as yet reluctant) white local and expatriate authorities.

In his bid to move (cautiously) toward social equality with the colony's social élite, Rupert's journey to ownership (rather than just management) of cocoa estates, to which we turn in the next chapter, is not conceived in terms of solidarity with others of nonélite origin such as the "East Indians who are landed proprietors and taxpayers in the southern district here assembled," hundreds of whom gathered in 1909 to present, "in Hindustani," an "address and purse" to the warden of Trinidad's Naparima district.[88] Rupert Gray aspires to social affinity with white (English or English-descended) Trinidadians and visitors. The novel seeks to release him from typicality in order to demonstrate that he is more properly to be understood as a friend of powerful people who take photographs, in a process that requires that these women be arrested in asynchronous time. Their journeys and transactions within Trinidad (including stopping to be posed, to anticipate, deflect, and protect their children from resident and visiting élite strollers, including those wielding cameras), and possibly also their regional and global journeys and transactions, are not meant be read as cosmopolitan, or as capable of driving the narrative forward. Their complexity must give way to Rupert's complex emergence.

4

PLOTTING INHERITANCE

By the end of *Rupert Gray: A Tale in Black and White* (1907) and *The Sword of Nemesis* (1909) each suave, well-read male protagonist—"a statue of Apollo carved out of ebony," and with a "cultured looking face of ebony"—has charmed one heiress (dead before the novel's end) into bequeathing him some or all of her fortune, and married another, the last of the line of a white Caribbean plantation family.[1] The process by which each man has come to own and preside over the great house while clarifying his credentials as one of the era's Caribbean New Negroes is one of the preoccupations of this chapter.[2] These fictional protagonists of the early twentieth century preside over unencumbered properties as both self-made (even though one of them is recovering the stolen inheritance of his parents) and uninterested in revenge.

The sometimes-violent redistribution of wealth by which this resolution is achieved must be rendered in the genteel and aesthetic terms demanded by the genre and conform to the norms of respectability of the Black lower-middle class from which the novelists have emerged: attempted lynching, but also crumpets, tea, and philosophical musings. How a white, eastern Caribbean heiress, groomed to give birth to offspring who will consolidate white futurity, is seduced by a Black beau's superior intellect and troubling virility, also interests us here. Her husband displaces her father as the legal as well as moral arbiter of an inheritance which she cannot be seen to claim and dispose of on her own terms; she is the (sometimes spectral) medium through which this wealth is transferred from one male to another. The generosity of dead heiresses suggests that older sources of wealth must be identified and secured, even as they are being rendered obsolete (fictionally, at least) by other systems of power. Throughout, the capacity to accumulate always seems to fall away from the social subject marked as Black and female even when, as in one instance, she ostensibly presides over the great house.

Even as this chapter shifts to neighborhoods and coasts as sites for the consolidation or unraveling of hierarchy and racial order, we have already seen that Trinidad's botanical gardens and the nearby Savannah are key locations for the rehearsal of imperial losses and gains, as the backdrop for Carnival bands' reenactments of the Boer War, the postures and patriotic songs of a police parade, and a countess's narration of her own bloody family history of accumulation by conquest. The collection and identification of specimens of flora, on the basis of which Rupert Gray bonds with the countess as they share their credentials as amateur botanists, is directly connected to the afterlife of enslavement and conquest. We might think of her intrusive photography, and the friendship that ensues nonetheless, as their era's reckoning with long-standing attempts at rendering labor, leisure, and the ownership of human and botanical property aesthetically and morally palatable. Botanical *gardens*, as sources of food, spaces of solace and creativity, and opportunities to display wealth and social position, evoke the well-kept grounds of an estate or a suburban garden, but they also gesture to the *yerbero*'s *el monte* that is the successor to *marronage* cultivation and to the provision grounds of slavery's plantation economy.[3]

The Savannah, through which the vacationing countess takes her daily constitutional from the nearby Queens Park Hotel, abuts streets and neighborhoods that cut across multiple social and cultural constituencies. Belmont, at the Savannah's eastern edge, is a thriving community of multi-class and -ethnic African-born and -descended Trinidadians, not unlike Laventille, Belmont's neighbor in the East Dry River district. Laventille, as we have seen, made a ruckus in the 1900 Carnival season with its Laventille Boers, but two decades earlier the Newgate Carnival band, "composed of an agglomeration of the worst characters who have arrived here from the neighboring English-speaking islands for their own countries' good but as a curse to this colony," was accused of attacking the "Venezuelan Soldiers" band in the February 1883 Carnival season.[4] The *Fair Play* editorial quoted here throws shade on Barbadian and other eastern Caribbean immigrants deemed to be polluting the Trinidadian landscape with rowdy outsiders. This cultural struggle over physical and symbolic space was multilayered; the rowdies in the Newgate band were said to be "boatmen, carters or loafers"; their name, invoking London's notorious prison, signaling opposition to law and order, similar to the Laventille Boers' nomenclature of imperial disloyalty. But Barbadian immigrants were also employed by the cynical colonial authorities as constables in the Trinidad police force, a terrorizing English-speaking buffer for the francophone Creole-speaking populace.

North of Laventille, the more respectable neighborhood of Belmont is also home to immigrants from the southeastern Caribbean—George Lamming would later marvel at its households in which "the only Trinidadians were the children"—while its shrines for Elegba and Agwé, its Rada/Dahomean social center, and its lanes and stick fight yards with Ewe/Fon and Kikongo names also identify it as a stronghold of migrants entering Trinidad from across West Africa after the abolition of the British slave trade and British slavery: both indentured laborers, and captives bound for slavery in Brazil and Cuba whom the Royal Navy released and resettled in Trinidad.[5] Praised for its well-laid-out streets, concrete sidewalks, and "artistic" houses, early twentieth-century Belmont is the sort of multi-ethnic and cross-class home of an emerging Black middle class from which the fictional Rupert Gray could come, though he might also be from another incubator for that class, several miles away, along the Arima Corridor in a town or village such as Tunapuna. In his accounts of his own intellectual formation, C. L. R. James, born a year after Lord Inventor sings "Climbing Majuba Hill," and six years old when *Rupert Gray: A Tale in Black and White* is published, roots himself squarely in the legacy of first-generation parents born to Protestant eastern Caribbean migrants in his own Tunapuna household and that of his aunts a few streets over.[6] He is *placed* in Tunapuna, inheriting a deep pleasure in books from his convent-schooled mother, and a strong sense, from family stories of a grandfather once frantically summoned by white estate managers to fix a problem in the boiler room (possibly on an estate in Barbados), that technical expertise, imagination, and creativity are the obvious gifts of a Black labor force that extends these to their white managers, and to the world.

Repeated to grandchildren in another place and time, this story about a Barbadian boiler room is a claim on the estate that cannot be *ownership*, but that can assert, *We run the estate, even if its profits are not shared with us and our expertise is not credited; these colonies are built on our skill, physical exertion, and theoretical calculation.* The plantation might demand productive time according to its strict schedule, from sunup to sundown, but even (or especially?) under duress its labor force inserts other times, imbued with other meanings and rhythms. Even as his family epitomizes the prim, starched respectability that James terms "Puritan" and that is more often designated "Victorian," he and his siblings are scolded for their attraction to Carnival and to ne'er-do-wells on the cricket field, suggesting that this new generation breaches linguistic and class boundaries. The James household is driven by divergent desires at the same time that it is firmly anchored in multiple regional geographies, and a strong sense of a significant legacy that can be narrated in all of its contradictions. While Cobham's novel keeps its eye trained on Rupert Gray's management skills, and his versatility as technical and financial supervisor, and intellectual aesthete, we remain curious about the silence regarding his genealogy, or even his borough of origin. Why must he be cut off from family and place, when Pierre, a character we are primed to patronize, can say that his parents are Barbadian and Yoruba (thereby making Belmont a possible birthplace)? Why is it that we can know where Rupert Gray *works*, but not where he *lives*?

West of the Savannah is Port of Spain's wealthiest neighborhood, St. Clair, on the edge of which is the cocoa estate that Rupert Gray's employer has renovated for his daughter. A rerouted river allows her to fish on the property, and the nearby St. Clair tramcar conveys passengers to Port of Spain: the city encroaches on the domain of the rural landowning class, or a rural landholding class inches toward "town." Rupert crosses and recrosses the border between this estate and his workplace at the Port of Spain docks, as the novel's plotline positions him to inherit both the estate and the business. In the early years of the century, the eastern Caribbean novel stakes out an *ebony* claim to political rights, interpreted in part as coming into possession of an *estate* (not a barracks and not a Belmont house, thank you very much), and with an owner who can plant his feet firmly on the ground, among the living.

Rather than doing away with or otherwise conquering estate time, then, there is a bid here to reframe it, to revivify it, just as that Cuban Revolution–era planter evoked in my introduction reinvested his money and kept things moving. In a time that turns toward Port of Spain's asphalted streets, the estate is kept visible and viable, inviting us to pay attention to space, time, and desire. Who can live in a mortal space, and at what cost? Who occupies mythic space (whether underground, in heaven, or a cabin in the woods) and is this liberating or imprisoning? In any case, a successful novel should end, as *Rupert Gray* does, with its eponymous Black middle-class protagonist *coming home* to St. Clair in the evenings, rather than leaving as a guest who is really an employee. In this era of upstarts, that is, the coordinates of estates and gardens are respecified, as new movements and gestures are rehearsed. Rupert's marriage to Gwendoline suggests a successful but precarious replotting, as he walks (or accepts transgressive carriage rides) between the city where he works, and an estate just beyond St. Clair, where a white father threatens to lynch him.

A *problem* identified in chapter 3, an anxiety about the intimate partners of Black professional men, reveals itself here in a more aspirational highbrow setting, though with no relief from either salacious newspaper reporting or the courtroom. Forged wills and broken betrothals are some of the ways in which these novels stage issues of masculine authority and inheritance. Marriage is a conundrum for these male protagonists. It is key to foundational fictions, to be sure, as in Latin America, though we are interested in non-white protagonists who wish to assert their authority in the face of white and near-white elite opposition or paternalism; and in an era in which US African American writers play out the fraught postabolition scenarios of attempting to reunite with or not recognizing one's spouse, we will attend to Caribbean versions of the *problem* of a first love.[7] The marriage plot is a placeholder for figuring out questions of cultural equivalence in imperial and colonial contexts. Rites and relations with the whiff of nonmodernity threaten the prestige of Black and brown men who must answer simultaneously to colonial authorities, local and metropolitan white wealth, their own local and global coterie of the Talented Tenth, and the working classes they claim to lead. A youthful betrothal or a first wife flags anxieties about obsolescence and atavism. A spouse who is a (white) New Woman also poses a threat to nonwhite masculine authority. The means by which this class of men chooses from among prospective marital partners (including wealthy and educated nonwhite women) has to be carefully plotted.

These texts are obsessed with questions of heredity and lineage; their conversations about Darwin and monkeys feel closer to mid-nineteenth-century preoccupations. In *The Negro in the New World* Harry H. Johnston proposes that "negroes" are unable "to start the children from a higher level than the parents" even though this racial group is hardy, or, as he put it, "unextinguishable," an image of stasis, even regression, that seems also innate.[8] In *Sword of Nemesis*, wealthy neighbors as well as journalists and religious leaders collude in ostracizing Mrs. Woodhouse and her son, Carl (a darker-skinned family in white and putatively white social circles), when they are turned out of their home. Carl, stripped of everything but his own intelligence, endurance, and goodwill (and thus, in a moral sense, stripped of nothing), has to start over, and thus by the time he recovers his parents' property he is *self-made*. Rather than some inherent deficiency in the Woodhouses, then, their loss of property redounds to social isolation—the moral failure of a community which ought to have supported them. Downplaying the entitlement of birth relative to moral and intellectual capacity, the novel still insists, or admits, that breeding rather than blood is innate. As one character puts it, "What is in de bones can' [can't] come out, and when a pusson is bring up a lady or a gentleman de real character will always shine 'bove de pot sut [soot]."[9] The working-class character who pronounces this concedes her own noneligibility for this category. Linking "real character" (breeding?) to physiognomy, she names aesthetic and moral considerations for Black and brown writers and their protagonists. Physical appearance or *countenance*, morality, and the conventional tropes that give pleasure to readers of fiction are all deeply entangled. The blackness of soot would seem to be a problem that must be solved, disavowed, or claimed defiantly.

Perhaps this is why, though his character is at least loosely based on H. Sylvester Williams, the Trinidadian founder of the Pan-African Association, Rupert Gray steers clear of that continent, except for the world tour that he takes with the countess's nephew, one leg of which skirts the Nile. Africa is invoked cautiously, if at all, by a Black character who must listen politely while a kodaking countess recites her family's exploits in Pretoria, or in a social world in which a Jamaican audience titters when Sydney Olivier chides Sylvester Williams for claiming the right to speak on Africa's behalf. Part of what is being negotiated in Black-authored texts are the terms on which the African continent can be represented—explicitly or obliquely, but certainly without rancor—as part of an ongoing engagement with questions of origin and heritage, as well as the violent displacements of the contemporary moment. Allusion to the continent or to people of African descent can cast Black people as regressive in relation to discourses of modernity, or position diasporic communities as modern in relation to a presumed continental stasis. Olivier's rebuke of Williams underlines the sense in which the continent is viewed as being under the jurisdiction of white imperial authorities. In this sense Rupert Gray's declaration of self-generation in the botanical gardens could be read as a brisk pragmatism, rather than betokening shame or disavowal, in a world in which white experts speak for both continental and diasporic blackness. As we will see, West African discussions of equivalence in this period are framed by a sense that European domination, though unavoidable, is also morally and spiritually deficient relative to local and regional mores.

But Caribbean middle-class men such as the authors of *Sword of Nemesis* and *Rupert Gray* demand of colonial authorities and dubious local élites the right to participate in political life as equals, and within the parameters of respectability. It would be unusual, that is, for an appeal *of equivalence* to be made on behalf of beliefs or practices deemed to be non-Christian, so delicate are the threads separating Black respectability from a presumption of savagery and, I am assuming, so distasteful are such beliefs, anyway, for many middle-class Black Caribbean Christians. At the same time, defending against the charge of heathenism entails a critique of Europe's moral hypocrisy. Caribbean people have not lost their souls by succumbing to a zealous investment in rationality that is unable to appreciate otherworldliness, coincidence, visits from the dead, ghosts. Still, it is usually white characters in the fiction under discussion here, for instance, who refer to non-Christian traditions, so precarious would a discussion of this by a middle-class Black character be held to be. Similarly, I would not expect that the Black Caribbean novelists I discuss would approve of working-class concubinage or advocate for the legality of Hindu marriage, even as they know that for white people in the region having children outside of marriage does not diminish the social power of whiteness.

"The Caribbean, it turns out, is a space that learned to 'read' itself in literature through Gothic fiction."[10] Lizabeth Paravisini-Gebert's reminder that the earliest authors of Gothic fiction owned property, including human property, in the Caribbean—that their desires and appetites made the space terrifying—suggests that Caribbean-authored texts, including by Black writers, must figure out the consequences of this terror and of its representation for Black life. If the Caribbean is where Europe displaces one troubling side of itself—brutal punishment, inappropriate consumption, usurped heirs—the extent to which the region's perceived belatedness makes possible Europe's timeliness, its modernity, must be reckoned with. Caribbean characters occupy space in the European novel as temporal and moral foils to Europeans. Bertha Mason Rochester bides time in an estate in rural England because she has outstayed her usefulness: her family's inheritance having been invested in her husband's financial security, she now stands in the way of his marital happiness and (presumably) reproductive future; she is the kind of "minor" character, Alex Woloch proposes, who, in objecting to her confinement, is disruptive in both a social sense and at the level of form.[11] What can traditionally confined characters become in this new time, and who remains confined to traditional roles—trapped in a subplot for comedic purposes, for example—to facilitate the movement of the *ebony* protagonists under consideration here?

With their frequent invocations of Cowper and Shakespeare and Mrs. Corelli, *Rupert Gray* and *Sword of Nemesis sound* out of time to us, as if they precede De Lisser's Jane or James Joyce's Stephen Daedalus by generations, instead of just a few years. It is possible that these novels might already be viewed as belated in their own time, just as Edwardians are ridiculed for cleaving to Victorian sensibilities in an age of modernism. Such ridicule, with its assumption of a clear distinction between a forward-looking age and another, ornery one obsessed with the past, can be valuable "as a symptom of the self-conscious awareness of living in a moment of transition that pervaded the Edwardian imagination."[12] We want to test a similar awareness in the Caribbean novel about being *in time*, and in which the protagonists' cultured sonority always signifies as modern and desirable, even as another time is also implied.

Some three decades earlier, the Trinidadian intellectual John Jacob Thomas lamented the continuing conflation of blackness with servitude, years after slavery's abolition; we might say that while he assumed that his postabolition plantation society needed to catch up to the present, it was he who was presumed to be speaking out of time.[13] He used the physical toll on his own body and his lack of access to resources that would have enabled him to move gracefully or to write wittily, to argue that it was a failure of imagination and a frivolous attachment to style at the expense of ethics to assume that he was deficient without these resources. But in this new age Thomas can only be claimed by someone like Rupert Gray in a politely admiring way, as a sort of prickly uncle. When Thomas is invoked in the novel it is deeply ambivalent, his name stuttered by a character we are invited to patronize. When this generation is admired for its erudition, it wants to look and sound suave. It also wants to befriend élite interlocutors (local or metropolitan) rather than fight righteously for a usurped inheritance as does Emmanuel Appadocca, the eponymous hero of the 1854 precursor to *Rupert Gray* and *Nemesis*.[14] Appadocca's erudite resentment failed to secure his stolen inheritance, and this generation is betting that a different strategy will win the day.

How to Court a "Spanish" and Then Get Rid of Her

At a key point in *The Sword of Nemesis* a mother and her young son, traveling by boat in the dead of night from Montserrat to Trinidad, are waylaid by kidnappers who whisk the little boy away in another boat.[15] As horrific as this experience is, the fact that they are traveling at all is already disastrous proof of their disinheritance. Turned out of their estate home by what we will come to learn is a false accusation that she has deceived her husband and brought about his murder, this "swarthy" mother and "ebony" son prompt a key question to which we will keep returning in different ways: what is it about them (and about her in particular) that sets them adrift? What prevents her social status as (at least) the wife of an estate owner from *sticking*? Is it that their nonwhiteness makes it difficult for accumulation to attach to them? I read *The Sword of Nemesis* as working out issues of inheritance, accumulation, and usable pasts, with Venezuela as a crucial nodal point even when Venezuela *qua* Venezuela is neither named nor implied, as it had been in *Emmanuel Appadocca*; *Nemesis* inherits *Venezuela* as an aspect of Trinidad's genealogy that must now take its place as a relic.

Here we could ask what it means to see Venezuela from Trinidad, as we track not only contemporary journeys taken by Trinidadians in the early twentieth century, but questions of governance and cultural inheritance. Getting or retrieving the estate requires not just a negotiation of Protestant whiteness but (at least in *Nemesis*) confronting the lingering question of the Spanish Catholicism of the earliest conquest in the region. To see Venezuela from Trinidad is to recognize the massive traffic between their coasts. If political exiles wait things out in Trinidad during the nineteenth century, then nonelites also go to Trinidad from Venezuela as agricultural laborers. So do *Warrahouns/Guaragons* traveling back and forth between mainland and island in canoes, making indigeneity dynamic and legible.

If Trinidad is the great regional and global magnet for labor, it is also the case that Trinidadians seek work in Venezuela, and Lara Putnam directs our attention to how African-descended Trinidadians fare, alongside other English- and French-speaking eastern Caribbean islanders, when they travel to Venezuela to seek employment.[16] Spurned by Trinidad and Venezuela in different ways, Black Trinidadians find themselves unwelcome beyond their ability to give military service to Venezuelan authorities or political rebels, while Black Grenadians and Vincentians traveling by boat between both territories are prevented from disembarking without paying fines. Many travelers thus find themselves at the receiving end of Venezuelan ire: forced to work in road-building gangs, beaten for protesting their situation, rounded up and boarded on coast guard vessels, and "forced at gunpoint overboard."[17] While many of these incidents occur in the early 1930s, some of the compensation claims brought by British Caribbean subjects to Venezuela refer to our moment. We might consider the case of Trinidad-born Benjamin, living in Venezuela from 1908: married to a Venezuelan, raising children, and paying taxes, he is arrested one day, conscripted to labor, then dumped off the coast of Point Icacos, where he has to find his way ashore.[18] As with Jamaican workers in Cuba, he appears vulnerable to the category of unwanted outsider, and we must wonder how his racial identity catapults him into this categorization. How are he and others to be understood as both exceeding the project of Venezuelan nationalism, and, from Trinidad's point of view, insufficiently British subjects?

The body of water between these territories is the site of a long history of contention among European powers, from Bolivar's 1819–1820 liberation of Gran Colombia (which until 1830 included Venezuela) to feuds among early twentieth-century German, British, and Haitian factions. Coastal towns, islands between other islands, islands between island and mainland, islands on the margins of mainland territories: these are visible or not, in relation to land disputes, as people travel back and forth—daily and for centuries—in the wake of the island's geographical break from the South American continent. From 1777 Trinidad was a province of the vice-captaincy of Venezuela; an invitation to Catholics to settle in Trinidad and receive land based on number of slaves and racial identification expanded the population, set the tone for its Catholic/Latin character, and cemented its racial hierarchies. The last Spanish governor ceded the colony to the British in 1797.[19] Becoming British meant severing a formal tie to South America, but a constant stream of migrants from Venezuela maintained the connection, including "*cocoa panyols*," the affectionate and disparaging term for workers on cocoa estates, who "arrived in Trinidad as 'mixed' people . . . African-Amerindian-Spanish," as well as upper-class Venezuelans who sent their children to school and shopped in Trinidad, or who lived there, supplementing Trinidad whiteness.[20] Sylvia Moodie-Kublalsingh refers to a "Hispanic Venezuelan ribbon" as part of Trinidad's cultural formation, noting its linguistic impact on Trinidad Creole.[21] For Aisha Khan, in Trinidad a "Spanish" signals an identity with shifting registers: texture of hair, color of skin, region of Trinidad, non-Protestant, non-British, having pride in Trinidadian culture, rural, and Afro- or Indo-Trinidadian depending on who is speaking. Venezuela, as an actual place or as a symbolic placeholder, registers alongside or as an alternative to indigenous constituencies, and as deployed through "Spanish" it can mark a "dilution" of potential antagonisms associated with a more obvious site of conflict.[22]

Emmanuel Appadocca's protagonist, whose description, compared to his "black" companions is "Quadroon," "in the infinity of grades connected with Spanish America," bequeaths a racial *casta* system to the early

twentieth-century novels that is either preserved in formaldehyde and waiting to be cast off, or lurking in designations such as "ebony."[23] A brilliant,
Paris-trained mathematician and philosopher, Appadocca presses his father,
a Trinidad plantation owner, to admit his exploitation and abandonment of
himself and his mother, the young woman whom he presumably owned.
Christopher Taylor reads the novel in terms of a tarrying with Venezuela
and with Trinidad's Spanish history that represents the failure to cathect;
he contends that in the wake of imperial abandonment to the free market,
as English-speaking Caribbean people experienced neglect rather than a
pathway to political and economic autonomy, they turned toward Spanish America and away from the British empire, and then toward the United
States by the end of the nineteenth century.[24] Taylor sees in Feliciana, the
young Venezuelan woman whom Appadocca meets when he washes up on
Venezuelan shores, an opportunity to acknowledge and accept her care, and
to move on from abandonment to mourning.

I am interested in what Feliciana can inherit and what space she can occupy in her movement from Venezuelan daughter to Appadocca's companion. She and her *ranchero* father and the *llaneros* he employs (cattle rancher
and herdsmen) live a "half barbarous" existence that is not driven by plantation capital—in a space of comfort in which Spanish saddles and indigenous
hammocks are fully incorporated. This is a rendering of Venezuela as a quasi-
mythical space that tests and proves Appadocca's heroism, as he wrestles with
sharks and wild animals to get to the mainland. But this hospitality exudes a
drowsy obsolescence that sends him back toward Trinidad. Following him
there, Feliciana seems to float above the ground, traveling only at night, accompanied by a Trinidadian warner-woman/*houngan* figure, and while this
demonstrates her openness to Black companionship this will not be the only
time that we will ask if it is the fate of Black women to bear up white women.
Like Feliciana, Appadocca also seems to skulk around the Trinidad city at
night, whereas his father walks freely through the Savannah to his home in
St. Ann. Ultimately, the Venezuelan solidity of haciendas that she offers him
feels insufficient, defunct.

Generations later *The Sword of Nemesis* reserves a place for "Spanish"
maidens, though this time on Trinidadian soil. Once again, as with Appadocca, a young man fighting for his inheritance washes up on shore after
almost drowning. Here he is rescued by the father of Rita, the "Spanish" who
becomes his first love. Her feet planted firmly on earth and fully inhabiting

the present (unlike *Appadocca*'s ghostly Feliciana who remains a Venezuelan revenant within the Trinidad landscape) *Nemesis*'s Rita must nevertheless be replaced if Carlito is to move forward. The wake marking her father's passing, which introduces us to their community, suggests moral disorder. Carlito (whom we soon discover is the little boy stolen from his mother on the boat) teaches Rita that Catholicism is equivalent to Protestantism, presumably a lesson in comparative religion that he had learned as a little boy from his father, who had also taught him about Buddhism. Rita is referred to at one point as an "Inca princess," suggesting how indigeneity gives way to and then joins "Spanish" in becoming defunct. Rita is a "Spanish" who promises wealth that, when attached to her living body, cannot buy anything in the modern world. While Feliciana spends the rest of her life mourning Appadocca's rejection of her companionship and then his death in the 1854 novel, Rita's devotion earns her a betrothal, though Carlito is bound by his good word to what is in effect a millstone. She will have to release him into the future, to a better match, and she does so, presiding over her own withering away, and giving her inheritance to Carlito on her deathbed. Unlike Appadocca, then, Carlito gets an inheritance out of this "Spanish" connection, and thus before retrieving his parents' stolen property he has begun a process of accumulation that makes him independent of both the parental inheritance he recovers and the one he acquires by marriage.

Since "Venezuelans" whether indigenous or élite, or as part of Afro-, Indo-, or any other constituency, are anything but defunct in Trinidad in the early twentieth century (or, for that matter, today) it is interesting that this novel focuses squarely on a Protestant-ish Trinidadian future (as does *Rupert Gray*) as if Britishness, or at least Englishness, has more to offer socially mobile Black social actors than a Spanish/"Spanish" identity. Though never explicitly invoked, then, I am suggesting that *Venezuela* (a term I am using in a deliberately nonspecific sense to imply something like a meaningful historical and geographical connection to mainland, indigenous, or hispanicized contexts that constitutes an inheritance that is worth accumulating and passing on) withers away fictionally from its role in the earlier novel as a parallel and largely off-stage place of respite, from which to return to Trinidad and attempt to claim one's birthright. After rescuing and enriching the protagonist it is as if *Nemesis* streamlines and puts "Spanish" origins in storage, with "Carlito de la Mar," the name given him when the community rescues him from the water, as the only trace.

But *Nemesis* rehabilitates another inheritance from *Emmanuel Appadoca* as Zac, the character who prophesies the misfortune that turns Mrs. Woodhouse and Carl/ito out of their home, parallels and updates both Feliciana's nighttime companion and Jack Jimmy, a character who seems drawn from the minstrel stage. Zac's home in the woods, on the property of the Woodhouse estate, becomes a space for Mrs. Woodhouse and those of her white and near-white neighbors who have not abandoned her. There they debate spiritual and theological questions that constitute the moral conscience of the novel (since the villainy that casts the Woodhouses from their home can be freely worked out and declared to be unjust) but that also veer perilously toward Obeah. We could read Zac as an updated Hamel, Cynric Williams's spiritual leader from an earlier fictional Gothic generation that, as Candace Ward has persuasively argued, represents both the threat of enslaved rebellion and the persuasive argument for the "revolutions in manners" by which a population not ready for freedom is supervised by a rational planter class.[25] Is such a figure loyal, or a violent threat; atavistic or modern? By the 1930s the fictional Obeah man is still a destructive figure who cannot be accommodated into the present and future and must be obliterated; even in complex renderings this figure exceeds the boundaries of an appropriate modernist present and future.[26] So how is it that, at a historical moment when Black men in the woods are precisely the figures who are demonized for kidnapping and sacrificing white children, Zac is recuperable, able to make it into the future, when Feliciana and ranchero-*llanero*-Venezuela, Rita and her father cannot, and when his employer, Mrs. Woodhouse, is redeemed, but precariously?[27]

Zac's cabin convenes a discussion of sorcery—"peculiarly a Negro art, and the unfortunate darky has often to hang down his head at the charge of being a representation of a race peculiarly noted for its superstitions"—that has to be recuperated within a careful comparativist contextualization of Greeks, Romans, Arabs, and Anglo-Saxons, and astrology, necromancy, crystallomancy, and hydromancy, and by the visiting lawyer whose white cosmopolitan liberalism allows him to make this translation that Zac and Carlito's mother cannot or dare not.[28] Nevertheless, Zac "has access to my law books, and is 'studying for the Bar,' he says."[29] Quietly biding time, aware of his visitors' patronizing image of him as the loyal, eternal estate retainer, Zac is headed toward a legal career. Utilizing what we recognize by now as a code for a defiant and versatile modernity (though without assuming that it will be legible as such to his interlocutors) Zac declares, "I am from the brave Zulu race, with no mixture," in a passage that invokes darkness and light, civilization and savagery, black skin, monkeys, and black tricks. Zac thus critiques and trades in ideas of blackness as requiring rehabilitation, and as apocalyptic transformation: "My appearance will some day change into the brightness of the stars of the morning."[30]

Zac is part of the novel's general contention that older theological and spiritual systems should not feel self-conscious in the face of the modernizing rationality of science. Dreams and portents drive the plot forward and also have to be carefully matched, as if *vetted*, to bodies in the social world, since all these systems jostling together are potentially precarious for bodies in Caribbean space. As a good reader of signs (that many respectable characters would interpret as his superstition or satanism) he prophesies the murder of Mrs. Woodhouse's husband that catapults her out of her home and into the wilderness. But élite cosmopolitan characters like Mrs. Woodhouse and Carlito, unable to read a wide array of signs, are susceptible to the schemes of forgery of racially prejudiced neighbors and classmates. This is a failure of literacy.

Nemesis must navigate between the generic convention that blackness strains the moral and physiognomical credibility of character delineation and this novel's insistence that its élite characters' African descent is an important part of their morality and their social entitlement. Thus Carl is "almost black," with his mother's "beautiful ebony complexion," his lips are "not thin" but it "could not be said" that they were Ethiopian, and he has a "finely-shaped head" suggesting a "well-developed brain," and a nose that while "not aquiline" is in proportion with his face.[31] Mary Highfield, Rita's successor for Carl's romantic interest, is a blue-eyed, Roman-nosed, golden-haired belle who, "though an octaroon . . . might have passed for white."[32] Daphne, a rival who threatens the romantic conclusion of the novel with her "black, lustrous eyes" and "beautiful brown" "complexion," accuses Carl of "marrying out of [his] own race," instead of [looking] near home."[33] Thus Mary Highfield appears to have been bumped "up" to white-without-question, illustrating the ideological predicament for a protagonist who must be simultaneously race-conscious and a visually credible heir to the Highfield estate.

Just as we will see for Rupert Gray, Carlito's engagement to Mary is socially transgressive, and both *Nemesis* and *Rupert Gray* allude to Shakespeare's *Othello* to underline this. In each case the protagonist's wish to marry the white or putatively white daughter of a local landed planter earns him the violent ire of the father, and Carlito has to insist to his future father-in-law that "God has made of one blood all nations," the Biblical line that provides the title of

Pauline Hopkins's novel of the same period.[34] In both novels the daughter is the only child and thus the last of the line, and wooing and winning her is a crucial part of addressing the acquisition and management of the estate, still a powerful repository for postabolition social relations in this era. Both novels are working out who can be represented as owning it, and under what conditions, including moral considerations still lingering from slavery, and aesthetic ones concerning the tension between utility and pleasure.[35] Thus the Montserrat and Trinidad estates described in the novel provide the picturesque setting of philosophical discussions and evening strolls, and yet they are also working sugar plantations with "thick black smoke."[36] Here strolling the plantation ends with a beverage in the boiling house, though for estate owners and their neighbors rather than for United Fruit Company tourists.

Carl's retrieval of his family's inheritance, and his successful wooing of a golden-haired heiress, comes with the important condition that he understands his indebtedness to the society that has made way for him (even though he is recovering property stolen from his parents). As if to reassure the community that they are not dangerous, both Carl and Zac save vulnerable white characters in parallel incidents involving runaway animals. Furthermore, Carl pays off the debts of the prospective father-in-law who had disapproved of his daughter Mary's interest in a nonwhite man. Carl rescues him from "villainous money-grabbers" by mortgaging the estates that Rita bequeathed to him, and then hires him to be his attorney.[37] To come into possession of the great house (whether the one stolen from his parents, or the one he now keeps in the possession of the family of Mary, his future wife) is to agree to subsidize its *traditional* owners, and to do so cheerfully.[38]

Returning to a scene of a mother and child whisked away by boat in the dead of night, then, we want to know why Carlito's mother, who, after all, begins the novel presiding over Elmsdale Cottage, cannot maintain the right to look out from an eminent position. Which spaces can accommodate her and which spaces render her presence untenable for others? In our earliest impression of her as mistress of Elmsdale, we learn that she is "a swarthy woman of dignified appearance," with the "delicate and refined" features that "the ancient Greeks and Romans loved to give to their goddesses," and with an accent "acquired on the Continent."[39] If Rita, a "Spanish," could not accompany an heir into the future, she certainly enriched that future, even while accommodating her own extinction, but Black women such as Carlito's mother seem to be *shackles* for the era's Black men, with both a "swarthiness" that must be carefully (and constantly?) qualified, and the "superstitious tendencies" that place her on the wrong side of a delicate spiritual equation.[40]

A lingering moral question from the generation of enslavement offers clues to the question of the eligibility of the Woodhouse family to inherit and maintain estate ownership, and to the particularity of Mrs. Woodhouse's eligibility. Her husband inherits his wealth from his white English father, who, like the Sav-la-Mar Clarkes, has stumbled into it; arriving in Montserrat from England he "worked hard until he became one of the potent sugar princes of the West Indies." With syntax that frames him as the object of her wiles and appears to elide the fact that she is also his property, he is "attracted by the eldest daughter of one of his slaves," and educates her, before she becomes a "victim to the passions of her benefactor." Though "he was not proof against one of the worst social crimes that prevailed then" (because it would have been hard not to succumb to what everyone else was doing?) it is nonetheless made clear that he has exploited his position, so that a common feature of Caribbean slavery is not rendered normal or acceptable.[41] After living in concubinage, they marry (he "repaired the wrong") after their son Burleigh Woodhouse is born. A *natural* son, he receives a continental European education, and inherits five or six plantations and seventy thousand pounds.

If the ease with which the Woodhouse family can be stripped of its inheritance is an outcome of this earlier event, it is striking that Mrs. Woodhouse, a newcomer to the family, comes to be partly or wholly the source or sign of its vulnerability. Could this be because her "swarthiness" connects her in a particular way to her mother-in-law's status? Or because she commits the social violation of not holding up someone else, as a Black female companion supports Feliciana's *ranchera*-walking in *Appadocca*? Mrs. Woodhouse is propertied and married and yet her very body appears to disclose a tainting vulnerability. We meet her again, years after the horrifying night in the boat, as the novel bides its time sorting out her son's attempt to extricate himself from his parents' mess—a mess that is putatively the fault of a villainous cousin, but which we can read as the stain of an inheritance from a white grandfather's union with a Black woman. This is the stain that, as we saw in the previous chapter, Rupert Gray is relieved of when he is described as "a gentleman with no ancestry—no history—no past." To claim "parentage," or a "past" is to risk unearthing a Burleigh Woodhouse story that does not affect the capacity of the white father to accumulate wealth and to pass it on but marks the wife and child as always-already "concubine" and "natural."

When *Nemesis* is ready for us to pick up the threads of her story, Mrs. Wood-house is unrecognizable, as if the wealth, breeding, and morality suggested in the novel's opening description are insufficient to overcome female blackness, or to do so in a way that will stick. She is (now) "a poor black woman standing on the bank with an Indian basket on her head.... She might not have been more than forty years old, yet she seemed worn with care. Her once sable ring-lets had been almost entirely converted into silver threads, and an expression of unmistakable sorrow rested on her face. Her clothes were none of the best and were stained with mud and dust."[42] Carl's immediate kindness, so differ-ent from the crowd's response to her, indicates an innate sensitivity and good-ness that elicits her own in response, and this likeminded sensitivity prefigures their eventual mutual recognition. What is crucial here is that bystanders read her as dangerous: they "cast insults at her. One man remarked that she was a witch who had come to dupe the place."[43] With her "silver" hair she ought at least to have been a granny-midwife.[44] Instead she elicits the community's active hostility. Even allowing for the fact that the plot is not yet ready for son and mother to recognize each other, the bystanders' cruelty is striking. Pointing out that Carl is a gentleman they ask him if he is really going to help the "she-devil." Even though he has already been absorbed into the community, her eventual integration will have to occur in spite of this initial experience. On a later trip to Grenada the ship's passengers are surprised that someone of her appearance is in his company. Turned out of her home, then, Mrs. Woodhouse quickly becomes an outcast; and in this new space she is immediately not just a stranger, but a reviled one, whom a crowd perceives as harming *Carl*. Here we are put in mind of Sara Ahmed's proposal that "Strangers are not simply those who are not known in this dwelling, but those who are, in their very proximity, *already recognized as not belonging*, as being out of place."[45] Thus she carries her capacity to stain others around with her. In this sense she re-mains "at sea," in a different way from her son. Outside of the already precari-ous protection that proximity to her property-owning husband had afforded her, she is adrift, suspect, and threatening.

African American and West African Netherworlds

Thus Mrs. Woodhouse, Carlito's mother, lives in a world that is not yet ready to accept that a body like hers could leave the boat as a free woman without question, that assumes that her European continental travel, her accent, and waltzing, must be a veneer. Perhaps Carlito's mother is a lesson, a reminder of what would have happened had he hung on to Rita—a warning that "swarthy" women, no less than Inca princesses who work with their hands, threaten to drag down the charismatic and accomplished inheritor. We must assume that Carlito's father intensifies the transgression of his parents' union by marrying and enabling a "swarthy" belle to preside over the great house. If Zac's future transformation is permissible because he does not transgress his present social boundaries—he keeps the social relations of the estate intact—Mrs. Woodhouse makes space abject. She propels herself into a sort of wilderness, an at-sea-ness, a void: a "nether world" to use a term from Casely Hayford's 1911 novel *Ethiopia Unbound*, discussed below. Though negative in Mrs. Woodhouse's case, such a space could also be a refuge, where one bides time waiting for the world to catch up. It could be viewed in terms of Gloria Anzaldúa's invocation of the "vague and undetermined place created by the emotional residue of an unnatural boundary . . . in a constant state of transition."[46] Perhaps those who reside here are resistant to being incorporated into a formal structure, such as the plantation, the empire, the nation-to-come. Such spaces are inhabited by social subjects who do not fit, or who are in danger of reminding us that we do not fit either, that our time has not yet come, or that (the world having changed around us) something that we are doing no longer makes sense.

We can pursue these spaces and their significance through Pauline Hopkins's portrayal of kinship and accumulation in her novel, *Of One Blood, Or the Hidden Self*, serialized in 1902–3. Hopkins suggests that the cabin in the woods of the US South is the moral conscience of Harvard Square; rather than the abode of mysticism that must wither away to make way for Zac's legal future, Hopkins's cabin holds the key to suppressed family histories and stolen inheritances that haunt the seat of power and knowledge. This is "the living who haunt as if they were dead," to use Avery Gordon's formulation—who hang around inconveniently.[47] Hopkins insists that the turn of the century is haunted by the estate, but while the Caribbean protagonists of *Sword of Nemesis* and *Rupert Gray* try to preside over it by making peace with a sometimes hostile white and near-white planter class, Hopkins is preoccupied with how bodies and psyches buckle under the weight of this haunting. Any hopeful future is overshadowed by the possibility that one's intimate partner could be one's sibling. Any dream of a liberal, leisured life in Harvard Square is haunted by the potential catastrophe underlying putatively legitimate marital partnerships, and by the cabin in the woods as the hidden source of Northern wealth.[48]

In this age of extraction, expeditions, and invasions across the African continent, perhaps the most well-known fiction of the era, Joseph Conrad's *Heart of Darkness*, celebrates this "discovery" of the continent's "interior," arguably questioning its ethical consequences but always firmly conscripting readers into its project of imperial visuality.[49] Hopkins shows how US histories of sexual violation and disinheritance, and European and US imperial exploitation of the African continent are imbricated. Where her Caribbean counterparts approach the African continent with caution in *Nemesis* and *Rupert Gray*, Hopkins takes us deep underground, transforming depredation into a powerful image of autonomy and endurance: an apparently defeated continent waiting for the fullness of time.

Hopkins places her African American protagonist—a brilliant medical student in Harvard Square who does not yet know that he is also the son of the matriarch of the cabin in the woods—on an expedition bound to the Horn of Africa, which provides an opportunity to debate the racial dimensions of US citizenship, and the place of the African continent in world history. As this traveler of African descent stumbles into a hidden kingdom of continental African people, we follow him underground into a place of blinding light. This blinged-out kingdom is an alternative inheritance to the cabin in the woods; the former redeems the latter. It is also a fictional restoration of a kingdom such as that seized from the Benin Oba; thus, a sovereign power can stake a claim without being vulnerable to having treasures stolen and being led away in chains by a European power.

But an African kingdom like Hopkins's fictional Telassar seeking its completion in a US African American savior *mimics* the imperial fantasies of European heroes discovering lost civilizations that it wants to critique. Questioning the efficacy of African American critiques of imperialism, Kwamankra (K), the protagonist of the 1911 novel *Ethiopia Unbound*, by the West African nationalist J. E. Casely Hayford, pronounces W. E. B. Du Bois's idea that two tormented souls, Negro and American, cleave the body apart "pathetic," in its position of weakness and supplication.[50] Anyone looking at the Sphinx, K declares, would see *one* undivided soul. Questioning the underlying assumptions of African American critiques of US and global racism and imperialism and reversing Hopkins's logic of Africans waiting for the arrival of their African American sovereign, K enjoins Africans in the Americas to abandon mimicry of the white man and to assert "African manhood" by looking to their true leaders as models: Western-educated "Ethiopians" in West Africa. Readers are guided in the novel's depiction of the Gold Coast under

British colonialism by a narrative focalization that, following Kwamankra's perspective, sees the irony of a British protectorate that fails to protect; a history of warring African factions exploited by Dutch and English interlopers is discerned by gazing out at contemporary landscapes within the colony. Kwamankra travels widely and his interactions with a range of characters in the Gold Coast, as well as during his studies in Europe, allow him to debate the merits of multiple systems. British civil servants in the Gold Coast are no match for his critique of colonial governance, while conversations in London with an English divinity student demonstrate Fanti's spiritual, cosmological, and philological flexibility and vigor, when compared with Christian, as well as classical, Anglo-Saxon, and Hebrew traditions. Thank goodness that he is a "poor benighted pagan," given Europe's spiritual and moral exhaustion.[51]

Through Kwamankra we learn that Africans in the diaspora are well positioned to learn industrial, technological, and agricultural skills from the West, while the West could learn to appreciate and preserve "national institutions, and the adoption of distinctive garbs and names, much as obtains among our friends the Japanese."[52] Kwamankra's London apartment is "furnished in the Oriental style" with an African-infused East Asian aesthetic: his rooms have silk cushions, leopard skin carpets, and "African weapons" decorating the walls.[53] Kwamankra feels "a thrill of Oriental pride" whenever he "[brushes] against an Asiatic in a garb distinctively Eastern. They aped no one."[54] Recall Partha Chatterjee's discussion, in the introduction, of Bengali's claiming of a superior cultural essence that cannot be penetrated by the West, even as colonized cultures must make peace with a public acknowledgement of the colonizer's advantage: a technological superiority thoroughly driven by the violence of expeditions such as those underway in the African continent. Kwamankra views Japan's imperial ambitions in terms of a Global South sibling that has managed to preserve its cultural soul: "the future of the world is with the East. The nation that can, in the next century, show the greatest output of spiritual strength, that is the nation that shall lead the world, and as Buddha from Africa taught Asia, so may Africa again lead the way."[55]

At the heart of *Ethiopia Unbound* is a debate about socially mobile men who abandon first or "cloth" wives married under traditional law instead of in the "ordinance marriages" recognized by colonial courts. Though Kwamankra seems personally opposed to having more than one spouse, he believes it is a terrible indictment on his society that women are thus abandoned, and he thinks that the British colonial attempt to cast polygyny as backward is misguided and dangerous. It signals a refusal to acknowledge that West Africans have been engaged for centuries in a dynamic process of weighing competing systems. The colonial project's insistence on a singular vision of modernity, which makes first wives out of date, thus creates the conditions for abandoning cloth women for "frock ladies," a desertion which is then condemned by the British as backward.

In arguing for a flexibility that would allow abandoned first wives to continue to be "protected"—"Call it polygamy if you like"—as more reasonable than colonial rigidity and cruelty, *Ethiopia Unbound* makes polygyny the key to its adjudication of an axis often posed as tradition/modernity.[56] Yogita Goyal demonstrates that a colonized territory's ability to gain rights means sacrificing traditions, which has implications for form, with the language of rights utilizing a realist mode, and that of tradition "[traversing] the terrain of romance," and so polygyny is part of the novel's contention that native African customs are more relevant than elaborate and irrelevant Victorian courtship rites.[57] For Donald Wehrs the ethical treatment of women shows the Gold Coast's successful dance with the colonial power, though the novel is silent about Kwamankra's class privilege.[58] But Kwamankra does not himself have more than one wife and we want to press this point, because it takes us beyond polygyny as such to the problem of *any wife* (first, second, or only) whose intellectual, sexual, or financial autonomy is a threat to her husband.

Kwamankra first meets his wife, Mansa, when she is touring Europe after her university studies in West Africa. She impresses him with her preference for Germany's "natural" Black Forest over England's "artificial" society.[59] The "slight tremor in [his] manly voice" when Mansa tells him she is going back to West Africa to be the headmistress of the junior section of the university is an affective response of sensitivity that is precariously demasculinizing, perhaps, but that I also take to be his involuntary reaction to the unbearable prospect of a marriage between two professionals.[60] This is why he must call her a dear "child" in the next moment, as he asks her to change her plans and devote her life to "guiding" him. She agrees to become the "childlike hand that shall guide" him, exchanging her own public professional life for the honor of nurturing the public professional at home. Thus his "tremor" is managed because both of them can cash in on the prestige of their advanced formal education in different gendered spheres. When they marry, Mansa is dressed in "a simple African costume of her own design" that she notes is "proper" and pleasing to her husband.[61] Even as this marks her as having the superior aesthetic tastes that make their community's fabric and styles preferable to European dress, we can also note here what Wehrs terms Hayford's general coyness regarding class. For though local fabric and design mark "cloth wives" as less sophisticated than their "frock lady" counterparts, élite West Africans of Mansa and Kwamankra's social group owned costly textiles from Africa, Europe, and Asia, carefully stored, gifted, and worn as precious heirlooms: that tasteful, "simple" wedding dress is undoubtedly expensive. It is certainly not the imported "Manchester home-spuns" contemptuously associated elsewhere in the novel with the "emasculated sentimentalities" and North American Sankey hymns that pass for Christianity, rather than the traditional Sankofu of a "healthy Fanti manhood."[62] Textile serves as a shorthand for imported inauthenticity as well as for the mass-produced and mass-wearing fabric that distinguishes one class from another.[63] The couple have a son, whom the father schools in the classics (as does Carl's father in *Nemesis*); here, besides *Aesop's Fables*, the recent Japanese victory over Russia in 1904 becomes a lesson in moral and ethnic, civilizational pride, as Ekra Kwow, Kwamankra's son, learns that Christians "claim a monopoly of culture, knowledge and civilization," and cry "Yellow Peril" or "Black Peril" when other groups resist them."[64]

Five years later Mansa dies in childbirth along with their unborn daughter. Kwamankra's grief sets the stage for a state of hypnotic unconsciousness that will allow him to visit Mansa in a vision. She resides in Nanamu-Krome, an otherworldly zone that allows her through a "thin veil" to oversee people on earth who have done their work with humility.[65] I read the consignment of Mansa to this sphere as a discomfort with female sexuality that is also evident when Kwamankra throws her spiritual kisses at her graveside: "Was it possible that the devotion and the trust and the love of his girl-wife had blossomed into a personality which was half god and half human even in the nether world?"[66] This discomfort may be a response to the pressure placed on African intimacies to live up to the religious and political scrutiny of the colonizing project in its various permutations, on the one hand, and to anxieties about "traditional" Fanti-modern or other alternatives, on the other. Colonial perceptions of hypersexual femininity and masculinity, or the queer desire that cannot be explored beyond student days abroad, such as the thrill of brushing against an "Asiatic" in London, are resolved by the chaste husband of an otherworldly, asexual "goddess."

Thus a reformist who wishes to save African women from an oppressive colonial rendering of intimate partnership cannot endure a marital relationship unless his wife is dead and looking on from Nanamu-Krome, from which position she can continue to "guide" him. As Stephanie Newell has shown, turn-of-the-century West African journalists and political reformers tackled marriage and female sexuality obsessively across a range of genres; reporting on marriage legislation and petitioning colonial officials, they also wrote fiction and drama that used "the discursive styles of newspaper editorials and articles, combining social realism with dilemma situations."[67] As a journalist, educator, and barrister in this period before his later career as a member of the Gold Coast legislative council, Casely Hayford, Gold Coast–born and Sierra Leone–and England-educated, was thus in line with, if not central to, the period's cross-generic debates on marriage, gendered roles, and inheritance. In the wake of formal British colonial rule after the "Scramble for Africa" in the 1880s, colonial ordinances governing marriage were among the earliest pieces of legislation, including marriage ordinances for the Gold Coast and for Lagos in 1884, and the 1900 Slander of Women Ordinance No. 12. For our purposes here, the relationship between marital union and the inheritance of property thickens the web of anxieties around marriages such as that between Kwamankra and Mansa, even as we are intrigued by the way that a "veil" separating a netherworld from an earthly one draws Hayford closer to Du Bois than he may have wished. Both men, and Hopkins as well, draw on the metaphor of the veil to theorize parallel states of existence, which in the fiction of Casely Hayford and Hopkins involves both a state of unconsciousness accessed through hypnosis, and a geographically separate state: enclaves of bling beyond earthly temporality and an accessible underground, for Hopkins, or (apparently) above the earth, for Casely Hayford. These are shimmering spaces of potentiality, housing realities too unbearable for everyday life. The world cannot (yet) accommodate social and intimate autonomy nor (West African women's and US African Americans') capacity to accumulate. Each space exceeds earth, creating a utopia that has to be discovered and acknowledged, a concealed place for depositing a spouse who has a cultural and intellectual power that threatens the patriarch, or a sovereign whose political power cannot be accessed within the present boundaries of US national life.

What ghosts are dislocated in this discovery of treasure deep down in the bowels of the earth, or above, or alongside it? Taking Hopkins's lead, as she links genealogy to mining and inheritance and suggests how the era's expeditions build on questions of slavery squelched away in the woods, and still unresolved, we want to see how such texts probe what is unethical about the tolerance of past inequities and the creation of new ones; how they press us to ask whether haunting is about the unevenness of transfer from one temporality to another. The novels in this chapter, from different locations and contexts, struggle to reconcile different systems: the legality of wills and land deeds or marriages and concubinage, older and newer orders of kinship. The novels of later generations are explicit (or perhaps differently explicit) about such struggles. The critique by colonial administrators and missionaries of the consignment of twins and Christian converts to society's netherlands, and the recognition of the critique as Europe's claim to a superior morality and generosity that entitles it to rule over others: this is the story of *Things Fall Apart*.[68]

But we also want to connect this attempt to reconcile different systems, or to resolve tensions (such as that between past and present, or "traditional" and "modern"), to unresolved issues from another source: the African continent's domestic and transatlantic trade in humans, even as neither (West African) *Ethiopia Unbound* nor (Caribbean) *Sword of Nemesis* or *Rupert Gray* appear to reference this explicitly. That is to say, if we can infer that these novels make slavery morally reprehensible for facilitating the seduction of a young woman who bears a "natural" son, this is a relatively understated reference; and Casely Hayford's eagerness to show that West African systems are equivalent or superior to European ones means that he "never mentions, much less critiques, either domestic slavery or slave trading."[69] Since these dislocations would be consolidated rather than resolved in the new African nation-states of the future (they enter independent nationhood at a political and economic disadvantage to European and US nation-states which, by comparison, profit from their imperial, colonial, and enslaving ties to Africa) for Taiwo Osinubi, African complicity ("implication") in the slave trade "does the additional work of cultural mourning [in the wake of] colonial conquest."[70] For Osinubi the African male-authored novel of a later period is more attentive to the sphere of relative visibility and maleness represented by the transatlantic slave trade than to a domestic sphere of enslavement in which women captured as prisoners of war, or as punishment for debt or adultery, are pressed into service as wives.

But perhaps the latter theme is already evident as an anxiety in the early twentieth century—in Casely Hayford's novel's discussions of cowives, first wives, and cloth wives; and in newspaper editorials, sermons, and songs about marriage, polygyny, women's labor, sexual autonomy, and gendered roles in public and private life. In West Africa as in the Americas, histories of dislocation are embedded in discussions of kinship. Here are excerpts from a court deposition published in the *Agos Standard* (Sierra Leone) in 1911:

My father's name is John Coker, born in England he was carried off as a slave and rescued in Sierra Leone. He died at Abeokuta. . . . [My mother] Sarah, an Egba woman, was carried off to the same place and returned with him. They were married at Sierra Leone. I was born at Abeokuta at the beginning of 1844, I never went to Sierra Leone with my parents. . . . [My wife] came from the West Indies, was born in Jamaica, of West African parents, who went from Sierra Leone to the West Indies and her parents returned with her to Sierra Leone and then she came to Lagos.[71]

These accretions of West African, European, and Caribbean sites that are recalled as birthplaces, final resting places, and ancestral locations speak to identities shot through with hybrid histories, as are verbs of displacement, return, and affiliation, their violence muted: "*carried off, went from, never went.*"

But this court deposition is also about marriage; it is Rev. R. A. Coker's testimony in court on behalf of his daughter, Adel, married to a Dr. Oguntola Sapara who had married another woman, Sarah Olaore Green, in an "ordinance marriage." This is the West African side of histories and migrations that renders fraught the claiming of inheritances, the assertion of the right to claim wealth as one's due, and the public narration of personal genealogies. In Cobham's *Rupert Gray*, Pierre's declaration of "Yarraba" and Barbadian parentage suggests a family history that crosses the Atlantic, in addition to southeastern Caribbean migrations. One explanation, of course, for the silence about enslavement in the novels on both sides of the Atlantic is that crossings and recrossings are so taken for granted that they do not generate shame, they do not have to be flagged. But Kwamankra's investment in Fanti authenticity and Rupert Gray's insistence on a genealogy that can only begin in the wake of abolition might also flag weddings and marriages as obstacles to (inasmuch as they are also generators of) prestige, posterity, and masculine authority.

Rupert Gray's Inheritance

While *Emmanuel Appadocca*'s 1854 protagonist had shunned intimate ties to concentrate on retrieving an inheritance that he was ultimately unsuccessful in acquiring, *The Sword of Nemesis* and *Rupert Gray: A Tale in Black and White* end with the marital consolidation of their protagonists' connections to élite white local families. To address the potential contradiction in the turn-of-the-century novels between protagonists' pride in their African descent and their choice of a white or putatively white spouse (recall that a "beautiful brown" love interest berates Carlito on this point), *Rupert Gray*'s concluding allusion to the warning about the danger of miscegenation made by the nineteenth-century intellectual Edward Blyden is reassuring rather than contradictory, as Belinda Edmondson persuasively contends: Blyden— and *Rupert Gray*—remind Black readers that Black marriages (or perhaps more specifically Black men's marriages) ultimately always consolidate Black identity.[72] This accumulation by marriage, moreover, is meant to suggest Rupert's capacity to attract local and global wealth solely on the basis of his moral and charismatic qualities; unlike Emmanuel Appadocca and Carlito, Rupert does not stake his claim to accumulation on being wrongfully denied an inheritance or other prior grounds.

If *Ethiopia Unbound*'s Kwamankra questions the capacity of diasporic institutions in the West to assert "African manhood" when they are beholden to US and European interests, then Rupert Gray fails this test: the list of donors for the Tuskegee-like institution he is establishing at the end of *Rupert Gray* includes the countess's nephew (the Earl of Rothberry), Baron Rothschild, and other members of the British peerage, and perhaps the era's most infamous imperialist, the politician and diamond magnate Cecil Rhodes, while a portrait of the British abolitionist William Wilberforce is slated to grace the walls of the institution.[73] But in *Rupert Gray* "African manhood" is precisely the understanding of the Talented Tenth leader or "race-man" of the necessity for the pragmatic wooing of the era's local and global white power brokers.

Rupert is an accountant who, by the end of the novel, completes his qualifications as a barrister in London, and is also appointed a member of Trinidad's senate. An invitation to read a paper at London's Linnaean Society—rescinded because of the scandal surrounding his relationship with the young heiress whom he eventually marries—is nevertheless a reminder of his credentials as an amateur botanist. These multiple roles speak to the covering of all possible bases for the turn-of-the-century leader who does not want to be subject to the shortcomings of previous generations.[74] Presumably a barrister-accountant will not be vulnerable (as Appadocca was, as well as Carlito's father, in previous generations) to losing what is rightfully his. Indeed, it falls to his legal acuity to find a hole in the court case that allows his future wife to recover the inheritance that is jeopardized because of her relationship with him.

Rupert Gray's epigraph, "*Secundus dubiisque rectus*," is accompanied by a note that the Latin phrase comes from Debrett's *Peerage*. The phrase can be parsed as upright in prosperous as well as perilous times or doubtful circumstances, with "*secundus*" having inflections that include inferior, substituted, favorable, smooth. The editors of *Rupert Gray* translate the phrase as "the second in line and in cases of doubt the right or direct heir." How is the certainty implied by "right," "direct," "favorable," "upright," undercut by "doubt," "inferiority," "peril"? *Rupert Gray* explores the challenges of inheritance outside of entail (the restriction of inheritance to keep property within specific families or lines within families) in the early twentieth century, alongside English fiction that is also working out these questions, as when readers of the 1904 edition of *Strand Magazine* followed the plot of Arthur Conan Doyle's "Adventure of the Priory School," in which a resentful "natural" son kidnaps his half-brother, the legal heir of their father's estate, hoping, in exchange for the latter's safe return, to convince their father to break the entail and allow him to inherit instead of his half-brother, born into a legal marriage.[75] E. M. Forster's 1910 novel *Howard's End* suggests that more than tradition or legality, more than the assertion of rights by a property owner, a consciousness of being a "steward" of culture should animate the transfer of property.[76]

Thus Mary Jo Parker's conclusions about the eighteenth- and early nineteenth-century English novel still hold: that the much-needed rejuvenation of tradition never dislodges the fact that any putative social impostor turns out to be the person who ought to have been there; and relatedly, that the recourse to affirming morality over property still produces the outcome that it is the propertied class that turns out to be the class that is the most moral: "The inheritance plot invariably demonstrates that the proper heir to a material estate is also the proper heir to what is, in effect, a moral estate."[77] At the beginning of the novel, "the protagonist, deprived of his or her rightful inheritance, must embark on a quest for security and position; by the end, he or she has been revealed or recognized as the proper heir and has come into wealth—or, at least, an elevation in social position."[78]

Rupert Gray wants to be neither the object of an élite family's good deeds, let in from the outside, nor an infant heir biding time. He does not ground his entitlement in biological descent but on moral and intellectual grounds. Though they are biological heirs who might thus be considered superior to Rupert, Appadocca and Carlito have a similar vulnerability to disinheritance, which I have tied to unmarried Black female forbears. Rupert rejects origin narratives that would tie him to slavery and abolition. He does not want to be connected to "increase by two births and acquisition," to invoke the language of estate compensation claims.[79] Rupert Gray must confront at least three obstacles successfully, to claim his rightful place: the countess, a wealthy single woman and friend, and who, as the last chapter made clear, also embodies the perils of demeaning visuality and imperial slander; Jacob Clarke, a member of Rupert's social group, whose capacity to harm him is framed as the most immediate and violent; and the Serles, the local white anglophone Creole family of cocoa planters (Rupert's employers) whose daughter, the last of the line of the family, he wishes to marry. Each obstacle requires his keen attentiveness to the exchange of money and other gifts, and to the performative acts in which his reputation and genealogy are couched, in a racial transfer of wealth that appears to be socially unprecedented.

An elaborate circuit of letters and newspaper articles, variously seeking either to tarnish or to rescue Rupert Gray's reputation, involves a proposed gift of one thousand guineas from the proceeds of the lecture on imperial botany he is purported to have given at the Linnaean Society. This money moves toward and away from Rupert's possession in a sequence of events that involves reports from Trinidad that Rupert is not fit to be a member of the society, the countess's declaration that she does not believe the slander, her offer to replace the lost amount from her personal funds, and Rupert's refusal of her check. This money is allocated instead to the Indian famine fund, though when the countess dies suddenly in London while laying the cornerstone for a "home for stranded natives from the colonies and Africa," "the thousand guineas fell back into residue and went to the residuary legatee accordingly."[80] In the morass of scandal that plagues Rupert, therefore, the countess may be said to redeem her original role as a perpetrator in the circulation of imperial slander that haunts their initial encounter in the botanical gardens, as she urges her elite peers to ignore attempts to impugn Rupert's character: "'Black, and that was all,' she said. 'But comely.'"[81] Prospective recipients of aristocratic donations, whether "stranded" in the metropole or elsewhere, compete with each other for recognition and funding from a circulation of imperial largesse that positions Rupert Gray (much like Booker T. Washington in this era) as both personal friend and recipient of institutional sponsorship.

Jacob Clarke is the villainous lower-middle-class foil to Rupert Gray's moral perfection. His attempts to accumulate wealth, unlike Rupert's, can only be read as crass, as he furtively applies for the US position earmarked for Rupert, spreads slander that leaves Rupert and the colony vulnerable to international yellow journalism, and forges the will that guarantees a local white heiress's entitlement to her (and thus ultimately also Rupert's) inheritance. As with Tack Tally, a figure in McKay's *Banana Bottom* who returns to the Caribbean with wealth acquired from Panama, Jacob Clarke's vilification is such that it seems to exceed both the community's censure and that of the omniscient narrator—curious in these Black-authored novels about the unfair castigation of Black middle-class aspiration and social mobility. Why should their accumulation be interpreted as not only crass, but dangerous? It is Clarke who calls Rupert an *exceptional* Negro early on, when Rupert offers him a job as a clerk in his firm, resuming a relationship begun as classmates. For the rest of the novel his resentment of Rupert's popularity and his determination to undermine him bears out this reading of Rupert's exceptionality, as Jacob joins the colony's naysayers in wishing to retard the progress of the chosen representative of this social group. There is room for only one favored member of socially mobile Black men in the imperial hierarchy of origin of the species, it would seem: Rupert Gray, whose successful procurement of the Serle family's wealth is cast as both accidental and born out of true love, rather than ambition.

Thus Rupert's relationships with the countess and with Jacob Clarke are precarious encounters in which Rupert risks losing his distinguished reputation to the ignominy of a photograph of imperial ethnic types and media accounts of his purported sexual salaciousness in order to gain the bigger prize. While Jacob Clarke is publicly horsewhipped at his own wedding by Rupert Gray, in an extraordinary scene of violent Black-on-Black punishment, the white prospective father-in-law who attempts to murder Rupert Gray in order to keep him from his daughter is never publicly identified as doing so. Rupert's silence about the details of the scene at the Serles' residence comes at great personal cost, since it feeds public perception that the media's tawdry portrayal of him is correct. In this sense Rupert's silence is a gift to the Serle family that we can read as part of an elaborate circuit of exchange in which Rupert must accept his perpetual indebtedness to the Serles. Rupert is also embedded in a series of monetary and moral negotiations that involve the countess and Jacob Clarke: she mails him a check for a thousand guineas, and he mails her a response in which he refuses the check, refuses to explain that his alliance with his white beloved was sedate and not the scandal reported in the media, but also professes to the countess his everlasting friendship, thus absolving her of any participation in demeaning his character, social status, and capacity to accumulate. Clarke's lies and forgeries are eventually disclosed in both the courtroom and the court of public opinion.

Rupert's very entry into the Serle firm, and the basis for his social legibility, is rooted in his return of a dropped coin to his future employer, in a sort of reverse-reparations moment that confirms white ownership as the proper locus of wealth. The story of a young Rupert returning a half-sovereign that Mr. Serle drops in the city streets is told fifteen years later by his daughter, Gwendoline, who has fallen hopelessly in love with Rupert: "This coin . . . got you into my father's service. . . . You, then quite a lad, picked it up and restored it to him. . . . He declared he never meant to part with it. It was to have gone down for an heirloom."[82] But why is this return of money so important to Serle, and how does Rupert's wooing of his daughter violate the relationship begun in that moment in the past? (This is what happens when you let them in!) In gratitude for Rupert's enhancing the value of almost a decade of European schooling by tutoring her in the practical skills of bookkeeping and typing, Gwendoline has the coin fashioned into a brooch. This is a regifting meant to confirm the earlier return of money to her father, but that can also be read as severing the earlier exchange and establishing a new relationship. The brooch could be viewed as a return of what rightfully belonged to Rupert and his community in the first place, in a gesture of reparations. It adds value, as an aesthetic, artisanal transformation of crass currency, or alternately replaces the use value of money with an impractical bauble. His beloved Gwendoline now becomes the giver who is beholden to the recipient, or she is the heiress who now supplants her father in adjudicating giving and receiving. The brooch is a tender token of her love, or (also) a collar marking ownership.

Does Rupert's original return of the coin cast him as honest, as powerful, as self-abnegating? Does it entangle his future employer uncomfortably in a circuit of gift-giving and reparations, where the question of whose wealth the coin represents in the first place is put on the table? The 1833 Act of Parliament that ended British Caribbean slavery provided for compensation of twenty million pounds to slaveholders, paid by the British crown as an acknowledgement of their loss of valuable property, as well as a period of apprenticeship whereby newly freed workers would continue to provide unwaged labor under the guise of being acclimatized to freedom. The end of several centuries of dehumanizing conditions of unwaged labor, that is, was cast as a debt owed to planters instead of laborers, and an opportunity for the latter rather than the former to learn to adjust to Black freedom.[83] References in *Rupert Gray* to Black Trinidadians' preference for "fine clothes to Crown lands" over saving money to purchase small plots of land, continue this theme.[84] In this use of Rupert as an example to cast other Black people as responsible for their nonaccumulation, the suggestion is that the colonial state has given them a fair chance to accumulate.

The "restoration" of Serle's coin by young Rupert sees a descendant of enslaved people (whose personal narration will later be detached from a genealogy of enslavement) returning money as a condition of a future transfer of wealth. Mr. Serle treasures this family heirloom, perhaps intending to pass it on to be similarly cherished by multiple generations. In so treasuring the coin he rehearses a particular relationship; it is not just that Rupert Gray will eventually work for his firm as a trusted accountant of the firm's cocoa estates in southern Trinidad and its headquarters in Port of Spain, but that in doing so Rupert continues to affirm white prosperity and futurity. In becoming an accountant, he scripts the futurity of the Black socially mobile subject as the capacity to build Black wealth in the context of the constant revitalization of white wealth.

Recalling from chapter 3 the countess's speculation that Trinidadians were "far behind the Māoris" (a reference that arguably underlines Māori backwardness, if the statement means "*even* the Māoris") then Marcel Mauss's discussion of Māori gift-giving would question these terms of belatedness in relation to what is lost with the advent of a capitalist economy.[85] Jane Anna Gordon discusses the tendency to recode the gift-giving of colonized subjects as indebtedness: "To be a colonized or a post-colonial person is to be forever indebted. . . . To be in debt casts a perpetual shadow over one's ability to give."[86] In this discussion Black intellectuals are the source of the gift of insight rather than mimics who are in a derivative relation to *actual* intellectuals. If we could read *Rupert Gray* as working out the gestures of gift-giving, gratitude, and reparations in a colonial setting, then Gordon presses us to think of its protagonist not only in terms of wealth-building (or thwarted wealth-building) but as "co-workers" of culture, to use Du Bois's phrase, exchanging intellectual generosity with the countess, Gwendoline, and others.[87] This relation is in tension with what is enacted when Rupert returns money in *Rupert Gray*, or when Carlito bails out his future wife's father in *Sword of Nemesis*. In exchange for affiliation and friendship, Rupert and his class must keep traditional holders of wealth afloat.

If Mr. Serle cannot ultimately handle Rupert's transformation from his employee to his daughter's beau, we can read his daughter as open to new relations of gift-giving that are disastrous to her family and class but that make possible new social relations and a new circulation of wealth. Here we could note Gwendoline's openness to and capacity for transformation. Turning a half-sovereign representing the maintenance of the status quo into a gold scarf pin, she transfers it from her "low square fronted bodice" to his necktie, which she has had to undo and rearrange, in a sexually charged moment of trembling limbs, dress sleeves, and curtains flapping in the wind, her "deep and full" breathing on his brow.[88] Taking flowers from one of her many élite white suitors, in this case "an English laird ... willing ... to clothe her with his ancient title," she withdraws a bachelor's button that she gifts Rupert, transforming a gesture of courtship meant to lead to approved white social coupling into the coaxing of a Black bachelor to join her in breaching social convention.[89]

If Gwendoline is a threat to her father and their caste, she is also a potential threat to Rupert's Black male ascendancy, assuming the masculine position, as when she penetrates him with a brooch or gives him flowers from a bouquet given to her by a prospective suitor: what does it mean for Rupert to receive flowers from her? From the time of her return to Trinidad at the opening of the novel, her father's Black employees get straight to the heart of the matter: Rupert's late arrival to work (because he has spent the previous day collecting and settling her in) makes them speculate that her arrival means that he will be replaced by her as accountant, or that having "overhauled" the books, she has discovered irregularities and has had him fired.[90] This suggests Rupert and Gwendoline's interchangeability, on the one hand; as with the countess, they have parallel lines of nonauthority, taking their place as amateurs alongside each other. On the other hand, the suggestion here is that Rupert was just biding time at the firm until the boss's daughter returned to take her rightful place. Gwendoline gardens, puts on theatricals, and types; she is neither a traveling photographer-botanist nor a physician like her visiting friend, Florence Badenock. Yet a canny working-class Black workforce may get to the heart of things as they grapple with Gwendoline's nonmale whiteness and Rupert's Black masculinity. There is a feminization understood to be emasculating here, as the novel deals with women with careers, women without careers who are nevertheless world-traveling heiresses, and women (such as Edith Pierre, the Black woman who is Gwendoline's maid) whose racial status occludes the fact of their careers and marital status.

If the countess is a New Woman, transforming the Queen's Park Hotel veranda when she invites Rupert to tea, Gwendoline creates in her home a parallel sphere of both limited movement and fertility, in relation to the infertile movement of the countess. Her friend Florence Badenock represents a middle ground: traveling but not alone, a physician but betrothed, marking the limit of the New Woman that someone like Rupert can withstand— "Florence Badenock played her cards with the skill of a goddess. What did it matter that she held a physician's diploma. Profession or no profession, women's profession is marriage."[91] The countess is free to meet Rupert in public while Gwendoline remains cloistered, but Gwendoline's very relegation to a domestic sphere is what makes her more appealing in this era of the troubling New Woman.

Represented as endangered and endangering, white Caribbean femininity helps to contextualize Gwendoline, who also represents an interesting departure from some of its tropes.[92] In *With Silent Tread*, an 1894 Antiguan novel, the social consequences of proximity to blackness for white Caribbean women are made horrifyingly clear: complete social isolation because of marriage to a Black man; Black women who dress as if they think they are ladies rather than de facto maids for white women; and face-changing leprosy that originates with being kissed in infancy by a Black employee.[93] This suggests an imperiled Caribbean whiteness that surfaces in Gwendoline's anxious conversations with her father and discussions with Florence of dreams about blood. Gwendoline worries that in inserting her golden money pin into Rupert she has jeopardized not only a gendered etiquette, but her social caste's racial contract: "She had paid the purchase money before the article was forthcoming. . . . Were there any other white girls in Trinidad in a parallel situation?"[94] Ultimately, she is betraying the obligation to reproduce white femininity as virtuous, exalted, and scarce. Transferred from one male (her father) to another (Rupert) Gwendoline Serle has value, as someone who is valuable to claim, to be affiliated with, and as deserving to be cherished, and she is also a medium through which wealth passes.

I am interested in connecting this capacity to be a conduit of wealth to the inability (or disinclination) to touch the ground. While New Women such as the visiting countess can walk around in real time, their feet planted on the soil, Gwendoline is a sort of spectral medium, connected to images of encasement that are imprisoning, or protective, or both.[95] This image of cloistered wealth brings to mind the apparition of nuns from the Venezuelan mainland seen in Monos, part of a group of offshore islands belonging to Trinidad and situated in the Bocas del Dragón between Trinidad and Venezuela, as represented in *Child of the Tropics: Victorian Memoirs* (1988), in Yseult Bridges's memoir of her childhood in mid-nineteenth-century Trinidad.[96] Kathryn Burns discusses the important alternative reproductive work of Spanish conquest enacted by convents in Cuzco, Peru, whose residents were children born of unions between Spanish men and Andean women.[97] As a prong of conquest, the convent held "its young charges off the marriage market while it was decided exactly what role they would play in the new society taking shape in Cuzco."[98] Shadowy figures who ultimately inhabit the landscape by languishing in forgotten graves, or by continuing to float above it, the nuns in Yseult Bridges's account pinpoint Venezuela as a sort of netherworld or wilderness, a holding area for inhabitants who cannot join society, and perhaps a source of Trinidad's spectral remains. We could read these Venezuelan nuns (as well as Rita in *Sword of Nemesis* and perhaps also *Emmanuel Appadocca*'s Feliciana) as wealth on the margins, their chastity and finances carefully preserved. They make wealth possible for others by opting out of reproduction and out of sociality.

Gwendoline does not venture out beyond her home after her initial return to Trinidad from a decade spent in Europe (not, at any rate, until the racial crisis that propels her father to turn her out). Presumably if she did so she would be appropriately veiled and conveyed in a carriage, rather than walking back and forth like Rupert. A staff of indoor and outdoor workers maintains her life at home. Presumably they have placed the "upturned bottles, blue, green, and colorless" in this garden that is otherwise a shrine to élite femininity, though it is intriguing to imagine that Gwendoline tolerates or endorses these objects "'mounted' with Obeah" to repel theft and negative spirits, as the novel's annotation explains.[99] Stamping their own will on the landscape and imbuing estate space with multiple times and procedures, these laborers who likely cannot own their own land or move beyond the confines of the estate make possible Gwendoline's comfortable, cloistered life. Their shock when she skirts the rules by sitting in a carriage beside Rupert confirms the sense that intimate congress with people like themselves would be improper; perhaps the bottles are meant to keep the estate safe from intruders like him.

Gwendoline has returned to a future that must be carefully curated, as the last of the line of "a proud old family, without a trace of intermixture," after the requisite time in Europe just before their coming-out ball, "pale and washed out," in Bridges's account of this social group.[100] England allowed women like Bridges the opportunity "to eradicate the insidious singsong Creole accent and acquire that poise and complexion, that *cachet*, which would enhance her chances of making a 'good match.'"[101] For such young women, it was preferable to return to Trinidad "just before the Ball, their looks as well-guarded a secret as the style of their frocks, hurried ashore into hooded Victorias by their mothers, heads down, faces concealed by Leghorn hats—but wearing their prettiest ensembles!"[102] Strong public interest adds glamour to the event and casts the young women as valuable and important, but also depends on their being withheld from the public's gaze; they are displayed, in effect, as not available for display. At home they are forced into gowns, their "godgiven" waists transformed from twenty-two inches to eighteen, to the soundscape of the Black women who wait on them, guard them, and help to support the present-in-absence condition of their charges. In Bridges's text, Creole-speaking Black women are deeply invested in white women's non-Creole-speaking public success and futurity within Trinidad, even as it is precisely this Creole-speaking blackness that causes white Caribbean degradation in the first place and creates the need for a lengthy European sojourn to root out this proof of the danger of proximity. (Recall that in *Sword of Nemesis* Mrs. Woodhouse also spends time in Europe and returns with an accent that reflects this; she is an anomaly, since her race casts her as more properly an *attendant* to female whiteness.) The Black women who dress these debutantes are narrated as sustaining rather than undermining, and as happily and fully committed to the public thriving of white femininity. A lot of labor is needed to ensure that this critical sonic difference adds value on the return to the Caribbean.

Notably, it is Rupert Gray's sonic magnificence that first draws Gwendoline to him. "Not an hour ago the poignant vigor of a man's voice—masculine, musical—floated around her, and turning—the voice spoke as she leaned against the deck rails—she faced a full-blooded negro."[103] As much as the novel is about Rupert's future, it also flags Gwendoline's return to Trinidad as monumental, particularly because her father intends to return to Europe after he retires. In this sense Rupert's intervention makes possible her Caribbean futurity as long as it is intertwined with his, and also undermines the father's desire to have a future in Europe, since the latter is so devastated by their romance that he languishes and dies in Trinidad. A hot commodity on the marriage market, Gwendoline is a conduit through which money passes, allowing it to be amassed. For Rupert the question is whether, since she is groomed to be sold to the highest bidder, she will choose him when the men in her social circle throw themselves at her feet.

In lieu of venturing beyond her gate, like traveling countesses and veiled US tourists, Gwendoline re-creates the experience of public spaces such as the botanical gardens and the theater in her own expansive domain at the edge of Port of Spain's suburbs, in a home newly renovated by a doting father: "It stood on a knoll, hidden among ancient trees, in the centre of a broad cocoa field."[104] If she cannot touch urban soil in Port of Spain, she is at least grounded in rural prosperity. Such a home may well be outfitted with one of the era's modern plunge baths, the household feature that helped to justify the steep rise in water rates, and in turn united Port of Spain's residents (whether they used plunge baths or standpipes) in the protests leading to the Water Riot in 1903. As part of the renovation, Mr. Serle has altered the course of a river so that it runs through the property. If this is the kind of use of water that the authorities had in mind when they applied the disputed rates, the location of the home beyond Port of Spain and its suburbs would mean that it would not be subject to the tax. As future patriarch of this home, then, Rupert Gray the politician will go into "town" every day to fight for legislation such as fair water rates and return in the evenings to an estate that is not subject to that legislation. This union of "poor negro boy" and "highborn lady" secures the modernization and apparent democratization of the estate-owning class, and simultaneously the incorporation of a few exceptional types into the ranks of this class, as the price of guaranteeing its futurity.[105]

The patronage afforded by Gwendoline's "theatricals" guarantees that an otherwise indifferent public will support the work of local artists but also reinforces the status of her estate as a stage on which social performances of racial equality can be tried out. The rehearsal for the theatrical evening in which Gwendoline listens to Rupert recite Walter Scott and Alfred Tennyson is an opportunity for him to exercise the charisma that has mesmerized her since she first saw him at the Port of Spain docks.[106] Gwendoline thrills to the sound of his voice, as it powerfully recapitulates the canonical texts, familiar to him, which are woven into her play just as the countess delighted in his enumeration of the proper Latin names of plants. This voice always speaks appropriately, whether in public gardens or on the factory floor, and it now schools Gwendoline to look rapturously up at him in her own home, as her future master. With the allure of its sonic and sartorial physicality, Rupert's body forces a reconsideration of Black masculinity as violent, fit only for manual labor, lacking in sensitivity and intellectual capacity. This is a Black masculinity from which emanates apt but also pleasing sounds. Seductive, Rupert wreaks "havoc" on Gwendoline's "self-control," producing a "despair" that she is not worthy of him.[107]

It is precisely under the ecstatic effect of these sounds, as Gwendoline exchanges her first kiss with Rupert in her garden, that they are reminded of the transgressive nature of this particular performance. Someone like Rupert must be an intruder in this space when he exceeds his role as an employee hired to tutor the daughter of the house; persons looking like him in this space should be gardeners. Indeed, it had been the shock of the gardener and the rest of Gwendoline's staff that constituted the proper social reaction to the couple's breach of racial etiquette, and the figurative "fire" of the gardener's beard on that occasion prefigures Rupert's clothing set alight by the report of the gun.[108] The inevitable playing out of *these* theatricals is Mr. Serle's attempted lynching of Rupert, when a tip from Jacob Clarke alerts him to the scene of the couple's garden tryst.[109] In the violent scene that ensues, Gwendoline is "like a maiden-martyr tied to the stake" as she attempts to defend her beau—a beau who in effect *is* her "stake," since she is clutching him behind her. Rupert is shot twice, his clothing set on fire, and when the gun accidentally fires again, it strikes "the coagulum of blood which marked the spot where Rupert Gray was shot." It is not enough to shoot Rupert, but his blood has to be attacked as well.[110] The ritualistic character of the attack on both suggests that not only Rupert but Gwendoline too has initiated this *hataclaps*, as her errant desire makes her social group vulnerable. Blood suffuses these theatricals literally and figuratively to mark murderous intent and near loss of life, the cleavage of daughter from father, and also the organic fusion of Rupert and Gwendoline, whose mingling of blood defies the supposed interracial catastrophe that her father declares everyone abhors: "Not one in a thousand of all the whites in the island would condemn me. Two-thirds of the blacks would vote solid against that scoundrel.... a nigger kissing my daughter—no, sir, I must lynch him."[111] Here we can note that as with a bedroom in Sav-la-Mar Jamaica in 1910, the intimate relations transformed into public salacious sexuality are intertwined with long-standing narratives of race, courtroom justice, and electoral politics.

The scene of crisis also demonstrates the resilience and imagination of two women who protect Gwendoline and enable a happy ending of private relations for her and Rupert. In the first place, Florence Badenock rescues the couple not only with critical medical attention, but with a story for the newspapers that will quell rumors about what really happened in the garden. Crucially, that is, she addresses the issue of reputation for both the Serle family and Rupert Gray, though the latter's character is further smeared by Jacob Clarke. Florence invites Gwendoline to Scotland to recuperate and then helps engineer an extraordinary scheme for her return to Trinidad and the recovery of her inheritance. Secondly, Edith Pierre, normally charged, as her personal maid, with facilitating Gwendoline's ability to thrive, literally oversees her passage from life to death and then back to life. In doing so, her earthiness continues to shield Gwendoline from public view, a crucial part of the social apparatus that, as we saw in Yseult Bridges's description, keeps white women from touching the ground of public space. As with the Black women servants in Bridges's description, Edith Pierre is fiercely loyal and admiring. Her malapropisms are meant as a comic foil to her white employers and to Rupert Gray, and also suggest the untimeliness of Black social aspiration.

Guarding Gwendoline's spectrality, Edith is the go-between who acts as lookout for the liaison with Rupert Gray, and since "none but my trusty maid had access to my room," as Gwendoline explains in court, Edith is the "jewel of a maid" who presides over the lie.[112] In this sense Edith shares with Catherine Stewart, whom I discussed in chapter 3, the labor of being fully accessible at every moment to her employer, charged with sensitive responsibilities, simultaneously loyal and prone to making the élite household vulnerable to public scandal. Edith works tirelessly on Gwendoline's behalf, telling the public that her employer will not see anyone, going into town to deliver a note to Rupert, and keeping the lie going about Gwendoline's death. Gwendoline is veiled during her father's attack on Rupert, and later too she enters the courtroom "in deep black, thickly veiled."[113] So even as she supplants the authority of the (now-dead) countess and her (now morally disgraced) father and leads the colony in recognizing and consecrating this man whose voice has so transfixed her, the life available to her outside the estate is destined to be cloistered, and it is facilitated by Edith, who, unveiled, exposed, and laboring strenuously, must bear up Gwendoline or explain her absence.

In figuring out that a new day is dawning, that a Black man can be "a kindred spirit . . . a God-given second self," Gwendoline joins Rupert in being out of time though they are differently punished.[114] The new day of Black autonomy which the novel seeks to usher in is thwarted by all classes, and for her employees this could be a pragmatic understanding that the new day that potentially promises Rupert social mobility means that *they* can now expect that he will join the authorities in surveilling them. This recalls a midnight woman's reservations about who is required to "wait fe you glass."

In the scene in which Gwendoline's father attempts to murder Rupert, it is Edith who notices that he is on fire, and who, in stumbling with the lantern, causes the light to flicker out. As she continues to react to what we must presume is not only a horrific scene, but a lesson about Black transgression that bears on her personhood in particular, her frightened exclamations are drawn from the Church of England Litany: "Lord have mercy upon us. . . . From battle and murder and from sudden death, good Lord deliver us."[115] At this point Florence Badenock appeals to Edith: "Will you not try to save Miss Gwendoline. She was good and kind to you, Edith. She loved you, loved your race. Edith, go, do you hear?"[116] If this is a rebuke connected to Edith's perceived failure to act quickly, or to act at all, it underlines the sense that not only Edith's time, but her emotional and affective repertoire are forcibly tethered to her employer and to her employer's best friend. What space is there for a conception of herself that is separate from bearing up her employer at every turn, and who will sacrifice all or nearly all, in order to guarantee the flourishing of Edith's life and relationships?

"You and I next," Pierre tells Edith after the shock of seeing Rupert and Gwendoline in the carriage together early in the novel.[117] It would seem that this transgressive sight facilitates their own romance, though another way of framing this is that their employers' romance, however it turns out, theoretically opens up a space for Edith to conceive of a life for herself outside of bearing up Gwendoline. Meant to be bathetic, the setting of their courtship is anything but picturesque: "That night two lovers sat under the bamboo clump beside the fishing basin . . . [a hillside teeming] with roofs of galvanized iron . . . Port of Spain is a pretty town, but not as seen from the sea."[118] But *their* union, unlike that of their employers, is socially permissible: "this time there was no disparity of class, or color; no let to their romance. Romeo and Juliet were both black."[119] Rupert and Gwendoline are destined to have the *private* life that is on the one hand befitting of the élite household but that also entails social ostracism. Barred, as servants, from bourgeois privacy, Edith and Pierre can enjoy their union in public.

Sound anchors this couple's (im)proper social grounding; her malapropisms and his stutter are meant to be a foil to Rupert Gray's suave sonority. The charge of ignorant and dangerous mismanagement of language directed for generations at lower middle-class Black men such as Rupert, in order to mock their political aspirations, is here deflected onto Pierre and Edith as working-class characters who cannot manage their diction and who will be the moral charges of Rupert's political class. But speaking out of turn, they threaten to derail the plotting of inheritance and futurity that sidelines them. In the botanical gardens Rupert Gray was declared to be self-generated, suggesting that the heirs of emancipation ("freedom's children," to use Colin Palmer's phrase) had no recourse to a narratable past; but Pierre "proudly" names his parentage as "Yarraba" and "Bajan" [Yoruba and Barbadian], a forthright public narration of his first-generation claim to Trinidadianness.[120] Listening to Pierre, "the voice that may come," this "speech caught in the mouth," trains us to appreciate the linguistic hesitation common to all speakers (and which we learn to mask with the schwa: *aaahm, er, um*); "it is a preparation for common recognition."[121]

Pierre's reduplicated interjections bring narratives of the past (whether it is his family's genealogy, or the brilliant lawyers and schoolteachers of African descent in Trinidad's history) into the present. Even if these are rendered old-fashioned by comparison to Rupert Gray's generation, poised for local and transnational leadership, they are models of kinship and morality that anchor Pierre, and that run counter to the intraracial bickering and competitiveness among Black Trinidadians in his present. Simultaneously ethical and comical, Pierre's speech is meant to augment Rupert's *gravitas*, at the expense of his own. But what if his stutter is the sign of neither failed speech nor the incapacity for leadership or personal sovereignty? What if his repeated syllables and the echoes they create serve to reimagine received narratives, much as the B-side of a reggae recording repeats and lengthens notes and riddims, creating its own momentum rather than merely imitating an original?

Edith's exuberant misapplication of words similarly threatens to cast her as a buffoon; instead of telling visitors that Gwendoline is "indisposed," for example, she says that she is "interposed." As Emrys Jones points out in an analysis of Richard Sheridan's eighteenth-century character Mrs. Malaprop, we assume that we know what a character such as Edith means, or ought to have meant, when she gets a word "wrong"; the joke, and our appreciation of the mistake, turn on this assumption.[122] But the supposed mistake gestures toward more complex possibilities opened up by the dissonance between not only the wrong use of the right word (or the wrong use of the wrong word) and the correct option, but a new way of thinking about the originally intended word and its displacement. How does Edith's utterance of "interposed" capture the intercessory, intervening, mediating register of her own role (and Gwendoline's potential role) in the social transformation promised by the emerging courtship with Rupert? If Edith is "transgressing against a linguistic inheritance" when she misspeaks, then she gestures toward "the impossibility of ever policing the channels of inheritance with absolute authority."[123]

Generations later, in a project that is critical of the postcolonial nation's vision of modernity, Christopher Cozier connects the construction of regimented and soulless suburban housing to the soundscape of Trinidadian schoolchildren being instructed to sing the national anthem with the hyperaspiration of *good English*.[124] Cozier asks us to listen to the sound of progress, and I want to extend the invitation to the earlier moment—to listen to a "Black Romeo and Juliet" who claim a future that is neither tragic nor comedic. Listening carefully to Edith and Pierre, "despite the sonic color line's narrowed definition of black listening abilities," as Jennifer Lynn Stover frames it in another context, trains us to hear this couple as exuberant, conservative, complex, rather than as socially subordinated mimics.[125]

In the future that is being ushered in by the novel's ending, Gwendoline and Rupert can live in the privacy made possible by suburban wealth in St. Ann, and by the labor of those who have neither privacy nor the benefit of a domesticity that can be narrated without tittering. Rupert has attained both private and public membership in the élite as a member of the senate, as the head of a new Tuskegee-like institution that can count on distinguished patronage, and as a marital heir of significant wealth, but he also shares with Gwendoline the "splendor of loneliness," in a world of sociality with others to which they look forward but that is not yet possible.[126] The narrator's scoffing at Edith's social transformation—"a swarthy empress of some kingly harem" who "since her marriage seems to have become left-handed"—indicates that her time is still conceived of as Gwendoline's.[127] But Edith has her own visions of the future. "No longer in [Gwendoline's] service," she is deeply attached to Rupert's proposed Negro-Industrial Institute, dreaming that her infant son will be trained as a botanist who will abjure "frock coats and beaver hats." Edith and Pierre's marriage is an interesting prefiguring of Jane's wedding at the close of De Lisser's *Jane's Career* a few years later, in which premarital pregnancy is an accepted part of unfolding events (which we can read as the critique of bourgeois norms that De Lisser shares with McKay), but Black-led social institutions and activism are ridiculed. In *Rupert Gray*, Edith's sartorial and occupational dreams for her son suggest a practical bent, not unlike the aesthete-as-accountant-botanist modeled by Rupert Gray himself, and perhaps indicating a Caribbean agnosticism about the humanist-versus-vocational tension embedded in debates about education by W. E. B. Du Bois and Booker T. Washington. We might also hear in Edith's remarks about "frock coats and beaver hats" a judgment of a performance of masculinity that just does not come together respectably enough for the scrutinizing Black woman, as in McKay's "Midnight Woman to the Bobby," or as in the queer dandies of the immediate future.[128]

The future political leaders who are the protagonists of the early twentieth-century novels in this chapter have differing ideas about the extent of the intimacy that it is necessary to pursue with local and metropolitan whiteness, even as all struggle to navigate its power in the process of speaking for local or diasporic Black constituencies. We have seen that the intimate and the political are deeply entangled. I think that Edith and Pierre would join Rupert and Gwendoline in disapproving of Catherine Stewart and Fred Evans from chapter 2. Kwamankra's disapproval would change to sympathy if Stewart were an abandoned first wife. If Edith and Pierre are Rupert's supporters but not his clones, they press us to think of multiple constellations of imagined futures—they occupy a colonial present that we sometimes narrate as a nodal point in the genealogy of a future nation, but Edith's dream may well be a third term that is different from Rupert's, Gwendoline's, or her husband's dreams, even as it is firmly rooted in colonial Trinidad.

When a man washes up on La Bocas, having been turned out of Venezuela, we might think of him as uncertainly tied both to the country he has just left and to the colony of his birth to which he has returned unceremoniously. These hazy itineraries and dreams keep the wilderness in view—placeholders beyond imagination, beyond utterance, illegible to onlookers or to us. As we have seen, some fictional characters cannot be assigned a future—because they are illegible or because their legibility is threatening. Some spaces remain hidden from view, imbued with divergent sources of power: cloistered and powerful whiteness; a non-Protestant Spanish and indigenous past; and mystical spaces of truth and reckoning in cabins in the Caribbean and the southern United States and in underground African kingdoms. We could think of the room of a single Black woman—so public in one sense—as another enclosure of reckoning where pasts and futures are being imagined. These spaces generate meditations on usable pasts, and on the timeliness of actual and alternative arrangements of power.

CODA

In a remarkable video accompanying her 2016 exhibition *Alchemy of the Soul*, Cuban-American artist Magdalena Campos-Pons strolls through the ruins of a sugar estate in her hometown of Matanzas, Cuba, exchanging warm greetings with former neighbors. Her exploration of the terrible legacies of sugar's chemical and social properties does not preclude her exuberant insistence on claiming an inheritance of place and experience, along with the ongoing sociality of her birthplace.[1] Perhaps I am drawn to Campos-Pons's disposition to exuberance because it is neither mine nor, for the most part, that of the texts examined in this book. As if the contemporary moment could not be narrated without keeping the earlier period close at hand, I found that the late twentieth- and early twenty-first-century novelists I was reading paid keen attention to the earlier turn-of-the-century moment, whether it was Ramabai Espinet's mournful engagement with familial silence and loss, or Nelly Rosario's return to the beginning of US occupation in the Dominican Republic to excavate the intimate histories of occupation.[2] In Zadie Smith's *White Teeth*, Clara silently recalls a family story of Jamaica's 1907 earthquake at a moment when the patronizing liberalism of the Chalfens requires a genealogical narrative from her that parallels the photographs, diagrams, and written accounts that stabilize, solidify, validate, and preserve for posterity a family in which "everybody knew whose children were whose [and] the marriages were singular and long-lasting."[3] By contrast, Clara's family tree, as well as that of her white working-class husband, is marked with births described as "haphazard" "paternity unsure," "copulated with," "brought up by grandmother," and "child's name unknown," and one conclusion that we could draw is that diasporic subjects in the United Kingdom have no corresponding monuments that can deliver family histories from furtiveness or transience. But Smith is careful to ground Clara's maternal history in the freedom of white Englishmen to impregnate Black women in Jamaica and simultaneously generate white children in "singular and long-lasting" unions if they wish to do so. Thus Smith shows that a willed blindness permits nationalist accounts of English genealogies to excise imperial relations and their violating consequences; as another character, Alsana, notes, the English "want to teach you and steal from you at the same time."[4] Thus on a January 1907 day when the earthquake strikes Kingston, Clara's grandmother is pregnant and in labor with one Victorian gentleman's child, while another Victorian gentleman's hand is up her dress. This is a *hataclaps* of "haphazard" consequences that is borne on *her* body, and that she bequeaths to succeeding generations.

If these novels are a reminder that Caribbean, British, US, and Canadian histories of exploitation still mark the present, even when (or because) they are not acknowledged, then other writers suggest that postcolonial African societies must also wrestle with the connection between patriarchal privilege and accumulation in the present, and histories of enslavement in the past. In Helen Oyoyemi's *The Icarus Girl* (2005) the figure of Tilly-Tilly, a "long-armed woman" smelling of coconuts, seems to emerge from a "rough drawing" in "black charcoal," her vengeance rooted in the dis-ease of dispossession, which seems at least partially marked by histories of the Atlantic slave trade.[5] The protagonist, Jessamy, learns that her Yoruba name, Wuraola, means gold, and that the compound built by her great-grandfather in the 1870s is shadowy, "except for the top floor and the balcony roof, which during the day were bathed constantly in waterfalls of gold." The "Boys Quarters," built to house the "troop of boys" needed to secure her great-grandfather's comforts (work done by Jessamy's aunts for her grandfather in the present), still bears these traces: "there might be fragments of bone, maybe people had died in here." Oyoyemi cautions that someone, spectral or living, is always paying the cost of this golden prosperity.

The fictional characters at the dawn of the twentieth century whom we have been considering in this book secure a particular kind of futurity by taking legal control of the accumulated wealth of the plantation, but the cautionary tales of the last two decades suggest that after the experience of dispossession, repair cannot be defined unproblematically as the right to possess. For the descendants of Marie Ursule and Bola in Dionne Brand's At *the Full and Change of the Moon* (1999), including a veteran of the Boer War, possession and resistance can never be claimed and celebrated unreservedly. They are always deeply entangled with loss, because of what is set in motion after the enslaved matriarch of their family deprives the owner of her plantation of his human property in the most radical and devastating way possible. Photography is enfolded into the novel's meditation on bequests, inheritance, and posterity: the plantation owner possesses "photographs that would speak of a great family," whereas "What Marie Ursule is leaving she knows she cannot put into a face," and so we have to look for Marie Ursule's bequest "in the bones or gestures muscular with dispossession."[6] The image of Bola's maternity—"The line of children stretched out unending on the beach"—would seem to bear out Black women's bequest of a legacy that is legible as "disorganized," "far out of line" with the norm, and the worst nightmare of respectable nation-building and public policy initiatives, for not only are her children numerous and of multiple paternities, but she has no interest in feelings of shame.[7]

I am riveted by Bola's charcoal drawing, a stick figure fought over by two of her children in their desperate struggle to claim a maternal inheritance. This is an aesthetics of image-making that is parallel and ostensibly inferior to photography, and that feels closer to Tilly-Tilly's traumatic artistic practice than to the refashioning of West African family heirlooms discussed by Erin Haney. Bola models a disinterest in possessiveness that makes her children's desire to hold on to her memory through the drawing all the more poignant; a mother who is not interested in possessiveness is fine, even virtuous, as long as you are not one of her children. Bola's response to her children's eagerness to make a claim of paternity on her serial lovers—"No one is anyone's. How much time I must tell you"—is harsh but can be understood as lovingly strategic when we appreciate her theorization of the particular terms of her social condition: "That woman Bola who spread her children around so that all would never be gathered in the same place to come to the same harm."[8] Because she is on intimate terms with the lesson that her peculiar personhood as a Black woman bequeaths disaster—that precarity is entangled with the freedom gifted by her enslaved mother—her loved ones must be kept at arm's length for the sake of their own thriving.

Bola presses us to disentangle issues of belonging from *possession* (what it means to *care for* without *possessing*); to imagine relief from the past as a burden that is both freeing and not necessarily experienced as freedom; and to reimagine the working-class Black woman's intimate and child-related choices (including choices that eschew children) as carefully considered and exercised.

This feels at odds with the discourses of the commentators and reformers of the period that is the focus of this book, and with the social scientist investigators of their intimate lives in the following decades. But it also feels at odds with postcolonial feminist investments that critique or advocate for her right to mother or not mother.[9] We must also apprehend Bola exercising a love of herself.[10] On that beach off the coast of the mainland (a down-the-islands netherworld), on that street, opening her trunk in a small bedroom/outhouse, or smashing a window of a business in downtown Port of Spain on Pretoria Day, what does she want, and how does she own that desire?

Brand (because she is reading the past through her jaded post-post-postcolonial present, or because this present allows her to see and acknowledge what optimistic narrators of the past have refused to see) gives us a character marked by what Kaiama Glover would identify in terms of "antisociality," "moral ambiguity," "unmediated and unrestricted by group affiliation."[11] Unlike her children and grandchildren, Bola already knows that the future will not be better. She has already apprehended a "past that is not past, [that] reappears, always, to rupture the present," but has calculated that between privileging her own desire, and understanding the harm caused by proximity to her personhood, her children are least harmed by the consequences of being tied too closely to her.[12] If these are the "skewed life chances and . . . premature death" of the "afterlife of slavery," and if these descendants *are*, "too," the "afterlife of slavery," then *Strolling in the Ruins* presses on the question of the specificity of periodization—each generation's particular experience of this afterlife.[13] How did the turn of the twentieth century, shaped by the particularity of its negotiation of imperial violence, both register constraint and subjugation, and exert its will and imagination?

Introduction

1 "We have seen in our lifetime an activity called writing, in the form of the novel, come to fruition without any previous native tradition to draw on." Lamming, *Pleasures of Exile*, 38.

2 On the Morant Bay uprising, see Wilmot, "The Road to Morant Bay," and Heuman, *Killing Time*. On the Hosay/Muharram massacre on October 20, 1884, see Singh, *Bloodstained Tombs*.

3 Appadurai and Breckenridge, "Public Modernity in India," 16.

4 Neptune, *Caliban and the Yankees*, 201n10. "Understudied" it may be, but it will be clear that I draw on a rich matrix of scholars for my own exploration of the cultural formation of this turn-of-the-century period, including Neptune.

5 On reading "beyond resistance," and for "quiet," see Puri, "Beyond Resistance," and Quashie, *Sovereignty of Quiet*. On quiet as an élite entitlement, see Samuel, "'Right to Quiet.'"

6 See Paton's discussion of the "low-level Magistrate-enforced [or police-enforced] law" outside of the scope of judge and jury, targeting those most likely to be without access to private space, in the postabolition period of the British Caribbean. "Small Charges," 2, 3–4.

7 Campt, *Listening to Images*, 4.

8 The quotation is from Stephens, *Black Empire*, 280. Generally, this book's references to 1915 or 1916, including two quotations by Marcus Garvey and Mahatma Gandhi in this chapter, and public statements by prominent men in Jamaica in chapter 2, fall just outside of many of the events and texts discussed in this book, and in the Jamaican case at least, may well mark the beginning of a distinctive moment of public debate.

9   "At one stage Port of Spain was peopled mainly by single women ... They did
    all kinds of things [before] Victorianism leveled everyone into a kind of aspir-
    ing middle-class attitude to life," Espinet in *My Mother's Place*, dir. Richard Fung,
    minute 35. On Trinidadian jamettes as both Carnival representation of female-
    identified disorder and Black female working-class unruliness and sexual auton-
    omy, see Franco, "'Unruly Woman'" and King, *Island Bodies*.

10 Hall and Massey, "Interpreting the Crisis," 57; Morfino, trans. Jason Smith, cit-
    ing or parsing Louis Althusser in "An Althusserian Lexicon."

11 Putnam, *Radical Moves*, 196.

12 Francis, Rosenberg, and Cobham-Sander, "Researching and Teaching with the
    Digital Archive"; Cobham-Sander, Francis, and Rosenberg, "Panama Silver,
    Asian Gold." See also Frederick, *Colón Man a Come*; Senior, *Dying to Better
    Themselves*; and Owens, "Hard Reading."

13 This is Stephens's phrase, from "What Is This *Black* in Black Diaspora?," 26. On
    reimagining the temporal, geographical, and canonical contours of modern-
    ism, see, for instance, Mao and Walkowitz, "New Modernist Studies"; Fried-
    man, "Periodizing Modernism" and *Plantetary Modernisms*; and Wollaeger and
    Eatough, *Oxford Handbook of Global Modernisms*. I am grateful for Kaylee Hall,
    Dominick Knowles, and Chih-Chien Hsieh's refreshing cynicism in their con-
    versations with me about these debates.

14 H. Johnson, "Cuban Immigrants in Jamaica;" M. Smith, *Liberty, Fraternity,
    Exile*; Brereton, *History of Modern Trinidad*. On unrest in reaction to increased
    taxes and rates in Montego Bay, Jamaica, and Port of Spain, Trinidad, see *Daily
    Gleaner*, "Montego Bay Under Mob Law," April 7, 1902; *New York Times*, "Riot-
    ing in Jamaica: Serious Conflict at Montego Bay," April 8, 1902; Bryan, *Jamaican
    People*; Laurence, "Trinidad Water Riot of 1903."

15 Meikle, *Confederation of the British West Indies*, 43. Meikle's specific British
    Caribbean context echoes an earlier call by an English colonial official who
    had served in the eastern Caribbean, Salmon, *Caribbean Confederation*. Nep-
    tune points out Meikle's text's connection to more well-known Caribbean
    and Latin American writers' concerns about the United States in the region
    including Martí, "Our America"; Rodó, *Ariel*; Darío, "To Roosevelt," 1904.
    See Neptune, *Caliban and the Yankees*, 60–64. If this articulation of "confed-
    eration" affirmed (or conceded) British imperial power in imagining alterna-
    tives to the United States, it also reminds us that single-territory nationalism
    was not always the desired endpoint across the region, and that federation was
    not only an elusive dream of the 1950s and 1960s. See Martínez-San Miguel's
    contention that there was always a richer range of political options indicating
    an "alternative post-colonial imaginary that questioned the master narrative
    of independence and sovereignty of archipelagic colonial regions," such as the
    nineteenth-century transimperial collaborations of Anténor Firmin, Ramón
    Betances, Eugenio María de Hostos, and José Martí. Martínez-San Miguel

urges us to examine their proposals in tandem with the anglophone Caribbean federation of the late 1950s. Martínez-San Miguel, "Spanish Caribbean Literature," 76.

16   The [Trinidad] *Indian Kohinoor Gazette*, April 8, 1899, reported that Carnegie proposed that the Philippines should be exchanged for Jamaica; see also [Jamaica] *Daily Gleaner*, "Julian Hawthorne and Jamaica," August 8, 1899, 7; and Wall, *Andrew Carnegie*, 695. Carnegie also offered to ensure Filipino independence by paying the $20 million purchase price for the Philippines that the United States was about to pay Spain.

17   See Plummer, *Haiti and the Great Powers* and *Haiti and the United States*. Harvey Neptune notes that the US presence in the anglophone Caribbean tended to be different from its "imperious and comprehensive reformist mission" in other parts of the Caribbean in the early twentieth century, and that this remained the case during its military presence in Trinidad decades later. Neptune, *Caliban and the Yankees*, 12. Discussing this period as "the beginning of the 'American century' in the greater Caribbean region," Bonham Richardson gives many examples of British and other European powers and the United States facing off against or working alongside each other in naval and other maneuvers in the context of surveillance and assistance after earthquakes, hurricanes, and fires in the eastern Caribbean. Richardson, *Igniting the Caribbean's Past*. I am grateful to Shalini Puri for this reference.

18   See D. Thomas, *Political Life in the Wake of the Plantation*, 1.

19   [Trinidad] *Port of Spain Gazette*, February 13, 1909, 5.

20   Stewart, "Kumina."

21   D. Brown, "Afro-Cuban Festival 'Day of the Kings,'" 54; Campbell, "Carnival, Calypso and Class Struggle"; Cowley, *Carnival, Canboulay, and Calypso*.

22   Gaspar, *Bondmen and Rebels*, 3–4 and 249–50. For Gaspar, such events showed how African captives "refashion[ed] something of the Akan world within the interstices of the Antigua slave system" (236).

23   Finch, *Rethinking Slave Rebellion in Cuba*. Thanks to Greg Childs for this reference.

24   Ferrer, *Freedom's Mirror*; Fischer, *Modernity Disavowed*; Palmié, *Wizards and Scientists*. Aponte was executed alongside other alleged conspirators in April 1812, and his severed head and hand were displayed near his home in Havana.

25   For theatrical productions related to Haitian sovereignty (proof that its assertions of monarchical sovereignty continued to be worked through and worked out in succeeding generations) see Riley, *Performing Race and Erasure*; Hamner, "Dramatizing the New World's African King"; Baptiste, *Darkening Mirrors*.

26   The Boston-based *Colored American Magazine* carried an etching of Emperor Menelik in December 1900; see Hill, "King Menelik's Nephew," 31. The *Baltimore Afro-American* covered the US visit of Prince Fushimi of Japan in mid-1904.

27 Psalm 68: 31 (*King James Version*); "The Ethiopian tradition derives from the Biblical verse, 'Princes shall come out of Egypt; Ethiopia shall soon stretch forth her hands unto God' [Psalm 68:31]. . . . It made repeated appearances during the nineteenth century and by World War I, Ethiopianism had become not only a trans-Atlantic political movement, but a literary movement well-known among all black people from the Congo basin to the mountains of Jamaica to the sidewalks of New York." Moses, *Golden Age of Black Nationalism*, 23–24.

28 By 1908–9 Prince Ludwig (born in Mulgrave, St. Elizabeth in southwestern Jamaica) was in Chicago, Illinois as Crown Prince Johannes of Ethiopia. Hill, "King Menelik's Nephew"; *Daily Gleaner*, "The Bogus Prince," May 5, 1904, 6.

29 Hill, "King Menelik's Nephew," 16 and 40, quoting from a 1937 directive by Garvey.

30 Gikandi, "Africa and the Epiphany of Modernism," 34; and see Josephine Baker performing "African" and "Vietnamese" roles as a "universal feminine colonial other" in the 1920s; B. Edwards, *Practice of Diaspora*, 162.

31 *Daily Gleaner*, October 21, 1904, 2.

32 E. Johnson, "Black Performance Studies," 447.

33 All kinds of sovereigns, or none at all: "For me, returning to the source didn't lead to the great courts and the regalia of kings and queens." Hartman, *Lose Your Mother*, 234. "Canvasses of dissent" in Brooks, *Bodies in Dissent*, 297.

34 Bonilla, "Ordinary Sovereignty" and *Non-sovereign Futures*.

35 Francis, *Fictions of Feminine Citizenship*, 8; Eng, *Feeling of Kinship*, 59.

36 Lewis, "Party Politics in Jamaica"; Jaffe, "Crime and Insurgent Citizenship"; D. Thomas, Bell, and Wedderburn, *Bearing Witness*; D. Thomas, *Political Life in the Wake of the Plantation*.

37 The name of the inaugural ship gives its name to the thousands of British Caribbean people who entered the United Kingdom from the late 1940s to the early 1970s and transformed a labor force depleted by the Second World War. On Windrush-generation migrants and their children whose landing documents were found to have been destroyed when some of them were deported to the Caribbean as illegal immigrants beginning around 2010, see Gentleman, *Windrush Betrayal* and Grant, *Homecoming*. For historians on the financial trail of Caribbean enslavement, see C. Hall, Draper, McClelland, Donington, and R. Lang, *Legacies of British Slave-Ownership*, and the Center for the Study of the Legacies of British Slave Ownership at the University of London, https://www.ucl.ac.uk/lbs/.

38 Landler, "Britain Grapples with Its Racist Past, from the Town Square to the Boardroom," *New York Times*, June 18, 2020; Rawlinson, "Lloyd's of London and Greene King to Make Slave Trade Reparations," [London] *Guardian*, June 18, 2020.

39 C. Hall et al., *Legacies of British Slave-Ownership*, 1.

40 On February 6, 2009, seven persons were arrested in Georgetown, Guyana under this 1893 act, and after years of appeals by four—Gulliver McEwan, Angel

Clarke, Peaches Fraser, and Isabella Persaud—the Caribbean Court of Justice struck down the 1893 law as invalid. See Matthews and Robinson, "Modern Vagrancy"; Paton and Romain, "Gendered Clothing Legislation"; Trotz, "A Historic Decision"; Rowley, *Feminist Advocacy and Gender Equity*, 201–2.

41 See Eng's proposal that it is shortsighted to think of *Lawrence v. Texas* (the 2003 US ruling striking down the Texas law banning same-sex "sodomy") as solely "queer liberalism's victory, rather than in terms of race, miscegenation, and segregation, unresolved in the past and persisting in the present." *Feeling of Kinship*, 41.

42 See Alexander, "Not Just (Any) Body," and Francis, *Fictions of Feminine Citizenship*.

43 On "black intentionality for, black agency for, and black intimacy with occupation, border policing, surveillance, and detention" in the United States, see E. Edwards, "Of Cain and Abel," 191; note also the "internationalization of the civil rights movement, in Condoleeza Rice's hands, meant occupation and Western domination, rather than racial equality and national autonomy," C. Young, "Black Ops," 36.

44 D. Scott, *Omens of Adversity*, 2; Abdur-Rahman, "Black Ecstatic," 345.

45 Russert, "Disappointment in the Archives of Black Freedom."

46 Walcott, "Ruins of a Great House"; Rhys, *Wide Sargasso Sea*; A. Clarke, *Polished Hoe*; and Collins, *Angel*.

47 Wynter, "Novel and History: Plot and Plantation"; Forbes, "Between Plot and Plantation," 24.

48 Forbes, "Between Plot and Plantation," 26. For a discussion of twenty-first-century Caribbean people of all classes as strongly identified with an antiblack great house ethos, see Levy and Irvine-Sobers, "The River Is in Spate and the Bridge Is Inundated."

49 In the first instance, De Lisser, *Jane's Career*, briefly discussed in chapter 2, and Roberts, *The Single Star*, discussed in chapter 1; and in the second, Cobham, *Rupert Gray*, set in Trinidad, and Tracy, *Sword of Nemesis*, set in Trinidad and Montserrat. Here, as elsewhere, my racial categorizations will irritate or bewilder some readers. I've tended to use the term *Black* to refer to Cobham, Tracy, and their protagonists, even though at least Tracy's protagonist's near-whiteness more correctly classifies him as something like *mixed-race*, *Colored*, or *of color*, and I've done so because of this character's ideological claim on the significance of African descent in his genealogical narration of himself. Thus light-skinned persons who identify with whiteness or don't affirm African descent as significant aren't Black (unless they cannot socially and legally claim "whiteness-without-question"). I mobilize terms such as *light-skinned*, *near-white*, and *nonwhite*, knowing full well that *light-skinned*, for example, may depend on who is in the room, and that *nonwhite* (usually as a way to group together persons across categories of Indigenous/First Nation, African, and Asian descent or affiliation who could not be designated white or white-appearing and

for whom that lack of access to whiteness is socially significant), like the designation *of color*, centers whiteness as a norm. I am arguably beholden to "one-drop" ideas (about the legally enforced distance from whiteness) that are sometimes associated with US contexts, and to late twentieth-century modes of address and identification in which *Black* is a socially legible and valorized categorization. But in the anglophone Caribbean, *Black* is not widely used as a self-designation before the early 1970s; neither is *Caribbean*, as a descriptor of the region's people (rather than *West Indian*); and so I am mobilizing both terms anachronistically. In opting to diminish or erase a *Colored* categorization that would have been understood and asserted, I am failing to take advantage of the intermediary and flexible categorization of *brown/Brown*, but this is simultaneously specific and all-embracing. In Maziki Thame's discussion, the "brown nationalism" of a Jamaican light-skinned class sought "to reorder racial hierarchy and center brownness" from the 1950s; and for Belinda Edmondson, *Brown*, whether condemned or celebrated, flags fewer actual people than the conjoining of characteristics of "quasi-elite status and humble origins" of middle-class identity in the English-speaking Caribbean. Maziki Thame, "Racial Hierarchy, 111; and Belinda Edmondson, *Caribbean Middlebrow*, 7. *Brown* may be the best term for De Lisser, whom I would describe as part of a light-skinned middling middle-class category of journalists and artists identified as of Jewish or partly Jewish descent, and who is sometimes described as *white* because of his increasingly white-elite-identified stance during his sojourn as the editor of the *Jamaica Daily Gleaner*, a stance that Rhonda Cobham-Sander helpfully discusses in relation to patronage. See Rhonda Cobham-Sander, "Creative Writer and West Indian Society," chap. 1; on the "'middling' classes of urban colonial society," see Stuart Hall, "Legacy of Anglo-Caribbean Culture," 179; and see also Leah Rosenberg, *Nationalism*, chap. 3; Kwame Dawes, "An Act of 'Unruly' Savagery"; and Matthew Smith, "H. G. and Haiti."

50 "As if to refuse the possibility or reality of their homelessness, southern whites displaced that visual sign of their landlessness onto black bodies hanging from trees. . . . Hanging, as most of these black bodies are—a few feet, sometimes only a few inches—above ground, the opportunity to count, to matter, to belong, to occupy a plot of land, by simple virtue of standing on that solid ground, is summarily denied them." Alexandre, *Properties of Violence*, 25; Thompson, *Eye for the Tropics*; for the connection between militarized strolling and photography, see Sontag, *On Photography*, 55.

51 Gaonkar, *Alternative Modernities*; Ramos, *Divergent Modernities*; "timelag" is part of Harootunian's critique of the language of "deformed" development, *Overcome by Modernity*, xii.

52 See R. Williams's 1958 description of the three decades before World War I as an "interregnum" in the time line of post-Victorian cultural formation, in which "we shall not find . . . anything very new: a working out, rather, of unfinished lines; a tentative redirection. Such work requires notice, but suggests brevity," in *Culture and Society*, 161–62. It is now more common to account for the rever-

berations of imperial and colonial accumulation and kinship in British novels of this historical moment, as in Jameson's and Z. Smith's engagements with E. M. Forster and Esty's reading of the "jagged effects" on the *bildungsroman* and its ideals of humanism caused by imperialism's "unsettling" of the "politics and poetics of subject formation." Jameson, "Modernism and Imperialism"; Z. Smith, *On Beauty*; Jed Esty, *Unseasonable Youth*, 2, 3.

53   "What are the ways in which an act of 'remembering the wrong things at a wrong moment' might generate an unlearning that critically unsettles the way we believe we know our history?" Yoneyama, *Cold War Ruins*, 49.

54   On stigma and silence regarding enslavement in West Africa, see Hartman, *Lose Your Mother*, and Greene, *Slaveowners of West Africa*.

55   Even if African institutions "lose," in the Africa/Europe encounters narrated by African writers, there is also significant symbolic loss on the European side. Cobham-Sander, "'Mwen Na Rien, Msieu,'" 874.

56   Chatterjee, *The Nation and Its Fragments*, 120.

57   Wynter, "We Must Learn to Sit Down and Discuss a Little Culture," 24.

58   Césaire, *Notebook of a Return to the Native Land*, 43. See also Walter Mignolo on coloniality as "the hidden face of modernity and its very condition of possibility"; Mignolo, "Many Faces of Cosmo-polis," 158. On "temporal distancing" and the denial of "coevalness," see Fabian, *Time and the Other*, 30–31. On Caribbean elites' participation in the representation of the Caribbean as not quite modern, for an emerging tourist industry, see Thompson, *Eye for the Tropics*. On the Caribbean and the US South as ethnographically disappointing, see Trouillot, "Caribbean Region," 20–21; and Palmié, *Wizards and Scientists*, 39–41.

59   Asad, "Conscripts of Western Civilization," 334; D. Scott, *Conscripts of Modernity*, 117, 119.

60   Lowe, "Intimacies of Four Continents," 207–8. See also Scott's more recent invocation of "a sensibility of time that, however forgotten, is not forgetful," in his discussion of the past of the Grenada Revolution. D. Scott, *Omens of Adversity*, 96.

61   Newton, "Returns to a Native Land," 112. "Scourging" and "empty lands" are from Mintz's discussion of how Europe's conquest of the Caribbean differed from its conquests elsewhere. Mintz, "Caribbean as a Socio-cultural Area," 918, emphasis in original. Following Newton we could think of spaces of indigeneity in the region at the turn of the century, including the Miskito Nation's complex relationship with the Nicaraguan state, with the British empire by way of colonial Jamaica, and with US banana interests. The Miskitos' King Clarence had been living in exile in Jamaica from the late 1890s. See Olien, "Miskito Kings and the Line of Succession." Such spaces of indigeneity occupy the "*internal* South" of the nation and the colony, as Shona Jackson points out in a discussion of indigeneity in the postcolonial present: as both a south of the Global South, and as mainland territory that challenges the privileging of island spaces in the theorization of the Caribbean imaginary. Jackson, *Creole Indigeneity*, 12–14; Mintz, "Enduring Substances, Trying Theories," 295–96.

62 King Henri I, sovereign of Haiti from 1811 to 1820; Shaka kaSenzangakhona, sovereign of the Zulu kingdom from 1816 to 1828; Ovonramwen Nogbaisi, Oba of Benin from 1888, before being deposed by a British expedition and exiled to Calabar in 1897; Yaa Asantewaa, Ashanti queen who led the final of five wars of Ashanti independence against the British in 1900; Asantehene Prempeh (Prempeh I), Ashanti sovereign dethroned and exiled between 1896 and 1900; Cixu, empress dowager of China until 1908; Puyi, emperor of China from 1908 to 1912. When the British sovereign Queen Victoria died in 1901 (having occupied the throne since 1837 and been most recently fêted globally in Diamond Jubilee celebrations in June 1897), Empire Day began to be celebrated throughout the British imperial world the following year on May 24, 1902.

63 "Invisible" begs the question of vantage point ("Invisible to whom? Not to me," is Toni Morrison's contention that the work of a generation of African American writers including Ralph Ellison was directed at a white audience), Als, "Toni Morrison and the Ghosts in the House." Louis Althusser suggests that capitalism seeks to "conceal," to render invisible, the variety of experiences of time, and that in unearthing this multiplicity of "rhythms" we must attend to how they are corralled to serve the time of capital. Althusser, "Errors of Classical Economics," 112; and see Pratt's discussion of this passage in *Archives of American Time*, 44–45.

64 See Anderson's conception of how the novel and the newspaper came to convene nineteenth-century citizens in Spanish America and the Spanish Pacific in a nation-time of "temporal coincidence" in which, aware of though never in personal contact with each other, they shared an "imagined community," *Imagined Communities*, 24–25; and see Chatterjee's critique that since people "can only imagine themselves" but "do not live in" such an abstract, empty "time-space" that "linearly connects past, present and future," he prefers a more realistic sense of "heterogeneous, unevenly dense" time; Chatterjee, "Anderson's Utopia," 166. For other critiques of Anderson, see Bhabha, *Location of Culture* and McClintock, *Imperial Leather*, chap. 10.

65 See Tageldin's discussion of the "unevenness of Egyptians' temporal self-understanding," *Disarming Words*, 215, Tageldin's emphasis.

66 Patterson, "Slaves differed from other human beings in that they were not allowed *freely* to integrate the experience of their ancestors into their lives, to inform their understanding of social reality with the inherited meanings of their natural forebears, or to anchor the living present in any conscious community of memory," *Slavery and Social Death*, 5, my emphasis. Language connecting people of African ancestry to the status of property and the status of noncitizenship in nineteenth-century US law notes that "they had no rights which the white man was bound to respect," and here I understand "bound to respect" to be parallel to Patterson's "freely," Carbado, "Racial Naturalization," 642–43.

67 See Gloria Rolando's Cuban interlocutors remembering the brutal repression of the Partido Independiente de Color in 1912, in the film *Las raíces de mi corazón*;

and the discussion of Confederate statuary in New Orleans in 2018: "Up until a few years ago, my mother wouldn't talk about what she had heard about her grandmother's life on the plantation. My mother was born in 1904 and so you couldn't just talk about white people in those days." Topsy Chapman quoted in Robertson and Reckdahl, "Stories of New Orleans"; *New York Times*, "As Monuments Go Down, Family Histories Emerge," May 24, 2017.

68 Mintz, "Enduring Substances, Trying Theories," 296. Mintz is not celebrating this capacity, but showing how, under "coercion," the Caribbean's plantation processes made the region modern before Europe in distinctive ways. See also D. Scott, "Modernity That Predated the Modern."

69 "'Kinship' loses meaning, since it can be invaded at any given and arbitrary moment by the property relations." Spillers, "Mama's Baby, Papa's Maybe," 74.

70 Morgan, "*Partus Sequitur Ventrem*," 1, 13; Hunter, discussing 1643 Virginia legislation and Black women's presumed capacity for "arduous physical fieldwork," which distinguished them from untaxed white female laborers perceived to be weak and dependent, and added a significant financial burden to Black families' capacity to "advance economically or purchase their freedom." Hunter, *Bound in Wedlock*, 9.

71 Trotman, *Crime in Trinidad*, 240–46; Zeuske, "Hidden Markers, Open Secrets," 214–15. This did not mean that such persons did not use a second surname (that is, the name of their father or of the person who had owned them or their mother), but that official religious and legal records would not recognize it. This terminology became the polite replacement for other designations ("former," "*libre*," "*pardo*," "*moreno*") that indicated a history of enslavement and indentureship, or nonwhiteness: in postabolition Cuba such persons "operate as juridical persons," able to purchase land legally, and so on, "but they are simultaneously being marked as illegitimate. See also Loichot's reminder that in the French Caribbean, Article 9 of the 1724 *Code Noir* states that "the biological father whether black or white could not transmit his name to the child of a woman of color." Loichot, *Orphan Narratives*, 98.

72 The quotations and emphases are from Hong's discussion of the foregrounding of the male social subject and the occlusion of women's reproductive capacity in Patterson's theorization of natal alienation, in *Death beyond Disavowal*, 103, 104.

73 Halberstam, *In a Queer Time and Place*, 54; Sharpe, *Monstrous Intimacies*, 13–23.

74 Quotation from Woloch, *The One vs the Many*, 13.

75 Froude, *English in the West Indies*, 65.

76 Mahabir, "Communal Style," 114–15; and see the discussion of this jewelry as "the Indian way of banking," Rayman, "Indian Jewellery in British Guyana." On the "mystical" and "enigmatic" commodity concealing labor under capitalist relations, see Marx, "The Fetishism of the Commodity and Its Secret" in *Capital*, vol. 1, trans. Ben Folkes, 164–65. When Caribbean merchants advertised "sterling silver Indian jewelry made by our own Indian silversmith" to tour-

ists and local monied élites, were they validating (migrant or Caribbean-born) Indo-Caribbean imagination and artistry? Or, in severing artisans ("our own") from dynamic social relations with their communities, and no doubt also from the profits of mark-up pricing, were they rendering this jewelry exotic and "enigmatic"? See advertisement for "Gold and silver high class jewelry" by J. H. Milke and Bros., *Daily Gleaner*, February 22, 1899, 1.

77 "The African and the Asiatic will not mix," Froude, *English in the West Indies*, 65; "socializing without recourse . . ." is from Mintz, "Enduring Substances," 295–96.

78 Quotation from Ford-Smith, "Women and the Garvey Movement in Jamaica," 74. On the contradictions of middle- and upper-class women's reformist activism, see also Reddock, "Feminism, Nationalism, and the Early Women's Movement"; Vassell, "The Movement for the Vote for Women 1918–1919"; Gregg, *Caribbean Women*.

79 Both statements were made, coincidentally, in February 1916, after the period that is the focus of this book. Garvey is writing to the president of Tuskegee Institute, Robert Russa Moton, on the eve of the latter's visit to Jamaica in 1916: page 6 of an eight-page typewritten letter dated February 29, 1916, addressed to Major Moton, included in the irregularly paginated "The Perilous Road of Marcus M. Garvey" in *Eight Negro Bibliographies*, comp. Daniel T. Williams; see F. Smith, "Good Enough for Booker T To Kiss." Gandhi is referring to ships leaving India with indentured laborers: *The Leader*, "Indentured Labour," February 2, 1916; *Collected Works of Mahatma Gandhi*, vol. 13, 249. See Niranjana, *Mobilizing India*, chap. 2.

80 On "erotic autonomy," see Alexander, "Not Just (Any) Body," 6, and *Pedagogies of Crossing*, 22–23.

81 McClintock, "No Longer in a Future Heaven," 90, 92.

82 Women as "unproductive," Alexander, "Not Just (Any) Body"; consuming women as disquieting for feminists, leftists, and nineteenth-century male commentators, Felski, *Gender of Modernity*, 61–90.

83 McKay, "Midnight Woman to the Bobby," *Songs of Jamaica*, 74–76, and *Complete Poems*, 51–52. See W. James's reading of this poem, *Fierce Hatred*, 104–6.

84 "Law 12 of 1902: A Law to Consolidate and Amend the Laws Relating to Vagrancy, 1902," *Laws of Jamaica Passed in the Year 1902*, chap 12, page 3, https://ufdcimages.uflib.ufl.edu/AA/00/06/39/18/00064/Laws%20of%20Jamaica%201902%20pdf%20Opt.pdf.

85 Nicolazzo, "Henry Fielding's *The Female Husband*," 336; and see Matthews and Robinson, "Modern Vagrancy in the Anglophone Caribbean."

86 See Trotman's discussion of the impact of vagrancy laws on Indian migrants and Indo-Trinidadians, *Crime in Trinidad*.

87 On the "waiting room of history" prescribed for "Indians, Africans, and other 'rude' nations," see Chakrabarty, *Provincializing Europe*, 8.

88 Edmondson, "Brown women's sexuality is pivotal to the understanding of these early romances because brown men's social status hinged on the status of their women, and their women were *compromised subjects*." *Caribbean Middlebrow*, 60, my emphasis; Carby, the Black mother as bestowing a "hereditary weight of betrayal" in "Treason-Workers."

89 Hell and Schönle, *Ruins of Modernity*, 5.

90 Trouillot, "The Odd and the Ordinary," 4.

91 Walcott, "Ruins of a Great House"; it may be that the United States did not have significant or discernible managerial interests in the southeastern Caribbean context that Walcott was mapping in the early 1960s.

92 On Havana's ruins, see Birkenmaier and Whitfield, *Havana beyond the Ruins*; and on Cuba's estate ruins specifically, see Paravisini-Gebert, "The Caribbean's Agonizing Seashores."

93 Gosine, "My Mother's *Baby*," 51. On moving away from *injury* in framing postenslavement identities, and Black female sexuality in particular, see, for instance, Nash, *Black Body in Ecstasy*.

94 For example, many of my citations come from the [Trinidad] *Port of Spain Gazette* and the [Jamaica] *Daily Gleaner*, newspapers associated with the views of powerful local white élite classes; as opposed to papers such as the [Jamaica] *Times* and the [Trinidad] *Mirror*, both owned or managed by (local or UK-born) white editors who tended to support and promote the views and institutions of a nonwhite and respectable middle class; or papers run by Black journalists, such as the *Jamaica Advocate*, founded and edited by Dr. Robert Love.

95 See Jaji's discussion of "the visual and conceptual polyphony [and] cacophony" of early newspapers. Jaji, *Africa in Stereo*, 25.

96 See the discussion of "incommensurability" and the "[conflation] of the ground of comparison with the basis of equivalence." Melas, *All the Difference*, 36.

97 See the comparison of Chinese laborers in the Transvaal to Indian laborers in Jamaica, *Daily Gleaner*, "Labor Problem: The West Indian Coolie and Chinese for the Transvaal," April 12, 1904, 5; and of Indian laborers in Trinidad to both Indians "at home" and to Japanese and Korean immigrants in Peru, *Port of Spain Gazette*, March 18, 1909.

98 Lowe, "Intimacies of Four Continents," 193.

99 I am thinking, for instance, of Saidiya Hartman's harrowing accounts of Black life in New York City at this historical moment, *Wayward Lives*. On Caribbean people in North America, see Watkins-Owens, *Blood Relations*, and Nottage, *Intimate Apparel*. On Caribbean whiteness specifically, in a later generation, see Cliff, *No Telephone to Heaven*.

100 These novels are Cobham's *Rupert Gray* and Tracy's *Sword of Nemesis*, both set in the eastern Caribbean; Hopkins's *Of One Blood* (1903–4), set in the US Northeast and South as well as a mythical African kingdom; and Hayford's *Ethiopia Unbound* (1911), set in British-ruled West Africa.

101 Benjamin, "Theses on the Philosophy of History," 255; and Cadava, *Words of Light*, 64. On the relationship of past to present, see also Leigh Raiford's invocation of the "backward glance at forward motion" that may "grow beyond what we see," Raiford, *Imprisoned in a Luminous Glare*, 236; and S. Hall's sense of "the new" as "reconfiguring the elements of the past," rather than "breaking completely with the past," in *The Stuart Hall Project*, dir. John Akomfrah, minute 26.

102 Brathwaite, "Poetry, 11-9-82" (uploaded Nov 6, 2020?), min. 1:58, https://www.youtube.com/watch?v=_KVm1cNv4yo.

103 Lowe, *Intimacies of Four Continents*, 175; Coronado, *A World Not to Come*, 18.

104 See James, *Beyond a Boundary*, chap. 1. Other figures born early in that first decade include Cuban-born Nicolás Guillén, Wilfredo Lam, and Eusebia Cosme; Trinidad-born George Padmore (Malcolm Nurse), and Adrian Cola-Rienzi (Krishna Deonarine Tewari); Puerto Rican–born Margot Arce; Jamaican-born Una Marson; and Gold Coast–born Mable Dove. Figures born in the teen years of the new century include Aimé Césaire, Claudia Jones, and Marie Vieux Chauvet, while Neville Dawes, Sylvia Wynter, Stuart Hall, Paule Marshall, Edouard Glissant, George Lamming, V. S. Naipaul, and Maryse Condé were born in the late 1920s to early 1930s in Caribbean households in the region or in North America or West Africa.

105 On attending to the present, see Gikandi, "*Arrow of God*: The Novel and the Problem of Modern Time"; Wright, *Physics of Blackness*, 4; and Abdur-Rahman's discussion of a fleeting ecstatic present in "Black Ecstatic."

1. Cuba, South Africa, and the Anglophone Caribbean's New Imperial Century

1 Lord Inventor's [Henry Forbes's] calypso for the 1900 Trinidad Carnival season; the Duke of Marlborough's [George Adilla's] calypso for the 1900 or 1901 Carnival season; Trinidad respondents' memories of parents' or grandparents' Congolese lyrics about serving in the British forces in southern Africa, sung in the 1960s. Here and below discussions of these songs are drawn from Rohlehr, *Calypso and Society*, 45–46; Davies, "The Africa Theme in Trinidad," 70; and Warner-Lewis, *Central Africa in the Caribbean*, 53–54.

2 *Port of Spain Gazette* [Trinidad], "The Pronunciation of South African names," July 17, 1900, reprinted from London's *Standard*. Here I am using the era's terminology instead of the later names "Mafikeng" or "Mahikeng." Afrikaaner terms such as *kopke* (hill), *veldt* (grassland), *trekboers* (nomadic farmers), and *laager* (encampment of encircled and protected wagons) discursively reflected a pioneering claim to difficult territory that had been earned by blood and grit over time. When used by the British, these same terms (suggesting hills that were obstacles to clear sight of the enemy, or endless grasslands that provided no shelter from enemy fire) indicated an intractability that would be penetrated heroically. With these terms both white (settlers and would-be settlers) colonial groups effaced or subordinated nonwhite communities and their claims to the land.

3 "The Pronunciation of South African names." On Afrikaans, which has Malay, Khoisan, and other linguistic features in addition to Dutch, and which was designated an official language in 1918, see McClintock, *Imperial Leather*, 100; and Hofmeyr, "Building a Nation from Words."

4 Iglesias Utset, *Cultural History of Cuba*, 133.

5 Pérez, *On Becoming Cuban*, 99–100; van Heyningen, *The Concentration Camps of the Anglo-Boer War*.

6 See van Heyningen, *The Concentration Camps of the Anglo-Boer War*; and Jaji's discussion of court interpreter (and future Setswana-language newspaper founder, politician, and novelist) Solomon Tshekisho' Plaatje's observations of the war, *Africa in Stereo*, 55–56.

7 Hayes et al., introduction to *Comparatively Queer*, 6.

8 Dimock, "A Theory of Resonance," 1601.

9 This and following quotations, Allan [Charles W. Willis], *"Buckra" Land*, 8, 44, 45, 80.

10 See, for instance, Chomsky, *West Indian Workers and the United Fruit Company*.

11 Allen, "Constellations in Sugar," 88–89. For an account of Cuban estate ownership as devastating multigenerational ruination, see Pérez, *On Becoming Cuban*.

12 Stubbs, "Political Idealism and Commodity Production"; C. Jacobs, "Jamaica and the Cuban Ten Years War"; Hulme, *Cuba's Wild East*.

13 Hulme, *Cuba's Wild East*, 243, 268. H. Thomas recalls the "rigid quarantine" by the Jamaican authorities "against Cuba, for both hygienic and political reasons." *Story of a West Indian Policeman*, 390; Allan refers to Spanish gunboats patrolling Cuban waters and expresses support for Cubans' attempt to throw off "damnable Spanish rule." *"Bukra" Land*, 7.

14 On Cubans and Haitians in Jamaica, see De Lisser's *In Jamaica and Cuba*, and his early journalism, collected in Moore and M. A. Johnson, *Squalid Kingston*, 65; M. Smith, *Liberty, Fraternity, Exile*; Sheller, *Democracy after Slavery*; Bryan, "Émigrés: Conflict and Reconciliation"; H. Johnson, "Cuban Immigrants in Jamaica, 1868–1898"; McGarrity, "Cubans in Jamaica."

15 Hulme, *Cuba's Wild East*, 268–69. The Morant Cays off the coast of St. Thomas would make the most sense as a destination for Reid's characters, though Jamaica's cays are not only in this eastern location.

16 Walcott, "Henri Christophe: A Chronicle in Seven Scenes." First produced in London in 1953, the play was performed the following year at the University College of the West Indies, Mona.

17 See Wynter's discussion of *New Day*, capital, and literary form in "Novel and History, Plot and Plantation"; Brodber's and Cobham-Sander's discussions of the novel's return to 1865 in the late 1940s in order to capture what the historical archive could not and "to establish the basis for a national myth" as the colony began its push for self-government, and in the specific context of 1944, the beginning of universal adult suffrage in Jamaica, Brodber, "Oral Sources." Cobham-Sander,

"Fictions of Gender, Fictions of Race," 17; and see also Wilmot, "Road to Morant Bay"; Heuman, *Killing Time*; C. Hall, *White, Male and Middle Class*; Rosenberg, "New Woman and 'The Dusky Strand'"; Rizutto, *Insurgent Testimonies*.

18   D. Scott, "Sovereignty of the Imagination, Interview with George Lamming," 89.

19   Lamming, *In the Castle of My Skin*, 1953.

20   On life in Martinique during the Vichy régime, see Capécia's fictional 1948 account, *Je Suis Martiniquaise* ("I Am a Martinican Woman"), trans. Beatrice Stith Clark; on Trinidad, see Neptune, *Caliban and the Yankees*.

21   Mais, "Now We Know," *Public Opinion* [Jamaica], July 11, 1944.

22   Césaire, *Notebook of a Return to the Native Land*, 1939/1947.

23   Bonilla, *Non-sovereign Futures*; Wilder, *Freedom Time*.

24   This and the following quotations are from Reid, *New Day*, 164, 204, 168, 212.

25   Reid, *New Day*, 232.

26   He was allowed to enter Jamaica as a tourist. Roberts, *These Many Years*, 314–16.

27   Another text about the region is Roberts, *Lands of the Inner Sea*.

28   Hulme, *Cuba's Wild East*, 262–65.

29   Roberts, *The Single Star*, 295, 329; Hulme, *Cuba's Wild East*, 264–65.

30   For Roberts in 1949 Cuba's experience in the 1890s is a lesson in heroism from which anglophone neighbors should learn; but Fidel Castro, recalling past humiliation in order to forecast victory, would declare on January 1, 1959, that unlike 1895, when US forces prevented them from doing so, Cuban guerillas would enter Santiágo. Louis Pérez, *Cuba: Between Reform and Revolution*, 126–27.

31   Linebaugh and Rediker, *The Many-Headed Hydra*; Gilroy, *The Black Atlantic*; Reckin, "Tidalectic Lectures." Roberts's marine mapping and regional solidarity is central to Gillman's discussion of the archipelagic conceptualization of the "Mediterranean" in the Americas; she notes Roberts's strategic use of New Orleans in his work, for example, and his use of the term "Mediterranean of the West" in *The Caribbean: Story of Our Sea of Destiny*. Gillman, "It Takes an Archipelago." See also DeLoughrey's view, that a "[mystification of] the importance of the sea and the migrations across its expanse reinforces the colonial "'trope of the isolated island.'" *Routes and Roots*, 2.

32   This "slot" is continuous with the British Caribbean–born person of nebulous hispanophone connections, ethically shallow and reeking of new money (Bustamante himself was a money-lender) in the person of a character such as Tack Tally, in Claude McKay's 1933 novel *Banana Bottom*, set in Jamaica. Note Frederick's critique of McKay's harsh treatment of this character, in *Colón Man a Come*. The returnee from Cuba reappears in Jamaican fiction (though not negatively) with Michael Thelwell's 1980 novel *The Harder They Come*. A similar outsider is Manuel, in Jacques Roumain's 1944 novel, *Masters of the Dew*, who accumulates physical and emotional abuse that is politically radicalizing, rather than wealth, during his cane-cutting years in Cuba.

33   F. Smith, "Between Stephen Lloyd and Estaban Yo-eed."

34 Roberts, *The Single Star*, 24.

35 Roberts, *These Many Years*, 17–18.

36 Helg, "Black Men, Racial Stereotyping, and Violence in the U.S. South and Cuba"; Helg, *Our Rightful Share*; Scott is discussing an earlier, nineteenth-century period of anticolonial insurgency; R. Scott, "Race, Labor, and Citizenship in Cuba," 85.

37 See Rolando, *Las raíces de mi corazón*; and Melina Pappademos, "The Cuban Race War of 1912."

38 *Daily Gleaner* [Jamaica],"Romance of a War Hero: Boer Wins Belle of the West Indies," January 4, 1906, reprinted from the *New York Evening Journal*.

39 Muhammad points out that whereas blackness would continue to be criminalized *as blackness*, "ethnic" whites gradually became free of both the hyphen mediating their claim on Americanness and the moral taint implied by it. Muhammad, *The Condemnation of Blackness*.

40 Gillman, "It Takes an Archipelago," 141, 135.

41 Gillman, "The Afterlives of *Free State of Jones*."

42 *Daily Gleaner* [Jamaica], December 13, 1946, 16; June 12, 1948, 14; readers may have pondered the irony of the "ardent young warrior" being invited to return to Cuba for an official visit when his first visit in 1895, moonlighting as a war correspondent for the *Daily Graphic*, was as a soldier in the British flank of colonial Spanish forces attempting to suppress revolutionary Cuban forces. *Daily Gleaner*, "Churchill and Cuba," February 2, 1946, 8.

43 This and following quotations, De Lisser, *In Jamaica and Cuba*, v, 73, 78.

44 *Daily Gleaner*, "Jobless West Indians in Cuba Should Be Settled in British Guiana or British Honduras," September 6, 1947, 10. On Jamaican cane-cutters in Cuba, see Knight, "Jamaican Migrants and the Cuban Sugar Industry"; de la Fuente, "Two Dangers, One Solution"; and on the era's regional migrants more generally, see Putnam, *Radical Moves*.

45 Rohlehr, *Calypso and Society*, 45; Rohlehr, "Calypso Reinvents Itself," 214.

46 [Trinidad] *Port of Spain Gazette*, February 7, 1900.

47 *Port of Spain Gazette*, "Riotous Behavior—The Queen of the Brigade Fined," July 31, 1900. This name is "Lazaro" or "Cazaro."

48 Rohlehr, *Calypso and Society*; Franco, "The 'Unruly' Woman"; Gill, *Erotic Islands*. On the claims for the carnivalesque as a challenge to the dominant classes in early modern Europe, see Bakhtin, *Rabelais and His World*; and on the limits of Carnival's capacity for radical critique in Trinidad, see Lovelace, *The Dragon Can't Dance*.

49 The quotation is from McClintock, *Imperial Leather*, 100.

50 Pierre, *Predicament of Blackness*, 197.

51 Collis-Buthelezi, "Caribbean Regionalism," 40. Here it is worth noting that South Africa has been studied in relation to other periods and spaces in the Americas, as in Collis-Buthelezi's "Case for Black Studies in South Africa," and Stéphane

Robolin's study of apartheid-era South African and US African American writers, *Grounds of Engagement*; and also that the impulse to position South Africa in relation to the Americas has been critiqued: Barnard, "Of Riots and Rainbows."

52 The quotation is from Collis-Buthelezi, "Caribbean Regionalism," 37.

53 Sherwood, *Origins of Pan-Africanism*; Geiss, *Pan African Movement*, 177; Hooker, "The Pan-African Conference 1900." Garvey says the passengers were a West Indian man and Basuto woman and that they were traveling from Basutoland to their home in the East Indies. This would have been on his 1914 return to Jamaica from a two-year stay in Europe. This is recalled in the autobiographical document "The Negro's Greatest Enemy," written from Tombs Prison in New York City, and published in 1923. See the UCLA African Studies Center document: https://www.international.ucla.edu/asc/mgpp/sample01.

54 B. Edwards opens *The Practice of Diaspora* by pointing out that Du Bois's address to this London gathering in July 1900, in a speech entitled "To the Nations of the World," begins with the declaration "The problem of the twentieth century is the problem of the color line," which we have come to associate with *The Souls of Black Folk*, published three years later. For Edwards it is key to situate Du Bois's words at an international event, in Europe, addressing delegates from Africa, Europe, and the Americas, since Du Bois tends to be claimed in US-centered contexts.

55 My discussion of the proceedings is drawn from *Port of Spain Gazette*, "The Pan African Conference," July 28, 1900.

56 The *Port of Spain Gazette*, September 22, 1900, drawing on a [London] *Times Weekly* July 28, 1900 report, noted the success of the London conference, and that Williams wanted branches in both Trinidad and Jamaica, besides his headquarters in Chancery Lane, London.

57 [Jamaica] *Daily Gleaner*, March 30, 1901, 9.

58 *Daily Gleaner*, June 4, 1901.

59 *Daily Gleaner*, "The Cry of Race," May 22, 1906, 8–9.

60 Haggard, *King Solomon's Mines*; and Conrad, *Heart of Darkness*. I am thinking here of Joseph Roach's discussion of surrogation or substitution, to address "actual or perceived vacancies . . . in the network of relations that constitutes the social fabric"; these "performance genealogies" include "imaginary movements dreamed in minds." *Cities of the Dead*, 2, 26. As part of his argument, Roach discusses Zulu masquerade in New Orleans Carnival.

61 Smith, "Things You'd Imagine Zulu Tribes to Do," 24–25; Abbott and Seroff, *Ragged but Right*, 86.

62 Magubane, "Mines, Minstrels, and Masculinity."

63 North, *The Dialect of Modernism*, 10.

64 Brooks, *Bodies in Dissent*, 238, 240.

65 *Daily Gleaner*, "Zulu Outbreak," July 6, 1906, 11; *Daily Gleaner*, "An Extraordinary Letter," July 6, 1906, 8–9; *Daily Gleaner*, "Keir Hardie's Queer Letter,"

July 21, 1906, 18; *Daily Gleaner*, "Zulu Prince's Success," April 7, 1906, 13; *Daily Gleaner*, "Local Notes" (a concert billed as a tale of the Zulu war), April 24, 1903, 10; *Daily Gleaner*, "The Battle of Zulu" (a performance at the Rockfort Gardens in Kingston), January 6, 1910, 2; *Daily Gleaner*, "Lost and Found," October 23, 1906, 13; *Daily Gleaner*, "Action Brought in Circuit Court to Recover Land," October 13, 1911, 13; *Daily Gleaner*, "Spring Garden Races," June 19, 1911, 14.

66   Howard Rosenberg reviews the South African Broadcasting Corporation's 1986 television mini series with this title that was aired globally, *Los Angeles Times*, "'Shaka Zulu': Negative Metaphor for South African Blacks," November 21, 1986. For responses to this television program in Jamaican popular music that reflect "positive and negative" ideas about the African continent, see Mel Cooke, "Singing about Shaka: Zulu's Musical Role Changes from Ugly to Warrior," [Jamaica] *Daily Gleaner*, February 19, 2012.

67   Jaji, *Africa in Stereo*; Emery, "Caribbean Modernism," 60, 61; McKay, *Banjo*.

68   Aching, *Masking and Power*, 17, 32, 33; Gill, *Erotic Islands*, chapter 1.

69   Hearst's *New York Journal-American* supported the British against the Boers, and Pulitzer's *New York World* sided with the Boers and encouraged the United States to step in officially to play a mediating role. Terms such as "yellow journalism" presume a more heightened sensational or racist tone (relative to papers such as the *New York Times*) than is necessarily the case.

70   This is McClintock's critique of the privileged role assigned to print nationalism in Anderson's *Imagined Communities*. *Imperial Leather*, 374–75.

71   Schwarz, *Memories of Empire*. This and the following quotations are on page 217.

72   L. Doyle and Winkiel, *Geomodernisms*, 1.

73   The quotation is from R. Williams, *Marxism and Literature*, 132.

74   [Jamaica] *Daily Gleaner*, "Photography as an Aid to Scouts," November 23, 1899, 7; *Daily Gleaner*, July 9, 1900, 6; [Trinidad] *Port of Spain Gazette*, March 12, 1909, 4.

75   *Port of Spain Gazette*, "Pretoria Day In Trinidad," August 9, 1900; [London] *Black and White*, July 14, 1900. The *Black and White* (or *Black and White: A Weekly Illustrated Record and Review*) was a British illustrated weekly periodical that ran from the early 1890s to 1912, when it was incorporated with *The Sphere*. This periodical is not to be confused with another British periodical, the *Black and White Budget* (or *Black Illustrated Budget*, or *Illustrated Budget*), which ran from 1899 to 1905 and covered the Boer War primarily if not exclusively. An advertisement in the *Daily Gleaner*, May 10, 1900, 4, announced the availability of maps and atlases of the "Boer Republics," showing the details of the war, railway lines, and gold fields, as well as the latest issues of the *Black and White Budget*, from shops in the colony. The title of the novel *Rupert Gray: A Tale in Black and White*, published in Trinidad in 1907 and discussed in chapter 4, probably had this visual and sonic resonance in addition to its more obvious interracial allusion.

That is, for contemporary readers "Black and White" may have suggested not just a source of news about the Boer War, but an Anglo-Boer conflict eliciting loyalty from global British subjects.

76 Thompson, *An Eye for the Tropics*.

77 Photograph of capture of Benin Bronzes: https://www.alamy.com/the-benin -expedition-of-1897-was-a-punitive-expedition-by-a-british-force-of-1200-under -admiral-sir-harry-rawson-in-response-to-a-massacre-of-a-previous-british -led-invasion-force-his-troops-captured-burned-and-looted-the-city-of-benin -bringing-to-an-end-the-west-african-kingdom-of-benin-during-the-conquering -and-burning-of-the-city-much-of-the-countrys-art-including-the-benin -bronzes-was-either-destroyed-looted-or-dispersed-image344230067.html; Liu, "Desire and Sovereign Thinking," and "Conclusion: The Emperor's Empty Throne."

78 *Daily Gleaner*, "Great Parade: Odd Fellows Have Procession Seven Miles Long," October 1, 1912, 3, reprinted from the *Atlanta Constitution*.

79 *Port of Spain Gazette*, "Barbadian Going to Cartagena," August 23, 1900. This article notes that De Vine is headed to the United States of Colombia, but in 1900 this would have been the Republic of Colombia.

80 See the brutal response of the authorities to Canboulay/Carnival and Hosay/ Muhurram in Trinidad in the late nineteenth century: Rohlehr, *Calypso and Society*; Singh, *The Bloodstained Tombs*. On clashes with the authorities in Jamaica over the celebration of Hosay, see Shepherd, *Transients to Settlers*.

81 Thompson, "'Our Good Democracy,'" 34.

82 See Warner-Lewis, *Central Africa in the Caribbean*; Rohlehr, *Calypso and Society*; Gill, *Erotic Islands*, chap. 3.

83 *Port of Spain Gazette*, March 4, 1909, 5, reprinted from [Demerara, British Guiana] *Sportsman Argosy*.

84 Collis-Buthelezi, "Caribbean Regionalism," 53; Laurence, "The Trinidad Water Riot of 1903," 12.

85 Cobham, *Rupert Gray: A Tale in Black and White*, 55.

2. Ruination's Intimate Architecture

1 De Lisser, *Twentieth Century Jamaica*, 73; and see Pigou-Dennis's discussion of this passage, "Island Modernity: Jamaican Urbanism and Architecture."

2 De Lisser, *Twentieth Century Jamaica*, 76.

3 Seacole, *Wonderful Adventures of Mrs. Seacole in Many Lands*, 16; see also Firmin's 1885 riposte to Count Gobineau: *De l'égalité des races humaines: anthropologie positive*, translated (Asselin Charles) as *The Equality of the Human Races*; Trinidadian J. J. Thomas's response to James Anthony Froude, *Froudacity: West Indian Fables by J. A. Froude*. Quotation from Walcott, *Antilles: Fragments of Epic Memory*.

4   For harrowing survivors' accounts, see M. Smith, "A Tale of Two Tragedies."

5   See *Daily Gleaner*, "The Speeches of Mr. M Garvey and the Comments of our Correspondents," April 6, 1921, 13 (articles in that day's issue and the next deal with critics and defenders of Garvey's recent public appearances in Kingston and Montego Bay); and see Hill, *The Marcus Garvey and Universal Negro Improvement Association Papers*, vol. 3 (September 20 to August 1921), 338–39. Attempts to recover insurance claims (see, for instance, *Daily Gleaner*, "On Insurances: An Important Appeal to Policy-Holders," February 20, 1907, 1; *Daily Gleaner*, "The Second Day's Hearing of the First Insurance Case at Mandeville," October 30, 1907, 1 and 4) continued for another two years until insurers agreed to pay, Jacobs, *From the Earthquake to 1944*, 103. As Jamaicans began to ponder the finer points of wind direction, the precise nature of damage caused by fire, and the timing of fires in relation to tremors, they joined San Francisco's residents, who were in the midst of determining such questions after an April 1906 earthquake (see R. James, "Six Bits or Bust") and no doubt anticipated similar discussions in Ecuador and Cuba, both of which had earthquakes in June 1907.

6   On what came to be known as the "Swettenham Affair," see, for instance, *Daily Gleaner*, "Closing Scene: Alleged Apology from Jamaica's Governor," February 16, 1907, cover page; Tilchin, "Theodore Roosevelt, Anglo-American Relations, and the Jamaica Incident of 1907"; and Willock, "Caribbean Catastrophe."

7   See *Daily Telegraph*, January 19 and 21, 1907, http://www.jamaicanfamilysearch.com/Samples/earthqu4.htm; M. Smith, *Liberty, Fraternity, Exile*, 364n60; and the recollection of Haitian assistance to Jamaica in 1907 after the 1928 hurricane in Haiti, M. Smith, "Capture Land," 194.

8   See, for instance, the editorials *Daily Gleaner*, "The Church and Bedwardism," August 10, 1907, 6; and *Daily Gleaner*, "Earthquake, Credulity and Drift," August 13, 1907, 6.

9   Treves, *The Cradle of the Deep*, 279. Five years before this trip Treves had performed the first surgical treatment of appendicitis on Edward VII, shortly before the latter's coronation.

10 Treves, *Cradle of the Deep*, 279.

11 Treves, *Cradle of the Deep*, 286. For another example of the distinction between local and visiting white people acting decisively and Black Kingstonians who are mewling, see Willock, "Caribbean Catastrophe," citedabove.

12 Treves, *Cradle of the Deep*, 282.

13 Treves, *Cradle of the Deep*, 282.

14 Hunt, "An Acoustic Register," 42.

15 Cobb, *Picture Freedom*, 95.

16 D. Williams, "The Perilous Road of Marcus M. Garvey."

17 See Ford-Smith's discussion of McKenzie, Ashwood, and others who cofounded or held leadership positions in organizations that championed women's educational and political advancement, such as the People's Convention and the

UNIA in Jamaica. Ford-Smith connects these middle-class female activists' increasing organizational insignificance from the late 1920s onward to the conundrum of championing the franchise and other issues without a cross-class consciousness that would allow them to perceive, identify with, and tackle social issues facing working-class women. Ford-Smith, "Women and the Garvey Movement in Jamaica." On middle- and upper-class Jamaican women and the vote, see Vassell, "The Movement for the Vote." On Amy Ashwood, see Taylor, *The Veiled Garvey*, chap. 2.

18   McKenzie, "Women's Rights," 102–3; and see Gregg, "Catherine McKenzie," 98. This article appears to be the text of McKenzie's address to the annual 1901 People's Convention, organized by the *Advocate*'s editor, Robert Love, beginning in August 1898 (to mark the sixtieth anniversary of full abolition in 1838) and ending in 1903. See Lumsden, "Jamaican Constitutional and Political Developments, 1866–1920."

19   "The problem of the twentieth century is the problem of the color line," is Du Bois's characterization of the problem (and his prescription of the moral preoccupation) of the new century, in his address to Sylvester Williams's Pan-African conference in London in the summer of 1900, and in *Souls of Black Folk* (1903). Du Bois, "To the Nations of the World," 639, and Du Bois, *Souls*, 359, 372.

20   Nicholas Mirzoeff distinguishes between "visuality . . . the exclusive claim to be able to look" and the Derridean "right to look" that "must be mutual, each person inventing the other, or it fails." *The Right to Look*, 1–2. I pursue the question of the credibility of the female estate owner's right to look when she is not white in chapter 4.

21   H. A. Jacobs, *Incidents in the Life of a Slave Girl*.

22   McKittrick, *Demonic Grounds*, 44.

23   Campt, "The Loophole of Retreat."

24   *Daily Gleaner*, "A Case against Mary Jane Robinson, 'Warning Given,'" April 26, 1907, 5.

25   Brodber, "Clarendon: Kellits: A Woman Come Down in the World," 13, 15, 16, 17.

26   *Daily Gleaner*, letter from "Why Our Young Men Do Not Marry?," February 11, 1899; Moore and M. A. Johnson, *Neither Led nor Driven*, 373n50.

27   Moore and M. A. Johnson, *Neither Led nor Driven*, 110. This is a 1904 letter.

28   *Jamaica Times*, "The Working Girl in Jamaica," February 18, 1911, 3.

29   *Jamaica Times*, May 15, 1915, 13.

30   From a series of articles by De Lisser entitled "How Kingston Lives and Moves and Has its Being" in 1899–1900 for the *Jamaica Times* or the *Daily Gleaner*, and collected in B. Moore and M. A. Johnson, *Squalid Kingston*, 72.

31   See, for instance, the discussion of fiction in the 1920s in Rosenberg, "The New Woman and "'The Dusky Strand,'" 95.

32   Zubel, "Anti-colonial Flânerie"; Ramos, *Divergent Modernities*, 119; Ramos cites Sarmiento's 1851 essay "Los Temblores de Chile," 347.

33 Ramos, *Divergent Modernities*, 124, 125.

34 Césaire, *Notebook* and *Cahiers*.

35 Césaire, *Notebook*, 15, 11; *Cahiers*, 72, 58.

36 Césaire, *Notebook*, 2, 3, 21; *Cahiers*, 42, 38, 85.

37 Lowe, *Intimacies of Four Continents*, 39.

38 On walking in Port au Prince and Paris, see Firmin, *Equality of the Human Races*, 178–79, 197–98; on the wonder and anxiety of the "boisterous intimacy" of New York's Coney Island, see Martí, "Coney Island," 1881, *José Martí: Selected Writings*, trans. Esther Allen (New York: Penguin, 2002), 89–94; on walking in Kingston and Havana, see De Lisser, *In Jamaica and Cuba*.

39 Condé, "Habiter Ce Pays." I am grateful to Carolle Charles for this citation.

40 Condé, "Habiter Ce Pays," 7.

41 Condé, "Habiter Ce Pays," 8.

42 C. Carnegie shows that for nonelite Jamaican pedestrians who were always disdained, higher and higher residential and commercial walls now also increasingly keep them out of sight; for Cadogan walking in New Orleans and Manhattan as a Black man is so terrifying that the hazards of Kingston's streets feel more manageable by comparison; and perhaps with the long history of transgression attached to walking in Jamaica in mind, Colin Channer's fictional protagonist revels in his ability to exercise his right and his desire to walk—in Kingston, but also elsewhere in Jamaica and the world—as a kind of postcolonial freedom and inheritance. See C. Carnegie, "Walk-Foot People Matter" and "Walking Kingston"; Cadogan, "Walking While Black"; Channer, *Waiting in Vain*. I have in mind also terms from francophone Caribbean Creole languages—*dérive*, *drivet*—with a range of inflections from running away during slavery to meandering to loitering. Thanks to Patricia Saunders and other participants in the Symposium on the Jamaican Sixties in October 2015, as well as Dionne Brand and Njelle Hamilton, for bringing these to my attention. On related concepts of *errance* (wandering) and *traceés* (less well-traveled paths) in Caribbean literature in French, see Dash, "Textual Error and Cultural Crossing." And see Haigh on the figure of "*le driveur*," from the one who resisted staying in place before and after abolition, to the Haitian and Dominican migrants and artists in Guadeloupe and Martinique today. Haigh, "From Exile to Errance," 63–64.

43 "He floats with no material base, living on his wits, and lacking the patriarchal discourse that assured him of meaning, is compelled to invent a new one." This is E. Wilson, "The Invisible Flaneur," 109. See also Felski, *The Gender of Modernity*, chap. 3.

44 See McClintock's discussion of Charles Baudelaire, Émile Zola, and Walter Benjamin; this and following quotation, McClintock, *Imperial Leather*, 82.

45 The second quotation is from Sontag, *On Photography*, 55.

46 On this and other objections to postcards, see Thompson, *Eye for the Tropics*, chap. 1. There is an advertisement for *Pepper-Pot*, presented by Mr. H. Thornley

Stewart, in *Daily Gleaner*, December 4, 1914, 7, and see *Daily Gleaner*, "Book Review: *Pepperpot* is declared to be a most creditable Production," January 22, 1915, 10. The University of the West Indies-Mona Library lists *Pepperpot*—a "Magazine depicting mainly the personal and lighter side of Jamaican life"—as a publication that ran from 1915 to 1975. https://www.mona.uwi.edu/library/pepperpot. This means that the league was responding to the inaugural issue. On the reactions, see *Jamaica Times*, January 16, 1915, 15; and *Jamaica Times*, "The Dialect Question," January 23, 1915, 14; and see *Daily Gleaner*, January 9, 1915, 10 with a report of the Jamaica League's annual meeting; *Daily Gleaner*, January 22, 1915, 10; and *Daily Gleaner*, "Criticism of an Editorial which lately appeared in the *Gleaner*," January 29, 1915, 10. It appears that the league's January 7 meeting coincided with at least two other events that magnified the issue: the Jamaica Union of Teachers was addressed by Rev. C. A. Wilson, a Black Presbyterian minister who was identified with race-specific rhetoric, *Daily Gleaner*, "Jamaica Union of Teachers," January 6, 1915, 14; and Kingston's mayor addressed a meeting of the Negro Improvement Association, condemning the postcards and the use of "Negro dialect" in published "sketches"—see letter from E. Brown, *Daily Gleaner*, January 18, 1915, 13.

47 *Daily Gleaner*, January 28, 1915, 4.

48 *Daily Gleaner*, "The Latest Protest," January 11, 1915, 8. In my notes I have typed out most of this editorial under my notation "found it but very badly printed." This may mean that I read it on microfilm at the National Library, and the poor condition of the edition would explain why I cannot get access to this issue of the paper online to check the reference. I think that these are De Lisser's editorial remarks on the league's activities, in an editorial entitled "The Latest Protest," part of which also refers to Austria and Germany. The next day's *Daily Gleaner* (available and legible online) carries a letter to the editor from "Tom Strokes" (January 12, 1915) under the heading "The Jamaica League," which refers to "this morning's" commentary on the Jamaica League, and which helps me confirm that the *Daily Gleaner* carried De Lisser's editorial on the previous day.

49 On *Sketches of Character, In Illustration of the Habits, Occupation, and Costume of the Negro Population, in the Island of Jamaica, Drawn from Nature, and in Lithography* including a reproduction of "Milkmaid," and the social contexts of its Jewish Jamaican artist, Isaac Mendes Belisario, see Barringer, Forrester, and Martinez-Ruiz, *Art and Emancipation in Jamaica*.

50 "[The Black man] burns to be regarded as a scholar, puzzles himself with fine words, and addicts himself to religion for the sake of appearance, and delights in aping the little graces of civilization," Trollope, *The West Indies and the Spanish Main*, 56.

51 On Creole speech in a cross-racial public sphere in the Caribbean, see Edmondson, *Creole Noise*.

52 This is the period just before De Lisser's editorship at the *Daily Gleaner* began in 1904. See the series of newspaper articles for the *Jamaica Times* entitled "How

Kingston Lives and Moves and Has its Being," carried in the August 19, 26, December 16, 23, 30, 1899 editions, and January 6, 20, 27, February 10, 24, 1900. These are collected in Moore and M. A. Johnson, *Squalid Kingston*, chap. 3. Quotations are from 52–53. In 1899–1900 Paulus Kruger was president of the South African Republic or Transvaal, and General Redvers Buller was a commander of the British forces during a well-publicized routing of the British by the Boer side.

53 Moore and M. A. Johnson, *Squalid Kingston*, 60.

54 I am thinking of photographs such as "At Half Way Tree" and "Women on the Way to Market": https://www.historymiami.org/exhibition/awakening-jamaica -photographs-by-valentine-and-sons-1891/; https://digitalcollections.nypl.org /items/510d47df-8916-a3d9-e040-e00a18064a99. See Campt's meditation on those forced to pose for such photographs as embodying "a tense response that is not always intentional or liberatory, but often constituted by miniscule or even futile attempts to exploit extremely limited possibilities." Campt, *Listening to Images*, 59.

55 For discussions of early novels with Black women as their focus such as *One Brown Girl And—*, by Thomas McDermott, editor of the *Jamaica Times*, and published under the pseudonym Tom Redcam, and De Lisser's *Jane's Career* and *Susan Proudleigh*, see Ramchand, *The West Indian Novel and Its Background*; Cobham-Sander, "The Creative Writer and Jamaican Society, 1900–1950"; Rosenberg, *Nationalism and the Formation of Caribbean Literature*; Edmondson, *Caribbean Middlebrow*.

56 Duffy, *The Subaltern Ulysses*, 84, 87.

57 Felski discusses the department store in Émile Zola's 1883 novel *The Ladies' Paradise* (*Au Bonheur des dames*). *The Gender of Modernity*, 67, 62. On the flâneur's relationship to the department store, see Benjamin, "Paris: The Capital of the Nineteenth Century," 10.

58 De Lisser, *Jane's Career*, 39.

59 McKay, *Banana Bottom*.

60 I am drawing on the discussion of a fictional portrayal of the misguided expectation of justice. Kafka, "Before the Law" (first published in 1915); Derrida, "Before the Law." For Derrida, successful revolutionary violence can initiate a "yet to come" of a new law that is closer to justice. Thanks to Nijah Cunningham for discussing these texts with me.

61 Here I am drawing on a conversation with Rivke Jaffe. On being hailed, in the Althusserian sense of interpellation, see Althusser, "Ideology and Ideological State Apparatuses," 117–19.

62 S. Hall, Critcher, Jefferson, J. Clarke, and Roberts, *Policing the Crisis*.

63 Davis notes that Marissa Alexander was unable to use Florida's "Stand Your Ground" defense when she was imprisoned for firing a warning shot at her abusive partner, but the same defense buttressed George Zimmerman's ability to

avoid imprisonment for the shooting of Trayvon Martin. Davis, "Policing the Crisis Today."

64 H. Thomas, *The Story of a West Indian Policeman*; McKay, *Songs of Jamaica*; *Constab Ballads*; *My Green Hills of Jamaica*. On Thomas, see Paton, "The Trials of Inspector Thomas." On McKay, see for instance Lewis and Lewis, "Claude McKay's Jamaica."

65 As used in McKay's poem "The Malingerer," "Beat de eight" is parsed in the glossary (probably written by Walter Jekyll) as putting in eight hours of "beat-duty." McKay, *Constab Ballads*, 70, 82.

66 Here I do not mean territories that were part of France's empire, but territories such as Grenada that were, like Trinidad, officially English-speaking but whose histories and linguistic registers were shaped by francophone Caribbean inflections.

67 See, for instance, Harry Johnston's photograph "Street in Port Maria," *Photos and Phantasms: Harry Johnston's Photographs of the Caribbean*, cat. 66.

68 Allan [Charles W. Willis], *"Buckra" Land*, 40.

69 Bryan, *The Jamaican People*, 276.

70 Washington, "The Negro in the New World," 176.

71 Du Bois, "An Amazing Island," 80.

72 Du Bois, "An Amazing Island," 80.

73 Hill, "The First England Years"; F. Smith, "Good Enough for Booker T to Kiss."

74 This and following quotations, Thomas, *Story of a West Indian Policeman*, 354–57.

75 H. Thomas, *Story of a West Indian Policeman*, 339–40, 122; Bryan, *The Jamaican People*, 276.

76 H. Thomas, *Story of a West Indian Policeman*, 364.

77 H. Thomas, *Story of a West Indian Policeman*, 367.

78 McKay, *My Green Hills*, 47. The story quoted here is "The Woolseys." "Naked-'kin" is from line 33 of the poem "The Midnight Woman to the Bobby."

79 McKay, "Crazy Mary," *My Green Hills*, 132, 133.

80 See, for instance, Hathaway, *Caribbean Waves*, chap. 2. Jekyll was part of a bohemian upper-class movement that championed the rural authenticity of British folk music, rural working people, and gardens over the "tawdriness of sham jewelry and shoddy clothes, pawnshops and flaming gin-palaces" of the cities—a movement that included his sister, Gertrude Jekyll, who designed hundreds of gardens in Europe and North America. Barringer, "'There's the Life for a Man Like Me,'" 142. Jekyll published *Jamaican Song and Story* in 1907.

81 Holcomb, *Claude McKay: Code Name Sasha*; Cobham-Sander, "Jekyll and Claude"; Cobham-Sander, "Fictions of Gender, Fictions of Race"; W. James, *A Fierce Hatred of Injustice*.

82 McKay, *My Green Hills*, 61. All of my discussion of McKay's life is drawn from the essays gathered in *My Green Hills of Jamaica*.

83 McKay, *My Green Hills*, 60, 61; see a discussion of this passage and the implications for the exercise of extrajudicial justice in Paton, *No Bond but the Law*, 180.

84 On Bita see Cooper, "'Only a Nigger Gal!'"

85 Snorton, *Nobody Is Supposed to Know*, 47.

86 On the role of women in men's homosocial desire, see Sedgwick, *Between Men*. On the strategic, contingent humanizing of enslaved Black women so that sexual congress with them would not cast white men as bestial, see Tinsley, *Thiefing Sugar*, 12.

87 McKay, *Constab Ballads*, 15–25. For an extraordinary reading of these extraordinary poems and this period of McKay's work and life, see Macharia, *Frottage*.

88 Muñoz, "Gesture, Ephemera, and Queer Feeling," 423.

89 The quotation is from Ellis's brilliant parsing of homophobic lyrics in the queer early twenty-first-century dancehall, in "Out and Bad," 17. In teasing out McKay's queerness and heterosexual policing I am indebted here to a conversation with Ronald Cummings and Donette Francis.

90 McKay, "A Midnight Woman to the Bobby," 74–76. I assume that by "midnight woman" we are meant to understand her to be a sex worker. Here it is important to note that colonial Jamaican law gave the police the capacity to *produce* her as a prostitute, by naming her as such in a sworn statement and then compelling her to be medically examined for venereal disease. She could be examined for up to a year and possibly also detained in hospital, or face imprisonment or hard labor. See Moore and M. A. Johnson, "Fallen Sisters?"; and Franco, "The Unruly Woman."

91 H. Thomas, *Story of a West Indian Policeman*, 351.

92 Sharpe, *Monstrous Intimacies*, 21.

93 *Daily Gleaner*, "Night Marauders," "Memorial Clock," "The Work of a Gifted Jamaican," October 7, 1911, 6. The *Jamaica Times* of January 20, 1912, 22, also carries a photograph of McKay in his uniform, on the occasion of the publication of *Songs of Jamaica*.

94 McKay, "Pounding the Pavement," *My Green Hills*, 138.

95 McKay, *My Green Hills*, 139.

96 If the cook's domain was the kitchen and the pantry, the butler would greet and seat visitors, offer them a "glass of ice-water," and serve meals. For an account of a cook who takes umbrage at being asked to assist the butler, see Brodber, "St. Catherine: Church Pen: The Bright Young Butleress," 22.

97 The following discussion of the case is based on these accounts from the *Daily Gleaner* and the *Jamaica Times*: *Daily Gleaner*, "The Litigious Summer Season Stirring Sav-La-Mar," Friday, August 26, 1910, 13; *Daily Gleaner*, "End of the Evans Case" Monday, August 29, 1910, 13; *Daily Gleaner*, "Evans Case Concluded" and "Conviction Supported" September 24, 1910, front page and 3;

Daily Gleaner, "Echo of the Recent Celebrated Hendon Case," November 15, 1911, 13, 29; *Daily Gleaner*, "Long Pending Charge Is Heard," June 21, 1912, 13; *Daily Gleaner*, "Appeal Court," December 7, 1912, front page; *Jamaica Times*, August 27, 1910, 17; *Jamaica Times*, "Sav La Mar Case," September 3, 1910, 13; *Jamaica Times*, "Sav La Mar Court Sensation," September 3, 1910, 18–19. The "theater" quotation is from the first *Jamaica Times* citation listed here, and "spicy" is from the first *Gleaner* citation. My initial impression, though unverified by extended comparison, is that the *Jamaica Times* was less sensational in its coverage, and more sympathetic toward Stewart and Evans. Its first story on the case on August 27 is tucked away in the lowest right-hand corner of the page. On page 13 of the September 3 issue the paper notes that the time had not yet come for commenting on the disagreeable case, and on page 18 of the same issue Stewart is described as "a well dressed woman who stood the fire of the eyes directed on her from every side of the crowded Court House as well as she could."

98 *Daily Gleaner*, letter to the editor, February 8, 1902.

99 *Daily Gleaner*, letter to *The Presbyterian*, April 4, 1902, 7.

100 *Daily Gleaner*, March 6, 1903, 13.

101 *Laws of Jamaica: Passed in the Year 1902*, chap. 12, section 16, page 7: https://ufdcimages.uflib.ufl.edu/AA/00/06/39/18/00064/Laws%20of%20Jamaica%201902%20pdf%20Opt.pdf.

102 On slavery in Westmoreland, including the high rate of mortality for enslaved people, see Dunn, *A Tale of Two Plantations*. Generations later Westmoreland was one of the earliest nodal points of the 1930s uprisings that swept through the anglophone Caribbean—at the Frome estate owned by Tate and Lyle. Post, *Arise Ye Starvelings*.

103 On the Beckfords, see, for instance, Curtin, *The Story of Westmoreland*, and Gikandi's discussion of William Thomas Beckford's anxiety about his father's Jamaican accent, as part of a new generation's investment in prestige without the taint of slavery. *Slavery and the Culture of Taste*.

104 D. Hall, *In Miserable Slavery*, 256, 259; Burnard, *Mastery, Tyranny and Desire*.

105 Walker, *In Search of Our Mothers' Gardens*.

106 On the display of heads in Sav-la-Mar, see Burnard, *Mastery, Tyranny and Desire*, 104.

107 *Daily Gleaner*, "Little London," June 13, 1900. 7.

108 Curtin, *Story of Westmoreland*, 148; Shepherd, *Transients to Settlers*, 171–75, 179. *Hosay* is also rendered as *Hossay*, and *tazia* as *tazzia, tadjah*, and *tajeah*. There appear to have been Hosay celebrations twice in the following year, *Daily Gleaner*, "General Notes," January 31, 1912, 14; *Daily Gleaner*, "East Indian Festival," July 29, 1912, 4. Tazia time conformed to but it also exceeded both the time and space that the plantocracy and other élite interests decided it merited. Long a confounder of ethnic and religious purity (the Muslim festival had been transformed into a pan-Indo-Caribbean festival across the Caribbean for genera-

tions), the festival involved days of preparation, and the visibility of processions along multiple routes leading to a river or to the sea. See a vivid description of a Hosay celebration in 1909, in Annotto Bay, St. Mary, on Jamaica's northeast coast: large processions with up to nine tazias, a large multiracial crowd of thousands, stick fighting, wrestling, twirling torches, drumming and dancing, rowdy competitions, and grand feasting after the tazias were set afloat. Moore and M. A. Johnson, *They Do as They Please*, chap. 12.

109 Curtin, *Story of Westmoreland*, 155–62; Walvin, *Life and Times of Henry Clarke*. Craton and Walvin note that the Clarkes "were not products of the traditional Jamaican ruling class, which had almost departed the Jamaican scene, but comparative newcomers who determinedly rose from the second rank of island society by taking advantage of that limited social mobility which tends to occur in periods of economic dislocation." *Jamaican Plantation*, 259. I am aware that my reading of the Clarkes, and especially Rev. Henry Clarke, risks jettisoning a nuanced portrait of Jamaican whiteness in favor of monolithic savage whiteness with its roots in slavery—I am thinking here of Gill's nuanced reading of Guyanese-born Peter Minshall's disidentifying whiteness in the context of Trinidad. *Erotic Islands*, 39, 40. But for me dissenting whiteness can still avail itself of the privileges of whiteness on offer. This liberalism may or may not make a difference to the Black women who work in their homes or bear their children.

110 Lumsden, "Jamaican Constitutional and Political Developments."

111 E. Clarke, *My Mother Who Fathered Me*.

112 Lumsden, "Jamaican Constitutional and Political Developments"; *Jamaica Times*, "Coming General Election," October 29, 2010.

113 *Daily Gleaner*, "The Litigious Summer Season Stirring Sav-La-Mar," Friday, August 26, 1910, 13. Both Cox and Clarke contributed to debates about the merits of indentured laborers from India and the sugar industry, debates that sometimes retailed racist stereotypes, *Daily Gleaner*, "Indian Labor: A Striking Letter from Mr. Hugh Clarke," January 10, 1910; *Daily Gleaner*, "About Coolies," June 19, 1911, 14.

114 This and the following quotations are from the *Daily Gleaner*, "The Litigious Summer Season," Friday, August 26, 1910, 13.

115 "A "veritable public place, so many boots were wiped on its threshold"—this is the description of Nana's bedroom in Zola's novel *Nana*, 439. Felski notes of nineteenth-century fictional figures such as Nana, that like her bedroom she is "the ultimate threat to class difference, her body a private site of public intimacy, within which the seminal fluids of workers, bourgeois men, and aristocrats indiscriminately commingle." *Gender of Modernity*, 75.

116 *Daily Gleaner*, "End of the Evans Case," August 29, 1910, 13.

117 *Daily Gleaner*, September 24, 1910, cover and 3.

118 *Daily Gleaner*, "Victory Gained by Mr. Fred R Evans by Wide Margin," January 19, 1911, 14.

119 *Jamaica Times*, "The Opening of the Council," February 18, 1911, 9.

120 McKay, "When I Pounded the Pavement," 135.

121 McKay, "When I Pounded the Pavement," 140.

122 *Daily Gleaner*, "The Litigious Summer Season," Friday, August 26, 1910, 13.

123 McKay, "When I Pounded the Pavement," 144.

124 Paton, *No Bond but the Law*, 141.

125 McKay, "When I Pounded the Pavement," 143.

126 Lowe, "The Intimacies of Four Continents," 195.

127 See Garvey's letter to Robert Russa Moton about "hundreds of Black prostitutes" on Kingston's streets, in D. Williams, "The Perilous Road of Marcus M. Garvey."

128 McKay, *Home to Harlem*.

129 M. A. Johnson, "Problematic Bodies."

130 Emery, "On the Verandah," 60, 61.

131 McKay, "When I Pounded the Pavement," 140.

132 *Daily Gleaner*, "The Litigious Summer Season Stirring Sav-La-Mar," Friday, August 26, 1910, 13.

133 See Altink, "I Did Not Want to Face the Shame of Exposure," 366; and M. A. Johnson, "Problematic Bodies."

134 Altink, "I Did Not Want to Face the Shame of Exposure"; de Barros, *Reproducing the British Caribbean*.

135 Altink, "I Did Not Want to Face the Shame of Exposure," 366, citing *Daily Gleaner*, February 15, 1908.

136 Higginbotham, *Righteous Discontent*, 187; Francis, *Fictions of Feminine Citizenship*, 12.

137 Hartman, Keynote Speech, "Second Exposure."

3. Photography's "Typical Negro"

1 Cobham, *Rupert Gray*, 52. Leah Rosenberg's discussion of this novel centers on the hog plum tree. Rosenberg, *Nationalism*.

2 *Daily Gleaner*, "Real Progress: An Interview with Sir Harry Johnston," January 13, 1909, 1. This interview continues under another title in the same issue, *Daily Gleaner*, "The Future: Some Impressions of Sir Harry Johnston," January 13, 1909, 13.

3 Washington, "The Negro in the New World," 174.

4 Johnston, *Negro in the New World*, 3, captioned "The Typical Negro: A Kru Man from the Kru Coast, Liberia," https://library.si.edu/digital-library/book/negroinnewworloojohn. The photograph is attributed to Samuel Hall.

5 On imperial friendship, see Gandhi, *Affective Communities*.

6 Ross, "The New Negro Displayed," 262.

7   "Visuality's first domains were the slave plantation, monitored by the surveillance of the overseer, operating as the surrogate of the sovereign." Mirzoeff, *The Right to Look*, 2.

8   Wexler, *Tender Violence*, 92.

9   Note that Frances B. Johnston is one of two photographer-Johnstons mentioned in this chapter, along with Harry H. Johnston. There is a third, James Johnston, who is discussed in the context of images of Jamaica, in Thompson, *An Eye for the Tropics*. On Frances Johnston at Hampton, see Wexler, *Tender Violence*; and Weems, *Carrie Mae Weems*.

10 Wexler, *Tender Violence*, 21. On the "Philippine question" and US imperialism, see Isaac, *American Tropics*.

11 The Gerhards' images can be found at https://www.loc.gov/pictures/search/?q =Gerhard+Sisters&sp=3.

12 Shannon, *Jean Price-Mars*, 19, 29. Shannon seems to assume that Price-Mars referred to Ota Benga, a Mbuti man (from the Congo) who was exhibited at this fair and then at the Bronx Zoo. But Price-Mars says Filipinos, which seems to imply that he met Moro-Filipinos and Igorot-Filipinos (terms that I am aware have or have had derogatory racial connotations). The delegation from the Philippines numbered in the hundreds, across multiple booths meant to demonstrate an internal racial hierarchy of Filipino national life that posited Price-Mars's interlocutors as less advanced than other Filipino groups: a "difference" that redounded to the triumph of US imperialism. For a discussion of this from the perspective of the delegation's constabulary band and its African American conductor, see Talusan, "Music, Race, and Imperialism."

13 "People outside the magic circle of nineteenth-century domesticity—for instance, slaves, Native Americans, Mexicans, and later Eastern European immigrants, Cubans, Filipinos, Hawaiians, and Chinese—posed an interesting problem of exclusion in relation to [photographs of bourgeois domesticity]." Wexler, *Tender Violence*, 66–67.

14 While in St. Louis, Price-Mars wrote to Booker T. Washington and spent two weeks at Tuskegee. Shannon, *Jean Price-Mars*, 20 and 29n27.

15 Sekula, "The Body and the Archive," 347.

16 This is S. Smith's suggestion in *Photography on the Color Line*, 44; see also Raiford's proposal that the use of lynching photographs in *anti*-lynching campaigns "reveals a crisis of representation." *Imprisoned in a Luminous Glare*, 17.

17 A "shadowed, even hooded" archive that is "housed on mantelpieces and in desk drawers across the United States," Mirzoeff, "Shadow and the Substance," 123.

18 On stillness, see H. Young, *Embodying Black Experience*.

19 Appadurai, "The Colonial Backdrop," 4–7; E. Edwards, "Looking at Photographs," 54.

20 Cobham, *Rupert Gray*, 92. See advertisements in *Post of Spain Gazette*, August 23, 1900, and March 2, 1909.

21 Paula Reyes, Uda. De Guzman to BTW, September 12, 1911, Reel #684, container 906–9, BTWT, Library of Congress. In her letter, sent from Havana and written in English, she says that she has learned that her son's health is not very good.

22 Thompson, *An Eye for the Tropics*, chap. 5; Modest, "The Affective Photograph," 22.

23 I owe this last insight to Michelle Rowley. See also Petrine Archer-Straw, "Photos and Phantasms," for a more flexible view than mine of visiting photographers.

24 E. Edwards, "Photographs and History," 23.

25 Tsinhnahjinnie's term for the agency of Indigenous people in ethnographic images taken by non-Indigenous people is "photographic sovereignty." Tsinhnahjinnie, "Dragonfly's Home." See also the Anishinaabe theorist Gerald Vizenor on *survivance*: "an active sense of presence, the continuance of native stories, not a mere reaction, or a survivable name." *Manifest Manners*, vii.

26 Willis, *A History of Black Photographers*, 182.

27 Campt, *Image Matters*, 124.

28 Akomfrah, *The Stuart Hall Project*.

29 Gikandi on West Indian planters in England in the eighteenth and nineteenth centuries, *Slavery and the Culture of Taste*, 119.

30 *Daily Gleaner*, "Roosevelt Wanted to Interfere in Hayti: Important Letter to Harry Johnston," March 16, 1909, 1. See Morillo-Alicea's observation that US historians think of empire as a European story best left to historians of Europe, "Looking for Empire in the US Colonial Archive," *Only Skin Deep*, 129–42.

31 Johnston, *Story of My Life*, 384.

32 Johnston, *Liberia*.

33 See, for instance, *Daily Gleaner*, "The Big Hunt: Roosevelt Bags His First Game in Africa," May 6, 1909, 4.

34 Johnston, *Story of My Life*, 401–3.

35 *Daily Gleaner*, "A World Factor," August 29, 1910, 8 (this is a review of *Negro in the New World*); *Montreal Gazette*, "An Expert on the Cuban Negro," May 21, 1909; *London Times Weekly*, "The Haitian Negroes," April 16, 1909, which Haitian statesman Anténor Firmin praised as proof of Johnston's "incontestable" competence in its views on the impractical education that Haitian doctors received in France. *Lettres de St. Thomas*, 200.

36 Gikandi, "Africa and the Epiphany of Modernism," 46–47.

37 Johnston, *Negro in the New World*, 60.

38 Johnston, *Negro in the New World*, 68–69.

39 In what Krista Thompson would call a "visual repatriation," the 1998 exhibition at the Royal Geographic Society in London traveled in that year to Kingston's National Gallery of Jamaica, Port of Spain's National Museum of Trinidad and Tobago, Queen's Park Gallery in Bridgetown, Barbados, Havana's Fototeca de Cuba, and Le Musée d'Art Haitien in Port au Prince, Haiti. *An Eye for the Tropics*, 253.

40 Johnston, *Negro in the New World*, 65; the caption is "Negroes at Work, Cuba" in *Photos and Phantasms*, cat. 49.

41 Johnston, *Negro in the New World*, 64; http://archive.org/stream. /negroinnewworloojohn#page/64/mode/2up; "A Cuban Negro," *Photos and Phantasms*, cat. 7 (a different shot of the same man in the same location).

42 Johnston, *Negro in the New World*, 269; http://archive.org/stream /negroinnewworloojohn#page/268/mode/2up; "A Jamaican Farmer or Bee-keeper," *Photos and Phantasms*, cat. 37.

43 *Daily Gleaner*, "Real Progress: An Interview with Sir Harry Johnston," January 13, 1909, 1.

44 Wilcox, *Sailing Sunny Seas*, 133.

45 Wilcox, *Sailing Sunny Seas*, 232.

46 Wilcox, *Sailing Sunny Seas*, 231.

47 Wilcox, *Sailing Sunny Seas*, 26.

48 Wilcox, *Sailing Sunny Seas*, 136.

49 *Daily Gleaner*, "The Future: Some Impressions of Sir Harry Johnston," January 13, 1909, 13; Wilcox, *Sailing Sunny Seas*, 121–23.

50 Wilcox, "Trinidad. Coolie Woman At Door of her House," *Sailing Sunny Seas*, facing 230; and 279 in the digital text: https://babel.hathitrust.org/cgi/pt?id =wu.89098878721&view=1up&seq=279.

51 Wilcox, *Sailing Sunny Seas*, 49.

52 Wilcox, *Sailing Sunny Seas*, 49.

53 Cobham, *Rupert Gray*, 52.

54 On the "troubling" assumption that Black expression is "exclusively public" and tied to resistance, see Quashie, *The Sovereignty of Quiet*, 143.

55 Froude, *The English in the West Indies*; Drayton, *Nature's Government*.

56 "Bay Tree Avenue, Royal Botanic Gardens Trinidad" and back of postcard. From the collection of the University of the West Indies, St. Augustine: https:// uwispace.sta.uwi.edu/dspace/bitstream/handle/2139/4771/GoldF8_68B.pdf ?sequence=1&isAllowed=y. But David Boxer argues that since white photographers were as likely to "[use] a white assistant in the same way," it is not racist to use Black children and adults to convey a sense of proportion. *Jamaica in Black and White*, 213. On human scale and machinery in Panama in the same era, see Cobham-Sander, Francis, and Rosenberg, "Panama Silver, Asian Gold." For a discussion of a similar postcard, see Cole, "Teaching and Research Guide."

57 Thompson, *An Eye for the Tropics*, 57.

58 Cobham, *Rupert Gray*, 55.

59 On amateur botanists, see Cole, "Teaching and Research Guide"; and Tobin, *Colonizing Nature*, chap. 6.

60 Cobham, *Rupert Gray*, 56, 54. She is a kindred spirit of Charles Kingsley, who made his own illustrations of the flora and fauna for his travelogue about his trip to Trinidad in the late 1860s, Kingsley, *At Last*.

61 Cobham, *Rupert Gray*, 54–55.

62 Cobham, *Rupert Gray*, 55.

63 Local readers would have connected fictional Rupert Gray's legal career, African diasporic interests, and white wife to Henry Sylvester Williams, who completed his training as a barrister in residence at Gray's Inn, London (perhaps one inflection of "Gray" in the novel's title), and returned to Trinidad to live with his English wife and their children in 1908, before his death in 1911. The novel's author, Stephen Cobham, toasted Williams and the Pan-African Association at a 1901 function in Port of Spain. See Cobham, *Rupert Gray*, xv, xxix, xxx.

64 Cobham, *Rupert Gray*, 53.

65 On McKinley, see Sundquist, *To Wake the Nations*, 414.

66 Cobham, *Rupert Gray*, 55; Patterson, *Slavery and Social Death*, 5.

67 Lady Eastlake, "Photography."

68 Armstrong, *Fiction in the Age of Photography*.

69 1864 letter to John Herschel cited in Rosen, *Margaret Cameron's Fancy Subjects*, 2.

70 Armstrong, *Fiction in the Age of Photography*, 112.

71 S. M. Smith, *Photography on the Color Line*, 108–12.

72 This and the following quotation, S. M. Smith, *Photography on the Color Line*, 110–11. Smith is citing a 1904 essay by Booker T. Washington in the *Colored American Magazine*.

73 A. Doyle, "Scandal in Bohemia"; Dickens, *Bleak House*; see R. Thomas, "Making Darkness Visible"; and see Armstrong, *Fiction in the Age of Photography*, for a different reading of *Bleak House*.

74 Cadava, *Words of Light*, 42–43; Benjamin, "The Work of Art," 221.

75 Benjamin, "Work of Art," 218, 224; Cadava, *Words of Light*, 43.

76 Mofokeng, *The Black Photo Album*.

77 See Campbell's "African Pass System," n.p., which closes Mofokeng, *The Black Photo Album*.

78 Santu Mofokeng, cited in Bajorek, "Then and Now," 222.

79 Mofokeng's introduction to *The Black Photo Album*; Bajorek, "Then and Now," 226.

80 See the discussion of the Lutterodt archive in Haney, "Film, Charcoal, Time."

81 Haney, "Film, Charcoal, Time," 123.

82 Osinubi, "Provincializing Slavery," 7.

83 Cobham, *Rupert Gray*, 103.

84 Cobham, *Rupert Gray*, 102. "The Great Penrhyn Quarry Strike: Capturing the Public Imagination. TUC 150 years," https://tuc150.tuc.org.uk/stories/the-great-penrhyn-quarry-strike/. Baron Penrhyn's personal wealth (as opposed to the Penrhyn property acquired through his wife's estate) was built on his inheritance of estates in Jamaica.

85 McClintock, *Imperial Leather*, 223.

86 "A Haitian Peasant Woman and her Children," Johnston, *Negro in the New World*, 191, http://archive.org/stream/negroinnewworloojohn#page/190/mode /2up; *Photos and Phantasms*, "Haitian Woman with Children, Haiti," cat. 25.

87 Cobham, *Rupert Gray*, 18.

88 *Port of Spain Gazette*, "Mass Meeting of East Indians at Gasparillo Village, Naparima," February 16, 1909.

4. Plotting Inheritance

1   Cobham, *Rupert Gray*, 27; Tracy, *Sword of Nemesis*, 316. Though a 1919 edition is all I have seen, and is possibly the date of publication, I use a 1909 publication year for *Sword of Nemesis* because of 1909 announcements of a forthcoming book: "by Dr. Archer Tracy of Trinidad" and "Dr. Archer Tracy of Trinidad, says the Jamaica *Gleaner*." See *Daily Gleaner*, "West Indian Book," March 11, 1909, 4; *Port of Spain Gazette*, "West Indian Book," March 23, 1909. Born in Montserrat, Tracy seems to have been raised in Trinidad, and practiced medicine in the United States.

2   Generations later an enraged poetic persona recalls the owners of the ruinate plantation *them* and *theirs*: the descendant of slaves and opponent of slavery cannot also be the patriarch of the great house. Walcott, "Ruins of a Great House."

3   *Yerbero* (herbalist); *el monte* (forested or mountainous domain of the spirits); *marronnage* (the process of escaping enslavement by running away or communities of persons who have escaped enslavement).

4   Rohlehr, *Calpyso and Society*, 28–29. The reference here is to a February 15, 1883 letter from Guzman, the leader of the attacked band, and a February 22, 1883 editorial, both in the newspaper [Trinidad] *Fair Play*.

5   George Lamming in Scott, "Sovereignty of the Imagination," 25, 72–100; Warner-Lewis, *Trinidad Yoruba*, 41, 74; Stuempfle, *Port of Spain*, 72.

6   James, *Beyond a Boundary*.

7   Sommer, *Foundational Fictions*; Harper, *Iola Leroy*; Chesnutt, "Wife of His Youth."

8   H. Johnston, *Negro in the New World*, 162.

9   Tracy, *Sword of Nemesis*, 218.

10 Paravisini-Gebert, "Colonial and Post-colonial Gothic," 233.

11 Brontë, *Jane Eyre*, 1847; Woloch, *One vs. the Many*.

12 Fletcher, "Victorians and Moderns," 99.

13 The specific reference here is to an 1871 letter to the editor. See F. Smith, *Creole Recitations*, 122–27.

14 Philip, *Emmanuel Appadocca*.

15 *Sword of Nemesis* is set mainly in a fictional world that approximates Trinidad and begins and ends in a neighboring island whose capital is identified as "P,"

that I take to be suggestive of Plymouth, the capital of Montserrat. I make this assumption because the author, "Dr. Archer Tracy of Trinidad," appears to have been born in Montserrat.

16 Putnam, *Radical Moves*, 17–18, 24, 39–48, 243n31.

17 Putnam, *Radical Moves*, 211.

18 Putnam, *Radical Moves*, 212.

19 Moodie-Kublalsingh, "Spanish in Trinidad and Tobago"; Moodie-Kublalsingh, *The Cocoa Panyols of Trinidad*; Khan, "What Is a 'Spanish'?"; Brereton, *A History of Modern Trinidad*.

20 Khan, "What Is a 'Spanish,'?" 192.

21 Moodie-Kublalsingh, "Spanish in Trinidad and Tobago."

22 Khan, "What Is a 'Spanish,'?" 198.

23 Philip, *Emmanuel Appadocca*, 12, 23.

24 Taylor, *An Empire of Neglect*; Taylor's reading of the significance of Venezuelan hospitality in the novel is different from mine. Other discussions of the novel include Selwyn Cudjoe and William Cain's commentary in Philip, *Emmanuel Appadocca*; Rosenberg, *Nationalism and the Formation of Caribbean Literature*; and Manjapra, "Necrospeculation: Postemancipation Finance and Black Redress."

25 [C. Williams], *Hamel, the Obeah Man*; Ward, "'What Time Has Proved," 50.

26 See Claude McKay's 1933 *Banana Bottom*.

27 See, for instance, Putnam, "Rites of Power and Rumors of Race."

28 Archer, *Sword of Nemesis*, 19.

29 Archer, *Sword of Nemesis*, 119.

30 Archer, *Sword of Nemesis*, 93.

31 Archer, *Sword of Nemesis*, 152–53.

32 Archer, *Sword of Nemesis*, 138.

33 Archer, *Sword of Nemesis*, 214, 294, 315.

34 Hopkins, *Of One Blood*.

35 See Tobin, *Colonizing Nature*; and also turn-of-the-century discussions about the garden as a "serious business," rather than merely "ornamental": Lady Broome, 1899, cited in Stuempfle, *Port of Spain*, 68.

36 Archer, *Sword of Nemesis*, 11.

37 Archer, *Sword of Nemesis*, 284.

38 On gratitude and debt, see Ahmed, *The Promise of Happiness*, 121–59; and Antwi, "On Labor, Embodiment, and Debt."

39 Archer, *Sword of Nemesis*, 14.

40 Archer, *Sword of Nemesis*, 26.

41 Archer, *Sword of Nemesis*, this and following quotation, 13.

42 Archer, *Sword of Nemesis*, 170.

43 Archer, *Sword of Nemesis*, 171.

44 On this figure, see Turner, *Contested Bodies*.

45 Ahmed, *Strange Encounters*, 21, Ahmed's emphasis.

46 Anzaldúa describes the U.S-Mexican border: "*Es una herida abierta* where the Third World grates against the first and bleeds." *Borderlands, La Frontera*, 25.

47 "What's living and breathing in the place hidden from view.... [prompting] a contest over the future, over what's to come next or later." A. Gordon, "Some Thoughts on Haunting and Futurity," 3.

48 *Of One Blood* illuminates a US South that is paralyzed or even actively under-developed by the North, underlining Aboul-Ela's assertion that "the South of Faulkner's formative years at the beginning of the twentieth century manifested many of the characteristics of a colonial economy." *Other South*, 15.

49 Conrad, *Heart of Darkness*, 1–95.

50 Hayford, *Ethiopia Unbound*, 180–81; W. E. B. Du Bois, *The Souls of Black Folk* in *Writings*, 364–65. For discussions of this novel in relation to Du Bois, see Hill, "The First England Years"; and Sundquist, *To Wake the Nations*, chap. 6.

51 Hayford, *Ethiopia Unbound*, 20.

52 Hayford, *Ethiopia Unbound*, 171–72.

53 Hayford, *Ethiopia Unbound*, 5–6.

54 Hayford, *Ethiopia Unbound*, 172.

55 Hayford, *Ethiopia Unbound*, 9.

56 Hayford, *Ethiopia Unbound*, 136.

57 Goyal, *Romance, Diaspora, and Black Atlantic Literature*, 107.

58 Wehrs, *Pre-colonial Africa*.

59 Hayford, *Ethiopia Unbound*, 36.

60 Hayford, *Ethiopia Unbound*, 34.

61 Hayford, *Ethiopia Unbound*, 36–37.

62 Hayford, *Ethiopia Unbound*, 73, 75.

63 See Manning, "Contours of Slavery," 852; M. Johnson, "Technology, Competition, and African Crafts"; and LaGamma and Guintini, *The Essential Art of African Textile*.

64 Hayford, *Ethiopia Unbound*, 109.

65 Hayford, *Ethiopia Unbound*, 51.

66 Hayford, *Ethiopia Unbound*, 52.

67 Newell, *The Power to Name*, 128.

68 Achebe, *Things Fall Apart*, 1958. I am calling them "explicit" in Achebe's fiction, but see Cobham-Sander's discussion of Achebe's reticence about gender as one of those "unnamed *things*" left unarticulated because they were beyond representation, or because the need for representation was not registered until they were lost. "Chasms," 240.

69 Wehrs, *Pre-colonial Africa*, 17.

70 Osinubi, "Provincializing Slavery," 7.

71 Newell, *The Power to Name*, 6; *Agos Standard*, September 20, 1911.

72 Edmondson, *Caribbean Middlebrow*, 75–76. A prominent Pan-Africanist editor, professor of classics and college president, diplomat, and politician (and thus whose versatility invites parallels with Rupert Gray's aspirations), Edward Wilmot Blyden was born in St. Thomas, in the Danish Virgin Islands, and spent much of his long career in Liberia and Sierra Leone. He died in 1912.

73 Cobham, *Rupert Gray*, 123.

74 In this sense Rupert Gray's address to the Linnaean Society alludes to John Jacob Thomas's lecture to the Philological Society in 1873, and suggests a later generation's claim to have Thomas's intellectual mastery but with a more equal relationship to metropolitan élites, and also demonstrates the precarity of intimate relations with élites at home and abroad. On Thomas, see Smith, *Creole Recitations*, 68, 102.

75 Doyle, "The Adventure of the Priory School."

76 Forster, *Howard's End*; Frank, *Law, Literature*, 21.

77 Parker, *Author's Inheritance*, 11, 13.

78 Parker, *Author's Inheritance*, 11.

79 This specific citation is from the claim of Don Antonio Gomez, a Spanish-born migrant from Venezuela who acquired a cocoa estate in Trinidad, and who collected compensation of over seventeen hundred pounds based on the claim submitted on the lost value of his human "property" when slavery was abolished. Claim #1296 by his son Philip, Legacies of British Slave-ownership, University College of London, Parliamentary Papers, p. 165. (This website is now "Legacies of British Slavery," as of May 2021, and does not seem to retain the Parliamentary Papers section.)

80 Cobham, *Rupert Gray*, 80.

81 Cobham, *Rupert Gray*, 78.

82 Cobham, *Rupert Gray,* 23.

83 Casting political independence as a dubious replacement for reparations in the anglophone Caribbean, David Scott has asked: "Now that we inhabit the dead end of the nation-state project, we can better ask, why should the spontaneous uprising of the black poor, the descendants of the enslaved, have given birth to a movement for political independence that has only enhanced the elite classes? Might it not better have given birth to a demand for reparations, to a demand for the moral and material repair for the generations of enslavement?" "On the Very Idea of the *Making* of Modern Jamaica," 46.

84 Cobham, *Rupert Gray*, 32, 132.

85 See Robbie Shilliam's use of Mauss's discussion of the Māoris to theorize Guyana's gift-giving to Haitians after the 2010 earthquake. "The Spirit of Exchange"; Mauss, *The Gift*.

86 J. Gordon, "The Gift of Double Consciousness," 144.

87 Du Bois, *Souls of Black Folk*, 365.

88 Here I am indebted to conversations with Gina Pugliese, Ashley Manchester, and Arianna Anaya.

89 Cobham, *Rupert Gray*, 39.

90 Cobham, *Rupert Gray*, 13.

91 Cobham, *Rupert Gray*, 42.

92 On white womanhood in the Caribbean, see O'Callaghan, *Women Writing the West Indies*.

93 Cassin, *With Silent Tread*.

94 Cobham, *Rupert Gray*, 27.

95 On spectral femininity, property ownership, and a non-Protestant location (Ireland) in English fiction, see Gaylin, "Ghostly Dispossessions."

96 Bridges, *Child of the Tropics*, 146; on the Monos and white futurity, see Kingsley's fantasy about a Scotsman's "paradise," *At Last: A Christmas in the West Indies*; and Kempadoo's discussion of photographs of family outings, *Creole in the Archive*, 94–99. Brand rehearses this down-the-islands scenario with slaveholding nuns who are also quasi-spectral, in *At the Full and Change of the Moon*.

97 Burns, *Colonial Habits*.

98 Burns, *Colonial Habits*, 31.

99 Cobham, *Rupert Gray*, 20, 129.

100 Bridges, *Child of the Tropics*, 161; Cobham, *Rupert Gray*, 9. Fictional Gwendoline is connected to creole English whiteness, her father having migrated to Trinidad from England to seek his fortune; her dead mother's specific ethnic whiteness is unidentified. Yseult Bridges conjoins francophone *and* anglophone through her mother and father, respectively.

101 Bridges, *Child of the Tropics*, 156.

102 Bridges, *Child of the Tropics*, 160.

103 Cobham, *Rupert Gray*, 8.

104 Cobham, *Rupert Gray*, 29.

105 Quotations from Cobham, *Rupert Gray*, 66.

106 On Caribbean charisma in a future political moment, see Allahar, *Caribbean Charisma*; on Black charisma and fiction in the US context, see E. Edwards, *Charisma and the Fictions of Black Leadership*.

107 Cobham, *Rupert Gray*, 37.

108 Cobham, *Rupert Gray*, 22, 69.

109 For a brilliant reading of this scene as a lynching, see Pugliese, "Intimate Scripts."

110 Cobham, *Rupert Gray*, 68–71.

111 Cobham, *Rupert Gray*, 70–71.

112 Cobham, *Rupert Gray*, 116, 37.

113 Cobham, *Rupert Gray*, 115.

114 Cobham, *Rupert Gray*, 27.

115 Cobham, *Rupert Gray*, 71.

116 Cobham, *Rupert Gray*, 71.

117 Cobham, *Rupert Gray*, 22.

118 Cobham, *Rupert Gray*, 93–94.

119 Cobham, *Rupert Gray*, 94.

120 Palmer, *Freedom's Children*; Cobham, *Rupert Gray*, 83, 150.

121 LaBelle, *Lexicon of the Mouth*, 131–32.

122 Jones, "Maternal Duties."

123 Jones, "Maternal Duties," 174–75.

124 Cozier, *Uncomfortable*; Cozier, "Unspeakable."

125 Stover, *The Sonic Color Line*, 61.

126 Cobham, *Rupert Gray*, 123; Pugliese, "Intimate Scripts."

127 This and following quotations Cobham, *Rupert Gray*, 123.

128 Miller, *Slaves to Fashion*.

Coda

1 "In Cuba with Maria Magdalena Campos Pons," Peabody Essex Museum, *Alchemy of the Soul*, https://www.youtube.com/watch?v=MULRM5OHid8.

2 Espinet, *The Swinging Bridge*; Rosario, *Song of the Water Saints*.

3 Z. Smith, *White Teeth*, this and following quotations, 280, 292.

4 Z. Smith, *White Teeth*, 295.

5 Oyoyemi, *The Icarus Girl*, this and following quotations, 78, 33, 77.

6 Brand, *At the Full and Change of the Moon*, 20.

7 Brand, *At the Full and Change of the Moon*, 298. On Black Caribbean families as disorganized because of the mother's centrality, see Reddock, *Women, Labour and Politics*, 7; for African American families as pathological because of the mother, see Moynihan, "Tangle of Pathology," 75; and Spillers, "Mama's Baby, Papa's Maybe," 58. See also Tracy Robinson's conclusion that "managing the Black family became a technology for managing colonialism." Robinson, "Properties of Citizens," 429.

8 Brand, *At the Full and Change of the Moon*, 198.

9 See Rowley's discussion of "maternal citizenship" in *Feminist Advocacy and Gender Equity*.

10 See Morrison's interrogation of the maternal obligation for Black women in the late nineteenth and early twentieth centuries: "What value did she place on herself?," *Source of Self-Regard*, 318.

11 Glover, *A Regarded Self*, 1.

12 Sharpe, *In the Wake*, 9, drawing on Trouillot, *Silencing the Past*, 15.

13 Hartman, *Lose Your Mother*, 6.

Abbott, Lynn, and Doug Seroff. *Ragged but Right: Black Traveling Shows, "Coon Songs," and the Dark Pathway to Blues and Jazz*. Jackson: University Press of Mississippi, 2007.

Abdur-Rahman, Aliyyah I. "The Black Ecstatic." *GLQ: A Journal of Gay and Lesbian Studies* 24, no. 2–3 (June 2018): 343–65.

Aboul-Ela, Hosam. *Other South: Faulkner, Coloniality, and the Mariátegui Tradition*. Pittsburgh, PA: University of Pittsburgh Press, 2007.

Achebe, Chinua. *Things Fall Apart*. Norton Critical Edition. Edited by Abiola Irele. New York: W. W. Norton, [1958] 2009.

Aching, Gerard. *Masking and Power: Carnival and Popular Culture in the Caribbean*. Minneapolis: University of Minnesota Press, 2002.

Ahmed, Sara. *The Promise of Happiness*. Durham, NC: Duke University Press, 2010.

Ahmed, Sara. *Strange Encounters: Embodied Others in Post-coloniality*. London: Routledge, 2000.

Akomfrah, John, dir. *The Stuart Hall Project: Revolution, Politics, Culture and the New Left Experience*. London: British Film Institute, 2013.

Alexander, M. Jacqui. "Not Just (Any) Body Can Be a Citizen: The Politics of Law, Sexuality, and Postcoloniality in Trinidad and Tobago and the Bahamas." *Feminist Review* 48 (Autumn 1994): 5–23.

Alexander, M. Jacqui. *Pedagogies of Crossing: Meditations on Feminism, Sexual Politics, Memory and the Sacred*. Durham, NC: Duke University Press, 2005.

Alexandre, Sandy. *The Properties of Violence: Claims to Ownership in Representations of Lynching*. Oxford: University Press of Mississippi, 2012.

Allahar, Anton, ed. *Caribbean Charisma: Reflections on Leadership, Legitimacy and Populist Politics*. Kingston, Jamaica: Ian Randle Publishers, 2001.

Allan, Eric [Charles W. Willis]. *"Buckra" Land: Two Weeks in Jamaica: Details of a Voyage to the West Indies Day by Day, and a Tour of Jamaica, Step by Step*. Boston: Boston Fruit Company, 1897.

Allen, Esther. "Constellations in Sugar." In *Maria Magdalena Campos-Pons: Alchemy of the Soul*, edited by Joshua Basseches, 82–99. Salem, MA: Peabody Essex Museum, 2016.

Als, Hilton. "Toni Morrison and the Ghosts in the House." *New Yorker*. October 27, 2003. https://www.newyorker.com/magazine/2003/10/27/ghosts-in-the-house.

Althusser, Louis. "The Errors of Classical Economics: Outline of a Concept of Historical Time." In *Reading Capital* edited by Althusser and Étienne Balibar, translated by Ben Brewster, 101–31. London: Verso Press, 2009.

Althusser, Louis. "Ideology and Ideological State Apparatuses (Notes Toward an Investigation)." In *Lenin and Philosophy and Other Essays*, translated by Ben Brewster, 85–126. New York: NYU Press and Monthly Review Press, 2002.

Altink, Henrice. "'I Did Not Want to Face the Shame of Exposure': Gender Ideologies and Child Murder in Post-Emancipation Jamaica." *Journal of Social History* 41, no. 2 (Winter 2007): 355–87.

Anderson, Benedict. *Imagined Communities: Reflections on the Origins and Spread of Nationalism*. London: Verso, 2006.

Antwi, Phanuel. "On Labor, Embodiment, and Debt in the Academy." *a/b: Auto/Biography Studies* 33, no. 2 (2018): 301–26.

Anzaldúa, Gloria. *Borderlands, La Frontera: The New Mestiza*. San Francisco: Aunt Lute Books, 1987.

Appadurai, Arjun. "The Colonial Backdrop." *Afterimage* 24, no. 5 (March–April 1997): 4–7.

Appadurai, Arjun, and Carol A. Breckenridge. "Public Modernity in India." In *Consuming Modernity: Public Culture in a South Asian World*, edited by Carol Breckenridge, 1–20. Minneapolis: University of Minnesota Press, 1995.

Archer-Straw, Petrina. "Photos and Phantasms: Harry Johnston's Photographs of the Caribbean." In *Photos and Phantasms: Harry Johnston's Photographs of the Caribbean*, 9–15. London: British Council and Royal Geographical Society, 1998.

Armstrong, Nancy. *Fiction in the Age of Photography: The Legacy of British Realism*. Cambridge, MA: Harvard University Press, 2000.

Asad, Talal. "Conscripts of Western Civilization." In *Dialectical Anthropology: Essays in Honor of Stanley Diamond*, vol. 1, *Civilization in Crisis*, edited by Christine Gailey, 332–51. Gainesville: University Press of Florida, 1992.

Bahadur, Gaiutra. *Coolie Woman: The Odyssey of Indenture*. Chicago: Chicago University Press, 2013.

Bajorek, Jennifer. "Then and Now: Santu Mofokeng's *Black Photo Album*." In *Distance and Desire: Encounters with the African Archive. African Photography from the Walther Collection*, edited by Tamar Garb, 217–27. New York: Steidl, 2013.

Bakhtin, M. M. *Rabelais and His World*. Translated by Helen Iswolsky. Bloomington: Indiana University Press, 1984.

Barnard, Rita. "Of Riots and Rainbows: South Africa, the US, and the Pitfalls of Comparison." *American Literary History* 17, no. 2 (Summer 2005): 399–416.

Barringer, Tim. "'There's the Life for a Man Like Me': Rural Life and Labor in Edwardian Art and Music." In *Edwardian Opulence: British Art at the Dawn of the Twentieth*

Century, edited by Angus Trumble and Andrea Wolk Rager, 133–57. New Haven, CT: Yale Center for British Art and Yale University Press, 2013.

Barringer, Tim, Gillian Forrester, and Bárbaro Martinez-Ruiz. *Art and Emancipation in Jamaica: Isaac Mendes Belisario and His Worlds*. New Haven, CT: Yale Center for British Art with Yale University Press, 2007.

Barthes, Roland. *Camera Lucida: Reflections on Photography*. Translated by Richard Howard. New York: Farrar, Straus and Giroux, 1981.

Batiste, Stephanie Leigh. *Darkening Mirrors: Imperial Representation in Depression-Era African American Performance*. Durham, NC: Duke University Press, 2011.

Benjamin, Walter. "Paris: The Capital of the Nineteenth Century." In *The Arcades Project*. Translated by Howard Eiland and Kevin McLaughlin, 3–13. Cambridge, MA: Belknap Press, [1935] 2002.

Benjamin, Walter. "Theses on the Philosophy of History." In *Illuminations*. edited by Hannah Arendt and translated by Harry Zohn, 253–64. New York: Schocken Books, [1955] 2007.

Benjamin, Walter. "The Work of Art in the Age of Mechanical Reproduction." In *Illuminations*, edited by Hannah Arendt and translated by Harry Zohn, 217–51. New York: Schocken Books, [1955] 2007.

Bennett, Louise. *Selected Poems*. Edited by Mervyn Morris. Kingston, Jamaica: Sangster's Bookstore, 1982.

Bhabha, Homi K. *The Location of Culture*. London: Routledge, 1994.

Birkenmaier, Anke, and Esther Whitfield, eds. *Havana beyond the Ruins: Cultural Mappings after 1989*. Durham, NC: Duke University Press, 2011.

Bonilla, Yarimar. *Non-sovereign Futures: French Caribbean Politics in the Wake of Disenchantment*. Chicago: University of Chicago Press, 2015.

Bonilla, Yarimar. "Ordinary Sovereignty." *Small Axe* 42 (November 2013): 152–65.

Boxer, David. *Jamaica in Black and White: Photography in Jamaica c.1845–c.1920: The David Boxer Collection*. London: Macmillan Caribbean, 2013.

Brand, Dionne. *At the Full and Change of the Moon*. New York: Grove Press, 1999.

Brantlinger, Patrick. *Taming Cannibals: Race and the Victorians*. Ithaca, NY: Cornell University Press, 2011.

Brathwaite, Kamau. "Poetry, 11-9-82." Uploaded November 6, 2020. https://www.youtube.com/watch?v=_KVm1cNv4yo.

Brereton, Bridget. *The Book of Trinidad*. Edited by Gerard Besson and Bridget Brereton. Newtown, Port of Spain: Paria Press, 1992.

Brereton, Bridget. *A History of Modern Trinidad 1783–1962*. Portsmouth, NH: Heineman, 1982.

Brereton, Bridget. "The White Elite of Trinidad, 1838–1950." In *The White Minority in the Caribbean*, edited by Howard Johnson and Karl Watson, 32–70. Kingston, Jamaica: Ian Randle Press, 1998.

Brickhouse, Anna. *Transamerican Literary Relations and the Nineteenth-Century Public Sphere*. Cambridge: Cambridge University Press, 2005.

Bridges, Yseult. *Child of the Tropics: Victorian Memoirs*. Edited by Nicholas Guppy. New York: Aquarella Galleries, 1988.

Brodber, Erna. "Clarendon: Kellits: A Woman Come Down in the World." In *Life in Jamaica in the Early Twentieth Century: A Presentation of Ninety Oral Accounts*, 13–17. Mona, Jamaica: ISER [Institute of Social and Economic Research], 1980.

Brodber, Erna. "Oral Sources and the Creation of a Social History of the Caribbean." *Jamaica Journal* 16, no. 4 (November 1983): 2–11. https://original-ufdc.uflib.ufl.edu /UF00090030/00041/4j?search=jamaica+%3djournal+%3dbrodber+%3doral+%3 dsources.

Brodber, Erna. "St. Catherine: Church Pen; The Bright Young Butleress." In *Life in Jamaica in the Early Twentieth Century: A Presentation of Ninety Oral Accounts*, 18–23. Mona, Jamaica: ISER [Institute of Social and Economic Research], 1980.

Brontë, Charlotte. *Jane Eyre*. New York: Penguin Books, [1847] 1984.

Brooks, Daphne A. *Bodies in Dissent: Spectacular Performances of Race and Freedom, 1850–1910*. Durham, NC: Duke University Press, 2006.

Brown, David H. "The Afro-Cuban Festival 'Day of the Kings' [by Fernando Ortiz]: An Annotated Glossary." In *Cuban Festivals: A Century of Afro-Cuban Culture*, edited by Judith Bettelheim, 41–93. Kingston, Jamaica: Ian Randle Publishers, 2001.

Brown, Vincent. *Tacky's Revolt: The Story of an Atlantic Slave War*. Cambridge, MA: Harvard University Press, 2020.

Browne, Katherine, Alla Kovgan, and Jude Ray, directors. *Traces of the Trade: A Story from the Deep North*. San Francisco: California Newsreel, 2008.

Bryan, Patrick. "Émigrés: Conflict and Reconciliation: The French Émigrés in Nineteenth Century Jamaica." *The Haiti-Jamaica Connection*. Seminar Proceedings, UWI Mona, April 3, 17–30. Kingston, Jamaica: Latin American-Caribbean Centre, 2004.

Bryan, Patrick. *The Jamaican People, 1880–1902: Race, Class and Social Control*. Kingston, Jamaica: University of the West Indies Press, 2000.

Buckridge, Steeve O. *The Language of Dress: Resistance and Accommodation in Jamaica, 1760–1890*. Kingston, Jamaica: University of the West Indies Press, 2004.

Burnard, Trevor. *Mastery, Tyranny and Desire: Thomas Thistlewood and His Slaves in the Anglo-Jamaican World*. Chapel Hill, NC: UNC Press, 2004.

Burns, Kathryn. *Colonial Habits: Convents and the Spiritual Economy of Cuzco, Peru*. Durham, NC: Duke University Press, 1999.

Cadava, Eduardo. *Words of Light: Theses on the Photography of History*. Princeton, NJ: Princeton University Press, 1997.

Cadogan, Garnet. "Walking While Black." In *Freeman's: The Best New Writing on Arrival*, edited by John Freeman. New York: Grove, 2015. https://lithub.com/walking -while-black/.

Campbell, Susan. "Carnival, Calypso and Class Struggle in Nineteenth-Century Trinidad." *History Workshop Journal* 26, no. 1 (1988): 1–27.

Campos-Pons, Maria Magdalena. *Maria Magdalena Campos-Pons: Alchemy of the Soul*. Edited by Joshua Basseches. Salem, MA: Peabody Essex Museum, 2016.

Campt, Tina M. *Image Matters: Archive, Photography, and the African Diaspora in Europe*. Durham, NC: Duke University Press, 2012.

Campt, Tina M. *Listening to Images*. Durham, NC: Duke University Press, 2017.

Campt, Tina M. "The Loophole of Retreat: An Invitation." *e-flux* 105 (December 2019). https://www.e-flux.com/journal/105/302556/the-loophole-of-retreat-an-invitation/.

Capécia, Mayotte. *I Am a Martinican Woman and the White Negress: Two Novelettes.* Translated by Beatrice Stith Clark. Pueblo, CO: Passeggiata Press, 1998.

Carbado, Devon W. "Racial Naturalization." *American Quarterly* 57, no. 3 (September 2005): 633–58.

Carby, Hazel. "Treason-Workers: Violators of Tradition and Other Unreasoning Women." Talk given at the "Idea of a Black Radical Tradition," Small Axe Symposium, Columbia University, New York, April 22–23, 2011.

Carnegie, Charles. "Walk-Foot People Matter: Part 1." [Jamaica] *Public Opinion*, May 31, 2018.

Carnegie, Charles. "Walk-Foot People Matter: Part 2." [Jamaica] *Public Opinion*, June 14, 2018.

Carnegie, Charles. "Walking Kingston." *Public Opinion*, June 28, 2018.

Carnegie, James. *Some Aspects of Jamaica's Politics: 1918–1938.* Kingston: Institute of Jamaica, 1973.

Casid, Jill H. *Sowing Empire: Landscape and Colonization.* Minneapolis: University of Minnesota Press, 2005.

Cassin, Frieda. *With Silent Tread.* London: Macmillan Caribbean, 2002.

Césaire, Aimé. *Cahiers d'un retour au pays natal.* Edited by Abiola Irele. Columbus: Ohio University Press, [1956] 2000.

Césaire, Aimé. *Notebook of a Return to the Native Land.* Edited and translated by Clayton Eshleman and Annette Smith. Middletown, CT: Wesleyan University Press, 2001.

Chakrabarty, Dipesh. *Provincializing Europe: Postcolonial Thought and Historical Difference.* Princeton, NJ: Princeton University Press, 2000.

Channer, Colin. *Waiting in Vain.* New York: One World-Ballantyne, 1998.

Chatterjee, Partha. "Anderson's Utopia." In *Grounds of Comparison: Around the Work of Benedict Anderson*, edited by Johnathan Culler and Pheng Cheah, 161–70. New York: Routledge, 2003.

Chatterjee, Partha. *The Nation and Its Fragments: Colonial and Postcolonial Histories.* Princeton, NJ: Princeton University Press, 1983.

Chesnutt, Charles W. "The Wife of His Youth." In *The Wife of His Youth and Other Stories of the Color Line*, 1–24. Ann Arbor: University of Michigan, [1899] 1968.

Chomsky, Aviva. *West Indian Workers and the United Fruit Company in Costa Rica 1870–1940.* Baton Rouge: Louisiana State University Press, 1996.

Clarke, Austin. *The Polished Hoe.* New York: Amistad, [2002] 2004.

Clarke, Edith. *My Mother Who Fathered Me: A Study of the Families in Three Selected Communities of Jamaica.* Kingston, Jamaica: University of the West Indies Press, [1957] 1999.

Cliff, Michelle. *No Telephone to Heaven.* New York: Plume, 1987.

Cobb, Jasmine Nichole. *Picture Freedom: Remaking Black Visuality in the Early Nineteenth Century.* New York: NYU Press, 2015.

Cobham, Stephen N. *Rupert Gray: A Tale in Black and White.* Edited by Lise Winer. Kingston, Jamaica: University of the West Indies Press, [1907] 2006.

Cobham-Sander, Rhonda. "Chasms and Silences: For Chinua Achebe." *PMLA* 129, no. 2 (March 2014): 240–43.

Cobham-Sander, Rhonda. "The Creative Writer and West Indian Society: Jamaica 1900–1950." PhD diss., St. Andrew's University, 1981.

Cobham-Sander, Rhonda. "Fictions of Gender, Fictions of Race: Retelling Morant Bay in Jamaican Literature." *Small Axe* 8 (September 2000): 1–30.

Cobham-Sander, Rhonda. "Jekyll and Claude: The Erotics of Patronage in Claude McKay's *Banana Bottom*." *Caribbean Quarterly* 38, no. 1 (1992): 55–78.

Cobham-Sander, Rhonda. "Jekyll and Claude: The Erotics of Patronage in Claude McKay's *Banana Bottom*." In *Queer Diasporas*, edited by Cindy Patton and Benigno Sánchez-Eppler, 122–53. Durham, NC: Duke University Press, 2000.

Cobham-Sander, Rhonda. "'Mwen Na Rien, Msieu': Jamaica Kincaid and the Problem of Creole Gnosis." *Callaloo* 25 (2002): 868–84.

Cobham-Sander, Rhonda, Donette Francis, and Leah Rosenberg. "Panama Silver, Asian Gold: Migration, Money, and the Making of the Modern Caribbean" and "Panama Silver, Asian Gold: Reimagining Diasporas, Archives, and the Humanities." Course syllabus, updated May 14, 2016. https://hcommons.org/deposits/item/hc:31065/.

Cole, Kenneth G. II. "Teaching and Research Guide to Stephen Cobham's *Rupert Gray*." Updated January 2016. https://www.dloc.com/AA00012883/00001?search =rupert+=gray%20(GoldF8_68B.pdf.jpg&search=rupert+=gray%20(GoldF8_68B .pdf.jpg.

Collins, Merle. *Angel*. Leeds, UK: Peepal Tree Press, 2011.

Collis-Buthelezi, Victoria J. "Caribbean Regionalism, South Africa, and Mapping New World Studies." *Small Axe* 46 (March 2015): 37–54.

Collis-Buthelezi, Victoria J. " "The Case for Black Studies in South Africa." *The Black Scholar* 47, no. 2 (2017): 7–21.

Condé, Maryse. "Habiter Ce Pays, La Guadeloupe." *Chemins Critiques* 1, no. 3 (December 1989): 5–14.

Conrad, Joseph. *Heart of Darkness* and *The Congo Diary*. Edited by Owen Knowles and Robert Hampson. New York: Penguin Books, 2007.

Cooper, Carolyn. "'Only a Nigger Gal!' Race, Gender, and the Politics of Education in Claude McKay's *Banana Bottom*." *Caribbean Quarterly* 38, no. 1 (1992): 40–54.

Coronado, Raúl. *A World Not to Come: A History of Latino Writing and Print Culture*. Cambridge, MA: Harvard University Press, 2013.

Cowley, John. *Carnival, Canboulay, and Calypso: Traditions in the Making*. Cambridge: Cambridge University Press, 1996.

Cozier, Christopher. *Uncomfortable: The Art of Christopher Cozier*. Directed by Richard Fung. Canada/Trinidad and Tobago: Video Data Bank, 2005.

Cozier, Christopher. "The Unspeakable State of Sliced Bread Sandwiches." *Public* 27 (Spring 2003). http://www.publicjournal.ca/shop/.

Craton, Michael, and James Walvin. *A Jamaican Plantation: The History of Worthy Park, 1670–1970*. Toronto: University of Toronto Press, 1970.

Curtin, Marguerite R. *The Story of Westmoreland: A Jamaican Parish*. Jamaica: Marguerite R. Curtin, 2010.

Darío, Rubén. "To Roosevelt." *Selected Poems of Rubén Darío*. Translated by Lysander Kemp, 69. Austin: University of Texas Press, [1904] 1965.

Dash, J. Michael. "Textual Error and Cultural Crossing: A Caribbean Poetics of Creolization." *Research in African Literatures* 25, no. 2 (1994): 159–68.

Davies, Carole Boyce. "The Africa Theme in Trinidad Calypso." *Caribbean Quarterly* 31, no. 2 (June 1985): 67–86.

Davis, Angela. "Policing the Crisis Today." Stuart Hall International Conference: Conversations, Projects and Legacies. Goldsmiths University of London. November 28, 2014. https://vimeo.com/113119921.

Dawes, Kwame S. N. "An Act of 'Unruly' Savagery: Rewriting Black Rebellion in the Language of the Colonizer: H. G. De Lisser's *The White Witch of Rosehall*." *Caribbean Quarterly* 40, no. 1 (March 1994): 1–12.

De Barros, Juanita. *Reproducing the British Caribbean: Sex, Gender, and Population Politics After Slavery*. Chapel Hill, NC: UNC Press, 2014.

Delaney, Martin R. *Blake: Or the Huts of America*. Boston: Beacon Press, [1859–61] 1970.

De Lisser, H. G. *In Jamaica and Cuba*. Kingston, Jamaica: Gleaner Co., Ltd., 1910.

De Lisser, H. G. *Jane's Career*. Kingston, Jamaica: Heinemann Caribbean Writers Series, 1980.

De Lisser, H. G. *Susan Proudleigh*. London: Methuen and Co., 1915.

De Lisser, H. G. *Twentieth Century Jamaica*. Kingston, Jamaica: Jamaica Times, 1913.

DeLoughrey, Elizabeth M. *Routes and Roots: Navigating Caribbean and Pacific Island Literatures*. Honolulu: University of Hawai'i Press, 2007.

Derrida, Jacques. "Before the Law." In *Act of Literature*, edited by Derek Attridge, 183–220. London: Routledge, 1992.

Dickens, Charles. *Bleak House*. London: Penguin Classics, [1853] 1996.

Dimock, Wai Chee. "A Theory of Resonance." *PMLA* 112, no. 5 (October 1997): 1060–71.

Doyle, Arthur Conan. "The Adventure of the Priory School." *Strand Magazine* 27, no. 158 (February 1904): 123–40.

Doyle, Arthur Conan. "A Scandal in Bohemia." *Strand Magazine* (July 1891): 61–75. https://www.arthur-conan-doyle.com/index.php?title=A_Scandal_in_Bohemia.

Doyle, Laura, and Laura A. Winkiel, eds. *Geomodernisms: Race, Modernism, Modernity*. Bloomington: Indiana University Press, 2005.

Drayton, Richard. *Nature's Government: Science, Imperial Britain, and the "Improvement of the World."* New Haven, CT: Yale University Press, 2000.

Du Bois, W. E. B. "An Amazing Island." *The Crisis* 10 (June 1915): 80–81.

Du Bois, W. E. B. *The Souls of Black Folk*. In *Du Bois: Writings,* edited by Nathan Huggins, 357–552. New York: Literary Classics of the United States, 1986.

Du Bois, W. E. B. "To the Nations of the World." In *W. E. B. Du Bois: A Reader*, edited by David Levering Lewis, 639–43. New York: Henry Holt, 1995.

Duffy, Enda. *The Subaltern Ulysses*. Minneapolis: University of Minnesota Press, 1994.

Dunn, Richard S. *A Tale of Two Plantations: Slave Life and Labor in Jamaica and Virginia*. Cambridge, MA: Harvard University Press, 2014.

Eastlake, Lady Elizabeth. "Photography." In *Classic Essays on Photography*, edited by Alan Trachtenberg, 39–68. New Haven, CT: Leete's Island Books, 1980.

Edmondson, Belinda. *Caribbean Middlebrow: Leisure Culture and the Middle Class.* Ithaca, NY: Cornell University Press, 2009.

Edmondson, Belinda. *Creole Noise: Early Caribbean Dialect Literature and Performance.* Oxford: Oxford University Press, 2022.

Edmondson, Belinda. *Making Men: Gender, Literary Authority, and Women's Writing in Caribbean Narrative.* Durham, NC: Duke University Press, 1998.

Edwards, Brent Hayes. *The Practice of Diaspora: Literature, Translation, and the Rise of Black Internationalism.* Cambridge, MA: Harvard University, 2003.

Edwards, Elizabeth. "Looking at Photographs: Between Contemplation, Curiosity, and Gaze." In *Distance and Desire: Encounters with the African Archive*, edited by Tamar Garb, 48–54. New York: Steidl and the Walther Collection, 2013.

Edwards, Elizabeth. "Photographs and History: Emotion and Materiality." In *Museum Materialities: Objects, Engagement, Interpretations*, edited by Sandra H. Dudley, 21–28. London: Routledge, 2013.

Edwards, Erica R. *Charisma and the Fictions of Black Leadership.* Minneapolis: University of Minnesota Press, 2012.

Edwards, Erica R. "Of Cain and Abel: African American Literature and the Problem of Inheritance after 9/11." *American Literary History* 25, no. 1 (Spring 2013): 190–204.

Ellis, Nadia. "Out and Bad: Toward a Queer Performance Hermeneutic in Jamaican Dancehall." *Small Axe* 35 (July 2011): 7–23.

Emery, Mary Lou. "Caribbean Modernism: Plantation to Planetary." In *The Oxford Handbook of Global Modernism*, edited by Mark Wollaeger and Matt Eatough, 48–77. Oxford: Oxford University Press, 2012.

Emery, Mary Lou. "On the Verandah: Jean Rhys' Material Modernism." In *Jean Rhys: Twenty-First Century Approaches*, edited by Erica L Johnson and Patricia Moran, 59–81. Edinburgh, UK: Edinburgh University Press, 2015.

Eng, David L. *The Feeling of Kinship: Queer Liberalism and the Racialization of Intimacy.* Durham, NC: Duke University Press, 2010.

Espinet, Ramabai. *The Swinging Bridge.* Toronto: Harper Perennial, 2004.

Esty, Jed. *Unseasonable Youth: Modernism, Colonialism, and the Fiction of Development.* New York: Oxford University Press, 2012.

Fabian, Johannes. *Time and the Other: How Anthropology Makes Its Object.* New York: Columbia University Press, [1983] 2002.

Fanon, Frantz. *Black Skin, White Masks.* Translated by Richard Philcox. New York: Grove, 2008.

Felski, Rita. *The Gender of Modernity.* Cambridge, MA: Harvard University Press, 1995.

Ferrer, Ada. *Freedom's Mirror: Cuba and Haiti in the Age of Revolution.* New York: Cambridge University Press, 2014.

Finch, Aisha K. *Rethinking Slave Rebellion in Cuba: La Escalera and the Insurgencies of 1841–44.* Chapel Hill, NC: UNC Press, 2015.

Findlay, Eileen J. "Love in the Tropics: Marriage, Divorce, and the Construction of Benevolent Colonialism in Puerto Rico, 1898–1920." In *Close Encounters of Empire: Writing the Cultural History of US-Latin American Relations*, edited by Joseph, Le-Grand, Salvatore, 139–72. Durham, NC: Duke University Press, 1998.

Firmin, Antenor. *The Equality of the Human Races*. Translated by Asselin Charles. New York: Garland, [1885] 2000.

Firmin, Antenor. *Lettres de St. Thomas*. Port au Prince, Haiti: Editions Fardin, [1910] 1986.

Fischer, Sibylle. *Modernity Disavowed: Haiti and the Cultures of Slavery in the Age of Revolution*. Durham, NC: Duke University Press, 2004.

Fletcher, Pamela. "Victorians and Moderns." In *Edwardian Opulence: British Art at the Dawn of the Twentieth Century*, edited by Angus Trumble and Andrea Wolk Rager, 99–107. New Haven, CT: Yale University Press, 2013.

Forbes, Curdella. "Between Plot and Plantation, Trespass and Transgression: Caribbean Migratory Disobedience in Fiction and Internet Traffic." *Small Axe* 38 (July 2012): 23–42.

Ford-Smith, Honor. "Women and the Garvey Movement in Jamaica." In *Garvey: His Work and Impact*, edited by Rupert Lewis and Patrick Bryan, 73–83. Mona, Jamaica: ISER and Department of Extra-Mural Studies, 1988.

Forster, E. M. *Howard's End*. New York: G. P. Putnam's Son, 1910.

Francis, Donette. *Fictions of Feminine Citizenship: Sexuality and the Nation in Contemporary Caribbean Literature*. New York: Palgrave, 2010.

Francis, Donette, Leah Rosenberg, and Rhonda Cobham-Sander. "Researching and Teaching with the Digital Archive"; "The Caribbean Digital: A *Small Axe* Event." Barnard College, December 4, 2014.

Franco, Pamela. "The 'Unruly Woman' in Nineteenth Century Trinidad Carnival." *Small Axe* 7 (March 2000): 60–76.

Frank, Catherine O. *Law, Literature, and the Transmission of Culture in England, 1837–1925*. Surrey, UK: Ashgate, 2010.

Frederick, Rhonda. *Colón Man a Come: Mythographies of Panama Canal Migration*. Lanham, MD: Lexington Books, 2005.

Friedman, Susan Stanford. "Periodizing Modernism: Postcolonial Modernities and the Space/Time Borders of Modernist Studies." *Modernism/Modernity* 13, no. 3 (September 2006): 425–43.

Friedman, Susan Stanford. *Planetary Modernisms: Provocations on Modernity across Time*. New York: Columbia University Press, 2015.

Froude, James Anthony. *The English in the West Indies or the Bow of Ulysses*. London: Longmans Green, 1888.

Fuente, Alejandro de la. "Two Dangers, One Solution: Immigration, Race, and Labor in Cuba, 1900–1930." *International Labor and Working-Class History* 51 (1997): 7–29.

Fung, Richard. *My Mother's Place*. Video Data Bank, 1990.

Gandhi, Leela. *Affective Communities: Anticolonial Thought, Fin-de-Siècle Radicalism, and the Politics of Friendship*. Durham, NC: Duke University Press, 2006.

Gandhi, M. K. "Indenture or Slavery?" In *The Collected Works of Mahatma Gandhi*, vol. 13, 146–48. Delhi: Publications Division, Ministry of Information and Broadcasting, Government of India, 1964.

Gandhi, M. K. "Indentured Labour." In *The Collected Works of Mahatma Gandhi*, vol. 13, 247–50. Delhi: Publications Division, Ministry of Information and Broadcasting, Government of India, 1964.

Gaonkar, Dilip Parameshwar, ed. *Alternative Modernities*. Durham, NC: Duke University Press, 2001.

Garraway, Doris. *The Libertine Colony: Creolization in the Early French Caribbean*. Durham, NC: Duke University Press, 2005.

Garvey, Marcus. *The Marcus Garvey and Universal Negro Improvement Association Papers*. Vol. 3 (Sept 20 to Aug 1921), Berkeley: University of California Press, 1984.

Garvey, Marcus. "The Negro's Greatest Enemy." UCLA African Studies Center. https://www.international.ucla.edu/asc/mgpp/sample01.

Gaspar, David Barry. *Bondmen and Rebels: A Study of Master-Slave Relations in Antigua*. Baltimore, MD: Johns Hopkins University Press, 1985.

Gaylin, Ann. "Ghostly Dispossessions: The Gothic Properties of *Uncle Silas*." In *Troubled Legacies: Narrative and Inheritance*, edited by Allan Hepburn, 87–108. Toronto: University of Toronto Press, 2007.

Geiss, Immanuel. *The Pan African Movement*. Translated by Ann Elizabeth Keep. London: Methuen, 1974.

Gentleman, Amelia. *The Windrush Betrayal: Exposing the Hostile Environment*. London: Guardian Faber, 2019.

Gikandi, Simon. "Africa and the Epiphany of Modernism." In *Geomodernisms: Race, Modernism, Modernity*, edited by Laura Doyle and Laura A. Winkiel, 31–50. Bloomington: Indiana University Press, 2005.

Gikandi, Simon. "*Arrow of God*: The Novel and the Problem of Modern Time." *Research in African Literatures* 49, no. 4 (Winter 2018): 1–13.

Gikandi, Simon. *Slavery and the Culture of Taste*. Princeton, NJ: Princeton University Press, 2011.

Gill, Lyndon K. *Erotic Islands: Art and Activism in the Queer Caribbean*. Durham, NC: Duke University Press, 2018.

Gillman, Susan. "The Afterlives of *Free State of Jones*." *Los Angeles Review of Books*, July 2016. https://lareviewofbooks.org/article/the-afterlives-of-the-free-state-of-jones/.

Gillman, Susan. "It Takes an Archipelago to Compare Otherwise." In *Archipelagic American Studies*, edited by Brian Russell Roberts and Michelle Ann Stephens, 133–53. Durham, NC: Duke University Press, 2017.

Gilroy, Paul. *The Black Atlantic: Modernity and Double Consciousness*. Cambridge, MA: Harvard University Press, 1993.

Glover, Kaiama L. *A Regarded Self: Caribbean Womanhood and the Ethics of Disorderly Being*. Durham, NC: Duke University Press, 2021.

Gordon, Avery F. "Some Thoughts on Haunting and Futurity." *Borderlands* 10, no. 2 (2011): 1–21.

Gordon, Jane Anna. "The Gift of Double Consciousness: Some Obstacles to Grasping the Contributions of the Colonized." In *Postcolonialism and Political Theory*, edited by Nalini Persram, 143–62. Lanham, MD: Lexington Books, 2008.

Gosine, Andil. "My Mother's *Baby*: Wrecking Work After Indentureship." In *Indo-Caribbean Feminist Thought: Genealogies, Theories, Enactments*, edited by Gabrielle Jamela Hosein and Lisa Outar, 49–60. New York: Palgrave, 2016.

Goyal, Yogita. *Romance, Diaspora, and Black Atlantic Literature*. Cambridge: Cambridge University Press, 2010.

Grant, Colin. *Homecoming: Voices of the Windrush Generation*. London: Jonathan Cape, 2019.

Greene, Sandra E. *The Slaveowners of West Africa: Decision Making in the Age of Abolition*. Bloomington: Indiana University Press, 2017.

Gregg, Veronica. "Catherine McKenzie." In *Caribbean Women: An Anthology of Non-fiction Writing, 1890–1980*, edited by Veronica Marie Gregg, 98. Notre Dame, IN: University of Notre Dame Press, 2005.

Gregg, Veronica Marie, ed. *Caribbean Women: An Anthology of Non-fiction Writing, 1890–1980*. Notre Dame, IN: University of Notre Dame Press, 2005.

Guridy, Frank. *Forging Diaspora: Afro-Cubans and African Americans in a World of Empire and Jim Crow*. Chapel Hill, NC: UNC Press, 2010.

Haggard, H. Rider. *King Solomon's Mines*. London: Penguin Classics, [1885] 2007.

Haigh, Sam. "From Exile to Errance: Dany Laferière's *Cette grenade dans la main de jeune Nègre est-elle une arme ou un fruit?*" In *The Francophone Caribbean Today: Literature, Language, Culture*, edited by Gertrude Aub-Buscher and Beverley Ormerod Noakes, 60–80. Kingston, Jamaica: University of the West Indies Press, 2003.

Halberstam, Jack. *In A Queer Time and Place: Transgender Bodies, Subcultural Lives*. New York: NYU Press, 2005.

Hall, Catherine. *White, Male and Middle Class: Explorations in Feminism and History*. Cambridge: Polity Press, 1992.

Hall, Catherine, Nicholas Draper, Keith McClelland, Katie Donington, and Rachel Lang. *Legacies of British Slave-Ownership: Colonial Slavery and the Formation of Victorian Britain*. Cambridge: Cambridge University Press, 2014.

Hall, Douglas, ed. *In Miserable Slavery: Thomas Thistlewood in Jamaica 1750–1756*. Kingston, Jamaica: University of the West Indies Press, 1998.

Hall, Stuart. "The Legacy of Anglo-Caribbean Culture—A Diasporic Perspective." In *Art and Emancipation in Jamaica: Isaac Mendes Belisario and His Worlds*, edited by Tim Barringer, Gillian Forrester, and Barbaro Martinez-Ruiz, 179–95. New Haven, CT: Yale Center for British Art with Yale University Press, 2000.

Hall, Stuart. "The West Indian Front Room." In *The Front Room: Migrant Aesthetics in the Home*, edited by Michael McMillan, 18–19. London: Black Dog, 2009.

Hall, Stuart, Charles Critcher, Tony Jefferson, John Clarke, and Brian Roberts. *Policing the Crisis: Mugging, the State, and Law and Order*. London: Macmillan, 1978.

Hall, Stuart, and Doreen Massey. "Interpreting the Crisis: Doreen Massey and Stuart Hall Discuss Ways of Understanding the Current Crisis." *Soundings: A Journal of Politics and Culture* 44 (Spring 2010): 57–71.

Hamner, Robert. "Dramatizing the New World's African King: O'Neill, Walcott, and Césaire and Christophe." *Journal of West Indian Literature* 5, no. 1–2 (August 1992): 30–47.

Haney, Erin. "Film, Charcoal, Time: Contemporaneities in Gold Coast Photographs." *History of Photography* 34, no. 2 (2010): 119–33. http://dx.doi.org/10.1080/03087290903361464.

Harootunian, Harry D. *Overcome by Modernity: History, Culture, and Community in Interwar Japan*. Princeton, NJ: Princeton University Press, 2000.

Harper, Frances E. W. *Iola Leroy, or Shadows Uplifted*. Boston: Beacon Press, 1987.

Hartman, Saidiya. *Lose Your Mother: A Journey along the Atlantic Slave Route*. New York: Farrar, Straus and Giroux, 2007.

Hartman, Saidiya. *Scenes of Subjection: Terror, Slavery, and Self-Making in Nineteenth-Century America*. Oxford: Oxford University Press, 1997.

Hartman, Saidiya. "Second Exposure." Keynote Speech at the Dark Room Collective. Northeastern University. April 2014.

Hartman, Saidiya. "Venus in Two Acts." *Small Axe* 26 (June 2008): 1–14.

Hartman, Saidiya. *Wayward Lives, Beautiful Experiments: Intimate Histories of Riotous Black Girls, Troublesome Women, and Queer Radicals*. New York: W. W. Norton, 2019.

Hathaway, Heather. *Caribbean Waves: Relocating Claude McKay and Paule Marshall*. Bloomington: Indiana University Press, 1999.

Hawkins, Sean. "'The Woman in Question': Marriage and Identity in the Colonial Courts of Northeastern Ghana, 1907–1954." In *Women in African Colonial Histories*, edited by Jean Allman, Susan Geiger, and Nakanyike Musisi, 116–43. Bloomington: Indiana University Press, 2002.

Hayes, Jarrod, Margaret R. Higonnet, and William J. Spurlin, eds. "Introduction: Comparing Queerly, Queering Comparison." In *Comparatively Queer: Interrogating Identities across Time and Cultures*, 1–19. New York: Palgrave Macmillan, 2010.

Hayford, J. E. Casely. *Ethiopia Unbound: Studies in Race Emancipation*. London: Frank Cass and Co., Ltd., [1911] 1969.

Helg, Aline. "Black Men, Racial Stereotyping, and Violence in the U.S. South and Cuba at the Turn of the Century." *Comparative Studies in Society and History* 42, no. 3 (July 2000): 576–604.

Helg, Aline. *Our Rightful Share: The Struggle for Cuban Equality, 1886–1912*. Chapel Hill, NC: UNC Press, 1995.

Hell, Julia, and Andreas Schönle, eds. *Ruins of Modernity*. Durham, NC: Duke University Press, 2010.

Herskovits, Melville. "The Negro in the New World: The Statement of a Problem." *American Anthropologist* 32, no. 1 (1930): 145–55.

Heuman, Gad. *The Killing Time: The Morant Bay Rebellion in Jamaica*. Knoxville: University of Tennessee Press, 1994.

Heyningen, Elizabeth van. *The Concentration Camps of the Anglo-Boer War: A Social History*. Auckland Park, New Zealand: Jacana, 2013.

Higginbotham, Evelyn Brooks. *Righteous Discontent: The Women's Movement in the Black Baptist Church, 1880–1920*. Cambridge, MA: Harvard University Press, 1994.

Hill, Robert A. "The First England Years and After, 1912–1916." In *Marcus Garvey and the Vision of Africa*, edited by John Henrik Clarke, 38–70. New York: Vintage, 1974.

Hill, Robert A. "King Menelik's Nephew: Prince Thomas Mackarooroo, aka Prince Ludwig Menelek of Abyssinia." *Small Axe* 26 (June 2008): 15–44.

Hill, Robert A., ed. *The Marcus Garvey and Universal Negro Improvement Association Papers*. Vol. 3, *September 20 to August 1921*. Los Angeles: University of California Press, 1984.

Hirobayashi, Lane Ryo, and Evelyn Hu-Dehart, eds. "Asians in the Americas Transculturations and Power." *Amerasia Journal* 28, no 2 (2002): iv.

Hofmeyr, Isabel. "Building a Nation from Words: Afrikaans Language, Literature and Ethnic Identity, 1902–1924." In *The Politics of Race, Class and Nationalism in Twentieth-Century South Africa*, edited by Shula Marks and Stanley Trapido, 95–123. New York: Routledge, 1987.

Holcomb, Gary Edward. *Claude McKay: Code Name Sasha: Queer Black Marxism and the Harlem Renaissance*. Gainesville: University of Florida Press, 2007.

Hong, Grace Kyungwon. *Death Beyond Disavowal: The Impossible Politics of Difference*. Minneapolis: University of Minnesota Press, 2015.

Hooker, J. R. "The Pan-African Conference 1900." *Transition* 46 (1974): 20–24.

Hopkins, Pauline. *Of One Blood: The Hidden Self*. New York: Washington Square Press, [1902–1903] 2004.

Hu-Dehart, Evelyn. "Diaspora." In *Keywords for Asian American Studies*, edited by Cathy J. Schlund-Vials, Linda Trinh Vo, and K. Scott Wong. New York: NYU Press, 2015. https://keywords.nyupress.org/asian-american-studies/essay/diaspora/.

Hulme, Peter. *Cuba's Wild East: A Literary Geography of Oriente*. Liverpool, UK: Liverpool University Press, 2011.

Hume, David. "Of National Characters." In *Essays Moral, Political, and Literary*, edited by Eugene F. Miller. Indianapolis, IN: Liberty Fund, [1753–54] 1987.

Hunt, Nancy Rose. "An Acoustic Register: Rape and Ruination in Congo." In *Imperial Debris: On Ruins and Ruination*, edited by Ann Stoler, 39–66. Durham, NC: Duke University Press, 2013.

Hunter, Tera. *Bound in Wedlock: Slave and Free Black Marriage in the Nineteenth Century*. Cambridge, MA: Belknap Press, 2017.

Iglesias Utset, Marial. *A Cultural History of Cuba During the US Occupation, 1898–1902*. Translated by Russ Davidson. Chapel Hill, NC: UNC Press, 2011.

Isaac, Allan Punzalan. *American Tropics: Articulating Filipino America*. Minneapolis: University of Minnesota Press, 2006.

Jackson, Shona. *Creole Indigeneity: Between Myth and Nation in the Caribbean*. Minneapolis: University of Minnesota Press, 2012.

Jacobs, Charles C. "Jamaica and the Cuban Ten Years War." *Jamaica Journal* 44 (1980): 81–91.

Jacobs, H. P. *From the Earthquake to 1944*. Kingston, Jamaica: Pioneer Press, n.d.

Jacobs, Harriet A. *Incidents in the Life of a Slave Girl, Written By Herself*. Boston, c. 1860. https://docsouth.unc.edu/fpn/jacobs/jacobs.html.

Jaffe, Rivke. "Crime and Insurgent Citizenship: Extra-State Rule and Belonging in Urban Jamaica." *Development* 55, no. 2 (2012): 219–23.

Jaji, Tsitsi Ella. *Africa in Stereo: Modernism, Music, and Pan-Africanism*. Oxford: Oxford University Press, 2014.

James, C. L. R. *Beyond a Boundary*. Kingston, Jamaica: Sangster's Book Store, with Hutchinson, 1963.

James, Robert A. "Six Bits or Bust: Insurance Litigation Over the 1906 San Francisco Earthquake and Fire." *Western Legal History* 24, no. 2 (Summer/Fall 2011). https://

www.pillsburylaw.com/images/content/5/2/v2/5251/Six-20Bits-20or-20Bust
-20Insurance-20Litigation.pdf.

James, Winston. *A Fierce Hatred of Injustice: Claude McKay's Jamaica and His Poetry of Rebellion.* London: Verso, 2000.

Jameson, Frederic. "Modernism and Imperialism." In *Nationalism, Colonialism, and Literature,* edited by Terry Eagleton, Frederic Jameson, and Edward W. Said, 43–66. Minneapolis: University of Minnesota Press, 1988.

Jekyll, Walter. *Jamaican Song and Story: Annancy Stories, Digging Sings, Ring Tunes, and Dancing Tunes.* London: David Nutt, 1907. https://archive.org/details /jamaicansongandoobroagoog/page/n5/mode/2up.

Johnson, E. Patrick. "Black Performance Studies: Genealogies, Politics, Futures." In *The SAGE Handbook of Performance Studies,* edited by D. Soyini Madison and Judith Hamera, 446–65. Thousand Oaks, CA: Sage Publications, 2006.

Johnson, Howard. "Cuban Immigrants in Jamaica, 1868–1898." *Immigrants and Minorities* 29, no. 1 (March 2011): 1–32.

Johnson, Marion. "Technology, Competition, and African Crafts." In *The Imperial Impact: Studies in the Economic History of Africa and India.* Vol. 21 of *Commonwealth Papers,* edited by Clive Dewey and A. G. Hopkins, 259–69. London: The Athlone Press, Institute of Commonwealth Studies, 1978.

Johnson, Michelle A. "Problematic Bodies: Negotiations and Terminations in Domestic Service in Jamaica, 1920–1970." *Left History* 12, no. 2 (Fall/Winter 2007): 84–112.

Johnston, H. (Harry) H. (Hamilton). "A Journey up the Cross River, West Africa." *Proceedings of the Royal Geographical Society and Monthly Record of Geography* 8 (July 1888): 433–38.

Johnston, H. (Harry) H. (Hamilton). *Liberia.* 2 vols. London: Hutchinson and Co., 1906.

Johnston, H. (Harry) H. (Hamilton). *The Negro in the New World.* London: Methuen and Co., 1910.

Johnston, H. (Harry) H. (Hamilton). "The Origin of the Bantu." *Journal of the Royal African Society* (1907): 329–40.

Johnston, H. (Harry) H. (Hamilton). *The Story of My Life.* Indianapolis, IN: The Bobbs-Merrill Company, 1923.

Jones, Emrys. "Maternal Duties and Filial Malapropisms: Frances Sheridan and the Problems of Theatrical Inheritance." In *Stage Mothers: Women, Work, and the Theater, 1660–1839,* edited by Laura Engel and Elaine M. McGirr, 159–78. Lanham, MD: Bucknell University Press and Rowan and Littlefield, 2014.

Kafka, Franz. "Before the Law." In *The Collected Stories,* 3–4. New York: Shocken, 1971.

Kempadoo, Roshini. *Creole in the Archive: Imagery, Presence and the Location of the Caribbean Figure.* London: Rowan and Littlefield, 2016.

Khan, Aisha. "What Is a 'Spanish'? Ambiguity and 'Mixed' Ethnicity in Trinidad." In *Trinidad Ethnicity,* edited by Kevin Yelvington, 180–207. London: Macmillan and University of Warwick, 1993.

King, Rosamond S. *Island Bodies: Transgressive Sexualities in the Caribbean Imagination.* Gainesville: University of Florida Press, 2014.

Kingsley, Charles. *At Last: A Christmas in the West Indies*. 2 Vols. London: Macmillan, 1871.

Klein, Herbert. "African Women in the Atlantic Slave Trade." In *Women and Slavery in Africa*, edited by Clare C. Robertson and Martin A. Klein, 29–38. Portsmouth, NH: Heinemann, 1997.

Knight, Franklin. "Jamaica Migrants and the Cuban Sugar Industry, 1900–1934." In *Between Slavery and Free Labor: The Spanish-Speaking Caribbean in the Nineteenth Century*, edited by Manuel Moreno Fraginals, Frank Moya Pons, and Stanley L. Engerman, 94–114. Baltimore, MD: Johns Hopkins University Press, 1985.

Kriz, Kay Dian. *Slavery, Sugar and the Culture of Refinement: Picturing the British West Indies 1700–1840*. New Haven, CT: Yale University Press, 2008.

LaBelle, Brandon. *Lexicon of the Mouth: Poetics and Politics of Voice and the Oral Imaginary*. New York: Bloomsbury, 2014.

LaGamma, Alisa, and Chrisine Guintini. *The Essential Art of African Textiles: Design without End*. New York: The Metropolitan Museum of Art, 2008.

Lamming, George. *In the Castle of My Skin*. Ann Arbor: University of Michigan Press, [1953] 1991.

Lamming, George. *The Pleasures of Exile*. Ann Arbor: University of Michigan Press, [1960] 1992.

Laurence, K. O., ed. "The Trinidad Water Riot of 1903: Reflections of an Eyewitness." *Caribbean Quarterly* 15, no. 4 (December 1969): 5–22.

Levy, Carol, and Alison Irvine-Sobers. "The River Is in Spate and the Bridge Is Inundated." Pree. July 5, 2020. https://preelit.com/2020/07/05/carol-irvine-levy-and-alison-irvine-sobers/.

Lewis, Rupert. "Party Politics in Jamaica and the Extradition of Christopher Dudus Coke." *Global South* 6, no. 1 (2012): 38–54.

Lewis, Rupert, and Maureen Lewis. "Claude McKay's Jamaica." *Caribbean Quarterly* 23, no. 2–3 (June/September 1977): 38–53.

Linebaugh, Peter, and Marcus Rediker. *The Many-Headed Hydra: Sailors, Slaves, Commoners, and the Hidden Histories of the Revolutionary Atlantic*. Boston: Beacon, 2000.

Liu, Lydia H. "Conclusion: The Emperor's Empty Throne." In *The Clash of Empires: The Invention of China and Modern World-Making*, 210–28. Cambridge, MA: Harvard University Press, 2004.

Liu, Lydia H. "Desire and Sovereign Thinking." In *Grounds of Comparison: Around the Work of Benedict Anderson*, edited by Jonathan Culler and Pheng Cheah, 91–223. New York: Routledge, 2003.

Locke, Alain. "The New Negro." 1925. In *The New Negro: Voices of the Harlem Renaissance*, edited by Alain Locke, 3–16. New York: Touchstone, 1997.

Loichot, Valérie. *Orphan Narratives: The Postplantation Literatures of Faulkner, Glissant, Morrison and Saint-John Perse*. Charlottesville: University of Virginia Press, 2007.

Long, Edward. *1774. History of Jamaica*, vol. 1. New York: Arno Press, 1972.

Lott, Eric. *Love and Theft: Blackface Minstrelsy and the American Working Class*. Oxford: Oxford University Press, 1993.

Lovelace, Earl. *The Dragon Can't Dance*. London: Andre Deutsch, 1979.

Lowe, Lisa. "The Intimacies of Four Continents." In *Haunted by Empire: Geographies of History in North American History*, edited by Ann Laura Stoler, 191–212. Durham, NC: Duke University Press, 2006.

Lowe, Lisa. *The Intimacies of Four Continents*. Durham, NC: Duke University Press, 2015.

Lumsden, Joy. "Jamaican Constitutional and Political Developments, 1866–1920." *My Jamaican History Articles*. Posted September 28, 2012. https://sites.google.com/site/myjamaicanhistoryarticles/jamaican-constitutional-and-political-developments-1866–1920.

Macharia, Keguro. *Frottage: Frictions of Intimacy across the Black Diaspora*. New York: NYU Press, 2019.

Magubane, Zine. "Mines, Minstrels, and Masculinity: Race, Class, Gender and the Formation of the South African Working Class, 1870–1900." *Journal of Men's Studies* 10, no. 3 (June 2002): 271–89.

Mahabir, Joy. "Communal Style: Indo-Caribbean Women's Jewelry." *Small Axe* 53 (July 2017): 112–22.

Mais, Roger. "Now We Know." [Jamaica] *Public Opinion*. July 11, 1944.

Manjapra, Kris. "Necrospeculation: Postemancipation Finance and Black Redress." *Social Text* 37, no. 2 (June 2019): 29–65.

Manning, Patrick. "Contours of Slavery and Social Change in Africa." *American Historical Review* 88, no. 4 (October 1983): 835–57.

Mao, Douglass, and Rebecca L. Walkowitz. "The New Modernist Studies." *PMLA* 123, no. 3 (May 2008): 737–48.

Martí, José. "Coney Island." In *José Martí: Selected Writings*, translated by Esther Allen, 89–94. New York: Penguin, [1881] 2002.

Martí, José. "Our America." In *José Martí: Selected Writings*, translated by Esther Allen, 288–96. New York: Penguin, [1881] 2002.

Martínez-San Miguel, Yolanda. "Spanish Caribbean Literature: A Heuristic for Colonial Caribbean Studies." *Small Axe* 51 (November 2016): 65–79.

Marx, Karl. *Capital*, vol. 1. Translated by Ben Folkes. London: Penguin Books, 1976.

Matthews, Janeille, and Tracy Robinson. "Modern Vagrancy in the Anglophone Caribbean." *Caribbean Journal of Criminology* 1, no. 4 (April 2019): 123–54.

Mauss, Marcel. *The Gift: Forms and Functions of Exchange in Archaic Societies*. Translated by Ian Cunnison. London: Routledge and Kegan Paul, 1966.

McClintock, Anne. *Imperial Leather: Race, Gender and Sexuality in the Colonial Contest*. New York: Routledge, 1995.

McClintock, Anne. "No Longer in a Future Heaven: Gender, Race, and Nationalism." In *Dangerous Liaisons: Gender, Nation, and Postcolonial Perspectives*, edited by Anne McClintock, Aamir Mufti, and Ella Shohat, 89–112. Minneapolis: University of Minnesota Press, 1997.

McGarrity, Gayle. "Cubans in Jamaica: A Previously Neglected Segment of the Cuban Diaspora." *Caribbean Quarterly* 42, no. 1 (March 1996): 55–83.

McKay, Claude. *Banana Bottom*. New York: Harvest Books, [1933] 1961.

McKay, Claude. *Banjo*. New York: Harvest, 1929.

McKay, Claude. *Complete Poems*. Edited by William J. Maxwell. Urbana: University of Illinois Press, 2004.

McKay, Claude. *Constab Ballads*. London: Watts and Co., 1912.

McKay, Claude. "Crazy Mary." In *My Green Hills of Jamaica and Five Jamaican Short Stories*, edited by Mervyn Morris, 126–33. Kingston, Jamaica: Heinemann Educational Books (Caribbean) Ltd., 1979.

McKay, Claude. *Home to Harlem*. Boston: Northeastern University Press, [1928] 1987.

McKay, Claude. "A Midnight Woman to the Bobby." In *Songs of Jamaica*, 74–76. Kingston, Jamaica: Aston W. Gardner, 1912.

McKay, Claude. *My Green Hills of Jamaica and Five Jamaican Short Stories*. Edited by Mervyn Morris. Kingston, Jamaica: Heinemann Educational Books (Caribbean) Ltd., 1979.

McKay, Claude. *Songs of Jamaica*. Kingston, Jamaica: Aston W. Gardner, 1912.

McKay, Claude. "When I Pounded the Pavement." In *My Green Hills of Jamaica and Five Jamaican Short Stories*, edited by Mervyn Morris, 133–44. Kingston, Jamaica: Heinemann Educational Books (Caribbean) Ltd., 1979.

McKenzie, Catherine. "Women's Rights." In *Caribbean Women: An Anthology of Nonfiction Writing, 1890–1980*, edited by Veronica Marie Gregg, 99–103. Notre Dame, IN: University of Notre Dame Press, 2005.

McKittrick, Catherine. *Demonic Grounds: Black Women and the Cartographies of Struggle*. Minneapolis: University of Minnesota Press, 2006.

McKittrick, Catherine. "Plantation Futures." *Small Axe* 42 (November 2013): 1–15.

Meikle, Louis S. *Confederation of the British West Indies versus Annexation to the United States of America: A Political Discourse on the West Indies*. London: S. Low, Marston and Co., 1912.

Melas, Natalie. *All the Difference in the World: Postcoloniality and the Ends of Comparison*. Stanford, CA: Stanford University Press, 2007.

Mignolo, Walter D. "The Many Faces of Cosmo-polis: Border Thinking and Critical Cosmopolitanism." In *Cosmopolitanism*, edited by Carol A. Breckenridge, Sheldon Pollock, Homi K. Bhabha, and Dipesh Chakrabarty, 157–88. Durham, NC: Duke University Press. 2002.

Miller, Monica L. *Slaves to Fashion: Black Dandyism and the Styling of Black Diasporic Identity*. Durham, NC: Duke University Press, 2009.

Mintz, Sidney W. "The Caribbean as a Socio-cultural Area." *Journal of World History* 9, no. 4 (1966): 912–37.

Mintz, Sidney W. "Enduring Substances, Trying Theories: The Caribbean Region as *Oikoumenê*." *Journal of the Royal Anthropological Institute* 2, no. 2 (June 1996): 289–311.

Mirzoeff, Nicholas. *The Right to Look: A Counter History of Visuality*. Durham, NC: Duke University Press, 2011.

Mirzoeff, Nicholas. "The Shadow and the Substance: Race, Photography, and the Index." In *Only Skin Deep: Changing Visions of the American Self. International Cen-*

ter for Photography, edited by Coco Fusco and Brian Wallis, 111–26. New York: ICA and Abrams, 2003.

Modest, Wayne. "The Affective Photograph: Museums and the Emotional Afterlife of Colonial Photography." In *Uncertain Images: Museums and the Work of Photographs*, edited by Elizabeth Edwards and Sigrid Lien, 21–42. Abingdon, UK: Routledge, 2016.

Mofokeng, Santu. *The Black Photo Album/Look at Me: 1890–1950*. Göttingen, Germany: Steidl Verlag, 2013.

Moodie-Kublalsingh, Sylvia. *The Cocoa Panyols of Trinidad: An Oral Record*. London: British Academic Press, 1994.

Moodie-Kublalsingh, Sylvia. "Spanish in Trinidad and Tobago." STAN. https://sta.uwi .edu/stan/article14.asp.

Moore, Brian L., and Michelle A. Johnson. "Fallen Sisters? Attitudes to Female Prostitution in Jamaica at the Turn of the Twentieth Century." *Journal of Caribbean History* 34, no. 1–2 (2000).

Moore, Brian L., and Michelle A. Johnson. *Neither Led nor Driven*: *Contesting British Cultural Imperialism in Jamaica, 1865–1920*. Kingston, Jamaica: University of the West Indies Press, 2004.

Moore, Brian L., and Michelle A. Johnson, eds. *Squalid Kingston, 1890–1920: How the Poor Lived, Moved, and Had Their Being*. Kingston, Jamaica: University of the West Indies Press, 2000.

Moore, Brian L., and Michelle A. Johnson. *"They Do as They Please": The Jamaican Struggle for Cultural Freedom after Morant Bay*. Kingston, Jamaica: University of the West Indies Press, 2011.

Morfino, Vittorio. "An Althusserian Lexicon." Translated by Jason Smith. *Borderlands e-Journal* 4, no. 2 (2005). http://www.borderlands.net.au/vol4no2_2005/morfino _lexicon.htm.

Morgan, Jennifer B. *"Partus Sequitur Ventrem*: Law, Race, and Reproduction in Colonial Slavery." *Small Axe* 55 (March 2018): 1–17.

Morillo-Alicea, Javier. "Looking for Empire in the US Colonial Archive." In *Only Skin Deep: Changing Visions of the American Self. International Center for Photography*, edited by Coco Fusco and Brian Wallis, 129–42. New York: ICA and Abrams, 2003.

Morrison, Toni. *The Source of Self-Regard: Selected Essays, Speeches, and Meditations*. New York: Knopf, 2019.

Moses, Wilson. *The Golden Age of Black Nationalism 1850–1925*. Hamden, CT: Archon, 1978.

Moynihan, Daniel Patrick. "The Tangle of Pathology." In *The Negro Family: A Case for National Action*. Office of Policy Planning and Research, US Department of Labor. March 1965. https://www.dol.gov/general/aboutdol/history/webid-moynihan /moynchapter4.

Muhammad, Kahlil Gibran. *The Condemnation of Blackness: Race, Crime, and the Making of Modern Urban America*. Cambridge, MA: Harvard University Press, 2011.

Muñoz, José Estéban. "Gesture, Ephemera, and Queer Feeling: Approaching Kevin Aviance." In *Dancing Desires: Choreographing Sexualities On and Off the Stage*, edited by Jane C. Desmond, 423–42. Madison: University of Wisconsin Press, 2001.

Naipaul, V. S. "Power?" In *The Overcrowded Barracoon*, 248–50. New York: Knopf, 1973.

Nash, Jennifer C. *The Black Body in Ecstasy: Reading Race, Reading Pornography*. Durham, NC: Duke University Press, 2014.

Neptune, Harvey R. *Caliban and the Yankees: Trinidad and the United States Occupation*. Chapel Hill, NC: UNC Press, 2007.

Newell, Stephanie. *The Power to Name: A History of Anonymity in Colonial West Africa*. Athens: Ohio University Press, 2013.

Newton, Melanie J. "Returns to a Native Land: Indigeneity and Decolonization in the Anglophone Caribbean." *Small Axe* 41 (July 2013): 108–22.

Nicolazzo, Sarah. "Henry Fielding's *The Female Husband* and the Sexuality of Vagrancy." *The Eighteenth Century* 55, no. 4 (2014): 335–53.

Niranjana, Tejaswini. *Mobilizing India: Women, Music, and Migration between India and Trinidad*. Durham, NC: Duke University Press, 2006.

North, Michael. *The Dialect of Modernism: Race, Language and Twentieth-Century Literature*. New York: Oxford University Press, 1994.

Nottage, Lynn. *Intimate Apparel and Fabulation, or the Re-Education of Undine*. New York: Theater Communications Group, 2006.

O'Callaghan, Evelyn. *Women Writing the West Indies, 1804–1939: A Hot Place Belonging to US*. London: Routledge, 2004.

Olien, Michael D. "The Miskito Kings and the Line of Succession." *Journal of Anthropological Research* 39, no. 2 (Summer 1983): 198–241.

Osinubi, Taiwo Adetunji. "Provincializing Slavery: Atlantic Economies in Flora Nwapa's *Efuru*." *Research in African Literatures* 45, no. 3 (Fall 2014): 1–26.

Owens, Imani. "'Hard Reading': US Empire and Black Modernist Aesthetics in Eric Walrond's *Tropic Death*." *MELUS* 41, no. 4 (Winter 2016): 96–115.

Oyoyemi, Helen. *The Icarus Girl*. New York: Anchor Books, 2005.

Palmer, Colin. *Freedom's Children: The 1938 Labor Rebellion and the Birth of Modern Jamaica*. Chapel Hill, NC: UNC Press, 2014.

Palmié, Stephan. *Wizards and Scientists: Explorations in Afro-Cuban Modernity and Tradition*. Durham, NC: Duke University Press, 2002.

Pappademos, Melina. "The Cuban Race War of 1912 and the Uses and Transgressions of Blackness." In *Breaking the Chains, Forging the Nation: The Afro-Cuban Fight for Freedom and Equality, 1812–1912*, edited by Aisha Finch and Fannie Rushing, 241–71. Baton Rouge: Louisiana State University Press, 2019.

Paravisini-Gebert, Lizabeth. "The Caribbean's Agonizing Seashores: Tourism Resorts, Art, and the Future of the Region's Coastlines." In *The Routledge Companion to the Environmental Humanities*, edited by Ursula Heise, Jon Christensen, and Michelle Neiman, 278–88. Abingdon, UK: Routledge, 2017.

Paravisini-Gebert, Lizabeth. "Colonial and Post-colonial Gothic: The Caribbean." In *The Cambridge Companion to Gothic Literature*, edited by Gerrold Hodges, 229–57. New York: Cambridge University Press, 2003.

Parker, Jo Alyson. *The Author's Inheritance: Henry Fielding, Jane Austen, and the Establishment of the Novel*. DeKalb: Northern Illinois University Press, 1998.

Paton, Diana. *No Bond but the Law: Punishment, Race, and Gender in Jamaican State Formation, 1780–1870*. Durham, NC: Duke University Press, 2004.

Paton, Diana. "Small Charges: Law and the Regulation of Conduct in the Post-slavery Caribbean." The Elsa Goveia Memorial Lecture to the Department of History and Archaeology at the University of West Indies, Mona, Jamaica, 2014.

Paton, Diana. "The Trials of Inspector Thomas: Policing and Ethnography in Jamaica." In *Obeah and Other Powers: The Politics of Caribbean Religion and Healing*, edited by Diana Paton and Maarit Forde, 172–97. Durham, NC: Duke University Press, 2012.

Paton, Diana, and Gemma Romain. "Gendered Clothing Legislation and Trans Experience in Guyana." *Histories of the Present* (blog). *History Workshop*, March 21, 2014. http://www.historyworkshop.org.uk/gendered-clothing-legislation-trans-experience-in-guyana/.

Patterson, Orlando. *Slavery and Social Death*. Cambridge, MA: Harvard University Press, 1982.

Pérez, Louis A., Jr. *Cuba: Between Reform and Revolution*. Oxford: Oxford University Press, 1988.

Pérez, Louis A., Jr. *On Becoming Cuban: Identity, Nationality and Culture*. Chapel Hill, NC: UNC Press, 1999.

Phelan, Peggy. *Unmarked: The Politics of Performance*. New York: Routledge, 1993.

Philip, M. M. *Emmanuel Appadocca; or, Blighted Life: A Tale of the Boucaneers*. Amherst: University of Massachusetts Press, [1854] 1997.

Photos and Phantasms: Harry Johnston's Photographs of the Caribbean. Exhibition Catalog. London: The British Council and the Royal Geographical Society, 1998.

Pickens, William. *The New Negro: His Political, Civil, and Mental Status, and Related Essays*. New York: Neale, 1916.

Pierre, Jemima. *Predicament of Blackness: Postcolonial Ghana and the Politics of Race*. Chicago: University of Chicago Press, 2012.

Pigou-Dennis, Elizabeth. "Island Modernity: Jamaican Urbanism and Architecture, Kingston, 1960–1980." *Urban Island Studies* 3 (2017). http://www.urbanislandstudies.org/UIS-3-Pigou-Dennis-Modernity-Jamaican-Urbanism.pdf.

Plummer, Brenda Gayle. *Haiti and the Great Powers: 1902–1915*. Baton Rouge: Louisiana State University Press, 1988.

Plummer, Brenda Gayle. *Haiti and the United States*. Athens: University of Georgia Press, 1992.

Post, Ken. *Arise Ye Starvelings: The Jamaican Labour Rebellion of 1938 and Its Aftermath*. The Hague, Netherlands: Martinus Nijhoff, 1978.

Pratt, Lloyd. *Archives of American Time: Literature and Modernity in the Nineteenth Century*. Philadelphia: University of Pennsylvania Press, 2010.

Pugliese, Gina. "Intimate Scripts and the Early Twentieth-Century Black Transnational Romance." PhD diss., Brandeis University, 2018.

Puri, Shalini. "Beyond Resistance: Notes Towards a New Caribbean Cultural Studies." *Small Axe* 14 (September 2003): 23–38.

Putnam, Lara. *The Company They Kept: Migrants and the Politics of Gender in Caribbean Costa Rica, 1870–1960*. Chapel Hill, NC: UNC Press, 2002.

Putnam, Lara. *Radical Moves: Caribbean Migrants and the Politics of Race in the Jazz Age*. Chapel Hill, NC: UNC Press, 2013.

Putnam, Lara. "Rites of Power and Rumors of Race: The Circulation of Supernatural Knowledge in the Greater Caribbean, 1890–1940." In *Obeah and Other Powers: The Politics of Caribbean Religion and Healing*, edited by Diana Paton and Maarit Forde, 243–68. Durham, NC: Duke University Press, 2012.

Quashie, Kevin. *The Sovereignty of Quiet: Beyond Resistance in Black Culture*. New Brunswick, NJ: Rutgers University Press, 2012.

Radhakrishnan, R. *Theory in an Uneven World*. Hoboken, NJ: John Wiley and Sons, 2008.

Raiford, Leigh. *Imprisoned in a Luminous Glare: Photography and the African American Freedom Struggle*. Chapel Hill, NC: UNC Press, 2011.

Ram, Kalpana. "Maternal Experience and Feminist Body Politics: Asian and Pacific Perspectives." In *Maternities and Modernities: Colonial and Postcolonial Experiences in Asia and the Pacific*, edited by Ram and Margaret Jolly, 275–309. Cambridge: Cambridge University Press, 1998.

Ramchand, Kenneth. *The West Indian Novel and Its Background*. London: Faber and Faber, 1970.

Ramesar, Marianne Soares. "The Significance of Changing Dress Styles among Indo-Trinidadians (1845–1945)." *Journal of Caribbean Studies* 1–2 (1999): 117–30.

Ramos, Julio. *Divergent Modernities: Culture and Politics in Nineteenth-Century Latin America*. Translated by John D. Blanco. Durham, NC: Duke University Press, 2001.

Rayman, Evelyne. "Indian Jewellery in British Guyana: Guyana Mirror." *Guyana: Land of Six Peoples*, September 24, 2000. https://www.landofsixpeoples.com/news/nmoo9242.htm.

Reckin, Anna. "Tidalectic Lectures: Kamau Brathwaite's Prose/Poetry as Sound-Space." *Anthurium: A Caribbean Studies Journal* 1, no. 1 (2003). http://doi.org/10.33596/anth.4.

Redcam, Tom. *One Brown Girl and—*. Kingston: All Jamaica Library, Times Printery, 1909.

Reddock, Rhoda. "Feminism, Nationalism, and the Early Women's Movement." In *Caribbean Women Writers: Essays from the First International Conference*, edited by Selwyn Cudjoe, 61–81. Amherst: University of Massachusetts Press, 1990.

Reddock, Rhoda. *Women, Labour and Politics in Trinidad and Tobago: A History*. London: Zed Books, 1994.

Reid, V. S. *New Day*. London: Heinemann Educational Books, [1949] 1973.

Rhys, Jean. *Wide Sargasso Sea*. New York: W. W. Norton, [1966] 1982.

Richardson, Bonham C. *Igniting the Caribbean's Past: Fire in British West Indian History*. Chapel Hill, NC: UNC Press, 2004.

Riley, Shannon Rose. *Performing Race and Erasure: Cuba, Haiti, and US Culture, 1898–1940*. London: Palgrave Macmillan, 2016.

Rizutto, Nicole. *Insurgent Testimonies: Witnessing Colonial Trauma in Modern and Anglophone Literature*. New York: Fordham University, 2015.

Roach, Joseph. *Cities of the Dead: Circum-Atlantic Performance*. New York: Columbia University Press, 1996.

Roberts, W. Adolphe. *The Caribbean: The Story of Our Sea of Destiny*. Indianapolis, IN: The Bobbs-Merrill Co., 1940.

Roberts, W. Adolphe. *Lands of the Inner Sea: The West Indies and Bermuda*. New York: Coward-McCann, 1948.

Roberts, W. Adolphe. *The Single Star: A Novel of Cuba in the '90s*. Indianapolis, IN: Bobbs-Merrill Company, Inc., 1949.

Roberts, W. Adolphe. *These Many Years: An Autobiography*. Edited by Peter Hulme. Kingston, Jamaica: University of the West Indies Press, 2015.

Robertson, Campbell, and Katy Reckdahl. "Stories of New Orleans: As Monuments Go Down, Family Histories Emerge." *New York Times*, May 24, 2017. https://www.ny-times.com/2017/05/24/us/new-orleans-monuments-confederate-history.html?hp&action=click&pgtype=Homepage&clickSource=story-heading&module=second-column-region&region=top-news&WT.nav=top-news.

Robinson, Tracy. "The Properties of Citizens: A Caribbean Grammar of Conjugal Categories." *Du Bois Review* 10, no. 2 (2013): 425–46.

Robolin, Stéphane. *Grounds of Engagement: Apartheid-Era African-American and South African Writing*. Urbana: University of Illinois Press, 2015.

Rodó, José Enrique. *Ariel*. Translated by F. J. Stimson. Boston: Houghton Mifflin, [1900] 1922.

Rohlehr, Gordon. *Calpyso and Society in Pre-Independence Trinidad*. Port of Spain, Trinidad and Tobago: Gordon Rohlehr, 1990.

Rohlehr, Gordon. "Calypso Reinvents Itself." In *Carnival: Culture in Action—The Trinidad Experience*, edited by Milla Cozart Riggio, 213–27. New York: Routledge, 2004.

Rolando, Gloria, dir. *Las raíces de mi corazón, Roots of My Heart*. DVD. Havana: Imágenes del Caribe, 2001.

Rosario, Nelly. *Song of the Water Saints*. New York: Vintage, 2003.

Rosen, Jeff. *Margaret Cameron's Fancy Subjects: Photographic Allegories of Victorian Identity and Empire*. Manchester, UK: Manchester University Press, 2016.

Rosenberg, Leah. *Nationalism and the Formation of Caribbean Literature*. New York: Palgrave, 2007.

Rosenberg, Leah. "The New Woman and 'The Dusky Strand': The Place of Feminism and Women's Literature in Early Jamaican Nationalism." *Feminist Review* 95 (2010): 46–63.

Ross, Marlon B. "The New Negro Displayed: Self-Ownership, Proprietary Sites/Sights, and the Bonds/Bounds of Race." In *Claiming the Stones, Naming the Bones: Cultural Property and the Negotiation of National and Ethnic Identity*, edited by Elazar Barkan and Ronald Bush, 259–301. Los Angeles: Getty Research Institute, 2003.

Roumain, Jacques. *Masters of the Dew*. Translated by Langston Hughes and Mercer Cook. Portsmouth, NH: Heinemann Educational Books, [1944] 1978.

Rowley, Michelle V. *Feminist Advocacy and Gender Equity in the Anglophone Caribbean: Envisioning a Politics of Coalition*. New York: Routledge, 2011.

Russert, Brit. "Disappointment in the Archives of Black Freedom." *Social Text* 33, no. 4 (2015): 19–33.

Salmon, Charles S. *The Caribbean Confederation*. New York: Negro Universities Press, [1888] 1969.

Samuel, Petal. "A 'Right to Quiet': Noise Control, M. Nourbese Philip and a Critique of Sound as Property." *Journal of West Indian Literature* 27, no. 1 (April 2019): 70–87.

Sarmiento, Domingo F. "Los Temblores de Chile." In *1842–53*, vol. 2 of Obras de D. R. Sarmiento, 346–54. Buenos Aires: Felix Lajouane, 1885. https://babel.hathitrust.org /cgi/pt?id=txu.059173018750741&view=1up&seq=368.

Schneider, Rebecca. *Performing Remains: Art and War in Times of Theatrical Reenactment*. New York: Routledge, 2011.

Schwarz, Bill. *Memories of Empire*. Vol 1, *The White Man's World*. Oxford: Oxford University Press, 2011.

Scott, David. *Conscripts of Modernity: The Tragedy of Colonial Enlightenment*. Durham, NC: Duke University Press, 2004.

Scott, David. "Modernity That Predated the Modern: Sidney Mintz's Caribbean." *History Workshop Journal* 58 (2004): 191–210.

Scott, David. *Omens of Adversity: Tragedy, Time, Memory, Justice*. Durham, NC: Duke University Press, 2014.

Scott, David. "On the Very Idea of the *Making* of Modern Jamaica." *Small Axe* 54 (November 2017): 43–47.

Scott, David. "The Sovereignty of the Imagination: An Interview with George Lamming." *Small Axe* 12 (September 2002): 72–200.

Scott, Rebecca J. *Degrees of Emancipation: Louisiana and Cuba after Slavery*. Cambridge, MA: Belknap Press, 2005.

Scott, Rebecca J. "Race, Labor, and Citizenship in Cuba: A View from the Sugar District of Cienfuegos, 1886–1909." In *State of Ambiguity: Civic Life and Culture in Cuba's First Republic*, edited by Steven Palmer, José Antonio Píqueras, and Amparo Sánchez Cobos, 82–120. Durham, NC: Duke University Press, 2014.

Seacole, Mary. *Wonderful Adventures of Mrs. Seacole in Many Lands*. London: Penguin Classics, [1857] 2005.

Sedgwick, Eve Kosofsky. *Between Men: English Literature and Male Homosocial Desire*. New York: Columbia University Press, [1985] 2015.

Sekula, Alan. "The Body and the Archive." In *The Contest of Meaning: Critical Histories of Photography*, edited by Richard Bolton, 343–88. Cambridge, MA: MIT Press, 1992.

Senior, Olive. "All Clear, 1928." In *Gardening in the Tropics*, 57–60. Toronto: Insomniac Press, 2005.

Senior, Olive. *Dying to Better Themselves: West Indians and the Building of the Panama Canal*. Kingston, Jamaica: University of the West Indies Press, 2014.

Shannon, Magdaline W. *Jean Price-Mars, The Haitian Elite and the American Occupation, 1915–35*. New York: St. Martin's Press, 1996.

Sharpe, Christina. *In the Wake: On Blackness and Being*. Durham, NC: Duke University Press, 2016.

Sharpe, Christina. *Monstrous Intimacies: Making Post-slavery Subjects*. Durham, NC: Duke University Press, 2009.

Sheller, Mimi. *Democracy after Slavery: Black Publics and Peasant Radicalism in Haiti and Jamaica*. Gainesville: University Press of Florida, 2000.

Shepherd, Verene. *Transients to Settlers: East Indians in Jamaica, 1845–1950.* Leeds, UK: Peepal Tree, 1994.

Sherwood, Marika. *Origins of Pan-Africanism: Henry Sylvester Williams, Africa, and the African Diaspora.* New York: Routledge, 2011.

Shilliam, Robbie. "The Spirit of Exchange." In *Postcolonial Theory and International Relations,* edited by Sanjay Seth, 166–82. New York: Routledge, 2013.

Silvera, Makeda. "Man Royals and Sodomites: Some Thoughts on the Invisibility of Afro-Caribbean Lesbians." *Feminist Studies* 18, no. 3 (Autumn 1992): 521–32.

Singh, Kelvin. *The Bloodstained Tombs: The Muhuarram Massacre in Trinidad 1884.* New York: Macmillan, 1988.

Smith, Faith. "Between Stephen Lloyd and Esteban Yo-eed: Locating Jamaica through Cuba." *Journal of French and Francophone Philosophy* 20, no. 1 (August 2012): 22–38.

Smith, Faith. "Coming Home to the Real Thing: Gender and Intellectual Life in the Anglophone Caribbean." *South Atlantic Quarterly* 93, no. 4 (Fall 1994): 895–923.

Smith, Faith. *Creole Recitations: Jacob Thomas and Colonial Formation in the Late Nineteenth-Century Caribbean.* Charlottesville: University of Virginia Press, 2002.

Smith, Faith. "Good Enough for Booker T to Kiss: Hampton, Tuskegee, and Caribbean Self-Fashioning." *Journal of Transnational American Studies* 5, no. 1 (2013). https://escholarship.org/uc/item/2jx0z2xq.

Smith, Faith. "Of Laughter and Kola Nuts: Or What Does Africa Have to Do with the African Diaspora?" In *Gendering the African Diaspora: Women, Culture, and Historical Change in the Caribbean and Nigerian Hinterland,* edited by Judith A. Byfield, La Ray Denzer, and Anthea Morrison, 21–37. Bloomington: Indiana University Press, 2009.

Smith, Felipe. "'Things You'd Imagine Zulu Tribes to Do': The Zulu Parade in New Orleans Carnival." *African Arts* 46, no. 2 (Summer 2013): 22–35.

Smith, Matthew J. "Capture Land: Jamaica, Haiti, and the United States Occupation." *Journal of Haitian Studies* 21, no. 2 (Fall 2015): 194.

Smith, Matthew J. "Footprints on the Sea: Finding Haiti in Caribbean Historiography." *Small Axe* 43 (March 2014): 55–71.

Smith, Matthew J. "H. G. and Haiti: An Analysis of Herbert G. De Lisser's 'Land of Revolutions.'" *Journal of Caribbean History* 44, no. 2 (2010): 183–200.

Smith, Matthew J. *Liberty, Fraternity, Exile: Haiti and Jamaica after Emancipation.* Chapel Hill, NC: UNC Press, 2014.

Smith, Matthew J. "A Tale of Two Tragedies: Forgetting and Remembering Kingston (1907) and Port-au-Prince (2010)." *Karib: Nordic Journal for Caribbean Studies* 4, no. 1 (November 2019). https://www.karib.no/articles/10.16993/karib.50/.

Smith, Shawn Michelle. *Photography on the Color Line: W. E. B. Du Bois, Race, and Visual Culture.* Durham, NC: Duke University Press, 2004.

Smith, Zadie. *On Beauty.* New York: Penguin, 2005.

Smith, Zadie. *White Teeth.* New York: Vintage, 2001.

Snorton, C. Riley. *Nobody Is Supposed to Know: Black Sexuality on the Down Low.* Minneapolis: University of Minnesota Press, 2014.

Sommer, Doris. *Foundational Fictions: The National Romances of Latin America*. Berkeley: University of California Press, 1991.

Sontag, Susan. *On Photography*. New York: Picador, 1977.

Spillers, Hortense J. "Mama's Baby, Papa's Maybe: An American Grammar Book." In *The Black Feminist Reader*, edited by Joy James and T. Denean Sharpley-Whiting, 57–87. Hoboken, NJ: Blackwell Publishers, 2000.

Stephens, Michelle A. *Black Empire: The Masculine Global Imaginary of Caribbean Intellectuals in the United States, 1914–1962*. Durham, NC: Duke University Press, 2002.

Stephens, Michelle A. "What Is This *Black* in Black Diaspora?" *Small Axe* 29 (July 2009): 26–38.

Stewart, Dianne. "Kumina: A Spiritual Vocabulary of Nationhood in Victorian Jamaica." In *Victorian Jamaica*, edited by Tim Barringer and Wayne Modest, 602–21. Durham, NC: Duke University Press, 2018.

Stover, Jennifer Lynn. *The Sonic Color Line: Race and the Cultural Politics of Listening*. New York: NYU Press, 2016.

Stubbs, Jean. "Political Idealism and Commodity Production: Cuban Tobacco in Jamaica, 1870–1930." *Cuban Studies* 25 (1995): 51–81.

Stuempfle, Stephen. *Port of Spain: The Construction of a Caribbean City, 1888–1962*. Kingston, Jamaica: University of the West Indies Press, 2018.

Sundquist, Eric J. *To Wake the Nations: Race in the Making of American Literature*. Cambridge, MA: Belknap Press, 1993.

Tageldin, Shaden. *Disarming Words: Empire and the Seductions of Translation in Egypt*. Berkeley: University of California Press, 2011.

Talusan, Mary. "Music, Race, and Imperialism: The Philippine Constabulary Band at the 1904 St. Louis World's Fair." *Philippine Studies* 52, no. 4 (2004): 499–526.

Taylor, Christopher. *An Empire of Neglect: The West Indies in the Wake of British Liberalism*. Durham, NC: Duke University Press, 2018.

Taylor, Ula. *The Veiled Garvey: The Life and Times of Amy Jacques Garvey*. Chapel Hill, NC: UNC Press, 2002

Thame, Maziki. "Racial Hierarchy and the Elevation of Brownness in Creole Nationalism." *Small Axe* 54 (November 2017): 111–23.

Thelwell, Michael. *The Harder They Come*. New York: Grove Press, [1980] 1994.

Thomas, Deborah. *Political Life in the Wake of the Plantation: Sovereignty, Witnessing, Repair*. Durham, NC: Duke University Press, 2019.

Thomas, Deborah, Deanne M. Bell, and Junior Wedderburn, curators. *Bearing Witness: Four Days in West Kingston*. Penn Museum, University of Pennsylvania. December 2017–July 2018.

Thomas, Herbert T. *The Story of a West Indian Policeman, or Forty-Seven Years in the Jamaica Constabulary*. Kingston, Jamaica: The Jamaica Gleaner Company, 1927.

Thomas, J. J. *Froudacity: West Indian Fables by J. A. Froude*. London: New Beacon, [1889] 1969.

Thomas, Ronald. R. "Making Darkness Visible: Capturing the Criminal and Observing the Law in Victorian Photography and Detective Fiction." In *Victorian Literature* and the Victorian Visual Imagination, edited by Carol T. Christ and John O. Jordan, 134–68. Berkeley: University of California Press, 1995.

Thompson, Krista A. An Eye for the Tropics: Tourism, Photography, and Framing the Caribbean Picturesque. Durham, NC: Duke University Press, 2006.

Thompson, Krista. "'Our Good Democracy': The Social and Political Practice of Carnival and Junkanoo Aesthetics." In En Mas': Carnival and Performance Art of the Caribbean, edited by Claire Tancons and Krista Thompson, 30–45. New York: Independent Curators International and New Orleans: Contemporary Arts Center, 2015.

Tilchin, William N. "Theodore Roosevelt, Anglo-American Relations, and the Jamaica Incident of 1907." Diplomatic History 19, no. 3 (Summer 1995): 385–405.

Tinsley, Omise'eke Natasha. Thiefing Sugar: Eroticism between Women in Caribbean Literature. Durham, NC: Duke University Press, 2010.

Tobin, Beth. Colonizing Nature: The Tropics in British Arts and Letters, 1760–1820. Philadelphia: University of Pennsylvania Press, 2005.

Tracy, Archer R. The Sword of Nemesis. New York: Neale Publishing, 1919.

Trades Union Congress. "The Great Penrhyn Quarry Strike: Capturing the Public Imagination. TUC 150 Years." https://tuc150.tuc.org.uk/stories/the-great-penrhyn-quarry-strike/.

Treves, Frederick. The Cradle of the Deep: An Account of a Voyage to the West Indies. New York: E. P. Dutton, 1913.

Trollope, Anthony. The West Indies and the Spanish Main. New York: Carroll and Graf, [1860] 1999.

Trotman, David. Crime in Trinidad: Conflict and Control in a Plantation Society, 1838–1900. Knoxville: University of Tennessee Press, 1986.

Trotz, Alissa. "A Historic Decision: The Caribbean Court of Justice and the Cross-Dressing Case." Stabroek News, November 26, 2018. https://www.stabroeknews.com/2018/11/26/features/in-the-diaspora/a-historic-decision-the-caribbean-court-of-justice-and-the-cross-dressing-case/.

Trouillot, Michel-Rolph. "The Caribbean Region: An Open Frontier in Anthropological Theory." Annual Review of Anthropology 21 (1992): 19–42.

Trouillot, Michel-Rolph. "The Odd and the Ordinary: Haiti, The Caribbean, and the World." Cimarrón, New Perspectives on the Caribbean 2, no. 3 (1990): 3–12.

Trouillot, Michel-Rolph. Silencing the Past: Power and the Production of History. Boston: Beacon Press, 1997.

Tsinhnahjinnie, Hulleah J. "Dragonfly's Home." In Visual Currencies: Reflections on Native Photography, edited by Henrietta Lidchi and Hulleah Tsinhnahjinnie, 3–16. Edinburgh, UK: National Museums Scotland, 1988.

Turner, Sasha. Contested Bodies: Pregnancy, Childrearing, and Slavery in Jamaica. Philadelphia: University of Pennsylvania Press, 2017.

Vagrancy Law 1902. "Laws of Jamaica Passed in the Year 1902." https://books.google.com/books?id=2SxFAAAAYAAJ&pg=PR35&lpg=PR35&dq=jamaica+vagrancy+law&source=bl&ots=xcklCibOfE&sig=wGo5vig4O1R6K91tecyEi368_fI&hl=en&sa=X&ei=VzWfUKrH9SuyASU6YDQAg&ved=0CFQQ6AEwCQ#v=onepage&q=jamaica%20vagrancy%20law&f=false.

Vassell, Linnette. "The Movement for the Vote for Women 1918–1919." *Jamaican Historical Review* 18 (January 1993): 40–54.

Vizenor, Gerald. *Manifest Manners: Narratives of Postindian Survivance*. Lincoln: University of Nebraska Press, 1999.

Walcott, Derek. *The Antilles: Fragments of Epic Memory*. The Nobel Lecture. London: The Nobel Foundation and Faber and Faber, 1992.

Walcott, Derek. "Henri Christophe: A Chronicle in Seven Scenes." In *The Haitian Trilogy*, 1–108. New York: Farrar, Straus and Giroux, 2002.

Walcott, Derek. "Ruins of a Great House." In *Collected Poems 1948–84*, 19–21. London: Faber and Faber, [1962] 1992.

Walker, Alice. *In Search of Our Mothers' Gardens: Womanist Prose*. Orlando, FL: Harvest Books, 1983.

Wall, Joseph Frazier. *Andrew Carnegie*. New York: Oxford University Press, 1970.

Walvin, James. *The Life and Times of Henry Clarke of Jamaica, 1828–1907*. Illford, UK: Frank Cass, 1994. https://www.amazon.com/Times-Henry-Clarke-Jamaica-1828–1907/dp/0714645516.

Ward, Candace. "'What Time Has Proved': History, Rebellion, and Revolution in *Hamel the Obeah Man*." *Ariel* 38, no. 1 (2007): 49–73.

Warner-Lewis, Maureen. *Central Africa in the Caribbean: Transcending Space, Transforming Culture*. Kingston, Jamaica: University of the West Indies, 2003.

Warner-Lewis, Maureen. *Trinidad Yoruba: From Mother Tongue to Memory*. Tuscaloosa: University of Alabama Press, 1996.

Washington, Booker T. "The Negro in the New World." *Journal of the Royal African Society* 10, no. 38 (January 1911): 173–78.

Washington, Booker T., Norman B. Wood, and Fannie Barrier Williams, eds. *A New Negro for a New Century: An Accurate and Up-to-Date Record of the Upward Struggles of the Negro Race*. Chicago: American Publishing House, 1900.

Watkins-Owens, Irma. *Blood Relations: Caribbean Immigrants and the Harlem Community, 1900–1930*. Bloomington: Indiana University Press, 1996.

Weems, Carrie Mae. *Carrie Mae Weems: The Hampton Project*. Edited by Vivian Patterson. Exhibition Catalog. Williamstown, MA: Aperture in association with Williams College of Art, 2000.

Weheliye, Alexander G. "Engendering Phonographies: Sonic Technologies of Blackness." *Small Axe* 44 (July 2014): 180–90.

Wehrs, Donald R. *Pre-colonial Africa in Colonial African Narratives: From* Ethiopia Unbound *to* Things Fall Apart, *1911–1958*. Aldershot: Ashgate, 2008.

Wexler, Laura. *Tender Violence: Domestic Visions in an Age of US Imperialism*. Chapel Hill, NC: UNC Press, 2000.

Wilcox, Ella Wheeler. *Sailing Sunny Seas: A Story of Travel in Jamaica, Honolulu, Haiti, Santo Domingo, Porto Rico, St. Thomas, Dominica, Martinique, Trinidad and the West Indies*. Chicago: W. B. Conkey, 1909. https://archive.org/details/sailingsunnyseasoowilc/page/n7.

Wilder, Gary. *Freedom Time: Negritude, Decolonization and the Future of the World*. Durham, NC: Duke University Press, 2015.

[Williams, Cynric.] *Hamel, the Obeah Man.* 2 vols. London, 1827.

Williams, Daniel T., compiler. "The Perilous Road of Marcus M. Garvey." In *Eight Negro Bibliographies.* New York: Kraus Reprint Co., 1970.

Williams, Raymond. *Culture and Society: 1780–1950.* New York: Columbia University Press, 1983.

Williams, Raymond. *Marxism and Literature.* Oxford: Oxford University Press, 1977.

Willis, Deborah. *A History of Black Photographers 1840 to the Present.* New York: W. W. Norton, 2002.

Willock, Col. Roger. "Caribbean Catastrophe: The Earthquake and Fire at Kingston, Jamaica, B. W. I., 17–19 January 1907." *American Neptune* 29, no. 2 (April 1969): 118–32.

Wilmot, Swithin. "The Road to Morant Bay." In *The Caribbean, the Atlantic World and Global Transformation,* edited by Jenny Jemmott, Aleric Joseph, and Kathleen Monteith. Kingston, Jamaica: Social History Project, 2010.

Wilson, Elizabeth. "The Invisible Flâneur." *New Left Review* 1, no. 191 (January–February 1992): 90–110.

Wilson, Mabel O. *Negro Building: Black Americans in the World of Fairs and Museums.* Berkeley: University of California Press, 2012.

Wollaeger, Mark, and Matt Eatough, eds. *The Oxford Book of Global Modernisms.* Oxford: Oxford University Press, 2012.

Woloch, Alex. *The One vs. the Many: Minor Characters and the Space of the Protagonist in the Novel.* Princeton, NJ: Princeton University Press, 2004.

Wright, Michelle M. *Physics of Blackness: Beyond the Middle Passage Epistemology.* Minneapolis: University of Minnesota Press, 2015.

Wynter, Sylvia. "Novel and History, Plot and Plantation." *Savacou* 5 (June 1971): 95–102.

Wynter, Sylvia. "We Must Learn to Sit Down and Discuss a Little Culture: Reflections on West Indian Writing and Criticism." *Jamaica Journal* 2, no. 4 (1968): 23–32.

Yoneyama, Lisa. *Cold War Ruins: Transpacific Critique of American Justice and Japanese War Crimes.* Durham, NC: Duke University Press, 2016.

Young, Cynthia A. "Black Ops: Black Masculinity and the War on Terror." *American Quarterly* 66, no. 1 (March 2014): 35–67.

Young, Harvey. *Embodying Black Experience: Stillness, Critical Memory, and the Black Body.* Ann Arbor: University of Michigan, 2010.

Zeuske, Michael. "Hidden Markers, Open Secrets: On Naming, Race-Marking, and Race-Making in Cuba." *New West Indian Guide/Nieuwe West-Indische Gids* 76 (2002): 211–42.

Zola, Émile. *Nana.* Translated by George Holden. Harmondsworth, UK: Penguin, 1972.

Zubel, Marla K. "Anti-colonial Flânerie in Césaire's *Notebook of a Return to the Native Land.*" Paper presented at American Comparative Literature Association, New York University, March 20–23, 2014.

Abdur-Rahman, Aliyyah, 13
Abyssinia/Ethiopia, 8–10, 31, 41, 162, 194n27; emperors, 8, 9, 41, 193n26
African Americans: as candid about slavery in relation to African and Caribbean reticence, 162; in Caribbean fiction and nonfiction, 95, 141; critiqued by Caribbean and West African intellectuals, 91, 162; and photography, 119, 123; as viewed with suspicion for instigating global Black insurgency, 57. *See also* Du Bois, W. E. B.; Hopkins, Pauline; Tuskegee Institute; Washington, Booker T.
African continent: Black diasporic connections to, 53–55, 60, 160; Caribbean residents in, 5, 9, 52, 58; Caribbean reticence or openness about, 147, 149–50, 162; coevality with Europe, 150, 162–68, 197n55; as discursive or material property of white people, 55–58, 136, 149; imperial deposition of royalty from, 5; as source of indentured labor, 53. *See also* Abyssinia/Ethiopia; Akan, Ashanti; Boer War; Benin; Congo; Ethiopia; Gold Coast; Hayford, J. E. Casely; Johnston, Harry H.; Liberia; Pan-African intellectuals; Sierra Leone; Southern Africa; United States; Washington, Booker T.; Williams, Henry Sylvester; Yoruba; Zulu

Ahmed, Sara, 160, 224n38
Akan, Ashanti, 5, 65; Coromantee, 7–8; Fanti, 163, 165, 168
Akomfrah, John, 126
Alexander, M. Jacqui, 200n80
Alexandre, Sandy, 196n50
Allen, Esther, 37–38
Althusser, Louis, 3, 18, 198n63, 213n61
Altink, Henrice, 116
Anderson, Benedict, 19
Anglophone Caribbean. *See* Caribbean, and sovereignty
Antigua, 7
Anzaldúa, Gloria, 161
Aponte, José Antonio, 8
Archer-Straw, Petrina, 130, 220n23
Armstrong, Nancy, 137–38
Ashanti. *See* Akan, Ashanti
Ashwood, Amy, 72
Asia, 16, 17. *See also* Ceylon; India; Japan

Bajorek, Jennifer, 140
Barbados, 65, 142–43, 146. *See also* Lamming, George
Beckford family (Westmoreland, Jamaica), 105
Bedward, Alexander, 70, 73
Belisario, Isaac Mendes, 82
Benin, 5, 65, 140–41, 162, 198n62, 208n77
Benjamin, Walter, 31, 139, 213n57

Bermuda, 6, 29, 47. *See also* Caribbean, and sovereignty; United States

Black men: as African royalty, 9–10; as estate managers and owners, 144, 174; as improperly prosperous, 171–72; and Indo-Caribbean people, 108, 143, 217n113; and opportunity and risk of white proximity, 157–58, 175, 180; as policemen, 87–90, 100–103, 111, 114; and political organizations, 81, 108; as presumed middle-class leaders of working-class Black and Indo-Caribbean people, 143; and sonic allure, 151, 178, 182; as vulnerable to violence, 113, 172, 180

Black women: as bequeathing or transmitting blighted prosperity and futures, 20, 152, 158–61, 186–87, 188; as betraying or embarrassing Black men, 25, 83, 109, 201n88; as heavily surveilled alongside Black men, 24–25, 114; as impervious to violence, 97–98, 114–15; and Indo-Caribbean and Indian women, 21–24, 142; as international travelers, 68–69, 142, 158, 164; as jamettes, 51–52, 66, 192n9; and political organizations, 8, 55, 72, 209–210n17, 210n18; as the presumed intimate partners of Black men, 72, 164; as social actors incurring arrest, 51, 73, 100–101, 107–8; as strategizing in straitened circumstances, 185, 188; and white femininity, 83, 102, 154, 178, 180–82

Blyden, Edward, 168–69

Boer War, 33–37, 46, 50–54, 61–67, 84, 105–6, 121. *See also* African continent; Carnival, Trinidad; Southern Africa; whiteness

Bolívar, Simón, 40, 43, 153

Bonilla, Yarimar, 11, 41

Braithwaite, Kamau, 31

Brand, Dionne, 187–89

Bridges, Yseult, 176, 177–78, 180

British Caribbean. *See* Caribbean, and sovereignty

Brodber, Erna, 73–74, 203n17, 215n96

Brooks, Daphne, 10, 60

Bryan, Patrick, 89

Burns, Kathryn, 176

Cadava, Eduardo, 31, 139

Cadogan, Garnet, 211n42

calypso(nians), 66; Duke of Marlborough (George Jamesie Adilla), 1, 6, 34, 50; Lord Inventor, 50; Lord Kitchener, 51. *See also* Carnival, Trinidad

Campos-Pons, Magdalena, 186

Campt, Tina, 2, 73, 115, 126, 213n54

Carby, Hazel, 26

Caribbean, and sovereignty: British monarchical empire in the context of multiple empires and monarchies, 2, 5, 8–9, 10, 15–16; Danish, 2, 3, 32; as destination for deposed or exiled African and First Nation royalty, 5, 197; as different from Africa and Asia, 16–17; Dutch, 2; French, 2, 41; as having a modern, English-speaking future in relation to a Spanish imperial past, 155; as nonsovereign, 11; Spanish, 2, 35, 43, 123; and US imperial ambitions, 6, 41, 127–28. *See also* Barbados; Bermuda; Cuba; Grenada; Guadeloupe; Guyana (British Guiana); Haiti; Martinique; Montserrat; St. Thomas; St. Vincent

Carnegie, Charles, 211n42

Carnival, Trinidad, 7, 34, 50–52, 61, 63, 66, 147, 192n9. *See also* calypso(nians); refusal

Césaire, Aimé, 17, 41, 77, 80

Ceylon (Sri Lanka), 9, 31, 137

Channer, Colin, 211n42

Chatterjee, Partha, 17, 163, 198n64

China: and British imperialism, 65; royalty, 18, 102, 198n62; as site of ethnic nationalism, 57; as source of indentured labor, 3, 52, 201n97

Chong, Albert, 126

Clarkes (Westmoreland, Jamaica), 93, 159, 217n109; Edith, 107; Henry, 106–7; Hugh, 105, 107, 108, 109; Julia, 107–8; Lee Morris, 105, 107, 108; Richard, 108

clothing and cloth, 21, 86, 93, 98, 101, 110, 163–65, 174–75

coastlines and cays, 31, 39, 44, 152–53, 154, 155, 176, 185, 189

Cobb, Jasmine, 71

Cobham, Stephen, 222n63. *See also* fiction
and nonfiction: *Rupert Gray: A Tale in
Black and White*
Cobham-Sander, Rhonda, 16–17, 192n12,
196n49, 203n17, 221n56, 225n68
Coke, Christopher "Dudus," 11–12
Collins, Merle, 195n46
Collis-Buthelezi, Victoria, 54, 58, 205–6n51
Colombia, 65, 153
Condé, Maryse, 78
Congo, 52, 71, 146, 202n1
consumers, female, as modern gendered
subjects, 85–86, 213n57. *See also* kinship:
single women; kinship: women's wages
Coronado, Raúl, 31
Costa Rica, 3, 94
Cozier, Christopher, 183
Creole speech: and Afrikaans, 34, 203n3;
and agential working-class futurity,
182–84; as excessive for modern nation or white femininity, 177–78, 183;
as fraught for middle-class Black men,
81–82, 89; as policed by white and light-
skinned elites, 82–83, 93; as working-
class foil to middle- and upper-class
speech, 178, 182
Cuba: destination for regional migrants,
49–50, 73, 94, 95, 130–31; part of regional
insurgency, 7, 8, 44; and racialized kinship, 20, 46, 199n71; radical example
for British Caribbean, 42, 44; and
travel writers, 129, 132; war of independence, 34, 36, 38. *See also* Campos-Pons,
Magdalena; Reyes, Paula; Roberts,
W. A.; Rolando, Gloria

Danish Caribbean. *See* Blyden, Edward;
Caribbean, and sovereignty; Firmin,
Anténor; St. Thomas
Davis, Angela, 88
De Lisser, H. G., 49, 68–69, 82–87, 118, 128,
195–96n49
Dominican Republic, 3, 38, 41, 186
Du Bois, W. E. B., 48, 123, 138, 162, 166

earthquakes, 193n17; California, 209n5;
Chile, 76; Haiti, 27; Jamaica, 69; as pre-
cipitating diplomatic incident between

British colonial authorities in Jamaica
and US military, 69–70
Edmondson, Belinda, 26, 169, 196n49
Edwards, Brent, 194n30, 206n54
Edwards, Elizabeth, 125, 126
Edwards, Erica, 195n43
Ellis, Nadia, 100
Emery, Mary Lou, 61, 115
Eng, David, 11, 195n41
Espinet, Ramabai, 3, 186, 192n9
estate: coterminous with whiteness, 46;
dynamic institution with potential to be
modernized and made equitable, 127,
158; managed and owned by Black men,
142, 144, 157–58; obsolescent or unjust
institution requiring extermination, 14;
past site of imperial accumulation in
the age of diamond extraction, 127; the
past of urban-based fiction, 31; viable
because of Black expertise, 146
Ethiopia. *See* Abyssinia/Ethiopia
Evans, Fred R., 103–13, 115, 116

Felski, Rita, 86, 213n57, 217n115
fiction and nonfiction: *At the Full and
Change of the Moon*, 187–89; *Banana
Bottom*, 96–98, 171; *Banjo*, 61; *Child of
the Tropics: Victorian Memoirs*, 176–77;
In Cuba and Jamaica, 49; *Emmanuel
Appadocca*, 153–54, 155, 156, 168; *Ethiopia Unbound: Studies in Race Emancipation*, 161, 162–68, 169; *Hamel*, 156;
Heart of Darkness, 162; *Home to Harlem*,
115; *Icarus Girl*, 187; *Jane's Career*, 76,
151, 184; *My Green Hills of Jamaica*,
94–95, 98–99, 102–3, 112–13; *Negro in
the New World*, 119, 129–31; *New Day*,
38–39, 41–42, 47; *Of One Blood: The
Hidden Self*, 161, 166; *Rupert Gray: A
Tale in Black and White*, 121, 127, 134–37,
141–43, 167, 168–85, 207–8n75; *Sailing
Sunny Seas*, 131–34; *Single Star*, 38–39,
42–46, 48; *Song of the Water Saints*, 186;
Swinging Bridge, 186; *Sword of Nemesis*,
145, 151–62, 167, 177; *Waiting In Vain*,
211n42; "Walking While Black," 211n42;
White Teeth, 186–87; *With Silent Tread*,
176

Filipinos. *See* Philippines
Finch, Aisha, 8
Firmin, Anténor, 32, 192n15, 211n38, 220n35
Forbes, Curdella, 14
Ford-Smith, Honor, 23, 209–10n17
France. *See* Caribbean, and sovereignty
Francis, Donette, 11, 117, 221n56
Franco, Pamela, 215n90
Francophone and French Caribbean. *See* Caribbean, and sovereignty; Guadeloupe; Haiti; Martinique.
Frederick, Rhonda, 204n32

Gandhi, Mahatmas, 23, 54, 191n8, 200n79
gardens: and Black vulnerability to lynching, torture, or photographic surveillance, 105, 124, 134–35, 148, 180; as elite-identified "plantation" in plot/plantation dyad, 112, 134–37, 145, 178–79; as nonelite-identified "plot" in plot/plantation dyad, 14, 105, 112, 130, 145, 177; as sites of transgressive romance, 179–80; Trinidad Botanical, 118, 121, 134–35. *See also* estates; Forbes, Curdella; markets; Wynter, Sylvia
Garvey, Marcus, 21, 23, 65, 69, 72, 75, 91, 114, 191n8
Ghana. *See* African continent; Akan, Ashanti; Hayford, J. E. Casely; Gold Coast
Gikandi, Simon, 9, 127, 128–29
Gill, Lyndon Kamal, 61, 66, 217n109
Gillman, Susan, 48, 204n31
Glover, Kaiama, 189
Gold Coast (Ghana), 5, 53–54, 140–41, 162–68. *See also* African continent; Akan, Ashanti
Gordon, Avery, 161
Gosine, Andil, 28
Goyal, Yogita, 164
Gregg, Veronica, 200n78, 210n18
Grenada, 13, 152, 160
Guadeloupe, 78
Guyana (British Guiana), 12–13, 66, 194–95n40

Haiti, 4, 38, 44, 81; and aid to Jamaica during 1907 earthquake, 70; King Henri

Christophe, 8, 39; and photographers, 130–31, 142; as source of migration, 3; and US occupation, 2. *See also* Caribbean, and sovereignty; Firmin, Anténor; Price-Mars, Jean
Halberstam, Jack, 21
Hall, Stuart, 3, 196n49; with Doreen Massey, 88
Hampton Normal and Agricultural Institute, 121
Haney, Erin, 140–41, 188
Harper, Frances, 32
Hartman, Saidiya, 117, 189, 194n33, 197n54, 201n99
Hawai'i, 2, 132
Hayford, J. E. Casely, 161, 162–68
Hill, Robert, 9, 225n50
Hong, Grace K., 20, 199n72
Hopkins, Pauline, 157–58, 161–62, 166. *See also* African Americans; African continent; kinship; slavery
Hosay, 66, 106, 208n80, 216–17n108
Hosay (or Muhurram or Jahaji) Massacre, 191n2
Hulme, Peter, 38, 43
Hunter, Tera, 20, 199n70
hurricanes, 27, 78, 193n17

Iglesias-Utset, Marial, 34–35
imperialism, as entangled with Black diasporic identity, 129. *See also* Caribbean, and sovereignty; United States
indentured labor, 4, 22, 23, 53, 54, 146, 201n97, 217n113
independence, political: as assumed endpoint for English-speaking Caribbean, 1–2. *See also* Caribbean, and sovereignty; time/temporality: the future
India, 16–17, 141, 163. *See also* Gandhi, Mahatmas; indentured labor; Indo-Caribbean community
indigeneity, 3, 126, 152–55, 176, 197n61. *See also* Māori; Miskito Nation; Spanish
Indo-Caribbean community: and accumulation as exoticized, critiqued, or ignored, 21, 143; as adjacent to Black people, 3, 4, 21–23, 142, 143; and appropriated artisanship, 199–200n76; assumed to

be transient, 22; as propertied taxpayers, 143; as subject to vagrancy and crossdressing laws, 12, 200n86; women, and photography, 132–33, 142. *See also* Hosay; kinship; refusal

inheritance: by Black men, through interracial friendship and marriage, 30, 144; and Black women, 150, 158–59, 170, 188, 189; as entailing Black gratitude and indebtedness, 158, 171–74; as entailing indigenous extinction, 155; as facilitated by white women, 144, 157–58, 177; as failed, 151–52; as lineage, 139–40, 147; as requiring confinement or death of heiress, 142, 155, 176–77; white British, as unimpeded by histories of racial violence, 15–16, 170

insurgency. *See* refusal

insurrection. *See* refusal

Inventor, Lord, 34, 51

Jacobs, Harriet, 73

Jaffe, Rivke, 213n61

Jaji, Tsitsi Ella, 28, 61

James, C. L. R., 32, 48, 146–47

Japan, 8, 57, 163, 165, 193n26

Jekyll, Gertrude, 214n80

Jekyll, Walter, 214n80

Johnson, E. Patrick, 10

Johnson, Michelle, 115

Johnston, Frances B., 121–22, 123. *See also* photography; whiteness

Johnston, Harry H., 90, 118, 119, 127–31. *See also* African continent; Caribbean, and sovereignty; photography

Jonkannu, 66, 106

Kinloch, A. V. (treasurer, Pan African Association), 55. *See also* Pan-African Association; Pan-African intellectuals; Southern Africa

kinship: claimed freely, 136, 168, 182; discussions of marriage as concerns about, 16–17, 47–48, 148, 163–64, 168–69; as impeding productivity, 19–20; inability to claim freely, 19, 198n66, 198–99n67, 199nn69–70; as precarious intimacy, 161; and reproduction of kinlessness,

20–21; rhetorical erasure of, 137; single women, 3, 14, 20, 45–46, 73, 76, 114; women's wages and, 21–23. *See also* inheritance

Kitchener, Lord (calypsonian Aldwyn Roberts and Horace Herbert), 6, 34

Lamming, George, 40, 146

law, colonial, 88; as minor and expansive, 2, 191n6; as postcolonial inheritance, 13; "cross-dressing" law, 12; Offenses of Persons Act, 116. *See also* Vagrancy Laws

Legacies of British Slave-Ownership (Hall), 12, 15, 194n37

Liberia, 119, 123, 128. *See also* African continent

Love, Robert, 106. *See also* Pan-African intellectuals

Lowe, Lisa, 17–18, 31, 77

Lumsden, Joy, 106

lynching, 124, 148

Magubane, Zine, 59

Mahabir, Joy, 21

Māori, 135–36, 174

markets, as key site of women's movement and agency, 3, 84–85, 142

marriage, 86–87, 148, 163–66, 184–85. *See also* inheritance; kinship

Marson, Una, 43, 202n104

Martí, José, 38, 77, 192n15, 211n38

Martínez-San Miguel, Yolanda, 192–93n15

Martinique, 5, 41, 70, 80, 204n20

McClintock, Anne, 23, 52, 62, 79, 142

McKay, Claude, 61, 76, 87–90, 91, 95–103, 111–16, 171–72; "A Midnight Woman to the Bobby," 24, 100–102. *See also* fiction and nonfiction: *Banana Bottom*; fiction and nonfiction: *Banjo*; fiction and nonfiction: *Home to Harlem*; fiction and nonfiction: *My Green Hills of Jamaica*; policing

McKay, U Theo, 82, 94

McKenzie, Catherine, 72. *See also* Black women; Pan-African intellectuals

McKittrick, Catherine, 73

Meikle, Louis, 5

Menelik II, Emperor of Abyssinia/
Ethiopia, 8–10
Mintz, Sidney, 19, 21, 197n61, 199n68
Mirzhoeff, Nicholas, 73, 210n20, 219n17
Miskito Nation, 197
Mofokeng, Santu, 139–40, 141
Montego Bay "Riot"/Protest, 4, 89, 103,
192n14
Montserrat, 27, 151, 158, 159, 195n49,
223–24n15
Moodie-Kubalsing, Sylvia, 153
Morant Bay, 1, 29, 39–40, 41, 43, 92, 96, 191n2
Morgan, Jennifer, 20
Morrison, Toni, 198n63, 228n10
Moton, Robert Russa, 72, 200n79. *See also*
Garvey, Marcus; Tuskegee Institute
Muñoz, José Estéban, 100, 114

neighborhoods, 51, 145–48. *See also* estates;
gardens; streets
Neptune, Harvey, 2, 192n15, 193n17
Newell, Stephanie, 165–66
Newton, Melanie, 18
Nicolazzo, Sarah, 24
Niranjana, Tejaswini, 200n79

Obeah, 91, 104, 156, 177
O'Callaghan, Evelyn, 227n92
Olivier, Sydney, 55–56, 128, 149
Osinubi, Taiwo, 141, 167

Pan-African Association, 55–57, 58, 108, 149
Pan-African Conference (July 1900), 55,
206n54
Pan-African intellectuals. *See* Ashwood,
Amy; Blyden, Edward; Garvey,
Marcus; Kinloch, A. V.; Love, Robert;
McKenzie, Catherine; Williams, Henry
Sylvester
Panama, 3, 4, 69, 94, 95, 104, 128
Paravisni-Gebert, Lizabeth, 150
Paton, Diana, 2, 113, 191n6, 215n83
Patterson, Orlando, 19, 198n66
Philip, M. M., 152–55, 156, 159. *See also*
fiction and nonfiction; inheritance
Philippines, 2, 61, 219n10; and proposed
exchange for British Caribbean, 6, 29,
193n16; and World's Fair, 122–23, 219n12

photography: and Black (dis)inheritance,
139–40, 188; as Black male middle-class
ignominy or triumph, 81, 110, 112, 135; as
class-marker within whiteness, 137–39;
and complex working-class female personhood read as static, quaint or embarrassing, 81, 84–85, 142; and Indian or
Indo-Caribbean women, 132–33, 142;
as making imperial wars palatable, 122;
and New Women, 121, 133; and non-
photographic media, 140, 187, 188; as
proof of imperial loyalty, 64; as a racializing technology, 127, 138; as record of
British usurpation of African royalty,
65, 140–41, 208n77; studios in Kingston
and Port of Spain, 85, 125; studios in
West Africa, 140; studios in southern
Africa, 139; and visual repatriation,
220n39; as white female inheritance, 121.
See also Armstrong, Nancy; Bajorek,
Jennifer; Benjamin, Walter; Cadava,
Eduardo; Campt, Tina; gardens; Haney,
Erin; Johnston, Frances B.; Johnston,
Harry H.; Mofokeng, Santu; Raiford,
Leigh; Reyes, Paula; Smith, Shawn
Michelle; streets; Thompson, Krista;
Wexler, Laura; whiteness
plot/plantation dyad, 14. *See also* estates;
Forbes, Curdella; gardens; markets;
Wynter, Sylvia
policing, 66, 87–117. *See also* McKay,
Claude; refusal; Thomas, Herbert;
Vagrancy Laws
Price-Mars, Jean, 122–23
Puerto Rico, 2, 37, 61
Pugliese, Gina, 227n109
Puri, Shalini, 2, 191n5
Putnam, Lara, 3, 152

Quashie, Kevin, 2, 191n5, 221n54
Queen Victoria Lazaro, 51, 63, 66–67

racial designation, as used in this book,
195–96n49
Raiford, Leigh, 202n101
Ramos, Julio, 76
Rastafari, 10. *See also* Abyssinia/Ethiopia;
kinship

Rayman, Evelyne, 199n76
Reddock, Rhoda, 200n78, 228n7
refusal, 1, 4–5, 7–8, 57, 59, 60, 65–67; police, 112; popular celebrations as, 30, 51–52, 63, 66–67, 106, 145. *See also* Montego Bay "Riot"/Protest; Water "Riot"/Protest; Zulu
Reid, V. S., 38–42, 48–49, 50
resistance. *See* refusal
Reyes, Paula, 125
Rhys, Jean, 195n46
Richardson, Bonham, 193n17
"riots." *See* Montego Bay "Riot"/Protest; Morant Bay; refusal; Water "Riot"/Protest
Roberts, W. A. R., 38–47
Robinson, Tracy, 12–13, 24, 228n7
Rohlehr, Gordon, 51, 202n1
Rolando, Gloria, 198n67
Rosenberg, Leah, 210n31, 218n1, 221n56
Ross, Marlon, 119
Rowley, Michelle, 12–13, 228n9
royalty, 7–10, 11–12, 18, 41, 55, 65–67. *See also* Abyssinia/Ethiopia; Akan, Ashanti; Benin; China; Haiti; Hopkins, Pauline; India; Japan; Miskito Nation; Zulu

Schwarz, Bill, 62
Scott, David, 13, 17, 195n44, 197n60
Seacole, Mary, 68–69
sexuality, heterosexual, death of female spouse as solution to, 165; queer, as not precluding heterosexual entitlement, 100; queer, and desire in suspended time, 99; women's, as troubling to male leadership, 23, 109, 164
Sharpe, Christina, 21, 189
Shepherd, Verene, 208n80
Sierra Leone, 166, 167–68
slavery: as central (even when elided) in fiction, 167; as embodied and reproduced by Black women, 20–21; as erased, in British culture, 12; as explicit in African American fiction, 16, 166; as implicit anxiety in marriage debates, 167–68; as never-ending, 189; as a past that eclipses other pasts, 53, 54; as primal scene in

Caribbean fiction, 159; as unending Black debt and white compensation, 173; as unutterable inheritance, 136–37, 167, 170–71
Smith, Matthew, 209n4, 209n7
Smith, Shawn Michelle, 138
Smith, Zadie, 186–87
Snorton, C Riley, 97
sound and the sonic: as complex spatial and temporal reverberations, 61; and middle-class Black masculinity, 178, 179; as modern or outdated, 151; and propertied (white or Black) femininity, 158, 178; and working-class Black femininity, 82–83, 178; as working-class sovereignty, 182–84
Southern Africa, 33–37, 46, 50–67. *See also* African continent; Boer War; Mofokeng, Santu; whiteness; Zulu
Spanish (Trinidad-Creole designation): as term and ethos specific to Trinidad, 151. *See also* Caribbean, and sovereignty; Colombia; Cuba; Dominican Republic; Panama; Puerto Rico; Venezuela
Spillers, Hortense, 20, 199n69
Stephens, Michelle, 2, 4
Stewart, Catherine, 103–17, 185
stickfighting, 52, 63, 66–67. *See also* Carnival, Trinidad; Queen Victoria Lazaro
streets: as boundaries between neighborhoods, 147–48; as connectors of rural and urban, 84–85, 98, 101; and gendered strolling, 68–69, 78–80, 89, 100–101; and nonelite insurgency or celebration, 4–5, 66–67, 106, 216–217n108; and vulnerability to formal or informal policing, 93–94, 100–102; and walking as fraught or freeing, 78, 211n42; and white photographers' entitlement, 80, 85, 120, 132–33
St. Thomas (Danish Virgin Islands until 1917), 32. *See also* Blyden, Edward; Caribbean, and sovereignty; Firmin, Anténor
St. Vincent, 5, 27, 152

Tageldin, Sheldon, 19
Taylor, Christopher, 154

Thames, Maziki, 196n49

Thomas, Deborah, 6, 12

Thomas, Herbert, 76, 88–89, 91–94, 99, 101, 114. *See also* policing; whiteness

Thomas, John Jacob, 6, 151

Thompson, Krista, 64, 66, 135, 197n58, 220n39

time/temporality: Black prosperity as anachronistic, 25–26, 181; as burden caused by past of enslavement, 15–16, 159; Caribbean's non-coevality, 15, 17, 150; as endless Black obligation to white people, 181–82; estate, 106, 216n108; first wives' obsolescence and, 148; the future, 1–2, 13, 184; gendered inheritance and, 20–26, 160; as haunted by the living, 161; imperviousness of imperial power to ruination by, 12, 16; indigenous obsolescence and, 152; literary genealogy and, 1, 131, 151; the past's uncertain future, 31–32; the past as never past, 189; the past as unavailable to suture to the present, 15, 19, 139–40; present, 13, 202n105; suspended and queer, 99. *See also* photography

Tinsley, Omise'eke Natasha, 215n86

Tracy, R. Archer, 144, 148–52, 154–61, 167, 168, 178. *See also* fiction and nonfiction: *Sword of Nemesis*; Montserrat

Trotman, David, 20, 24–25

Tsinhnahjinnie, Hulleah J., 126

Tuskegee Institute, and Caribbean people, 123, 169. *See also* Garvey, Marcus; Moton, Robert Russa; Price-Mars, Jean; Reyes, Paula; Washington, Booker T.

United Fruit Company, 6, 37, 68, 120–21, 158

United States: and African continent, 127–29, 162; and Boer War, 61–62; and Cuban War of Independence/Spanish American War, 130, 132; and European imperialism, 2, 3, 5–6, 127–28; and Haiti, 2; as home to Caribbean people, 43, 47, 65, 91, 201n99; and imperial relationship to Caribbean, 6, 41, 127–28; and internal colonization, 3; as object of Black diasporic interest, 136–37, 141; presidents, 127–28, 136. *See also* African Americans;

African continent; Caribbean, and sovereignty; Du Bois, W. E. B.; Hopkins, Pauline; Roberts, W. A.; Tuskegee Institute; Washington, Booker T.

uprisings. *See* refusal

Vagrancy Laws: and Black intimacy and political aspiration in Jamaica, 24–25, 103–5, 113; and Indian and Indo-Caribbean indentured labor, 200n86; 1902 Amendment (Jamaica), 200n84

Vassell, Linette, 200n78, 210n17

Venezuela, 3, 19, 25, 40, 152–55, 156, 176–77. *See also* Bolivar, Simón; Lamming, George

Volcano, Guadeloupe, 78; Martinique, 77; Montserrat, 27; St. Vincent, 27

Walcott, Derek, 39–40

walking. *See* Caribbean, and sovereignty; streets

Warner-Lewis, Maureen, 52, 53, 66, 202n1

Washington, Booker T., 119, 120, 138

water. *See* coastlines and cays

Water "Riot"/Protest (Port of Spain, Trinidad, 1903), 4–5, 67, 119, 135, 141, 179; organizers as veterans of earlier associations, 66–67

Wehr, Donald, 164

West Africa. *See* Akan, Ashanti; Hayford, J. E. Casely; Gold Coast; marriage

West Indian/West Indies. *See* Caribbean, and sovereignty

Westmoreland, Jamaica, 103–17, 216n102; and Boer War, 105; and Hosay, 106. *See also* Beckford family; Clarkes (Westmoreland, Jamaica)

Wexler, Laura, 121

whiteness: as arbiter of Creole speech and global Black identities, 55–56, 93, 128–29; female, as adjacent to Black men, 136, 175; female, as conduit of accumulation, 47–48, 175–76; as imperial lineage, 136; as landed and anti-imperial, 46; and New Women, 121, 133, 175; as object of Black diasporic friendship or intimacy, 14–15, 127; as requiring Black time, wealth, and bolstering, 113, 154, 158, 174, 178, 181–82;

as untainted by enslavement, 12, 15, 106–7, 159. *See also* Beckford family; Boer War; Clarkes (Westmoreland, Jamaica); inheritance; photography

Wilcox, Ella Wheeler, 131–34

Williams, Henry Sylvester, 54, 55–57, 66–67, 149, 222n63. *See also* Pan-African Association; Pan-African Conference; Pan-African intellectuals

Williams, Raymond, 15, 62–63

Wolloch, Alex, 21, 150

World's Fairs: Paris (Paris Exposition/Exposition Universelle, 1900), 119, 122, 138; St. Louis (Louisiana Purchase Exposition, 1904), 8, 62, 122–23

Wynter, Sylvia, 14, 17, 202n104

Yoneyama, Lisa, 16

Yoruba, 147

Young, Cynthia, 195n43

Zubel, Marla, 76

Zulu: and African American performance, 58–60, 206n60; Bambatha Uprising in Natal, 1906, 57; in Jamaican imagination, 46, 206–7n65, 207n66; as problematic synecdoche, 58–59; as symbolic identity for global Black diasporic subjects, 156–57; as symbolic identity for white supremacy, 34, 59, 60–61; in Trinidadian imagination, 61, 156–57. *See also* African continent; Boer War; Southern Africa